Alt-America

*The Rise of the Radical
Right in the Age of Trump*

David Neiwert

V
VERSO
London • New York

This paperback edition first published by Verso 2018
First published by Verso 2017
© David Neiwert 2017, 2018

•

The moral rights of the author have been asserted

1 3 5 7 9 10 8 6 4 2

Verso
UK: 6 Meard Street, London W1F 0EG
US: 20 Jay Street, Suite 1010, Brooklyn, NY 11201

versobooks.com

Verso is the imprint of New Left Books

ISBN-13: 978-1-78663-446-7
ISBN-13: 978-1-78663-424-5 (US EBK)
ISBN-13: 978-1-78663-425-2 (UK EBK)

British Library Cataloguing in Publication Data
A catalogue record for this book is available from the British Library

The Library of Congress Has Cataloged the Hardback Edition as Follows:

Names: Neiwert, David A., 1956– author.
Title: Alt-America : the rise of the radical right in the age of Trump / by
  David Neiwert.
Description: London ; New York : Verso, 2017. | Includes bibliographical
  references and index.
Identifiers: LCCN 2017035134| ISBN 9781786634238 (hardback) | ISBN
  9781786634252 (UK e-book)
Subjects: LCSH: White nationalism—United States—History—21st century. |
  White supremacy movements—United States—History—21st century. |
  Right-wing extremists—United States—History—21st century. |
  Radicalism—United States—History—21st century. | United States—Race
  relations—History—21st century. | United States—Politics and
  government—1989- | United States—Social conditions—1980-
Classification: LCC E184.A1 N365 2017 | DDC 305.800973—dc23
LC record available at https://lccn.loc.gov/2017035134

Typeset in Fournier by MJ & N Gavan, Truro, Cornwall
Printed and bound by CPI Group (UK) Ltd, Croydon, CR0 4YY

For Fiona
and her generation

Trust, a mighty god has gone, Restraint has gone from men, and the Graces, my friend, have abandoned the earth. Men's judicial oaths are no longer to be trusted, nor does anyone revere the immortal gods; the race of pious men has perished and men no longer recognize the rules of conduct or acts of piety.

—Theognis of Megara, describing the fate of men after Pandora opened her box

Contents

1

Into the Abyss

The day after Donald Trump announced his campaign for the presidency, Dylann Roof walked into a Charleston, South Carolina, church with a gun and killed nine black people because they were black.

It was purely a coincidence that one act followed the other, hundreds of miles apart: Roof apparently knew little about Trump and was not known to be a Trump follower. Trump had never met nor had any interaction with Roof.

Yet the two acts were inextricably connected—by the events and acts that had preceded them, and by those that followed in the ensuing weeks and months. Most of all, both acts signaled, in different ways, a deep change in the American cultural and political landscape.

The American radical right—the violent, paranoid, racist, hateful radical right—was back with a vengeance. Actually, it had never really gone away. And now it had a presidential candidate.

Hopefully, he's going to sit there and say, "When I become elected president, what we're going to do is we're going to make the border a vacation spot, it's going to cost you twenty-five dollars for a permit, and then you get fifty dollars for every confirmed kill." That'd be one nice thing.
—Supporter of Donald Trump, interviewed in the *New York Times*

This robocall goes out to all millennials and others who are honest in all their dealings ... The white race is being replaced by other peoples in America and in all white countries. Donald Trump stands strong as a nationalist.

> —William White (a white nationalist), pro-
> Trump robocall to Massachusetts voters

The march to victory will not be won by Donald Trump in 2016, but this could be the steppingstone we need to then radicalize millions of White working and middle class families to the call to truly begin a struggle for Faith, family and folk.

> —Matthew Heimbach, cofounder of the neo-Nazi
> Traditionalist Youth Network, at organization's website

Get all of these monkeys the hell out of our country—now! Heil Donald Trump—THE ULTIMATE SAVIOR.

> —Tweet from the *Daily Stormer*, a neo-Nazi website

Donald Trump was right, all these illegals need to be deported.
> —White man in Boston who with another man beat a homeless Latino
> to within an inch of his life with a metal pole and then urinated on him

People who are following me are very passionate. They love this country and they want this country to be great again. They are passionate.
> —Donald Trump, when asked about the Boston hate crime

Most Americans surveying the wreckage of the American political landscape in the aftermath of the 2016 presidential election are startled by the ugliness and violence that have crept into the nation's electoral politics. And they can recognize its source: the sudden appearance of the racist far right as players.

Almost as blindingly as Donald Trump appeared on the scene, so did an array of white nationalists and supremacists, conspiracy theorists and xenophobes, even Klansmen and skinheads and other violent radicals, who for decades had been relegated to the fringe of right-wing politics. Hadn't they gone extinct?

Most Americans did not realize that, far from going extinct, these groups had been growing and flourishing in recent years, fed by the rivulets of hate mongering and disinformation-fueled propaganda flowing out of right-wing media for at least a decade and the hospitable dark environment provided by a virtual blackout in mainstream media concerning the growth of right-wing extremism.

These tendencies dated back to the Bill Clinton administration, when the radical right first began to try to mainstream itself as a "patriot" and militia movement, but was derailed largely by the violent terrorism that the movement also brewed up. Simultaneously, right-wing media began appearing as a new propaganda type that openly eschewed the journalistic standards of mainstream news organizations: in a classic use of "Newspeak," they declared themselves "fair and balanced."

The organizational drive of the new "Patriot" movement largely went into a hiatus in the early part of the new century, during the conservative Republican administration of George W. Bush, but the extremism that originally fueled the movement in the 1990s remained very much alive. On the far right the conspiracist element found fresh life in the aftermath of the terrorist attacks of September 11, 2001, which produced an entire cottage industry devoted to proving that the attacks were part of a plot by the New World Order. Simultaneously, the mainstream rhetoric on the right became vociferous during the Iraq War, when any criticism of Bush and his administration's conduct of the war was denounced nastily as treason, and liberals were sneered at as "soft on terror."

This suffused extremism came roaring back to life with the nomination of Barack Obama as the Democratic Party's candidate for the presidency in 2008, and then his election, which sparked a virulent counterreaction on the radical right. The idea of a black man, let alone a liberal one, as president made them recoil in visceral disgust. The mainstream, business-establishment right—after years of right-wing-media conditioning during both the Clinton and Bush years—apparently could no longer abide the idea of shared rule with a liberal president and set out to delegitimize him by any means possible. And it was in that shared hatred that the extremist and mainstream right finally cemented their growing alliance.

This alliance found form in the "Tea Party," which was widely celebrated as a grassroots conservative phenomenon that sprang to life in 2009, in the wake of Obama's election. It was generally portrayed (following members' self-descriptions) as attached to the conservative ideal of small government, expressed as limited spending and taxes. In reality, however, their founding organizations were explicitly focused on opposing Obama and every aspect of his presidency. In the ensuing years, politicians and pundits inside the Beltway assumed that this was the Tea Party's raison d'être.

But it was more. In the rural and red-voting suburban districts where the Tea Party organized itself on the ground, it became the living embodiment of right-wing populism.

Right-wing populism in America—as distinct from its left-wing variety—has always been predicated on a narrative known as "producerism," in which the hard-working "producers" of America are beset by a two-headed enemy: a nefarious elite suppressing them from above, and a parasitic underclass of "others," reliant on welfare and government benefits, tearing them down and sucking them under from below. Right-wing populism has most often been expressed via various nativist anti-immigrant movements. In the twenty-first century, this brand of populism became expressed as a hostility to "liberal" elites and "parasitic" minorities and immigrants.

Thus, the Tea Party focused on conspiracy theories and the supposed "tyranny" of the president, and ardently embraced ideals that kept bubbling up from the extremist right: constitutionalism, nullification of federal laws and edicts, and even secession from the Union. The Tea Party movement became a major conduit into the mainstream of American conservatism of the most extreme, often outright nutty ideas that originated with the Patriot movement and its related far-right cousins.

The Patriots have always specialized in creating a kind of alternative universe, a set of alternate explanations for an entire world of known facts, made possible only by a willingness to believe in easily disprovable falsehoods. The Patriots describe themselves primarily as constitutionalists, but their understanding of the Constitution is based on a distorted misreading of the document and its place in the body of law. For example, Patriots believe that the Second Amendment prohibits all gun and arms regulation whatsoever; that the text of the Constitution prohibits the federal government from owning any kind of public lands and from creating any kind of federal law enforcement; that the sheriff of the county is the highest law-enforcement entity in the land; and that federal laws ensuring civil rights and prohibiting hate crimes are unconstitutional and thus moot. Thus, in the context of the Patriot movement, "constitutionalist" describes people who believe that most "constitutional" powers reside in local government, specifically county sheriffs—not in the national Constitution.

These beliefs about the Constitution are amplified by a panoply of conspiracy theories: A nefarious New World Order is plotting to enslave all of mankind in a world government that permits no freedom, and its many tentacles can be glimpsed daily in news events. President Obama is secretly an illegitimate president who was born overseas and falsified his birth certificate; he's also secretly a Muslim plotting to hand the United States over to Islamist radicals who plan to institute sharia law in the United States and around the world. Global warming is a hoax, a scam dreamed up by leftists and totalitarian environmentalists who want to control every facet of our lives. In this alternative universe, facts and the laws of political gravity do not apply.

In the alternative universe of right-wing populism, down is often up. Ultimately, the right-wing populist solution to the world's problems is to submit to an authoritarian "enlightened" ruler. Some of the leading figures of right-wing populist movements in American history—for example, Henry Ford—have been famous "captains of industry."

Early on, Donald Trump identified this belief system as being aligned with his own. "I think the people of the Tea Party like me, because I represent a lot of the ingredients of the Tea Party," he told a Fox News interviewer in 2011.

Trump was cannily tapping into a large voting bloc that had already been created by conservative activists and made large by the very rhetoric and ideology that nearly all of the movement's media organs embraced to some degree before his arrival on the scene.

The political establishment, however, has studiously ignored the existence of this bloc, and so it has been utterly befuddled by the Trump phenomenon and his ability to operate in this universe where the normal laws of reason do not seem to apply and to bring it onto the national political stage.

"He is defying the laws of political gravity right now," exclaimed the political consultant Michael Bronstein in January 2016, voicing what became the conventional wisdom. Regarding Trump's comments and tweets, Bronstein said, "Inside the presidential race, any one of these lines, if they were associated to another candidate, it would've ended the candidacy … I think the establishment, the punditry class, looks at him and a lot of them are just bewildered."

Before the Trump campaign, the true believers of the Tea Party were assumed to be on the fringe of the Republican Party, a tiny subset that had no voice and even less power. The Trump campaign revealed that their numbers were not tiny, nor were they powerless. These dark forces had been building for years, waiting for the right kind of figure—charismatic, rich, fearlessly bombastic—to come along and put them into play.

They manifested themselves on that very first day of Trump's campaign, June 15, 2015, at the press conference he called at Trump Tower, in New York City. The atmospherics were negative: Trump was boastful and blaming as he sketched a narrative of an America whose leaders' incompetence had allowed the nation to be beaten down in trade by foreigners. But what really stood out was his open, unapologetic expression of bigotry toward Latinos and other minorities.

"The US has become a dumping ground for everybody else's problems," he claimed, to loud applause, and then continued:

Thank you. It's true, and these are the best and the finest. When Mexico sends its people, they're not sending their best. They're not sending you … They're sending people that have lots of problems, and they're bringing those problems with us. They're bringing drugs. They're bringing crime. They're rapists. And some, I assume, are good people.

But I speak to border guards and they tell us what we're getting. And it only makes common sense. It only makes common sense. They're sending us not the right people.

It's coming from more than Mexico. It's coming from all over South and Latin America, and it's coming probably—probably—from the Middle East. But we don't know. Because we have no protection and we have no competence, we don't know what's happening. And it's got to stop and it's got to stop fast.

This was a signature trope of Trump's campaign: Trump didn't avail himself of the coded "dog whistle" signals that conservatives had learned to employ when they spoke about race, ethnicity, crime, and immigration. He called this kind of euphemistic prevarication "political correctness," and he intended to smash it to tiny pieces and say what he knew his listeners already thought.

Right-wing politicians had for years relied on this coy rhetoric because naked racial attacks hurt them in opinion polls. This rhetorical dancing around also spared them from being attacked for their racism while allowing them to communicate to their own audiences that their biases aligned with those of their white suburban and rural base—which, it emerged, continued to embrace racist tropes and stereotypes about people of color, regardless of the broader social stigma in doing so.

This was made manifestly clear by the ardent following that Trump immediately developed for his "anti-PC" style of campaigning: instead of plummeting in the polls, as many expected after Trump's wildly controversial opening speech, his approval ratings climbed. And climbed. And climbed.

Longtime nativists soon perceived in Trump a bandwagon they could jump on. Among the friends and admirers Trump acquired who were movement conservatives was one of their leading mavens, the syndicated columnist Ann Coulter. Coulter had long complained that immigration was an issue that Republicans kept overlooking and botching in national elections—because they hadn't gone far enough to the right.

In fact, Coulter had made that very argument in a book that came out on June 1, 2015, *Adios America: The Left's Plan to Turn Our Country into a Third World Hellhole*. She had been making the rounds of all the right-wing TV talk shows to promote it—and a few mainstream programs as well.

Coulter has a long history of citing far-right extremists and white nationalists in her work, and this one was no different. Retailing a hodgepodge of recycled nativist talking points, the book cited a number of white supremacist sources, and repeated the assertion of Richard Spencer, a white nationalist, that "immigration is a proxy war against America." She also claimed in the book that Latinos sustained a "culture of misogyny."

Coulter also credited another well-known white nationalist figure named Peter Brimelow—the founder of an openly racist website called *VDare* (named for Virginia Dare, the first white child born in North America)—for her anti-immigrant politics. These views were seconded by another well-known "academic racist," Jared Taylor, who declared that with her book Coulter "has established herself as the foremost advocate for immigration sanity in America—if not the world."

Meanwhile, on TV and elsewhere, Coulter did what she does best—serve up sound bites of outrageous commentary that stir up condemnation from mainstream liberals and that warm the hearts of her fellow conservatives. This time out, though, Coulter had grown beyond outrageous and become genuinely vicious, warning Americans they "better get used to having your little girls get raped" as a result of immigration and that "Americans should fear immigrants more than ISIS," and sneering that Mexican culture "is obviously deficient." She denied that there was anything bigoted about this: "Hispanics are not black," she countered, "so drop the racism crap."

Coulter, who had been an ardent Romney supporter, had begun to turn in Trump's direction, telling one interviewer that a Trump-Romney ticket would stop "foreigners" from outvoting "white Americans." It was apparently a mutual-admiration society: Coulter told a reporter that Trump had "asked for, and received, an advance copy of my book, and he told me … that he's read the book cover to cover." Trump tweeted out that Coulter's book was "a great read. Good job!"

One of the solutions to immigration from south of the border was to build an effective wall along the Mexican border. "Contrary to repeated assertions that fences don't work," Coulter asserted, "… after Israel completed a fence along its border in 2013, the number of illegal aliens entering the country dropped to zero."

When Trump announced his plans to run for president on June 15, he made the wall idea the centerpiece of his attack on Mexican immigration: "I would build a great wall, and nobody builds walls better than me, believe me, and I'll build them very inexpensively, I will build a great, great wall on our southern border. And I will have Mexico pay for that wall. Mark my words."

That was just the opening act.

Another ardent Trump admirer that weekend was a South Carolina man named Kyle Rogers, the thirty-something webmaster of the St. Louis–based Council of Conservative Citizens (CCC). A reincarnation of the white-supremacist Citizens Councils of the 1950s, Rogers's new council has been designated a white-supremacist hate group by the Southern Poverty Law Center.

Rogers was active in South Carolina Republican politics, although his presence was mostly seen as an embarrassment by party officials, who tried to exclude him as much as possible. He'd served as a delegate to the Charleston County Republican Convention in 2007, and in 2013 GOP officials in Dorchester County confirmed that he was a member of that county's Republican Executive Committee. They expressed chagrin about Rogers's participation, saying they had asked him to resign but were unable legally to eject him.

The CCC enjoyed influence even in the halls of South Carolina state government. A CCC national board member, Roan Garcia-Quintana, had run as a Republican nominee for a state senate seat in 2008, and sat on Governor Nikki Haley's reelection campaign steering committee until his CCC membership was exposed and he was asked to resign.

The CCC had suffered a major blow when its founder and longtime leader, Gordon Baum, died in March 2015, and younger members like Kyle Rogers were increasingly seen as the face of its future. Promoting fake statistics about black crime is one of Rogers's specialties. He maintains a section on the CCC website titled "The Color of Crime," devoted to claims that black criminals disproportionately target white victims.

Rogers seemed to make at least some of his living by selling things online, including flags at Patriotic-Flags.com, which is directly linked at the CCC site he manages. Among the flags he sells is one from the government of Rhodesia, which no longer exists; its banner is still widely considered a symbol of white-supremacist rule in Africa, similar to the Confederate flag in the United States. And he sold T-shirts. On June 16, the day after Donald Trump's announcement, Rogers posted to his Twitter account a link to the "Donald Trump 2016" shirts he was selling to his 40,000 Twitter followers.

But Rogers deleted his entire Twitter account later that same day—the day Dylann Roof went to Charleston.

Dylann Roof was a twenty-one-year-old resident of Columbia, South Carolina, who ran a website called "The Last Rhodesian," devoted to white nationalism. He liked to wear Rhodesian flag patches and posed on his Facebook page wearing one while waving a Confederate flag.

Roof was an ardent member of the South Carolina branch of the CCC, although it is not clear to what extent he had associated with Rogers or other CCC leaders. In the days before he walked into a Charleston church with a gun, he had put together his manifesto, which made clear that the CCC had informed and ultimately inspired his actions that day. "I was not raised in a racist home or environment," Roof wrote.

> Living in the South, almost every White person has a small amount of racial awareness, simply because of the numbers of negroes in this part of the country. But it is a superficial awareness. Growing up, in school, the White and black kids would make racial jokes toward each other, but all they were were jokes. Me and White friends would sometimes watch things that would make us think that "blacks were the real racists" and other elementary thoughts like this, but there was no real understanding behind it.
>
> The event that truly awakened me was the Trayvon Martin case. I kept hearing and seeing his name, and eventually I decided to look him up. I read the Wikipedia article and right away I was unable to understand what the big deal was. It was obvious that Zimmerman was in the right. But more importantly this prompted me to type in the words "black on White crime" into Google, and I have never been the same since that day. The first website I came to was the Council of Conservative Citizens. There were pages upon pages of these brutal black on White murders. I was in disbelief. At this moment I realized that something was very wrong. How could the news be blowing up the Trayvon Martin case while hundreds of these black on White murders got ignored?

The remainder of the manifesto—which does not mention Donald Trump or any other politician—appears to be more or less a distillation of CCC and other white-nationalist talking points. Roof defends the history of slaveholding, adopting talking points drawn from neo-Confederate organizations such as the League of the South and the pseudo-historians they deploy to minimize the harm of slavery and its legacy. He discusses the need for American and European white nationalists to link arms in what they see as the struggle against "multiculturalism."

And some of it is just unrestrained bigotry (spelling as in originals):

Niggers are stupid and violent. At the same time they have the capacity to be very slick. Black people view everything through a racial lense. Thats what racial awareness is, its viewing everything that happens through a racial lense. They are always thinking about the fact that they are black.

...

Segregation was not a bad thing. It was a defensive measure. Segregation did not exist to hold back negroes. It existed to protect us from them.

...

Anyone who thinks that White and black people look as different as we do on the outside, but are somehow magically the same on the inside, is delusional. How could our faces, skin, hair, and body structure all be different, but our brains be exactly the same? This is the nonsense we are led to believe.

...

Negroes have lower IQs, lower impulse control, and higher testosterone levels in generals. These three things alone are a recipe for violent behavior.

The CCC's website and other similar sites were cloacae of such ignorant rants. But Roof chose to take all this in his own direction.

To take a saying from a film, "I see all this stuff going on, and I dont see anyone doing anything about it. And it pisses me off." To take a saying from my favorite film, "Even if my life is worth less than a speck of dirt, I want to use it for the good of society."

I have no choice. I am not in the position to, alone, go into the ghetto and fight. I chose Charleston because it is most historic city in my state, and at one time had the highest ratio of blacks to Whites in the country. We have no skinheads, no real KKK, no one doing anything but talking on the internet. Well someone has to have the bravery to take it to the real world, and I guess that has to be me.

Roof's bizarre, rambling manifesto was reminiscent of a similar document penned in 2008 by a conservative Tennessee man named Jim David Adkisson, who also walked into a church with a gun. Adkisson was driven to anger by the looming nomination of a black man as the Democratic candidate for the presidency: "I'm protesting the DNC running such a radical leftist candidate. Osama Hussein Obama, yo mama. No experience, no brains, a joke. Dangerous to America, he looks like Curious George!" He was also appalled by the race-mixing mores of modern times as exemplified by Obama's mother: "How is a white woman having a niger [*sic*] baby progress?" he asked.

In July 2008, Adkisson walked into a Unitarian Universalist church in downtown Knoxville armed with a 12-gauge shotgun during a performance of a children's musical and opened fire. He killed two people and wounded seven more; when he stopped to reload, he was tackled and immobilized by members of the congregation until the police arrived.

Contrary to his expectations of being killed by police, Adkisson instead stood trial for murder, pleaded guilty, and is now serving a life sentence with no possibility of parole.

In the seven and a half years between Jim David Adkisson's 2008 rampage and Dylann Roof's in 2015, domestic terrorism in America spiked dramatically. But hardly anyone noticed.

During that time span, there were 201 total cases of domestic terrorism in the United States—almost three times the rate of the preceding eight years. The large majority of these crimes were committed by right-wing extremists—some 115 in all, compared to 63 cases of Islamist-inspired domestic terror, and 19 cases of left-wing-extremist terrorism.

Despite that disproportionate reality, the image most Americans have when they think of terrorism is an act committed by someone wearing a turban. That is mostly a result of the Al Qaeda attacks of September 11, 2001, and their lingering aftermath, especially a declared War on Terror that focused on battling radical Islamists in Afghanistan, Iraq, Syria, and elsewhere.

However, *domestic* terrorism—acts that are plotted and executed on American soil, directed at US citizens, by actors based here —is a different story. It has been there all along. The most damaging domestic terrorist attack ever committed on American soil was the April 19, 1995, bombing of the Murrah Federal Building in Oklahoma City, which killed 168 people and injured another 680. The perpetrators were a pair of white right-wing extremists,

Tim McVeigh and Terry Nichols. For at least a generation, such homegrown extremists have been far and away the largest source of terrorism in the United States. Even before Obama's election in 2008—but also in anticipation of that event—the rate of incidents began to rise dramatically, seemingly triggered by Jim David Adkisson's rampage. And it remained at that same high level for most of the Obama presidency.

Right-wing extremist terrorism was more often deadly than Islamist extremism: nearly a third of incidents involved fatalities, for a total of seventy-nine deaths, whereas just 8 percent of Islamist incidents caused fatalities. However, the total number of deaths resulting from Islamist incidents was higher—ninety—due largely to three mass shootings in which nearly all the casualties occurred: in 2009 at Fort Hood, Texas, and in 2015 in San Bernardino, California, and Orlando, Florida, in 2016.

Incidents related to left-wing ideologies, including ecoterrorism and animal rights actions, were comparatively rare: nineteen incidents resulted in five deaths.

Despite these statistics, officialdom and the media focused only on terrorism threats plotted by Islamist radicals. Right-wing pundits viciously attacked and silenced anyone who tried to bring up right-wing violence in the framework of terrorism; they had grown touchy about their own ideological and rhetorical proximity to the extremism that was fueling the violence.

After the elections of 2010, when the Republicans seized control of Congress, Republicans in both houses began demanding hearings on the threat of domestic terrorism—but when the House committee chairman overseeing the discussion, Congressman Peter King of New York, opened hearings in March 2011, he announced that they would not be bothering to consider anything other than Islamist terrorism:

> This Committee cannot live in denial, which is what some would have us do when they suggest that this hearing dilute its focus by investigating threats unrelated to Al Qaeda. The Department of Homeland Security and this committee were formed in response to the Al Qaeda attacks of

9/11. There is no equivalency of threat between al Qaeda and neo-Nazis, environmental extremists or other isolated madmen. Only Al Qaeda and its Islamist affiliates in this country are part of an international threat to our nation. Indeed by the Justice Department's own record not one terror related case in the last two years involved neo-Nazis, environmental extremists, militias or anti-war groups.

As it happened, an attempted bombing of the MLK Day parade in Spokane by a white supremacist had happened just the day before. King was abysmally misinformed about the overall number of terrorist acts and plots emerging from the sectors he claimed were inactive. He was reminded of this by his Democratic colleague, Congressman Bennie Thompson, who pleaded, "I urge you, Mr. Chairman, to hold a hearing examining the Homeland Security threat posed by anti-government and white supremacist groups. As a committee on Homeland Security, our mission is to examine threats to this nation's security. A narrow focus that excludes known threats lacks clarity and may be myopic."

King ignored this plea and did not permit any deviation from the hearings' announced focus. However, the next year the Senate did hold hearings on the subject of right-wing extremist violence in the wake of neo-Nazi Wade Michael Page's murderous rampage at a Sikh temple in Wisconsin in which six worshippers died. At that hearing senators heard from Daryl Johnson, a veteran domestic-terrorism analyst. Johnson was unequivocal:

The threat of domestic terrorism motivated by extremist ideologies is often dismissed and overlooked in the national media and within the US government. Yet we are currently seeing an upsurge in domestic non-Islamic extremist activity, specifically from violent right-wing extremists. While violent left-wing attacks were more prevalent in the 1970s, today the bulk of violent domestic activity emanates from the right wing.

The Southern Poverty Law Center (SPLC), which tracks hate groups and Patriot and other extremist organizations and monitors and reports on their activities, continued to track this right-wing violence. In conjunction with an upswing in domestic terrorism and hate crimes that began in 2008, the SPLC saw dramatic increases in the number of hate groups and extremist organizations that got their start in those years; the number steadily increased in each of the following years. In 2012–13, the SPLC counted 1,360 active Patriot groups and 873 other hate groups of various stripes, such as the Ku Klux Klan, skinheads, neo-Nazis, antigay groups, anti-Muslims groups, and so forth.

But then along came a sharp decline between 2013 and 2015, of Patriot groups in particular; the new total was 874. At first it looked like an aberration, but eventually the reason became clear: radicals were taking their acts out of organizations and going online. In March 2015, Mark Potok, a senior fellow at the SPLC, explained what the data was showing them: the advent of social media and other more dispersed means of sharing information had created a shift in how extremists shared their ideologies and how they recruited, too.

The evidence, he said, indicated "that large numbers of extremists have left organized groups because of the high social cost of being known to affiliate with them. Many of those people apparently now belong to no group, but operate instead mainly on the Internet, where they can offer their opinions anonymously and easily find others who agree with them—and where they can be heard by huge numbers of people without the hassles, dues, and poor leadership associated with membership in most groups." He continued, "In any event, as the movement to the Internet suggests, the importance of organized radical groups is declining for a number of reasons. In an age when ever more people are congregating on the web and in social media, the radical right is doing the same. With almost no charismatic leaders on the scene, there is little to attract radicals to join groups when they can broadcast their opinions across the world via the Internet and at the same time remain anonymous if they wish."

With these observations on the force of attraction of the Internet, he could have been describing Dylann Roof.

Dylann Roof hardly seemed to live in the real world, because before that day in Charleston he had made so little impact on it. The son of a carpenter and a barmaid, by the age of twenty-one he had never had an occupation other than landscaper, a job he only held for a few weeks. He couldn't be called a student, since he had dropped out after ninth grade. He had been married and divorced. Mostly he hung out in his room and played video games, taking drugs and getting drunk.

At some point in his late teens, though, a political bug kicked in, and he began posting online: mostly white-nationalist material, including memes promoting the "14 Words"—a white-supremacist creed about "ensuring the future of the white race"—and the symbol "88," which is a cipher for "Heil Hitler" (*h* is the eighth letter of the alphabet). Photos of Roof posing with guns, with a Confederate flag, with a Rhodesian flag deck, posing at plantations and at cemeteries in historic slavery sites decked the walls of his bedroom.

One of his favorite websites was a neo-Nazi forum called the *Daily Stormer*, which he seems to have first encountered after his discovery of the Council of Conservative Citizens website. Roof posted at the *Stormer* under the handle "AryanBlood1488," perhaps as early as September 2014, and his hatred of black people was already pronounced then. "White culture is World Culture," he wrote, "and by that I don't mean that our culture is made up of ones from around the world, I mean that our culture has been adopted by everyone in the world. This makes us feel as if it isn't special, because everyone has adopted it." A nearly identical passage appears in his manifesto.

He began making preparations for his big day. He bought a Glock 41 .45-caliber handgun, even though he had been busted for narcotics possession in February and, under normal circumstances, should have been prevented from buying any guns at all, but the FBI's background-check system failed to catch him.

He also began telling his friends that soon he was going to start shooting people. Two of his friends tried to hide his gun from him. Another old friend, Dalton Tyler, ran into him just a week before he took his fateful trip to Charleston. "He was big into segregation and other stuff," Tyler said. "He said he wanted to start a civil war. He said he was going to do something like that and then kill himself."

But no one took him seriously. No one called the police.

When he set out for Charleston the morning of June 17, Roof probably intended to carry out his shooting spree primarily at the College of Charleston, an elegant old-line Southern school in the older part of the city. That was what he had been telling his friends. But at some point he changed his mind, apparently because of the high levels of security at the college campus, and headed for Emanuel African Methodist Episcopal Church, one of the city's oldest churches and a historic center of civil-rights activism in South Carolina. Its pastor, the Reverend Clementa Pinckney, was a state senator and well-regarded spokesperson for the black community.

When Roof walked into the church at 8:20 p.m., a prayer service was under way with a large congregation in attendance. Roof sat down in a pew. Shortly afterward, the gathering broke up into smaller Bible study groups. Roof, the only white person in the church, joined the group that was being led by Rev. Pinckney. He sought out a seat next to Pinckney. There were eleven others in the group.

All were longtime members of the congregation and their family members. Daniel Simmons, seventy-four, the church's assistant pastor, had retired a few years before as the head pastor at a nearby African Methodist church. Cynthia Hurd, fifty-four, was the branch manager of St. Andrews Regional Library. Depayne Middleton-Doctor, forty-nine, a longtime singer in the church choir, was an admissions coordinator at the Charleston learning center of her alma mater, Southern Wesleyan University. Sharonda Coleman-Singleton, forty-five, also an assistant pastor at the church, was a track coach at Goose Creek High School. Myra Thompson, fifty-nine, a longtime churchgoer and Bible study teacher, was an active member of the Delta Sigma Theta sorority. Susie Jackson, eighty-seven, was a longtime member of the church. Felecia Sanders, fifty-eight, Jackson's younger sister, was attending the service to be with her family. Tywanza Sanders, twenty-six, Felecia's son, a

2014 graduate of Allen University, was an aspiring poet who was renowned for his broad smile. With them was Felecia's grand-daughter, five. Ethel Lance, seventy, was a longtime director of Charleston's Gaillard Auditorium who had worked at the church for thirty years. Polly Sheppard, seventy-one, was a church trustee.

For nearly an hour the group discussed Scripture among them-selves. Roof later told police that he nearly called off his plan because everyone "was so nice to him." But he eventually steeled himself, deciding he "had to go through with his mission."

No one is quite sure what set him off, but Felecia Sanders said later the group had just closed their eyes to begin the closing prayer when Dylann Roof stood up, began ranting that he was there to kill "niggers," and pulled out his Glock. He turned and fired point-blank at Rev. Pinckney, killing him instantly.

Then he pointed it at Susie Jackson, the oldest person in the room. Tywanza Sanders stood up and pleaded with Roof not to take out his hatred on innocent people. "You don't have to do this," he said.

"Yes I do," Roof answered. "I have to do it. You've raped our women, and you are taking over the country. You have to go. I have to do what I have to do."

Sanders dove across his elderly aunt, Susie Jackson, trying to shield her, and Roof opened fire, killing him first. Then he shot Susie Jackson too.

The room erupted in the sound of gunfire and screams. Roof was between the door and everyone else, so they had nowhere to go but to cower on the floor. He methodically roamed about the room, shooting all of the other occupants—first Rev. Simmons, and then the rest, shooting each victim multiple times. He reloaded the Glock five times. He screamed racial epithets at his victims, and taunted them: "Y'all want something to pray about? I'll give you something to pray about."

Somehow, when it was all over, he had missed Felecia Sanders and her five-year-old granddaughter, who lay still on the floor, pretend-ing to be dead, and Polly Sheppard, who also lay quivering on the floor. Roof stood over her.

"Did I shoot you?" he asked.

"No."

He paused, then said, "Good, 'cause we need someone to survive, because I'm gonna shoot myself, and you'll be the only survivor."

Then he turned away, pointed the gun to his head, and pulled the trigger—but it only clicked. He had run out of ammunition. So he walked out the door and into the night.

On the day after Dylann Roof's rampage, the flags over the South Carolina statehouse in Columbia flew at half-staff except for one, the Confederate battle flag at the nearby Confederate Monument, which was affixed atop a pole by state law and could only come down at the behest of the state legislature. Half-staff wasn't even an option. (The flag had been moved there after a controversy surrounding the flag's flying over the statehouse itself.) But even before Roof was caught, the photos of him waving Confederate flags began to appear, along with his manifesto, and suddenly that flag's position came into sharp focus.

Roof himself was captured the next morning in his car in Shelby, North Carolina. Another driver, Debbie Dills of Gastonia, North Carolina, spotted him while driving alongside him on US Route 74, and followed him for thirty-five miles while phoning the police with details of his whereabouts. Police surrounded his car and he surrendered without incident.

The massacre outraged and stunned the world. Most shocked were Americans, who had seemingly forgotten about the racial hatred that fueled white supremacism, both the street variety and the institutional kind. A number of acts of shocking terrorist violence had been committed for a variety of motives in recent years, but this one was fueled by pure old-fashioned racial hatred. It was as though Dylann Roof had summoned an ancient demon out of the American cellar that everyone had hoped had withered away out of neglect. Instead it had grown large and ravenous in the dark.

The shooting took place in the midst of rising racial turmoil in the United States. The Trayvon Martin shooting in February 2012 had sparked a growing national conversation about the disproportionate numbers of deaths of young black men while their murderers went free. Some of them had died while in police custody. The heated conversation turned into a bonfire when a young black man named Michael Brown was shot to death by a police officer in Ferguson, Missouri, in August 2014. The shooting sparked several days of civil unrest in Ferguson as large protest crowds confronted police riot forces. A grand jury's decision in November not to charge the police officer triggered another week of riots and some looting.

There were other similar incidents of inexplicable lethal force applied to black men and boys. In July 2014, Eric Garner died in a New York City policeman's chokehold. Tamir Rice, twelve, was shot in November 2014 by a Cleveland policeman for having a toy gun at a playground. Eric Harris was killed by Tulsa police detectives while trying to run away from an undercover sting in April 2015. Less than a week later, in Baltimore, Freddie Gray, twenty-five, died while in police custody after sustaining injuries to his neck and spine. The incidents kept mounting and drove the black community to become increasingly organized to push back. The movement called Black Lives Matter began making its presence felt in demonstrations around the United States.

South Carolina had had its own moment that spring in the unwelcome spotlight of racial strife—just weeks before Roof's attack: On April 4, Michael Slager, a white North Charleston police officer, confronted Walter Scott about the brake lights on Scott's 1991 Mercedes. Scott tried to flee; Slager caught up to him in a nearby vacant lot; Scott ran away again; Slager pulled his gun and shot him to death in the back. A bystander caught the shooting on video. Soon it went viral across the nation on social media and nightly newscasts.

But this time the policeman did not get away with it. After police viewed the video, Slager was arrested on April 7 and was indicted by a grand jury on June 8. Roof went on his rampage on June 17.

As it happened, Slager was Roof's cell-block neighbor at the detention center in North Charleston where police took him after his capture (the two were unable to communicate). Roof reportedly confessed immediately to his crime and told investigators it was his hope that he would start a race war.

But nothing of the sort happened. The black community did not rise up in violence and anger in response to the murders. Instead, the survivors and the victims' family members publicly forgave Roof and his fellow haters and urged the community to come together to heal. The black community chose to focus on helping that healing process happen. At the funerals for the victims, and in interviews with the survivors, forgiveness was the overriding theme.

"We welcomed you Wednesday night in our Bible study with open arms," said Felecia Sanders in a public statement she read aloud to Roof at his first court hearing. "You have killed some of the most beautifulest people that I know. Every fiber in my body hurts, and I will never be the same. Tywanza Sanders is my son, but Tywanza was my hero … May God have mercy on you."

Ethel Lance's daughter said, "I will never be able to hold her again, but I forgive you. And have mercy on your soul. You hurt me. You hurt a lot of people, but God forgives you, and I forgive you."

President Obama came to Charleston and delivered the eulogy at Rev. Pinckney's memorial. As for Dylann Roof's hopes for a race war, Obama called the massacre "an act that he presumed would deepen divisions that trace back to our nation's original sin. Oh, but God works in mysterious ways," Obama continued. "God has different ideas. He didn't know he was being used by God. Blinded by hatred, the alleged killer could not see the grace surrounding Rev. Pinckney and that Bible study group."

"We all have one thing in common. Our hearts are broken," said Mayor Joseph Riley Jr. at an interfaith prayer service. Riley received a standing ovation at the service when another speaker recalled a 120-mile march to Columbia that Riley led in 2000 to demand the removal of the Confederate flag from the statehouse grounds—a demand that was never fully met.

The Confederate flag had been hoisted over the South Carolina statehouse in 1962 on the orders of Governor Ernest Hollings, a

Democrat, at the behest of the state legislature, as a protest against desegregation. Everyone knew what the flag stood for, and they weren't afraid to say it: *White power. Segregation today, segregation tomorrow, segregation forever. Keep the niggers down.*

By 2000, no one was willing to say that anymore. Defenders of the flag's continued use relied on a set of euphemisms—"states' rights," "Southern heritage," "regional identity"—for what they all knew was an abiding belief in white supremacy. The historian Gordon Rhea explains:

It is no accident that Confederate symbols have been the mainstay of white supremacist organizations, from the Ku Klux Klan to the skinheads. They did not appropriate the Confederate battle flag simply because it was pretty. They picked it because it was the flag of a nation dedicated to their ideals: "that the negro is not equal to the white man." The Confederate flag, we are told, represents heritage, not hate. But why should we celebrate a heritage grounded in hate, a heritage whose self-avowed reason for existence was the exploitation and debasement of a sizeable segment of its population?

South Carolina's display of the Confederate flag from atop its statehouse dome was one of the more notorious examples of officialdom flaunting the symbol. The pressure remained intense to remove it from the grounds altogether, including boycotts of the state by both the National Collegiate Athletic Association and the National Association for the Advancement of Colored People.

Finally, after the Charleston massacre, South Carolina's Republican governor, Nikki Haley, was suddenly faced with the need for major damage control. Haley and others knew that it was time to act. On June 22, five days after the massacre, she held a press conference. "Today we are here in a moment of unity in our state without ill will to say it's time to move the flag from the capitol grounds," Haley said. The removal, she explained, was necessary to prevent the symbol from causing further pain.

Even some of the flag's staunchest defenders conceded the need for change. "With the winds that started blowing last week, I figured it would just be a matter of time," said Ken Thrasher of the South Carolina division of the Sons of Confederate Veterans. "Whatever the Legislature decides to do, we will accept it graciously."

On June 23, the Assembly began to consider a measure to remove the flag from the statehouse grounds. On July 10, in a solemn ceremony, the flag was taken down for the last time.

Not just in South Carolina but all around the South, the Confederate flag seemed to have taken on a much clearer, and much darker, meaning, and many Southerners decided it was time to be done with it. Governor Robert Bentley of Alabama ordered the removal of the Confederate flag flying over the statehouse in Montgomery. Governors in Virginia, North Carolina, and Maryland announced that they would cease offering state license plates featuring the flag. Mississippi legislators vowed to remove the symbol permanently from their own state flag.

Retailers around the country, including Wal-Mart, Amazon, eBay, Etsy, Sears, and Target, announced they would be pulling Confederate flags and related merchandise from their offerings. The largest flag manufacturers announced they were stopping their Confederate flag production line.

Monuments to the Confederacy and its heroes came under fire. In New Orleans, Mayor Mitch Landrieu ordered the removal of four statues, including the sixty-foot column in the heart of the city bearing the figure of General Robert E. Lee.

In Memphis, the city council voted to remove a memorial to General Nathan Bedford Forrest, a famed Confederate leader and the founder of the Ku Klux Klan.

In pop culture, too, the flag was being banned. Warner Bros. announced it was ceasing production of its "General Lee" toy cars. As for real cars, NASCAR's chairman announced the company would no longer sanction any use of the flag, and a number of prominent drivers, including Dale Earnhardt Jr. and Jeff Gordon, publicly supported the move. NASCAR races are traditionally a favored location to fly the Confederate flag, but in early July, all NASCAR tracks issued a joint statement asking for fans to refrain from flying or waving the Confederate flag at races.

Official proscriptions of the flag were one thing—reality on the ground, another. As the weeks went by, NASCAR's order was increasingly ignored. More and more Confederate flags started appearing in the stands. At the Coke Zero 400 in Florida on July 6, held at Daytona International Speedway, thousands of fans showed up with Confederate flags. Most of them angrily denounced NASCAR's "political correctness."

"NASCAR is too quick to try to be politically correct like everybody else," said Paul Stevens, of Port Orange, Florida.

Another NASCAR fan, Steven Rebenstorf, said, "The Confederate flag has absolutely nothing to do with slavery. It has nothing to do with divisiveness. It has nothing to do with any of that. It was just a battle banner until the Ku Klux Klan draped it around themselves. Now, all of a sudden, it represents slavery and that's not at all true."

"It's just a Southern pride thing," Larry Reeves from Jacksonville Beach, Florida, told the Associated Press. "It's nothing racist or anything."

The backlash to the backlash grew in volume. On July 17, one week after the flag came down at the South Carolina statehouse, the Ku Klux Klan held a protest in Columbia to demand that it be restored. Several hundred KKK protesters were met by an even larger crowd of counterprotesters, including a number of radical New Black Panthers. Police had trouble keeping the two sides from tangling, and five people wound up being arrested. Confederate flags were everywhere.

And it turned out to be a lovely day to recruit new members to the Klan.

"We're just trying to save our heritage," Roy Pemberton, a sixty-two-year-old Klansman, told potential recruits he met at the rally, most of them middle-aged white men. Pemberton handed them business cards with the group's hotline number and its slogan: "Racial Purity Is America's Security!"

"If they continue ... there will be a war, and we will fight for our heritage," Pemberton said. "There are things the South will fight for, and that is one of them. If it continues, there will be bloodshed."

The new backlash provided recruitment opportunities for the racist radical right, and not just the Klan.

Some of the most eager defenders of the flag were so-called neo-Confederates, far-right Southern ideologues who argue that the cause of the South was just, and agitate for modern-day secession. Two of their favorite organizations now leapt to the fore: the League of the South (LoS), an anti-black hate group, and the Sons of the Confederate Veterans (SCV), a formerly legitimate Southern-heritage group that in recent years has been hijacked by neo-Confederates. Michael Hill, the president of the League of the South, defended the Confederate banner, declaring, "The Confederate battle flag, along with our other cultural icons, is not merely an historical banner that represents the South. It is a shorthand symbol of our very ethnic identity as a distinct people—Southerners."

In Alabama, a joint protest in Montgomery by the Sons of the Confederate Veterans and the League of the South took place a week after Bentley removed the flag from the statehouse. William Flowers, vice chairman of the Georgia LoS, told the gathering, "We are pushing now to reach out and grab the hearts and minds of fellow Southerners to pull them in to believing that the politicians have betrayed them because it is true. They do not represent your interests. They have stabbed you in the back."

By the second weekend of July, more than seventy protests had been organized in eight states formerly in the Confederacy, drawing more than 10,000 participants. One rally, in Ocala, Florida, featured an eight-mile procession with more than 1,500 cars. These events quickly became recruitment magnets for groups eager to defend the flag and all that it represented.

James Edwards, host of the far-right radio show the *Political Cesspool*, charged that "our societal overseers" hated the South and the "symbol of our unique identity before the murders that took place in Charleston occurred." He accused these new "overseers" of "exploiting the tragedy in order to launch an attempt to completely eradicate the Confederate flag and any memory of the righteous cause for which it stood." The "righteous cause" included the defense of white supremacy. It was a reiteration of the beliefs that had lain behind the displays of the Confederate flag since the defeat in the Civil War.

The Klan became publicly involved in the campaign to remove the remains of Confederate war hero (and Ku Klux Klan founding father) from their Memphis monument. Thom Robb, head of the Knights of the Ku Klux Klan, offered via press release to move the general's statue and remains to Robb's Christian Revival Center near Harrison, Arkansas.

In Alabama, a nominally mainstream "heritage" group called the Alabama Flaggers congregated at the statehouse to protest the flag's removal there and extended an open invitation to League of the South members to attend. The Flaggers posted on Facebook: "We are rallying for the Secession from the United States of America. Bring your … secession flags [and] your secession signs."

The backlash soon spilled out of the South. Pro-Confederate flag rallies were held in such disparate locations as Phoenix, Spokane, and Warsaw, Indiana. By late August, there had been more than 200 such rallies, and by December the total had reached 356. The attendance was generally sparse, but it was often loud, with an ugly tone of anti-black and anti–civil rights animus.

On July 14, when President Obama traveled to Durant, Oklahoma, to speak to students at the high school, he was met by a cluster of protesters who were angry about the Confederate flag prohibitions.

"We're not gonna stand down from our heritage. You know, this flag's not racist. And I know a lot of people think it is, but it's really not. It's just a Southern thing, that's it," Trey Johnson told TV reporters. He had driven three hours from Texas to join the protest.

Things turned frightening in the Atlanta suburb of Douglasville on July 25. A family of African Americans was celebrating a child's birthday when a convoy of trucks bearing Confederate flags began trolling past, drawing the ire of several people at the party, who yelled at them to leave. At that point, more than seven pickup trucks circled and then parked in the field in front of their home, the passengers yelling racial epithets and threatening the families.

"One had a gun, saying he was gonna kill the niggers," the party's hostess, Melissa Alford, told a reporter. "Then one of them said, 'Gimme the gun, I'll shoot them niggers.'"

It was all caught on video. Later that fall fifteen people were indicted for making terrorist threats and engaging in "criminal street activity." Most of those indicted were members of a Georgia group, Respect the Flag.

Melissa Alford said, "If they want to make a statement that these flags mean something to them, I'm OK with that. But ... you can't go around just blatantly terrorizing people."

Actually, it was just getting started.

The movie *Trainwreck* is a mildly raunchy sex comedy, starring the comedienne Amy Schumer, that was doing boffo box office in the summer of 2015. But it was also coming in for its share of criticism. The *National Review*'s film critic, Armond White, ripped the film for promoting sexual immorality and feminism. "Schumer disguises a noxious cultural agenda as personal fiat," he wrote. "She's a comedy demagogue who okays modern misbehavior yet blatantly revels in PC notions about feminism, abortion, and other hot-button topics."

A young writer for Fox News chimed in: "As a young woman, yes, even younger than Schumer, all this attention and praise for raunchy behavior bothers me."

Those were all people who had bigger audiences than John Russell Houser, fifty-nine, with a history of bipolar disorder and other mental-health issues. Originally from Georgia and most recently from Alabama, he had moved to Lafayette, Louisiana, in early July and taken up residence at a Motel 6 near the freeway.

In his room, he scribbled his "random" thoughts about the moral state of America in his journal:

America is a filth farm. America is no longer America, i.e., all liberal political measures are approved without a vote of the people. These are the measures that lack logic, morality, or financial responsibility. It is this that boils the blood of the citizens, [and] which causes them to dig in their heals. If you have not stood against filth, you are now a soft target.

If the founders of this nation could have seen what the US would become, they would say, "Let us destroy it."

America is in the middle of celebrating filth, and as such they are the enemy. Those who have not stood are equally culpable.

Soft targets are everywhere.

I have hidden nothing and have hated the US for at least 30 years. It will soon be every man for himself. A global rearrangement comes soon.

America is in the business of
    1—making whores and prostitutes of girls and women.
    2—making niggers of black people
    3—breaking up families that could have survived in a society of decency
    4—making sexual deviants (homosexuals) of normal people
    5—censoring people who love what is normal
    6—creating division amongst people that could have lived in harmony based on logic (affirmative action)

America as a whole is now the enemy. All soft targets included.

Nowhere in the US is it safe.

Houser had a long online history of similar ravings. Most of his postings indicate his obsession with "the power of the lone wolf," a reference to terrorist attacks carried out by solo operators unconnected to any organization. It is a modality favored by far-right extremists. In 2005 he registered to attend a conference led by the former Ku Klux Klansman David Duke, and later praised Duke in his online comments. He also had a penchant for praising Adolf Hitler, penning lines such as "Hitler is loved for the results of his pragmatism."

Like Jim David Adkisson, Honser also loved to hate on liberals: "Liberals are in the last stage of killing the golden goose, moral people who pay their bills, most notably, the white MAN."

Once settled in Louisiana, Houser appears to have tried scoping out his "soft target"—the Grand 16 movie theater in Lafayette. He showed up at the theater a couple of times in disguises, once dressed as a woman, and behaving "erratically."

On July 23, he showed up ten minutes late for the 7:10 showing of *Trainwreck* and took a seat in the second-to-last row. He had a .40-caliber handgun in his pants pocket and two ten-round magazines. About ten minutes after he had arrived, he stood, pulled the gun from his pocket, and shot the two people sitting directly in front of him. Then he began walking down the stairway aisle, shooting people in their seats and as they fled. He reloaded once, firing in all at least thirteen rounds.

When the shooting subsided, Houser attempted to return to his car by mingling with panicked patrons. But then he himself panicked when police arrived with lights and sirens blazing, and he ran back inside, firing again randomly at patrons as he did so. Finally he stopped, put the gun in his mouth, and fired a last shot.

Houser killed two women and wounded nine people. The injuries ranged in severity from light to life-altering, and the victims ranged in age from teenagers to women and men in their sixties. One of the victims suffered four gunshot wounds.

The news of the mass shooting hit the networks that night. Fox News's Megyn Kelly, anchoring the news desk that evening, pondered the breaking story: "Any reason to believe there might be a connection to ISIS, or radical Islam, or terror as we understand it in this country?"

When investigators got to Houser's Motel 6 room, they found wigs and dresses and makeup for disguises. It looked as though he had planned to escape.

They also found his journal. It didn't explain precisely why he decided to target a theater showing *Trainwreck*, but the general direction of his thinking was easy to discern. It isn't hard to guess why he chose a theater showing that movie as a "soft target," since he likely figured the audience would be full of liberals and women of questionable moral values.

Investigators also noted that Houser had penned some thoughts on Dylann Roof, whom in one note he called "good but green."

"Had Dylan Roof reached political maturity he would have seen the word is not nigger, but liberal," Houser wrote, an eerie echo of Adkisson's views. "But thank you for the wake up call Dylann."

2

Alt-America

Ladies and Gentlemen: In American public life there is an alternative dimension, a mental space beyond fact or logic, where the rules of evidence are replaced by paranoia. Welcome to Alternative America—Alt-America, for short.

Alt-America is an alternative universe that has a powerful resemblance to our own, except that it's a completely different America, the nation its residents have concocted and reconfigured in their imaginations. It is not the America where the rest of us live. In this other America, suppositions take the place of facts, and conspiracy theories become concrete realities. Its citizens live alongside us in our universe, but their perception of that universe places them in a different world altogether, one scarcely recognizable to those outside it.

In Alt-America:

- Barack Obama is secretly a Muslim born in Kenya who conspired with a global elite and terrorist radicals to impose sharia law on America.
- Obama, Hillary Clinton, and most mainstream politicians are simultaneously the corrupt pawns of a nefarious New World Order (NWO) that seeks to impose a global government that will turn the world's population into their slaves.
- Global climate change is a hoax concocted by the NWO and

environmentalist elites who want to impose massive regulatory regimes on businesses and force ordinary Americans out of public lands.

- These same global elites want to gut the Second Amendment so that Americans' guns can be confiscated and the populace disarmed, all in the name of public safety, but really for the purpose of imposing its tyrannical dictatorship.
- The current American government is actually an illegal and unconstitutional entity that seized control of the United States in the 1930s and, through its corrupt Federal Reserve Bank, controls the nation's fiat currency for its own nefarious ends.
- Prejudice and oppression against white people now is a greater problem for the world than whatever bigotry minorities might face. White people are the primary targets of oppression by an elite that shames them with "political correctness" whenever they object to the rising tide of brown faces—especially foreign-language-speaking Muslims and Latinos—in their midst.
- Minorities, especially blacks and illegal immigrants, are busily sucking up taxpayer dollars through welfare programs while homeless veterans go hungry. Organizations like Black Lives Matter are just another chapter in minorities' claims to victimhood, while their adherents shoulder no responsibility themselves.
- Illegal immigrants, especially Latinos, are part of a conspiracy by liberals and Democrats to overwhelm the country with welfare-dependent parasites who eagerly vote for the liberal agenda in order to sustain their lifestyle.

The longer you dwell in this universe, the more likely you are to absorb some of its more exotic beliefs, such as the theory that chemtrails left by jet airliners are actually part of a New World Order plot to slowly poison the populace or spread mind-control drugs, or that federal emergency-management plans are in reality a cover for a plot to begin rounding up Americans and forcing them into concentration camps.

Once Alt-Americans start to believe some of these kooky ideas, it becomes a simple matter to persuade them of the reality of other kooky ideas, new threats, new conspiracies against them and the nation. When Donald Trump informs his followers that there's a massive media and establishment conspiracy to "rig the election" and deny him the presidency, they not only eagerly embrace the claim but begin talking about a "revolution" to overthrow or even assassinate Hillary Clinton.

Established facts supported by concrete real-world evidence are inconsequential to people inside the Alt-America universe—indeed, those facts are instead interpreted as further evidence of the conspiracy and its efforts to hide "the truth." Never mind that President Obama is a practicing, churchgoing Christian who was born in Hawaii and has produced both versions of his birth certificate to prove that. And if he really is sympathetic to Islamic radicalism and the installment of sharia law, he certainly has an odd way of showing it, having ordered the killing of the Al Qaeda leaders Osama bin Laden and Anwar al-Awlaki, as well as the ISIS (Islamic State in Iraq and Syria) leaders Abu Bakr al-Baghdadi and Hafiz Sayed Khan.

Never mind that the New World Order conspiracy has long been recognized as the product of the fevered dreams of the extremist Patriot movement and John Birch Society elements of the American right that have been claiming since the 1950s that society is on the brink of mass roundups and enslavement that have never materialized—ideas that keep finding fresh life under new guises.

It doesn't matter to Alt-Americans that a consensus of the world's climate scientists agrees that global climate change is a reality that is already upon us, nor that the world's ice caps and glaciers are measurably shrinking at an alarming rate, and that sea levels around the world have already begun rising, already begun inundating low-lying American states such as Louisiana.

You can try explaining to someone from this universe that, even though a number of liberals and Democrats have proposed minor regulatory measures in response to the epidemic of gun violence that costs 33,000 Americans their lives every year, no one has proposed any kind of mass gun-confiscation measures or any other law that might violate the Second Amendment. You might even point out that gun-rights advocates have been warning for eight years that President Obama planned such tyrannical measures in the imminent future—steps that never even came close to materializing. It won't matter to them.

You can explain to them that the Federal Reserve is a heavily regulated entity that mostly watches over interest rates and the monetary supply. You might even try explaining that abandoning the gold standard in 1971 ensured the value of the dollar, but far-right conspiracists still claim that it resulted from a one-world-government plot. You can try, but they will dismiss you.

And so it goes for the rest of the universe inside of Alt-America. In more than a few respects its strange reversal of realities resembles that of Planet Bizarro, the square planet sometimes visited by Superman. Planet Bizarro almost always appeared purely for its humorous effect; likewise the notions promulgated by Alt-Americans are ripe fodder for people who want to make fun of them.

The beating heart of Alt-America, however, is the ancient drumbeat of white identity politics, a fear of nonwhite people who speak foreign languages and follow alien creeds. These people embody the Other: non- or sub-human beings whose presence is felt as a form of degradation. Good Alt-Americans loathe and fear this Other. That may be partly because race in this universe is essentially a zero-sum proposition: if one race gains in status or power, then another must lose concomitantly.

So when confronted with a discomfiting civil-rights movement like Black Lives Matter, they do not hear the message its name communicates clearly: "Black lives matter, and white people must stop acting as if they did not." What racists hear instead is a zero-sum assertion: "Only black lives matter, and no one else's." Their reality is distorted by their inability to comprehend other people or have empathy for them.

The Alt-Americans view any attempts at parity in the value of a life as a direct threat to their own privileged position. And privileged they are: Even though whites are losing their long-standing ethnic dominance of American demographics, they have, through a combination of factors, maintained their powerfully privileged positions economically, politically, culturally, and especially within the law-enforcement and justice systems.

They are similarly impervious to the factual realities regarding immigration. You can demonstrate to them how immigrants actually pay large sums into the federal income-tax and Social Security systems through their paycheck deductions (while receiving few of the benefits of those taxes, since by law they are precluded from participating in most federal "welfare" programs), and in the end pay substantially more in taxes than they receive in benefits. You can explain to them that the primary reason there are so many undocumented immigrants outside the system is that the American economy generates hundreds of thousands of unskilled-labor jobs every year that businesses have difficulty filling because of their often difficult and unpleasant natures, and yet our immigration system, still awaiting comprehensive reform, only issues around 5,000 green cards annually to cover that labor. You can show them crime statistics proving that immigrants commit crime at a substantially lower rate than the general population, the white populace included.

Such information doesn't make a dent. Alt-Americans will continue to believe that immigrants suck away their taxpaying dollars and bring crime and disease to the country and that we must erect a big wall to keep them out. They will continue to insist that Americans not only can fill those jobs, they need them. Latinos are displacing American workers, Alt-Americans believe, and the border is a national security risk—so immigration "reform" must wait until the border is secure. Immigration experts understand that this places the cart before the horse—that the border will never be secure until a sane policy that encourages legal immigration is in place.

Alt-America is largely the creation of an increasingly entrenched conspiracy industry that generates one theory after another about the truth that lies behind the public narrative generated in the mainstream media. These theories' influence now reaches broadly into the mainstream itself. This conspiracism industry is composed mainly of a network of radio hosts and Internet entrepreneurs, who churn out a steady stream of New World Order plots and predictably Alt-American interpretations of daily news events. Alex Jones and his Infowars website are the best known of this group. Jones claims that a variety of global events, including the Boston Marathon bombing and the November 2014 Paris massacres, were in reality false flag operations carried out by agents of the New World Order.

It's a self-contained universe. While this network often differs on the precise details of the conspiracies that populate Alt-America—sometimes resulting in vicious internecine bickering and "purity tests"—the overarching story and general nature of The Enemy is always the same: namely, some variation on the New World Order, or "globalists," or any other term used to name the secretive cabal they believe is conspiring to rule mankind. This Alt-America universe has come to reflect most closely the far-right ideology of the Patriot-constitutionalist-militia movement.

The material this industry produces becomes grist for a hundred thousand conversations on Internet chat forums and on social media such as Facebook and Twitter. A horde of bloggers, homemade YouTube political preachers, and far-right ideologues echo and spread these theories. The volume and intensity of this material that's been generated, especially since 2008, is genuinely astonishing. Equally astonishing is the extent to which you can find these ideas being increasingly voiced by ostensibly mainstream right-wing pundits on the radio and in media such as Fox News.

The material spreads readily. Any corner of the Alt-American universe can suffice to attract new believers who, sometimes in very short order, become wholesale subscribers to the many different facets of Alt-America. For example, a staple of the occupiers of the January 2016 Patriot takeover of the Malheur National Wildlife Refuge was that the Constitution doesn't permit the federal government to own public lands outside of the District of Columbia. Someone who believes that may well start spouting other "constitutionalist" theories, such as that a county sheriff is the supreme law of the land, superior to federal authorities, and expressing fears that there is a plot to drive white men off the land and into the cities, to take away their guns and Second Amendment rights as well, and so on from there.

For Americans outside the Alt-America universe, "cockamamie" doesn't begin to describe how such ideas sound when Alt-Americans begin spouting unintelligible lingo at them. Some may question the Alt-Americans' sanity and their intelligence. Yet various studies and polls of subscribers to conspiracy theories and Patriot movement beliefs have shown that the majority of Alt-Americans are better educated than the average American and have incomes well above the median. Their beliefs and worldviews are frequently based on close readings of arcane documents (legal and otherwise); they also often possess an extraordinarily detailed knowledge of various putative "facts" that, on close examination, turn out not to be facts at all. Alt-Americans are neither stupid nor unlettered; what they are instead is oddly gullible, eager to absorb any "fact" if it supports their worldview, and insistent that people who believe official explanations or mainstream media narratives are the *real* gullible fools, or "sheeple," as their lexicon prefers.

Alt-Americans share a set of personality traits that distinguish them from people who are less prone to join them, yet they simultaneously operate in the same universe as everyone else. This is why they are able to function perfectly well alongside the rest of us, why they seem so normal, even likable at times—until those moments when their world bangs up against ours and they attempt to assert their ideas.

The political scientist Eric Oliver of the University of Chicago argues that conspiracy theories are "simply another form of magical thinking," Oliver explained in an interview. And as with all types of magical thinking, people engage in conspiracy theories in order to cope with difficult emotions. Usually this emotion is the apprehension that is triggered by an inexplicable or unusual event. In struggling to restore our emotional equilibrium, we search for patterns. In looking for patterns, we use mental shortcuts called heuristics. These heuristics include our tendency to ascribe intentionality to inanimate objects or to assume that things that resemble each other share core traits ... Because conspiracy theories articulate these heuristics, they may feel more intuitively compelling than other explanations, particularly to people in distress."

The legal scholars Cass Sunstein and Adam Vermeule explored the spread and pervasiveness of conspiracism in a widely read study of the subject. They say the phenomenon is perhaps best understood if first we "examine how people acquire information." They observe that there is an epistemic, real-world challenge for all of us in figuring out what is real information and what might be false or delusionary: "For most of what they believe that they know, human beings lack personal or direct information; they must rely on what other people think." This is no minor issue: What we believe to be true shapes how we view the world, the behavior of others, and the meaning of events. We have to depend on other people—our parents, friends, teachers, the people who write the books and newspapers we read, the people who produce the television and movies we watch—to provide us with that array of information, facts, and opinion.

We all have built-in methods for sorting through the blizzard of information the world confronts us with. Most of these begin with trial and error—we pretty quickly discover that false, misleading, or distorted information can bring us to grief from life experience. Eventually we settle into patterns of gathering information that we become comfortable with as we learn to recognize reliable sources of facts. For most of us, this system of sorting through and figuring out the world usually revolves around established sources of reliable facts such as educators, experts, and journalists, as well as our personal acquaintances and family members.

In an era of high-speed communications and instant technology, this task of sorting through information has become more acutely personalized and haphazard than it was in the past. The arrival of the Internet as many people's primary source of information has rendered much of the flow of our facts into 140-character tweets and video sound bites. As the Internet becomes cluttered with highly ideological propaganda mills and fake news sites, and as a flood of tweets and Facebook posts spread falsehoods alongside genuine information, it's become exponentially more difficult to sort out just what information is accurate and what is not.

Most people alive in the twenty-first century have developed a healthy skepticism toward what they're exposed to by a mainstream media landscape that is littered with biased "analysts" and representatives of corporate interests out to make a buck. But some people have elevated that skepticism to an unhealthy level, so that they view everything produced by the mainstream media or official government or academic sources with a typically self-reinforcing form of highly selective skepticism. They cannot believe any kind of official explanation for events, actions, or policies, but instead seek an alternative one. When this happens, their extreme skepticism flips into extreme gullibility, so that they become suckers for conspiracy theories that confirm the narrative they want to believe.

This shapes—or rather, distorts—their relationship to authority. Any kind of authority that exists outside of their universe, particularly sources with the taint of mainstream liberalism (embodied by Obama, Clinton, and the Democratic Party), is viewed as illegitimate and untrustworthy and is to be vehemently rejected and ardently opposed. In the meanwhile, any authority within the Alt-America universe, especially political figures, conspiracist pundits, and Patriot movement leaders, are revered as reliable authorities. Some of Donald Trump's followers refer to him as Glorious Leader, or GL.

The personality trait common to most conspiracists and dwellers in Alt-America is authoritarianism. Most people think of authoritarianism as a political phenomenon in which whole nations are subjected to dictatorial rule, and it's typically considered in light of the authoritarian leaders who lead such regimes. But it's also

41

a phenomenon studied in depth by psychologists, whose focus is on the masses whom they control, ordinary people who willingly sacrifice their personal freedoms in the name of an orderly society shaped to their personal beliefs and prejudices.

How could supposedly freedom-loving Americans subscribe to an authoritarian worldview? Psychologists have established that most people have some authoritarian tendencies, but these are balanced by such factors as personal empathy and critical thinking skills. In some personalities, however, a combination of factors such as strict upbringing, personal trauma, of a harsh rearing environment can produce people who are attracted to the idea of a world in which strong authorities produce order and stability, often through iron imposition of law and order.

The psychologist Robert Altemeyer of the University of Manitoba, one of the world's leading experts in this personality research, has compiled a list of authoritarian personality traits that help explain the motivations of Donald Trump's supporters. Not every authoritarian exhibits every trait, of course; conversely, everyone shares these traits, but not to the high degree of the authoritarian personality:

- Ethnocentric, strongly inclined to experience the world as a member of their in-group versus everyone else. Their strong commitment to their in-group makes them zealous in its cause.
- Fearful of a dangerous world. Their parents taught them, more than parents usually do, that the world is dangerous. They may also be genetically predisposed to experiencing stronger-than-average fear.
- Self-righteous. They believe they are the "good people"; this unlocks hostile impulses against those they consider bad.
- Aggressive. If an authority figures gives them the green light to attack someone, they lower the boom.
- Biased. Holding prejudices against racial and ethnic minorities, non-heterosexuals, and women.
- Contradictory beliefs. Opposite beliefs exist side by side in

separate compartments in their minds. As a result, their thinking is full of double standards.

- Poor reasoning skills. If they like the conclusion of an argument, they don't pay much attention to whether the evidence is valid or the argument is consistent.
- Dogmatic. Because they have gotten their beliefs mainly from the authorities in their lives, rather than thinking things out for themselves, they have no real defense when facts or events indicate they are wrong. So they just dig in their heels and refuse to change.
- Dependent on social reinforcement of their beliefs. They think they are right because almost everyone they know, almost every news broadcast they see, almost every radio commentator they listen to, tells them they are. That is, they screen out the sources that will suggest that they are wrong.
- Limited in their exposure to contrary viewpoints. Because they severely limit their exposure to different people and ideas, they overestimate the level of agreement with their ideas. Conviction of being in the majority bolsters their attacks on the undesirable minorities they see in the country.
- Easily manipulated. People may pretend to espouse their causes and dupe them to gain their own advantage.
- Weak power of self-reflection. They have little insight into why they think and do what they do.

The authoritarian personality's demand for leadership by powerful authority figures also helps explain their vehement rejection of the leadership of such liberal politicians as Barack Obama, Bill Clinton, and Hillary Clinton. An authoritarian by nature wishes to follow the orders of the president, but cannot do so when someone viewed as an illegitimate usurper holds the position. Proving the fundamental illegitimacy of these figures—as a sexual pervert, a Muslim foreigner, and a lying crook, respectively—has been the driving preoccupation of their various campaigns to attack these politicians.

Authoritarianism as a worldview creates a certain kind of cognitive dissonance, a feeling of unreality, because it runs smack into the complex nature of the modern world and attempts to impose its simplified, black-and-white explanation of reality onto a reality that contradicts and undermines it at every turn. Thus, conspiracism is appealing to the people who tell pollsters they "don't recognize their country anymore." They are bewildered by the new brown faces and strange languages that people their cultural landscapes. They may long for a 1950s-style suburban America and are angry that the world no longer works that way.

Conspiracy theories offer explanations as to why the country is no longer what they wish it to be, *why* it has become unrecognizable. These narratives come to represent deeper truths about their world, while repeatedly reinforcing their long-held prejudices. They help them to ignore the uncomfortable nature of the changes the world, the nation, and its society are undergoing. Simply put, conspiracism provides a clear, self-reinforcing explanation for a sense of personal disempowerment.

Oddly enough, projection—interpreting others as results of tendencies that are actually one's own tendencies—also is a factor in the spread of conspiracism. One study found that the people who were particularly inclined to suspect others of engaging in conspiracies were themselves inclined to conspire against others. Another study found that conspiracists—even as they accused activists on the political left (particularly black activists) of fomenting violence—were themselves more prone to engage in violence; hence their mounting threats to start a revolution and a civil war after the 2016 election if Hillary Clinton were to win, followed by the wave of ethnic violence they unleashed in the wake of their actual victory at the polls.

This propensity for projection is especially noticeable in the most important aspect of Alt-America: its real-world agenda, which is to impose its worldview on the rest of us. Alt-Americans fret and stew over imagined plots to round up Americans and place them in concentration camps or even execute them in a mass genocide, and fear the imposition of a dictatorial regime in which they have no

44

say. Yet their own political agenda would result in the rounding up and incarceration of millions of people, while imposing a dictatorial regime shaped in their own political image that would silence any kind of leftist impulse.

In fact, in print and on YouTube, many Alt-Americans freely fantasize about their desire to execute liberals, terrorists, "race mixers," and other traitors. I call this desire *eliminationism*—a politics, and its accompanying rhetoric, whose goal is to excise whole segments of the population in the name of making it "healthy." This mindset is a common feature of authoritarianism; the Holocaust was a particularly horrifying case of eliminationist genocide perpetrated by an authoritarian regime. Eliminationist rhetoric lays the groundwork by being dehumanizing, the kind of talk that reduces human beings to vermin and diseases, such as when you hear immigrants described as "rats in a granary," or Muslims as "a cancer"—beings fit primarily for elimination. The rhetoric gives tacit or explicit permission for the final essence, violent acts, beginning with hate crimes and escalating into mass roundups and genocide.

Eliminationist rhetoric is common to Alt-America, as the public frequently saw in the Trump campaign. It was, after all, a campaign initially predicated on a racially charged conspiracy theory that Barack Obama was not born in the United States (a requirement for any president). The campaign's opening salvo, against Mexican immigrants, was openly eliminationist in calling for their mass deportation, and soon included similar demands for Muslims and the LGBT community. Trump's constant campaign message was unmistakable as to just how he intended to "make America great again": get rid of these people, deport them, prevent them from ever entering the country in the first place, and lock up or silence the rest of them.

This is the point at which Alt-America represents a real danger to American democratic institutions, threatening to displace them with a crude and frightening authoritarianism, enforced by state-sanctioned vigilantism. One of Alt-America's most powerful and abiding effects is to displace people from a sense of concrete reality by putting them in an epistemological bubble that insulates them from facts, logic, and reason. From within this kind of bubble, objectifying other people, rendering those outside the bubble as the Other, and then demonizing them, is almost inevitable. Once other people are conceptualized this way, inflicting violence not only becomes simple but in fact may even appear to be necessary. Certainly, that is how they rationalize it.

As Alt-America has grown, so has the violence that inevitably accompanies it: acts of domestic terrorism, hate crimes, and threats of "revolution" and "civil war," backed by a wave of citizen militias. All of them gained impetus during the Obama years and there was a significant wave of such incidents in 2015 and 2016, very likely fueled by the Trump campaign.

Indeed, the Trump campaign itself had an effect on the ground similar to that of eliminationist rhetoric generally: it seemingly gave permission, in its stubborn refusal to bow to "political correctness," for people to act and speak in an openly bigoted and spiteful fashion. It was as though the campaign lifted the lid off the national id, and the violent, vicious tendencies that had been held in check for years came crawling right out.

It's difficult to put a finger on exactly how large the Alt-American universe is; at any one time there's no clear measure of how many people subscribe to its worldview. From ratings data we can see that Alex Jones's Infowars audience at times exceeds 2 million weekly listeners and viewers, but that doesn't indicate how many people actually believe what he says. Some listeners are critics and skeptics amused by his hyperemotional rants.

Polling data give us a clearer idea. A 2013 survey of American voters by Public Policy Polling about various conspiracy theories found the following:

- 37 percent of voters believed global warming is a hoax; 51 percent did not. Fifty-eight percent of Republicans versus 11 percent of Democrats said they thought global warming was a hoax. Among independents 41 percent said global warming was a hoax and 51 percent said it wasn't. Among Romney voters 61 percent believed global warming is a hoax.

- 6 percent of voters believed Osama bin Laden is still alive.
- 21 percent of voters said a UFO crashed in Roswell, New Mexico, in 1947 and the US government covered it up. More Romney voters (27 percent) than Obama voters (16 percent) believed in a UFO cover-up.
- 28 percent of voters believed that a secret power elite with a globalist agenda is conspiring eventually to rule the world through an authoritarian world government, or New World Order. A plurality of Romney voters (38 percent) believed in the New World Order compared to 35 percent who didn't.
- 28 percent of voters believed Saddam Hussein was involved in the 9/11 attacks. 36 percent of Romney voters believed Saddam Hussein was involved in 9/11; 41 percent did not.
- 20 percent of voters believed there is a link between childhood vaccines and autism; 51 percent did not.
- 7 percent of voters thought the moon landing was faked.
- 13 percent of voters (22 percent of Romney voters) thought Barack Obama was the Antichrist.

More recent polling related to the conspiracy theories that have swirled around the Trump campaign has revealed that these kinds of beliefs have become more established and widespread in the ensuing years, inflamed in many cases by Trump himself.

In 2014 political scientists J. Eric Oliver and Thomas J. Woods found that at least half of the general American public believes in one kind of conspiracy theory or another; 25 percent of the poll respondents believed that President Obama was not an American citizen. The most widely held conspiracy theory, believed by 40 percent of those polled, was that the Federal Drug Administration is secretly withholding cancer cures.

Survey figures strongly suggest that Trump's campaign drove these numbers up. By August 2016, a poll conducted by NBC News found that 72 percent of registered Republican voters doubted that Obama's citizenship was real. A May 2016 Public Policy Polling survey found that two-thirds of Trump's supporters believed that Obama was secretly a Muslim. Political issues weren't the only ones that surged: an October 2016 Fairleigh Dickinson poll found that 60 percent of Trump's supporters now also believed that global warming was a myth concocted by scientists.

In the countdown to the election, the propensity for conspiracism among Trump voters intensified. Encouraged by Trump's frequent campaign trail charges that the election was rigged and his refusal, in the third and final presidential debate on October 19, to say he would accept the results of the election were he to lose, his supporters quickly embraced the conspiracy theories ginned up by Alex Jones and other Trump supporters. An August 2016 Public Policy Polling survey found that 69 percent of Trump voters believed that if Hillary Clinton won the election, it would be because it was "rigged," whereas only 16 percent thought it would be because she got more votes than Trump.

The PPP poll had a peculiar finding related to the long-standing right-wing loathing of the Association of Community Organizations for Reform Now, better known as ACORN, a group primarily committed to enrolling minority voters. It had been driven out of existence in 2010 by a right-wing scandal involving heavily edited videos. The poll asked: "Do you think ACORN will steal the election for Hillary Clinton, or not?" The pollsters found that "40 percent of Trump voters think that ACORN... will steal the election for Clinton. That shows the long staying power of GOP conspiracy theories."

Indeed, this was not an overnight phenomenon. The dumpster Donald Trump's campaign set on fire in the 2016 election had been slowly filling for many years.

48

3

Black Helicopters and Truck Bombs

The arrangements for my first meeting with John Trochmann, in November 1994, were an exquisite exercise in paranoia. On the phone beforehand he had insisted he meet me at the bridge over the Clark Fork River near the little town of Noxon, Montana, where he lived. I had been waiting outside my car at the appointed spot for about ten minutes when he came driving across in his car.

He got out and we shook hands and sized each other up, chatting about the cold air and the freezing river. Trochmann was a slight, skinny man with a bristling gray beard and sharp eyes, with a slightly nervous demeanor. It was cold and our breaths formed little clouds of mist around our heads. I took some photos of him, and then he told me to follow him in his car.

There was nothing ultrasecret about our meeting place—a little restaurant-tavern in Noxon's main street business district, a comfy hewn-log joint of a type common in these parts of Montana. Over the course of the next couple of hours, over coffee and a few sandwiches, Trochmann frankly laid out his alternative universe and plied me with piles of evidence he claimed proved its existence. He was not unlikable, but his personality had a brittle quality that made him seem volatile, so I chose not to push him too hard that day with questions.

He seemed to have a lot of friends in town, including the restaurant's owner, who was working that afternoon behind the bar. A TV mounted high on the wall at the bar's end played news from CNN, which began running reports from Hurricane Gordon, which had slammed into Florida.

Trochmann and the bartender exchanged knowing looks. "Boy, that's really late, isn't it?" he said. The man nodded. I asked him what he meant. Was he suggesting that someone was manipulating the weather?

"Sure," Trochmann said. "Naples, Florida, got hit at the same time Naples, Idaho [site of the Ruby Ridge standoff], did."

Really? That wasn't just an odd coincidence?

"Yeah, right," he retorted. "And I have another bridge for sale for you."

John Trochmann believed in a lot of things. He believed the federal government was capable of manipulating the weather, even causing hurricanes, through a secret radar installation up in the Arctic. He believed the feds were building hidden concentration camps intended to house gun owners and right-wing Americans like himself. He believed they intended to recruit Bloods and Crips street-gang members to round them up into black helicopters. And that's a mere sampling.

Trochmann, more than any other person, was the primary wellspring and original source of many of the conspiracy theories that flourished in the 1990s. He gave people like Alex Jones not only their inspiration but the grist for their conspiracy mills. Trochmann's Militia of Montana (MOM), based out of his home in Noxon, was not a real militia—it was a mail-order operation that specialized in disseminating material explaining to people not only how they could form their own "citizen militias," but why they should do so (the New World Order). Trochmann himself—a follower of the white-supremacist religious movement Christian Identity—was prone to lifting ideas, claims, and "evidence" from his fellow Patriots, but he gave them such wide distribution that MOM became

known as the go-to source for conspiratorial explanations of virtually every modern problem and event.

It was Trochmann who first distributed maps showing the location of FEMA "concentration camps" where Americans would be
rounded up under the New World Order (NWO); who first suggested
that the government was using radio transmitters and chemtrails to
control the weather and people's behavior; and who first claimed
that the 1995 Oklahoma City bombing was a secret government
"false flag" operation designed to discredit the Patriot movement.

Trochmann had been living under the shadow of the law for many
years as a result of a custody dispute over his then-teenage daughter
Brandi. She had run away at age thirteen with her father from her
mother's custody in Minnesota in 1988, the same year that Trochmann had moved from there to Montana, following in the footsteps
of his brother Dave, another Identity member who had arrived in
the state four years earlier. The girl had been seen numerous times
with him around Noxon; eventually the local sheriff issued an arrest
warrant, and Trochmann spent some time in the county jail on
custodial-interference charges, but his daughter never did return
to Minnesota. Instead, she became a teen bride when she married
another member of their Christian Identity church.

The Trochmann brothers wound up playing a key role in one
of the Patriot movement's seminal events. Both brothers attended
Christian Identity gatherings at the Church of Jesus Christ–
Christian in Hayden Lake, Idaho, better known to the outside world
as the home compound of the neo-Nazi Aryan Nations. At those
gatherings they became friends with Randy and Vicki Weaver, a
young couple who in 1984 had fled Iowa to make a home in the deep
woods of the Idaho Panhandle, about two hours' drive from Noxon.
It was called Ruby Ridge.

Rumors that Dave Trochmann might be involved in smuggling guns into the United States from Canada brought Bureau
of Alcohol, Tobacco and Firearms agents sniffing around Ruby
Ridge in 1990. It soon emerged that Weaver had sold a sawed-off
shotgun—an illegal firearm—to an ATF informant. ATF agents

put the squeeze on the wiry survivalist: either he would provide information about the Trochmanns' activities or he would go to jail for selling an illegal weapon. Weaver walked away, telling them to go ahead and charge him.

And they did. In February 1991 Weaver was arrested in a roadside sting, taken to court in Coeur d'Alene, and charged. However, the judge released him on his own recognizance. Weaver then retreated to his remote cabin on Ruby Ridge and refused to come out for nearly an entire year, now facing federal warrants as a fugitive. Federal marshals began staking out the property, setting up surveillance equipment and trying to figure out the best way to arrest Weaver with a minimum of violence.

One day in August 1992 a team of six marshals went up to check the equipment. The Weavers' dog, Striker, heard them and took off into the woods to find them. Randy, his teenage son Sammy, and Kevin Harris, a family friend, followed the dog down the trail and directly to the marshals' hiding spot. Rather than let Striker reveal their position, the marshals shot the dog. Just then Sammy came into view and he witnessed the act. He began firing at the marshals, as did Kevin Harris. When the smoke from the exchange of gunfire cleared, both Sammy Weaver and Marshal William Degan lay dead.

So began one of the most infamous armed standoffs in law-enforcement history. It lasted ten days and also claimed the life of Vicki Weaver. She was shot by a sniper the day after Sammy and Degan were killed when she held the door open for her husband and Harris as they tried to escape an FBI barrage. She was holding a baby in her arms. Randy Weaver, his children, and Harris remained holed up in the cabin for another week. Then, on Day Six, Colonel James "Bo" Gritz, a former Green Beret and Vietnam vet, arrived at Ruby Ridge. Upon his arrival at the scene he announced his intention to negotiate an end to the standoff.

Gritz was a bluff, colorful camera hound who had made national headlines in the 1980s by leading a group of other Vietnam veterans back to Vietnam in an attempt to locate American prisoners of war who were rumored to be held secretly in deep jungle prisons by the Vietnamese government. It was basically a media stunt and was underwritten by the populist millionaire H. Ross Perot, among others (they found no missing POWs). It would later inspire the plot of Sylvester Stallone's wildly popular film *Rambo: First Blood Part II*. More recently Gritz had become involved in organizing survivalist training sessions for would-be Patriots.

Four days after Gritz's arrival, Weaver and his daughters surrendered. Both Harris and Weaver were put on trial on a total of ten charges, including murder and the original firearms charges, and both were acquitted on most charges by a jury in Boise a year later (Weaver was convicted on the lingering failure-to-appear charge). Despite the acquittal, their case lit a flame among the conspiracy-minded Patriots, and "Ruby Ridge" became an instant byword for "government overreaction and oppression." That winter, a cluster of Patriot and Christian Identity movement leaders, including Trochmann, gathered in Estes Park, Colorado, and discussed their forthcoming strategy: encourage like-minded followers to form "citizen militias" that could spring into action to defend ordinary gun owners and other citizens against a dictatorial federal government.

Less than a year later, in February 1993, another armed standoff with a lethal outcome took place near Waco, Texas, at the compound of the Branch Davidian cult run by a charismatic preacher named David Koresh. The incident began with a botched ATF raid—they were looking for illegal weapons—that resulted in four federal officers dead and sixteen wounded and the deaths of six Branch Davidians. For fifty-one days the ATF tried to get the compound leaders to come out, but they refused. On April 19, 1993, FBI agents moved in to arrest the leaders, who instead immolated themselves and their followers—seventy-six people in all. Videos of the horror played endlessly on all the television networks. For the early dwellers in the Patriots' alternative universe, the incident became compelling evidence that a totalitarian New World Order takeover of America was imminent.

Now Ruby Ridge and Waco were on a lot of people's lips, not just Patriots' lips but also those of a number of mainstream conservative figures such as Rush Limbaugh, his many imitators on the airwaves, and eventually the pundits at the conservative cable TV network Fox News, when it launched in 1996. They mainly used the incidents to bash the Bill Clinton administration for its alleged incompetence, even though the Ruby Ridge incident had not occurred on his watch. Indeed, the Patriot movement was tapping into a deep vein of antigovernment sentiment that had been simmering among conservatives for many years, beginning in the years of the Reagan administration and its admonitions that the "government can't solve problems, it is the problem."

Antigovernment sentiment had started to reach a boil in the early nineties, thanks to the growing prominence of a phalanx of right-wing radio talk-show hosts who were transforming the nation's broadcasting landscape. They were led by Rush Limbaugh, who had become the country's most famous talk-show host.

"The second violent American revolution is just about—I got my fingers about a quarter of an inch apart—is just about that far away," he said. "Because these people are sick and tired of a bunch of bureaucrats in Washington driving into town and telling them what they can and can't do with their land."

Limbaugh generally eschewed NWO-style conspiracy theories, but he was a virulent hater of Bill Clinton and his administration, and devoted endless hours to promoting the various drummed-up scandals and conspiracy theories about Clinton, including a "Clinton body count" of people connected with the Clintons who had died under murky circumstances and tales of Clinton running drugs while he was governor of Arkansas.

All of this was also readily absorbed into the Patriot universe, as proof of Clinton's participation in the New World Order plot. Now, the agitation over the Ruby Ridge and Waco standoffs became a major lightning rod. Alex Jones later told reporter Alexander Zaitchik that he began his Austin, Texas, public-access television program devoted to New World Order conspiracies in 1993 as a result of his outrage over the Waco standoff.

By the mid-nineties the Patriot movement quickly became populated with a number of speakers who spread the word. John Trochmann, operating mainly in the Pacific Northwest, was one of them. Using an overhead projector he would blitz his audiences with a fast-moving blizzard of photos and news articles—military vehicles on railroad cars, blurry images of black helicopters, peculiar-looking fences and signage—that, thrown together with little explanation, reinforced the idea that there was a conspiracy to round up Americans and place them in concentration camps.

Similar speakers popped up around the country—in the Midwest, the Southwest, the South—spreading the word in similar fashion, one small gathering at a time. Some of the early Patriot movement leadership have faded into obscurity, while some—along with their political views—have had more enduring success in getting their messages out. In the latter category were Richard Mack, LeRoy Schweitzer, Jack McLamb, and Samuel Sherwood.

Richard Mack has proved to be one of the movement's more durable figures. The sheriff of Graham County, Arizona, from 1988 to 1996, Mack gained notoriety for refusing to enforce the Brady gun-control law in his county because he is convinced that such laws are a facet of the NWO in action. A longtime member of the John Birch Society, Mack travels the nation giving seminars on how to resist the New World Order by resisting gun-control measures, and recommends forming militias as preparation for effective self-defense. He also proselytizes regarding the "constitutionalist" notion that the county sheriff is the supreme law of the land, superseding federal and state authorities. In 2009 Mack founded the Constitutional Sheriffs and Peace Officers Association, which became a major source of "constitutionalist" organizing in the following years and played a major role in the Bundy family's standoffs with federal authorities in Nevada and Oregon in 2014 and 2016.

LeRoy Schweitzer, a former crop-dusting pilot who grew up near Bozeman, Montana, was an early proponent of "sovereign citizen" ideology that posited that ordinary Americans could declare themselves free of financial and other obligations to the federal government by filing certain documents with the county clerk. On the basis of this premise Schweitzer developed a scheme for getting rich. He held small seminars where he explained the material benefits of his system: how to create phony liens and file them against public or banking officials on spurious "constitutional" grounds, and then open bank accounts based on those liens and purchase expensive items with the checking account. This could work until bank officials figured out that such an account had nothing behind it. Schweitzer used his "system" to purchase a large cabin near Roundup, eastern Montana. That was where he began gathering a collection of likeminded "Freemen."

Jack McLamb was a former Arizona policeman who had a long association with Bo Gritz and was involved with the Ruby Ridge incident. McLamb toured the country giving talks on why law enforcement officers should join the Patriot movement, activity that brought him national notoriety for his overt attempts to recruit law enforcement officers.

Samuel Sherwood had been president of the United States Militia Association, based in Blackfoot, Idaho. Sherwood, also a devotee of Mormon "constitutionalist" W. Cleon Skousen and his brand of conspiracism, considered himself a mainstream political operative with influence in the 1990s Idaho legislature, and generally only attended rallies prepared by others. Sherwood espoused militias as a way to counter political trends he said were leading to an imminent "civil war."

Some of the less enduring, but in some cases more colorful of the earlier Patriot figures included Mark Koernke, Gary DeMott, and Gene Schroder. Koernke was a University of Michigan janitor who espoused theories essentially identical to John Trochmann's and presented his ideas on speaking tours throughout the Midwest. His delivery, straight out of Rush Limbaugh's book of mannerisms, was downright engaging, but as the nineties wore on, Koernke's reputation became increasingly tarnished by failed predictions, and he eventually faded into obscurity.

Gary DeMott, of Boise, Idaho, was the president of the Idaho

Sovereignty Association and the creator of a one-man "constitution-alist" show who toured the region tirelessly, spreading the gospel of "common law" courts. Demott asserted that the idea of a "common law" court, which originated with the old far-right Posse Comitatus movement, was the basis of the "sovereign citizen" form of govern-ment, and he told audiences, "We are the law enforcers."

Gene Schroder, based in Campo, Colorado, was another advo-cate of "common law" courts and toured the country explaining to people how to set up such courts. His United Sovereigns of America was a leading Patriot group that specialized in the pseudo-legal activity of these courts. Militias were a basic ingredient of Schrod-er's model of a proper government, and of the solution for ending "unconstitutional" intrusions by the federal government.

Bo Gritz was one of the most prominent militia figures in the main-stream media, but he generally eschewed the speaking circuit. The gruff, charismatic ex–Green Beret preferred to concentrate on his traveling SPIKE (Specially Prepared Individuals for Key Events) paramilitary training sessions, in which he imparted his considerable knowledge of Special Forces techniques to average Patriots.

The Ruby Ridge and Waco chickens came home to roost two years to the day after the Waco tragedy, April 19, 1995. On that day a young Gulf War veteran named Timothy McVeigh drove a rental truck laden with fertilizer laced with diesel oil—a truck bomb—up to the Murrah Federal Building in Oklahoma City, walked away, and then watched from a couple of blocks away as the bomb detonated. The massive explosion ripped apart the building's façade and took the lives of everyone near it, including 19 children in a day-care center. In total, 168 people lost their lives, and another 680 were injured in the blast.

Initially, media speculation focused on Islamic radical terrorists as the possible source of the terrorist attack. Three days later, however, McVeigh was arrested and charged with setting off the bomb. He eventually confessed, explaining both his ruthlessness and his moti-vations: "I didn't define the rules of engagement in this conflict," he told an interviewer. "The rules, if not written down, are defined by the aggressor ... Women and kids were killed at Waco and Ruby Ridge. You put back in [the government's] faces exactly what they're giving out."

I called John Trochmann the morning after the Oklahoma bombing to get his take on events. At the time, analysts were still largely ruminating about the possibility of some kind of terrorism from the Middle East, and law enforcement was still days away from arresting McVeigh. Trochmann, of course, had a completely different view: it was a New World Order plot to discredit the Patriot movement.

"It's the track record of the federal government, the British government," he told me. "In 1993 Waco burned. In 1992 they tried to raid Randy Weaver the first time. In '43, Warsaw burned. In 1775, Lexington burned. That's when they tried to take our guns the first time."

This rant was stock MOM talk; Trochmann believed the conspiracy to confiscate Americans' guns predated the Revolutionary War and included actions taken in the Warsaw Ghetto. But that wasn't all.

"It is also the beginning day of the Satanic preparations for the grand climax, according to the Satanic calendar. And I got this from a witch, a former witch out of a coven in St. Cloud, Minnesota. Their preparation for the sacrifice is April nineteenth to twenty-sixth.

"The grand climax, which is what they're preparing for, is the twenty-sixth through the thirty-first, in which they have oral, anal or vaginal sex with females ages one to twenty-five. They don't take infants."

"What do you think happened yesterday?" I asked.

"Well, with the information that's rolling in, it becomes very interesting. We've got a seismographic machine that's recorded fifteen miles from the site: two separate blasts, eight seconds apart. One was the vehicle outside and one was the technical blast inside. High-tech blast, high, high, high-tech. We got a call at eleven thirty last night from Special Forces, being questioned, 'Where were you?' It continues today."

Special Forces? This was the first I had heard suggesting that Patriots might be implicated. Was that what he meant?

"Oh, I think they're going to try to use it. First off, they say that there's three olive-skinned people from the Middle East that were doing it with the rig parked outside. Then we find out that that same morning NORAD was under Level 2 Alert, which is lockdown, nobody comes or goes. Then we find out the *Kitty Hawk*, the carrier fleet the *Kitty Hawk*, is heading into the Indian Ocean. And another carrier fleet, is heading into the eastern Mediterranean. What is all this connected to? We have two witnesses now that say there was a black helicopter hovering over that building earlier in the day, earlier in the morning. I think the most significant thing is the seismographic machine measuring two blasts, and it does not measure echoes, as the FBI is trying to defend. We full well believe that it's an inside job to justify their future deeds here, to give them justification for coming after—whoever."

Per Trochmann, the blast was a false flag operation carried out by the NWO to justify neutralizing Patriots. That became the Patriot movement's story, and they stuck to it. In short order, the dozens of conspiracy theorists around the country who had previously promoted New World Order tales quickly adopted it and began spreading it. It soon came out that McVeigh was a full-fledged far-right Patriot believer who had deeply embraced the New World Order narrative.

But Trochmann's attempt at deflection—pinning the crime on the NWO instead of where it belonged, on its adversaries—did not work. McVeigh had hoped his murderous act in Oklahoma City would spark a Patriot uprising against the government, but it had largely the opposite effect, and instead turned out to be a powerful setback for the movement. Overnight, the image of militiamen such as McVeigh was transformed from bumbling armed men in the woods to menacing terrorists. Soon mainstream media reports were filled with accounts of the militias' threatening behavior and rhetoric, as well as their conspiracy-driven worldview. It was not a flattering view.

In a widely covered speech, Clinton addressed the Oklahoma City bombing: "In this country we cherish and guard the right of free speech," he said. "We know we love it when we put up with people saying things we absolutely deplore. And we must always be willing to defend their right to say things we deplore to the ultimate degree. But we hear so many loud and angry voices in America today whose sole goal seems to be to try to keep some people as paranoid as possible."

The president was not calling for suppression of such speech, though: "If they insist on being irresponsible with our common liberties, then we must be all the more responsible with our liberties," he continued. "When they talk of hatred, we must stand against them. When they talk of violence, we must stand against them."

Right-wing talk-show hosts, led by Limbaugh, immediately protested that Clinton was trying to pin the cause of the bombing on them. In a full-page column Limbaugh wrote for the May 8 *Newsweek*, "Why I'm Not to Blame," he stated: "Those who make excuses for rioters and looters in Los Angeles now seek to blame people who played no role whatsoever in this tragedy."

Now the Patriots' chief talking point was that the president was trying to exploit the tragedy as a way of silencing his critics; eventually, the charge became an established part of conservative lore. Years later, in her 2002 bestseller, *Slander: Liberal Lies about the American Right*, the right-wing pundit Ann Coulter would assert: "When impeached former president Bill Clinton identified Rush Limbaugh as the cause of the Oklahoma City bombing, he unleashed all the typical liberal curse words for conservatives. He blamed 'loud and angry voices' heard 'over the airwaves in America' that were making people 'paranoid' and spreading hate."

Limbaugh and his fellow conservatives deployed this line of argument to limit serious discussion of Clinton's subsequent anti-terrorism legislation, which included a proposal that would allow law enforcement to track large fertilizer purchases. The legislation was largely defanged in Congress. Limbaugh and Co. also shut off exploration of a deeper underlying issue: the increasing migration of ideas and agendas that originated on the racist far right into main-stream conservatism and the dynamic whereby rational anger and discontent with the federal government was being transformed into an irrational, visceral, and paranoid hatred of it.

This clampdown on rational discussion muddled the public's understanding of the actual threat that the Patriot movement posed to democratic institutions, even as the movement kept producing a string of antigovernment radicals acting out violently.

In Roundup, Montana, following a series of confrontations with local law enforcement, LeRoy Schweitzer moved his cadre of Freemen out of their cabin, northward to a ranch a few miles outside the town of Jordan, owned by two fellow Freemen, Ralph and Emmett Clark. The Clark ranch was under foreclosure proceedings because the Clarks had refused to pay their taxes. At the ranch Schweitzer resumed his seminar sessions on "sovereign citizenship" and "common law courts," even though he was wanted on a number of felony charges. People traveled from around the country to attend them. The Freemen also stepped up their "constitutional" actions against local law enforcement, threatening to hang a federal judge and the local prosecuting attorney. At this point the FBI stepped in.

On March 25, 1996, an FBI informant posing as an antenna installer convinced Schweitzer and one of his followers to check over the antenna installation a short distance from the cabin. The two Freemen soon found themselves surrounded by FBI agents and under arrest. FBI agents surrounded the Clark ranch and urged the Freemen remaining inside—about twenty people in all, including both Clark brothers and two children—to surrender. They refused, and another armed standoff had begun.

It lasted eighty-one days. The FBI—extremely sensitive to the criticism it had endured in the wake of Ruby Ridge and Waco—negotiated patiently with the Freemen. They enlisted the assistance of a number of third parties, even of some Patriot movement figures, Bo Gritz among them. They each negotiated for a few days, and then walked away in frustration, saying the Freemen were utterly unwilling to compromise, mendacious, and too paranoid to reason with.

The most successful negotiator turned out to be a moderate Republican legislator named Karl Ohs; his plainspoken style was the best bridge between the Freemen's universe and the world waiting outside with guns. First he persuaded some of the people inside the ranch compound who were not facing arrest to come out of the house on their own. A few days later, on June 14, the remaining sixteen people came out. The Clarks and four others were slapped with federal charges, while eight others faced an array of other charges. Eventually, all of the participants were convicted, and some of those arrested on federal charges pled guilty and wound up serving a variety of sentences. Schweitzer received a twenty-two-year term and died in prison in September 2011.

The Freemen standoff demonstrated that the FBI had learned some lessons about dealing with Patriots and other similar groups. Those lessons would later be critical in its handling of the armed standoff on the Malheur National Wildlife Refuge in Oregon in early 2016. It also demonstrated that the Patriot true believers were willing to spend prison time as the price of their beliefs.

Shortly after the Freemen standoff ended, on July 27, 1996, someone in Atlanta, Georgia, left a backpack bomb at the Centennial Park, the main gathering spot for the 1996 Summer Olympic Games. When it detonated, it killed a spectator, Alice Hawthorne, and injured 111 people; one man died of a heart attack while rushing to the scene. Initial suspicion fell on a security guard at the scene, Richard Jewell, who had been the first to spot the backpack before it exploded and had begun clearing the area. After first being hailed as a hero, Jewell became the FBI's prime suspect and was hounded by the media for weeks and even months afterward, until the investigating US attorney officially announced in October that Jewell had been exonerated. The investigation into the bombing remained officially open and unsolved, and the FBI admitted it had no other suspects.

On January 16, 1997, a bomb exploded outside an abortion clinic in the Atlanta suburb of Sandy Springs. An hour later, another bomb hidden nearby detonated, injuring seven. FBI investigators noticed the devices' similarity to that used in Centennial Park.

Then, on February 21, a bomb containing nails went off in a back room of the Otherside Lounge, a lesbian bar in downtown Atlanta, which was packed with about 150 people, though only four women were injured. More chillingly, the bomber left a second backpack bomb outside in a walkway, clearly intended to go off as the crowd exited the building in a panic. Fortunately it did not detonate, and investigators found it and promptly defused it.

By now, police figured one person might be responsible for all of the bombing incidents, but it took awhile before they were certain. Nearly a year later, on January 29, 1998, a security officer named Robert Sanderson was killed at a Birmingham, Alabama, abortion clinic, when he began examining a backpack bomb left outside the building, hidden beneath a shrub. Emily Lyons, a nurse standing nearby, was badly injured. A witness spotted a man sitting in a gray Nissan pickup near the bombing scene and, watching him drive away afterward, wrote down the license plate number. Soon the FBI had its first real suspect: Eric Robert Rudolph.

The day after the bombing the FBI announced it was seeking him as a person of interest in the case. A week later, Rudolph's gray Nissan pickup was found abandoned in the woods near Murphy, North Carolina, one of his childhood stomping grounds. Immediately, hundreds of law-enforcement officers descended on the woods, but Rudolph successfully eluded them. By May, he was on the FBI's 10 Most Wanted List, with a $1 million reward on his head, where he stayed for the next five and a half years.

Rudolph was seen periodically by residents of the area around Murphy. Investigators began to suspect that some locals were harboring and assisting Rudolph. Finally, on May 31, 2003, he was captured by a rookie police officer in Murphy. Eventually he agreed to a plea bargain: life in prison with no chance of parole in exchange for a guilty plea. He then wrote an explicit confession detailing the bombings and his motivations for them.

Rudolph, thirty-nine at the time of his capture, was a religious fanatic who had been raised in rural North Carolina. When he was eighteen he had spent time with his mother in a Christian Identity community in rural Missouri and had converted to that belief system then, as his papers and writings indicate. He spent time in the Army in the 1980s but was discharged for marijuana use, and spent the next several years drifting around the South, gradually finding his calling as an anti-abortion and anti-gay zealot. He explained in a statement he issued after his arrest:

Because I believe that abortion is murder, I also believe that force is justified in an attempt to stop it. Because this government is committed to maintaining the policy of abortion, and protecting it, the agents of this government are the agents of mass murder, whether knowingly or unknowingly. And whether these agents of the government are armed or otherwise they are legitimate targets in the war to end this holocaust, especially those agents who carry arms in defense of this regime and the enforcement of its laws. This is the reason and the only reason for the targeting of so-called law enforcement personnel.

By the time Rudolph wrote his confession, the world had changed significantly. In 2003, when people thought of terrorists they no longer thought of people like Eric Rudolph.

Although not much of the Patriot movement's New World Order conspiracism caught on with the general public, the Patriots kept working to mainstream their ideas, mainly by seizing on everyday news events and running them through the grist mill of their belief system.

Militia activity had dropped drastically. The Southern Poverty Law Center reported in 1999 that there were a total of 217 militia groups in the United States—just 25 percent of their 1996 number, 858.

But this didn't seem to discourage relentless self-promoters such as Bo Gritz. Gritz had been attracted to all the media attention surrounding the hunt for Eric Rudolph, and in August 1998 he had shown up at the scene in North Carolina and announced that he intended to organize an army of 100 searchers to find Rudolph and convince him to turn himself in under Gritz's auspices. Gritz planned to parlay the $1 million reward into Rudolph's legal defense.

But the plan was a flop. First of all, Gritz could only muster about forty people. Then three of his searchers stumbled into some hornets and had to be treated at the hospital. The locals—already snickering about Gritz's dreams of glory—dubbed the entourage Bo's Hornet Hunters. After a week spent looking for Rudolph, Gritz packed his bags and returned home to Almost Heaven, the Idaho Patriot retreat community he had founded outside rural Kamiah.

Only two weeks before, Gritz had been brimming with his usual outgoing optimism as he addressed a big crowd at a Preparedness Expo in Puyallup, Washington, with Randy Weaver in the audience. The expo was devoted primarily to selling survivalist gear and supplies to attendees who had bought into the Patriot movement's warnings about an impending mass social collapse. And in 1998, the focus of those fears was the Y2K Bug.

Computer scientists had realized that most of the world's computers had operating systems with a dating method that used just the final two digits of any year to represent it. When the systems operating with twentieth-century dates expired on the stroke of midnight on December 31, 1999, those dates would suddenly reset to double zeroes, the same as 1900. Computer programmers had no idea how serious the consequences might be for the world's computer systems, but to prevent potential havoc they began working on updates that would help the global computer network survive the glitch.

Viewed through the Patriot movement's prism, the Y2K bug soon became grist for a fresh round of apocalyptic fearmongering, as dozens of conspiracists rushed to predict that Western civilization would collapse on New Year's Eve. Some of the believers in this new catastrophe were Christian evangelicals who for their own reasons already anticipated that the change of the millennium would bring about apocalyptical events foretold in the Book of Revelation.

All of them traded books and videos describing the doom that was nearly upon them: trains derailing and crashing into each other, a black-helicopter-enabled New World Order takeover in the wake of the social collapse; proof that this was being planned in the form of ominous executive orders from President Bill Clinton; and eyewitness accounts of apocalyptic occurrences such as the appearance of the Four Horsemen.

Events such as the Preparedness Expo at the state fairgrounds in Puyallup were organized to help people prepare for Y2K and other dangers. Attendees could purchase a wide variety of food-storage systems; bulk foods such as beans, sugar, and flour; and security systems and surveillance equipment. One entrepreneur was selling a modern-day bomb-shelter system you could dig in your backyard.

Gritz's talk to the attendees was a typical Bo performance: he urged his audience to help swell the ranks of his Rudolph expedition, and sounded biblical warnings about "the Beast" of evil government about to devour them. At one point he said, "This is a spiritual war, and very soon, you are gonna get a choice and you cannot sit on the fence." He concluded the speech by setting fire to a paper United Nations flag.

Gritz knew then that he was in trouble, even as he evinced his usual bravado: "I have been blessed by Almighty God to fear nothing on this earth. I was put on this earth to be a warrior." But he also explained to the crowd that "my wife is mad at me" about his plans for North Carolina.

When he returned from the failed Rudolph expedition to Idaho, he found that his wife of twenty-four years, Claudia, had packed her bags and departed. She soon filed divorce papers. A week later, Gritz pointed a gun at his chest and fired, but the wound was non-fatal and he eventually recovered. A year later, he married again, this time to the daughter of a longtime Christian Identity pastor. He abandoned his Almost Heaven project and moved to Nevada, where he became a full-fledged Christian Identity believer. Gritz now lives a quietly retired life in rural Nebraska.

Gritz's stumble had little effect on the Patriot movement, whose frenzy about the Y2K Bug only intensified as New Year's Eve approached. In addition to foodstuffs and bomb shelters, thousands of people were also purchasing guns, just in case. A number of right-wing websites with a conspiracist bent, such as the World Net Daily, ran stories warning that the Clinton administration intended to impose martial law to control the Y2K chaos.

No one could quite match Alex Jones, though, who on New Year's Eve went on the air and warned that a Pennsylvania nuclear plant was being shut down because of Y2K (actually, it had experienced an insulator failure, a relatively common and minor issue). He claimed that the US military was rolling into Austin to quell rioters and troublemakers who were to be locked in the airport, FEMA was on the verge of taking over all AM and FM radio stations, and Russia was threatening nuclear war:

> Cash machines are failing in Britain and now other European countries. They're finding large amounts of explosives in France. Vladimir Putin, who is known as Vladimir the Ruthless, using all his profanity on national TV, you name it. We won't read the profanity here but we've got it— this person is on an unbelievable power trip and resembles a demon. He is a creature of the IMF and the World Bank and International Communism. He is a former KGB head and this information is vital, ladies and gentleman.
>
> We're seeing the New World Order really come out in full force. More wars than have been in the past fifty years are going on right now.

But the Apocalypse stayed home. No one's computers went down, the infrastructure remained intact, and the world proceeded on January 1, 2000, just as it had in the days and years before.

The failed prediction turned out to be a major embarrassment for the Patriot movement and its conspiracist cohort, who for the next couple of years, whenever they raised their heads in the media, were reminded of just how wrong they had been. The fiasco was especially damaging to their credibility among the hundreds of thousands of foot soldiers who had spent their hard-earned dollars on preparing for a mass social breakdown that then gave no whiff of actually occurring. And they were reminded of it every time they pondered what to do now with the stores of beans, rice, and canned goods they had tucked away in their safe shelters.

But then the terrorists of 9/11 struck, the political landscape shifted dramatically, and the Y2K fiasco was washed down the memory hole.

4

9/11 and the Dark Invaders

The smoke and dust from the terrorist attacks of September 11, 2001, were still in the air when Alex Jones went on his radio show in Austin that same day and declared the disaster to be a false flag operation perpetrated by the New World Order.

Prior to the events of 9/11, Jones had mostly been following in the footsteps of the Patriot movement's leading conspiracy-meisters, mimicking and amplifying what had become, for a small but growing national audience, the many theories that made up their alternative universe in the 1990s. That changed the day of the attacks.

Jones gave his audience what they later came to see as a prediction of the 9/11 attacks in his broadcast of July 25, 2001, while ranting about the Oklahoma City bombing and other false flag operations he claimed were perpetrated by the New World Order. He thought recent talk about Middle Eastern terrorists was a prelude to more of the same. "Call the White House and tell them we know the government is planning terrorism," he said. "Bin Laden is the boogeyman they need in this Orwellian phony system."

So in a sense Jones was thoroughly prepared six weeks later on the morning of September 11, when New York City's Twin Towers and the Pentagon in Washington were hit by jet airliners flown by Al Qaeda terrorists. He opened his show by declaring that what Americans were seeing on their televisions was a staged terror attack. "I'll tell you the bottom line," Jones said. "Ninety-eight percent chance this was a government-orchestrated controlled bombing."

Years later, Jones told *Rolling Stone*'s Alexander Zaitchik, "I went on the air and said, 'Those were controlled demolitions. You just watched the government blow up the World Trade Center.' I lost 70 percent of my affiliates that day. Station managers asked me, 'Do you want to be on this crusade going nowhere, or do you want to be a star?' I'm proud I never compromised." It wasn't in Jones's nature to change his tune—he had been building toward this for years, and he finally had a national event around which he could spin a conspiracy-theory empire all his own.

That's what he set about doing in the subsequent weeks and years, gradually building a nationwide audience for his now-independent Infowars website, one conspiracy theory at a time: The Towers were felled not by the airliners but by powerful explosives already in place when the attacks began. Military jets had been intentionally grounded to prevent them from intercepting the airliners. The Pentagon was hit not by a jet airliner crashing into it, but by a series of explosives designed to resemble a jet crash. Soon branches off the central theories began sprouting like kudzu.

The believers insisted that what they were seeking was the truth about the attacks, so it became known as the 9/11 Truth movement, or Truthers for short. And not all of them were right-wing Patriots like Jones. The conspiracist Patriot universe had always attracted an element of the fringe left, such as people who promoted theories about health cures and the claim that the FDA was hiding cancer cures, or claims about jet contrails secretly poisoning the public.

This element, and other conspiracists from across the political bandwidth, formed a major part of the early audience for the theories. After all, a major element of the 9/11 Truther theories was their inherent critique of the Republican Bush administration, and most of them were already inclined to distrust the conservative government's policies. The 9/11 theories gave them further ammunition. Other prominent 9/11 theorists included the French analyst

Thierry Meyssan, who wrote a book, *9/11: The Big Lie*, in which he hypothesized that the attacks had been staged by a faction of the US military intelligence complex in order to impose a military regime, and a former theology professor, David Ray Griffin, who published a series of books supposedly exposing the conspiracy. These commentators distanced themselves from Jones and his conspiracy mill, whose videos and website rants spread everywhere on social media and Internet chat forums.

In addition to his daily radio show, Jones began churning out what he called documentary films that explored the various conspiracies around 9/11, and selling the videotapes and DVD versions on his Infowars website. They bore titles such as *9/11: The Road to Tyranny*; *The Masters of Terror: Exposed*; *Matrix of Evil*; *Martial Law 9/11: Rise of the Police State*; and *Terrorstorm: The History of Government-Sponsored Terrorism*. Jones later claimed that this last film provided some of the key footage for the conspiracist documentary series *Zeitgeist*, which similarly explored 9/11 conspiracies with a somewhat artier tone. There were all kind of similar spin-offs and independent 9/11 ventures, including *Loose Change*, for which Jones served as executive producer.

Conspiracy theories had always been something of a dividing line between Patriot extremists and mainstream conservatives, and that line became sharper now. Figures such as Rush Limbaugh and Fox News's Bill O'Reilly became more pointed in distancing themselves from Jones and the 9/11 conspiracy theories, especially because so many of them were staunch defenders of the Bush administration. The notion that Bush might have been part of a New World Order plot to bring down the Towers was not just risible to them but bordered on treason.

Limbaugh in particular was scathing in his dismissal of the 9/11 theorists, labeling them "loons" and similar epithets. He once pulled the plug on a call-in listener for suggesting that Limbaugh look at the evidence that the attacks were an "inside job" by the government. Limbaugh went into a rant about "kookery":

We don't allow kooks. Kookery is never allowed here. And if you're gonna talk about 9/11 being an inside job, and Khalid Sheik Mohamed, and you're going to start agreeing with Rosie O'Donnell, I would suggest rehab and treatment, counseling and so forth. You know, like Rosie, ... you've probably got really deep issues from your childhood that needs to be resolved, because you, sir, are a glittering jewel of colossal ignorance, and I am simply intolerant of it.

At Fox News, the right-leaning cable news network that had grown to become the dominant voice and propaganda organ of the conservative movement during the Bush years, there was, similarly, little tolerance for 9/11 conspiracism, although one correspondent, Geraldo Rivera, and an on-air contributor, Andrew Napolitano, both had brief flirtations with "being open" to some of the theories. But most of its talking heads, particularly talk-show hosts Bill O'Reilly and Sean Hannity, treated any hint of 9/11 conspiracism as evidence of the speaker's vile character.

The radio pundit Michael Reagan, the son of Ronald Reagan, made the mainstream-conservative loathing for the Truthers explicit in one of his broadcasts:

There is a group that's sending letters to our troops in Iraq ... claiming 9/11 was an inside job—oh, yeah, yeah—and that they should rethink why they're fighting ... Excuse me, folks, I'm going to say this: ... Just find the people who are sending those letters to our troops to demoralize our troops and ... you take them out, they are traitors to our country, and shoot them. You have a problem with that, deal with it. But anyone who would do that doesn't deserve to live. You shoot them. You call them traitors ... and you shoot them dead. I'll pay for the bullet.

This became something of a recurring theme—though for the most part, it was not directed at right-wing "kooks," but mainstream liberals.

Eliminationist rhetoric had become popular with right-wing talk-show hosts in the 1990s, during the heyday of the militia movement from which so much of it originated, brewed up amid the virulent hatred of the government that both had reveled in. Even back then Rush Limbaugh liked to make little "jokes": "I tell people don't kill all the liberals. Leave enough so we can have two on every campus— living fossils—so we will never forget what these people stood for."

So even though the events of 9/11 had created a wedge between the conspiracist Patriot universe and the extreme pro-Bush war patriotism of mainstream conservatives, the anger and viciousness remained intact on both sides. It expressed itself in the crude demonization of a targeted Other as vermin and excrement and disease fit only for elimination, ultimately creating tacit permission for people to excise them, violently or by any other means, in the name of "protecting society."

Mainstream conservatives became especially hyperpatriotic in their defense of the Bush administration and its decisions to invade, first Afghanistan in October 2001 in the wake of the 9/11 attacks and then, more controversially, Iraq in March 2003, to overthrow the regime of the dictator Saddam Hussein. Critics of the war were early on dismissed as traitors who, in Fox News host Bill O'Reilly's favorite phrase of the time, "hated this country."

In one of his nightly Fox broadcasts on *The O'Reilly Factor*, O'Reilly, a former mainstream reporter who had gained prominence as the host of a syndicated "tabloid" news show called *Inside Edition* in the early 1990s, laid down his edict for the bounds of acceptable discourse:

> Everybody got it? Dissent, fine. Undermining, you're a traitor. Got it? So, all those clowns over at the liberal radio network, we could incarcerate them immediately. Will you have that done, please? Send over the FBI and just put them in chains, because they, you know, they're undermining everything and they don't care, couldn't care less.

Throughout right-wing media the defense of the Bush administration remained consistently eliminationist in tone. When critics questioned the administration's rationale for invading Iraq based on dubious information about weapons of mass destruction—which indeed were never found—they were accused of "hating America" and committing treason. At one point, O'Reilly hosted a discussion on whether Ward Churchill, a professor of ethnic studies at the University of Colorado and a critic of the Iraq War, should be charged with treason and sedition. Others received similar treatment if they critiqued the execution of the war: the botched occupation of Fallujah, or the scandal that arose when torture and inhumane conditions at a US-run prison in Abu Ghraib were revealed in a series of horrifying photos. For most right-wing commenters, the sin was never the incompetent or illegal behavior revealed, it was daring to reveal it at all. For example, the popular Fox Network talk-show host Sean Hannity accused the Democratic National Committee of conspiring to have the Abu Ghraib photos released to the public.

The eliminationist rhetoric became commonplace in movement conservatives' attacks on liberals, embodied in the book titles that flooded the marketplace. Sean Hannity's bestselling screed, *Deliver Us from Evil: Defeating Terrorism, Despotism, and Liberalism* (2004), summed up in its title the general conservative view that liberals were not just wrong, but evil. Other iterations of this meme were Dinesh D'Souza's *The Enemy at Home: The Cultural Left and Its Responsibility for 9/11* (2007); Michael Savage's *The Enemy Within* (2003), which claimed that the nation's real enemy was liberalism; Ann Coulter's *Treason: Liberal Treachery from the Cold War to the War on Terrorism* (2003), in which she argued that Senator Joe McCarthy was right about Communists infiltrating the government in the 1950s, and charged that today's liberals were actively undermining antiterrorism efforts.

Conservatives during the Bush years did not reserve their eliminationist rhetoric for antiwar liberals alone. During those same years their most popular and durable target became Latino immigrants.

By 2006, Americans were seeing many, many more Latino faces in their midst. Millions, in fact.

Between 1990 and 2000, the numbers of undocumented immigrants in the United States more than doubled, from 3.5 million to 8.6 million people. The vast majority of them were from Mexico:

the number of documented and undocumented Mexican immigrants in the United States doubled in that same time span from 4.5 million to 9.7 million.

Most of the deluge was a result of circumstances arising from twofold conditions: the North American Free Trade Agreement (NAFTA) had resulted in significant loss of employment in Mexico; meanwhile, the American economy was booming.

NAFTA, approved under the Clinton administration in 1993 and intended to spur business between the United States, Canada, and Mexico, had had a disastrous side effect: its requirement to lift protections for corn prices forced millions of Mexican corn farmers out of business, because they could not compete with cheap American prices. Moreover, the promised job gains in Mexico to compensate for any losses, mainly in the form of American auto and other manufacturers moving their factory operations there, turned out to be ephemeral: many of the corporations that opened plants in Mexico soon abandoned those expansions and shifted their manufacturing operations to plants in China and elsewhere in Asia.

Further, the booming American economy was creating a massive job market—not only in such skilled labor markets as the new tech economy, but also in the unskilled labor markets such as agricultural production (that is, managing and harvesting crops). There was a huge demand for labor to harvest crops and process meat that was largely going unfilled by American workers. The legal immigration system was not set up to accommodate this need: the US economy generally produces 500,000 unskilled labor jobs per year, but the US Immigration Service issues only about 5,000 green cards to foreign workers.

So the vast majority of the immigrants found themselves without legal status, having either crossed the border legally and overstayed their visas, or crossed the border illegally. These immigrants generally figured they could at least come and work for a few years and send their earnings to their starving families back home; some came intending to leave, others came intending to stay, and fate was often known to play jokes that undermined those intentions. Virtually all, however, came intending to work, and that was primarily what they did, laboring in the shadows with fake Social Security numbers that allowed their employers to pay taxes in their names—even though they, as undocumented immigrants, would never receive any direct benefits from the system they were paying into. Thus, anti-immigration forces who charged that immigrants were a burden on taxpayers because they were able to collect benefits while paying nothing into the system were turning reality on its head. Working immigrants were actually subsidizing those legally in the system.

Before the passage of NAFTA, most illegal border crossings had occurred near one of a handful of major border cities—Nogales on the Arizona border, Ciudad Juarez in Texas, and Tijuana in California being the primary crossing points—where crossing illegally had been a relatively simple matter of skirting barriers. But after NAFTA was passed and its effects began creating a wave of Mexican immigrants, the Clinton administration, under pressure from Congress, moved to crack down on illegal crossings in those towns, beginning in 1996.

The crackdown stanched the flow for a few months. Soon, however, the wave of attempted border crossings began spreading out into the surrounding deserts. Longtime "mules" who helped people cross illegally reported having to move their operations farther and farther away from the border towns. Eventually this meant that human smuggling was rising like a bad flood tide out in the remote reaches where it previously had been only a rare thing. Ranchers along these borderlands began reporting having more and more problems with border crossers, from thefts to vandalism to threatening encounters to deaths of migrants in the desert. Many people living along the border who had in previous years gone out of their way to help stray border crossers now avoided them out of fear, especially as Mexican drug cartels became involved in the human smuggling. At the same time, thousands of border crossers began dying out in the lethal deserts where they now crossed, mostly of exposure and water and food deprivation. Some met violent deaths at the hands of human smuggling vultures.

These changes at the border were creating waves inland. In rural America, economic changes had transformed the landscape as small family-run pig and dairy farms were replaced by large industrial food-production operations. Like the agricultural operations in California's Central Valley, these food-production plants also ran on cheap, low-skilled workers willing to do harsh and unpleasant work. Cheap and often illegal labor brought in from Mexico and Central America filled the bill. Soon small Midwestern towns in Nebraska and Ohio were filling up around the edges with more and more Latinos who spoke little English and for a number of reasons tended to keep to themselves. Now there were brown faces in places where for generations just about the only faces to be seen had been white.

Even in the suburbs, there suddenly were many more brown faces—people working in landscaping and construction, in housekeeping and child care. Most American suburbs were predominantly white, often according to their original designs in the 1940s and '50s when race-based exclusionary covenants were still perfectly legal, and so the arrival of a tide of brown faces came as something of a cultural shock for many whites living there.

By 2000, anti-immigration organizations were marshaling their forces to make the fresh tide of Latino faces in America into a political issue. Many of these groups, such as the Federation for American Immigration Reform and the Center for Immigration Studies, had their roots in various think tanks funded by John Tanton, a prominent white supremacist based in Michigan. Others, such as Numbers USA and Americans for Legal Immigration, were openly nativist; one of them, run by a California white supremacist, Glenn Spencer, claimed that the wave of Latinos was part of a sinister *Reconquista* conspiracy by globalist forces to return the American Southwest to Mexico. Spencer advocated forming citizen militias under the banner of his outfit, American Border Patrol. Simultaneously, white-supremacist organizations around the country began talking about immigration as the next big issue around which they could recruit and expand their movement.

David Duke, a former Ku Klux Klansman and neo-Nazi, wrote a screed that year that he distributed to his fellow white supremacists:

> We are fighting for the preservation of our heritage, freedom and way of life in the United States and much of the Western World. Ultimately, we are working to secure the most important civil right of all, the right to preserve our kind of life. Massive immigration and low European American birthrates coupled with integration and racial intermarriage threatens the continued existence of our very genotype. We assert that we, as do all expressions of life on this planet, have the right to live and to have our children and our children's children reflect both genetically and culturally our heritage.

The numbers of immigrants continued to rise, reaching a peak in 2007, when the population of undocumented workers hit 12.2 million, an increase of 3.6 million over the previous year. But by then, the backlash was well under way.

Much of this nativist backlash, which could be found on right-wing radio, on cable talk shows, on websites and blogs and YouTube videos, was predicated on a set of myths about immigrants that were largely created and promoted by nativist anti-immigrant organizations such as the Federation for American Immigration Reform (FAIR), myths that were stark inversions of factual reality. These myths nonetheless came to be widely embraced by conservative pundits and their audiences. Four of the most prevalent were the following:

- Immigrants bring crime to their communities. In reality, numerous studies of the crime rates among various ethnic and immigrant communities clearly demonstrate that immigrants generally, and Latinos especially, commit crime at a significantly lower rate than occurs in the white and general populations.
- Immigrants take jobs away from Americans. The vast majority of undocumented Latino immigrants are employed in low-paying, low-skilled jobs that require hard labor and that employers have extreme difficulty filling without an

immigrant labor pool. So in reality immigrants are doing jobs that Americans won't take. Numerous economic studies have demonstrated that having a substantial immigrant labor pool is an essential ingredient to creating more higher- and middle-wage jobs in the larger economy.

- Immigrants bring disease with them. This is a bald-faced lie unsupported by credible data. But it does serve as a rationale for eliminationist thinking. Disease rates in immigrant communities are roughly the same as in other communities, and the Centers for Disease Control has no data indicating that immigrants are prone to bringing exotic diseases with them.
- They don't want to become Americans by learning to speak English. Most immigrant communities in US history have been faced with this canard, dating back to when Germans and Japanese immigrants faced similar accusations that they didn't want to assimilate. Similarly they were told they would never be "real Americans," but history has shown this to be untrue. Immigrant communities are frequently made up of people with lower education levels who have not had the opportunity to study English. Moreover, because of the hostility they often generate, immigrant communities have also long tended to form insular neighborhoods where they speak their native languages freely. History has demonstrated time and again that this insularity always breaks down over time. And many non-immigrant communities, ethnic and otherwise, are also quite insular by choice.

The larger narrative arc created by these myths was that "white culture" was under attack in the form of this "invasion" of brown faces speaking foreign tongues. This narrative not only became the core of the nativist and white-supremacist assault on immigration but also was the essential story told to the public on right-wing media such as Fox News, as well as on such ostensibly mainstream networks as CNN, where Lou Dobbs for many years held forth on the dangers of immigration.

On one of his nightly Fox broadcasts, Bill O'Reilly angrily explained the problem:

> Now in 1986, President Reagan thought he could solve the [immigration] problem by granting about three million illegal aliens amnesty. The *New York Times* was in heaven, editorializing back then, quote, "The new law won't work miracles but it will induce most employers to pay attention, to turn off the magnets, to slow the tide." Of course, just the opposite happened. But the *Times* hasn't learned a thing. That's because the newspaper and many far-left thinkers believe the white power structure that controls America is bad, so a drastic change is needed.
>
> According to the lefty zealots, the white Christians who hold power must be swept out by a new multicultural tide, a rainbow coalition, if you will. This can only happen if demographics change in America.

The first attempt to start a border militia was made by David Duke and some pals of his from the Ku Klux Klan. "We believe very strongly white people are becoming second-class citizens. When I think of America, I think of a white country." Duke uttered those words in October 1977 while speaking to assembled newspaper and TV reporters at the US-Mexico border crossing in San Ysidro, California.

Duke had announced that he and a couple of carfuls of robed Klansmen would hold a press conference at the border crossing to tell the public about his latest project: a "Klan Border Watch" that he claimed would enlist KKK members from around the nation to show up armed and ready to catch illegal border crossers. But Duke's project quickly fell apart amid internecine bickering with his fellow neo-Nazis.

The concept, however, lingered on among white supremacists, played a role in some of the movement that took off in the 1990s, and eventually led to the idea of having ordinary patriots form citizen militias. One of the people who picked up the idea in that era was Glenn Spencer, a retired California businessman who began agitating against immigration in 1993 and formed his militia-oriented organization, American Patrol, in 1995. Its website spread *Reconquista* conspiracy theories, white-supremacist eugenics, and anti-Latino hatred. "The Mexican culture is based on deceit," I once wrote. "Chicanos and Mexicanos lie as a matter of survival."

Most of all, Spencer promoted the idea of having citizen militias to act as eyes and ears on the border so that more illegal crossers could be caught, and perhaps to arrest them themselves. In 2001, Spencer packed his bags and moved his operation to a ranch outside rural Sierra Vista, Arizona. At about the same time, the militia idea caught on with a couple of Arizona ranchers named Jack Foote and Casey Nethercott, who organized a militiaesque armed outfit called Ranch Rescue that prowled the Arizona borderlands from 2002 to 2003, harassing border crossers when they found them. They finally ran afoul of the law when they assaulted and sicced a dog on a couple of Salvadoran immigrants who were caught crossing ranchland that the militiamen were guarding. The two vigilantes eventually were put out of business by a lawsuit filed on behalf of the terrorized couple.

The border-militias story attracted some media attention, but Foote and Nethercott were sketchy characters whom reporters shied away from interviewing, and Spencer was not very mediagenic. It took a former schoolteacher from California to get the media's attention—a fellow who made his living in part by playing one of the doomed gunmen in the daily re-creation for tourists of the Gunfight at the OK Corral in Tombstone.

Chris Simcox was a youthful, slightly scruffy man who had moved to Arizona from California in the early 2000s and become an ardent desert rat. With a ready grin and a pleasant voice, he had an all-American demeanor that TV reporters who started coming in 2003 soon found appealing, as he described his adventures with his newly organized Tombstone Border Militia and the urgent need to have better border security because of the "invasion" from Mexico.

The attitudes that were roaming the desert with Simcox's patrols were voiced by one participant caught by a documentary filmmaker who filmed an exercise by Simcox's militia group, now renamed Tombstone Civil Defense Corps. As cattle roamed in the background, the militiaman turned to the cameraman and said, "No, we ought to be able to shoot the Mexicans on sight, and that would end the problem. After two or three are shot, they'll stop crossing the border. And they'll take their cows home, too."

Simcox was flamboyant—he had a penchant for posing with a pistol down the front of his pants—and in him the border-militia movement now had a figurehead who made for a good story. Pretty soon Simcox was getting broader media attention, appearing on CNN with Lou Dobbs in November 2002 and on Fox News shortly thereafter with Sean Hannity, both of whom described him and his endeavors to organize vigilante border watchers in admiring tones. He also began popping up on right-wing talk radio all over the country.

One of the people listening in was Jim Gilchrist, a retired real estate salesman from California who had decided to devote himself to immigration activism and was attracted to right-wing theories about the "invasion." Inflamed in part by a Simcox interview, he conceived the notion of creating a nationwide "citizen border watch" event that would draw people from all over the country to Arizona for a month in an attempt to stop the flow of border crossers.

Gilchrist called it the Minuteman Project, and got ahold of Simcox to ask if he'd be interested in playing a central role in the project, since it would all take place down south of Tombstone, in Simcox's stomping grounds. Simcox was all in, and in short order stories about the project naming Simcox and Gilchrist as its cofounders started appearing in the right-wing media.

Within a few weeks, the two men were back on national TV, telling Dobbs, Hannity, and a number of visiting reporters about their plan to bring "thousands" of Americans down to the desert for a month-long "border watch" that they hoped, if nothing else, would send a message to politicians that people were tired of seeing immigrants flooding over the Mexico border.

The media reportage about the Minutemen's planned month-long event drew concern from officials in Mexico, who feared that their citizens might be mistreated and targeted by armed militiamen in Arizona. President George W. Bush—never a favorite of the Patriot crowd—stepped in and, in a joint presser with Mexico's President Vicente Fox, denounced the Minutemen, calling them vigilantes.

The whole thing came together in a big circus near the border in April 2005 that drew a media horde of TV crews, newspaper reporters and photographers, radio reporters, and Internet journalists who outnumbered the 900 Minutemen who showed up. The media gamely recorded the photo-op site established near the Mexico border of motor homes and campers. Many of the Minutemen were photographed scanning the desert wastes with their binoculars from the comfort of their lawn chairs.

Over the course of the first week of April, the Minutemen proved far more successful at attracting media coverage than they were at catching border crossers, none of whom came within their sights that week (although a couple of men were caught late one night in the second week). Sean Hannity even flew out to Tombstone and held a live broadcast from the Minutemen's gathering site in which he interviewed both Simcox and Gilchrist. Less noticed but silently lurking in the encampment were neo-Nazis and white supremacists.

The most exciting thing to happen was a late-night alarm, spread through the Minutemen's operations center, that Salvadoran drug gang members were about to descend upon them with machine guns. The pickups scrambled, roaring through the dust with their floodlights glaring and their passengers' long guns at the ready. Then they gradually realized that it had been a false alarm, and everyone returned to their campers and motor homes and went to bed.

By the second week of April, most of the participants began clearing out, and so did the reporters. By the third week of April, the border watch had pretty much petered out, the Minutemen had gone home in their campers, and their leaders, Chris Simcox and Jim Gilchrist, had flown out to Washington, DC.

Actually, the two men had a deeply acrimonious relationship that had manifested itself only a few days into the April media circus, caused mostly by Simcox's intense jealousy of Gilchrist's genial way with reporters. By December the rift had grown so intense that the two men announced they were officially splitting into two separate organizations: Gilchrist's operation would still be called the Minuteman Project, while Simcox's outfit was now named the Minuteman Civil Defense Corps.

Within a few months, the two organizations had descended into open and intense rivalry and had begun competing for members. Initially, Simcox held something of an upper hand, because he was already putting together the events for which the Minutemen were now known: civilian border watches, as they liked to call them. And in addition to organizing several such watches along the California border, in the summer of 2006 his MCDC began organizing a Minuteman watch in Washington State, along the Canadian border near Blaine. Of course, Canadians or other undocumented immigrants coming over the border aren't really a problem in Washington State, but Simcox mainly wanted to be able to point to the Canadian watches as proof to reporters that the Mexico border watches weren't racist in nature.

One of the people drawn to these Washington border watches was Shawna Forde, a hairdresser and former Boeing worker from Everett. One day after returning from a long road trip to California and back during which she had gorged on right-wing talk radio most of the way, she told her husband she had decided what she wanted to do with her life: "save America from illegal immigrants."

Forde was a diminutive but brassy and busty blonde who liked to play the tough gal in the testosterone-laden world of the mostly male Minutemen border watches. Indeed, Forde had a rap sheet dating back to when she was eleven years old that included sex work, shoplifting, credit-card fraud, and car theft, though none of her colleagues were aware of that. She was ambitious, and soon began climbing the hierarchy of the state Minuteman organization by putting together immigration-related meetings around the state. When Chris Simcox came to Bellingham for a public hearing about the Minutemen, Forde attached herself to him and introduced herself around as the state MCDC's press secretary.

Her raw ambition, combined with her propensity for thievery, put her sideways with the state's MCDC leadership, even though she had formed a close relationship with Simcox. After a prolonged internal fight, they fired her; she walked away vowing that she would form her own anti-immigrant border watch organization.

Forde promptly jumped ship to Jim Gilchrist's Minuteman Project, and sponsored a couple of Gilchrist speaking appearances in Washington state. In return he helped publicize her new group, Minuteman American Defense (MAD), and its plans to organize border watches in Arizona. Forde subsequently oversaw a number of these watches in various Arizona locales, including in the Altar Valley of the Sonoran Desert, and often hung out at Glenn Spencer's ranch in south-central Arizona, near Hereford.

A little after midnight the morning of May 30, 2009, Forde and three men dressed up to look like Border Patrol officers approached the home of Raul Flores Jr. in Arivaca, with the intention of robbing him. One of the vigilantes, Jason Eugene Bush, fatally shot Flores in the chest and head and wounded his wife, Gina Gonzalez, hitting her twice, though both shots were nonfatal. Gonzalez collapsed to the floor in a fetal position and pretended to be dead, then listened to them interrogate her nine-year-old daughter, Brisenia, as to the whereabouts of her older sister before they shot her twice in the face and left. Gonzalez called 911, but as she was doing so the gang reentered the home to retrieve a forgotten AK-47. The chief gunman, Bush, was lightly wounded by Gonzalez, who had retreated to the kitchen with a handgun. The gang fled, and authorities arrived about fifteen minutes later. Shawna Forde, Jason Bush, and a third cohort named Albert Gaxiola were arrested two weeks later.

Two years later, in January 2011, Shawna Forde went on trial for the murders and was swiftly convicted and sentenced to death. Jason Bush's trial the next month was shorter, the verdict and the sentence the same. The third gang member, Albert Gaxiola, was convicted of murder but got a life sentence without parole. All are still in the Arizona penitentiary system.

Forde maintains to this day that she is innocent. She claims the whole crime was a setup created by the New World Order and the

Obama administration to defame and embarrass the Minuteman border watch movement. A website run by an admirer and onetime associate promotes these claims as a conspiracy theory.

The Minuteman name more or less died with the Forde gang's crimes. As one former Minuteman leader told a reporter, "A lot of people felt, well, you're a Minuteman, you're a killer." However, he didn't seem to blame Forde for this, saying, "The name Minuteman has been tainted by a lot of organizations that didn't want us at the border, that say we're killers, that we've done harm."

The final nail in the Minutemen's coffin came in 2013, when Chris Simcox was arrested on multiple counts for molesting his daughter, six, and her five-year-old playmate. Simcox was eventually convicted in 2016 and was sentenced to twenty years.

Border militias enjoyed a brief resurgence in 2015, when fears about border crossers began rising amid intensifying hysteria about a sudden surge in children crossing into the United States to escape political and gang persecution in Honduras and elsewhere in Central America. You might find a few groups dotting the Arizona landscape on weekends, with names like Arizona Border Reconnaissance and Three Percent United Patriots.

A reporter for *Mother Jones*, Shane Bauer, spent a year undercover with one of these militias and found that their paranoias and hatreds were similar to those of the Minutemen ten years before and, for that matter, of David Duke's Klansmen in 1977. What this was all about for them, really, beyond the camping and outdoor time and "hunting beaners," as they called it, was doing something to stop the tide of brown faces they were seeing everywhere.

One militiaman, code-named Captain Pain, explained his motives in a roundabout way by describing his hometown in Colorado for Bauer: "Saudi fucking Aurora is what it is," he said. "We need to kill more of those motherfuckers. I never seen so many fucking towelheads stateside."

Another militiaman, code-named Jaeger, chimed in: "I remember when the part of Aurora I lived in was just white people."

5

A Black President and a Birth Certificate

J im David Adkisson really hated liberals. He hated them so much he wanted to start killing them en masse. So one day he did.

On July 27, 2008, Adkisson—a graying, mustachioed man from the Knoxville, Tennessee, suburb of Powell—drove his little Ford Escape to the parking lot of the Tennessee Valley Unitarian Universalist Church in Knoxville, which had attracted media attention for its efforts to open a local coffee shop for gays and lesbians. Adkisson walked inside the church carrying a guitar case packed with a shotgun and seventy-six rounds of ammunition.

The congregants were enjoying the opening scene from the church's production of the musical *Annie Jr.* when Adkisson, in a hallway outside the sanctuary, abruptly opened the guitar case, pulled out the shotgun, fired off a round that alerted everyone to his presence, then walked into the sanctuary and began firing randomly, while saying "hateful things." Linda Kraeger, sixty-one, a grandmother and retired schoolteacher, was hit in the face with a shotgun blast. Greg McKendry, sixty, got up to shield others from the attack and was hit in the chest.

A group of men began to surround Adkisson. When he stopped to reload, three men tackled him and wrestled away his gun. Pinned to the ground, Adkisson complained that the men were hurting him.

Greg McKendry was dead at the scene. Linda Kraeger died the next day. Seven other congregants were wounded.

In his Ford Escape, Adkisson had left a four-page manifesto describing his hatred of all things liberal and his belief that "all liberals should be killed."

A detective who interviewed Adkisson and examined the manifesto reported to his superiors that Adkisson targeted the church "because of its liberal teachings and his belief that all liberals should be killed because they were ruining the country, and that he felt that the Democrats had tied his country's hands in the war on terror and they had ruined every institution in America with the aid of media outlets."

Adkisson explained to the detective that he'd decided that since "he could not get to the leaders of the liberal movement that he would then target those that had voted them into office."

At Adkisson's home in Powell, scattered among the ammunition, guns, and brass knuckles, investigators found a library straight from the right-wing canon: *Liberalism Is a Mental Disorder*, by Michael Savage; *Let Freedom Ring*, by Sean Hannity; and *The O'Reilly Factor*, by Bill O'Reilly, among others.

Adkisson's manifesto read like an angry and twisted regurgitation of the rhetoric ladled out by Fox News and Rush Limbaugh, boiled down to its logical conclusion.

> Know this if nothing else: This was a hate crime. I hate the damn left-wing liberals. There is a vast left-wing conspiracy in this country & these liberals are working together to attack every decent & honorable institution in the nation, trying to turn this country into a communist state. Shame on them …
>
> This was a symbolic killing. Who I wanted to kill was every Democrat in the Senate & House, the 100 people in Bernard Goldberg's book. I'd like to kill everyone in the mainstream media. But I know those people were inaccessible to me. I couldn't get to the generals & high ranking officers of the Marxist movement so I went after the foot soldiers, the chickenshit liberals that vote in these traitorous people. Someone had to get the ball rolling. I volunteered. I hope others do the same. It's the only way we can rid America of this cancerous pestilence …
>
> I thought I'd do something good for this Country Kill Democrats til the cops kill me … Liberals are a pest like termites. Millions of them.

Each little bite contributes to the downfall of this great nation. The only way we can rid ourselves of this evil is to kill them in the streets. Kill them where they gather. I'd like to encourage other like minded people to do what I've done. If life aint worth living anymore don't just kill yourself. do something for your Country before you go. Go Kill Liberals.

Adkisson's rampage shattered the congregation. "People were killed in the sanctuary of my church, which should be the holy place, the safe place. People were injured," Rev. Chris Buice told PBS's Rick Karr a couple of weeks later. "A man came in here, totally dehumanized us—members of our church were not human to him. Where did he get that? Where did he get that sense that we were not human?"

Eliminationism had become an established component of right-wing rhetoric, both in the mainstream and among extremists, during most of the preceding decade and longer. One of its most powerful effects is to create an atmosphere of permission for acts of violence and intimidation; over time, enough such rhetoric will cause some people to commit hate crimes and worse.

The year 2008 was when eliminationism ceased being mere rhetoric and started bubbling up into the real world. Incidents of right-wing domestic terrorism, such as Jim Adkisson's murderous spree, suddenly doubled compared to 2007. Racially motivated hate crimes, particularly those directed against Hispanic victims, also increased. Militia organizing, which had tapered off to minuscule numbers for the previous eight years, also more than doubled.

There were a number of reasons for these changes, but one sequence of news events in particular appears to have inspired this upswing: the announcement, in February 2007, by Barack Obama that he intended to run for the presidency of the United States, followed by his extraordinarily popular and successful campaign in the succeeding months.

Right from the start, the old racist right made clear its hatred of Obama. In June 2007, the grand dragon of the National Knights of the Ku Klux Klan, Railston Loy, predicted, "Well, I'm not going to have to worry about him, because somebody else down South is going to take him out ... If that man is elected president, he'll be shot sure as hell."

But as Obama's candidacy advanced, old-line racists began facing the prospect of the election of a black man to the presidency—in so many ways another major defeat for their ideology. In short order they began changing their tune. In fact, they began claiming that the election of Barack Obama would be a good thing for them. August Kreis, the national director of the Aryan Nations, told an Associated Press reporter, "Obama's done my group a lot of good. He's polarizing Americans, black and white ... Especially in Florida, affiliates have increased recently."

Tom Prater, Florida spokesman for the white power group Euro, said, "I've gotten more calls in the last two months about interest in our organizations than I got in all the years in the past."

Don Black, owner of the neo-Nazi website *Stormfront*, was optimistic when interviewed by the *Washington Post* about the opportunities offered by Obama's candidacy: "I get nonstop e-mails and private messages from new people who are mad as hell about the possibility of Obama being elected," Black said. "White people, for a long time, have thought of our government as being for us, and Obama is the best possible evidence that we've lost that. This is scaring a lot of people who maybe never considered themselves racists, and it's bringing them over to our side."

Mainstream conservatives chose to race-bait more subtly, through the use of "dog whistles"—code words that race-baiting politicians and pundits use to refer to red-meat issues for the rabid right, audible only to those who have ears already attuned to the frequency. Conservative pundits in short order began referring to Obama by his middle name, Hussein, in an attempt to emphasize his foreignness and also to create an association with the Iraqi dictator American forces had not so long ago toppled. Rush Limbaugh ran a ditty with the title "Barack the Magic Negro," whose lyrics suggested his entire candidacy was built on a foundation of white guilt. In the *Washington Times*, the columnist Steve Sailer, who has often espoused eugenicist ideas, wrote, "While some whites envisage

Mr. Obama as the Cure for White Guilt, blacks are in no hurry to grant the white race absolution for slavery and Jim Crow, since they benefit from compensatory programs like affirmative action." In their eyes, Obama's candidacy was all about race—and for the duration, that's all it ever would be.

At mainstream news websites, things quickly became ugly. CBS. com had to shut down comments on any Obama story on its website because the stories inevitably attracted vicious race-baiters and death threats. In real life, matters were even worse; Obama's campaign attracted so many threats he was assigned a Secret Service detail earlier in the campaign than any other candidate in history.

The intensity of the racial and ethnic animus directed at Obama picked up after he secured the Democratic Party nomination at the Democratic National Convention in Denver, on August 28. An early warning sign that this might occur came on August 24, one day before the convention, when three men who turned out to have white-supremacist backgrounds were arrested in a nearby suburb for allegedly plotting to assassinate Obama (in the end no charges were brought).

Obama's nomination probably influenced the outcome of the Republican National Convention, which took place a few days later in St. Paul, Minnesota, and the ensuing campaign. The Republican nominee, Senator John McCain of Arizona, selected as his running mate Alaska's governor Sarah Palin, a populist bomb thrower popular with the religious right. Palin now entered the national stage as America's newest right-wing heroine. Upon hitting the hustings the week after the convention, Palin began lobbing rhetorical grenades in Obama's direction, accusing him of "palling around with terrorists," a reference to his association with William Ayers, a onetime Weather Underground leader. She also emphasized that the difference between Barack Obama and John McCain—and herself, of course—was that they, being good Republicans, preferred to campaign in "pro-American places." She didn't hold back on rabble-rousing red meat meant to emphasize Obama's foreignness and his supposed radicalism.

And the crowds responded, shouting out "terrorist" in reference to Obama and, at one rally, "Kill him!" in reference to Ayers. An Al-Jazeera camera crew caught the honest sentiments of many McCain-Palin supporters as they were leaving an Ohio rally—that Obama was anti-white, that he was a terrorist, or, more basically, that he was a black man:

> "I'm afraid if he wins, the blacks will take over. He's not a Christian! This is a Christian nation! What is our country gonna end up like?"

> "When you got a Negra running for president, you need a first stringer. [McCain's] definitely a second stringer."

> "He seems like a sheep—or a wolf in sheep's clothing, to be honest with you. And I believe Palin—she's filled with the Holy Spirit, and I believe she's gonna bring honesty and integrity to the White House."

> "He's related to a known terrorist."

> "He is friends with a terrorist of this country!"

> "Just the whole, Muslim thing, and everything, and everybody's still kinda—a lot of people have forgotten about 9/11, but ... I dunno, it's just kinda ... a little unnerving."

> "Obama and his wife, I'm concerned that they could be anti-white. That he might hide that."

> "I don't like the fact that he thinks us white people are trash ... because we're not!"

Such sentiments weren't unique to Ohio. In Las Vegas, the videographer Matt Toplikar interviewed McCain-Palin supporters as they left a Palin rally. One camouflage-capped fellow captured the spirit of the event, declaring, "Obama wins, I'm gonna move to Alaska. Haven't you ever heard that the United States is gonna be taken down from within?" he continued. "What better way to get taken down from within than having the president of the United States be the one that's going to do it?"

Another man warned, "Don't be afraid of me! Be afraid of Obama! Obama bin Laden, that's what you should be afraid of!" When accused of being a racist, he responded, "Yes, I am a racist. If you consider me a racist, well [unintelligible]. Those Arabs are dirtbags. They're dirty people, they hate Americans, they hate my kids, they hate my grandkids."

On Election Day, 2008, much of the nation celebrated the election of the first African American to the country's highest office. John McCain's supporters naturally felt the usual loser's bitterness and disappointment.

For many Americans, however—especially those who had opposed Obama on racial grounds—the reaction went well beyond despair. For them, November 5, 2008, was the end of the world. Or at least, the end of America as they knew it, or thought they knew it.

So maybe it wasn't such a surprise that they responded to that day with the special venom and violence peculiar to the American right.

In Texas, students at Baylor University in Waco discovered a noose hanging from a tree on campus the evening of Election Day. At a site nearby angry Republican students had gathered a bunch of Obama yard signs and burned them in a big bonfire. That evening, a riot nearly broke out when Obama supporters, chanting the new president's name, were confronted by white students outside a residence hall who told them: "Any nigger who walks by Penland [Hall], we're going to kick their ass, we're going to jump him." The Obama supporters stopped and responded, "Excuse me?" Somehow they managed to keep the confrontation confined to a mere shouting match until police arrived and broke things up.

On the North Carolina State University campus in Raleigh, some students spent Election Night spray-painting graffiti messages such as "Let's shoot that Nigger in the head" and "Hang Obama by a

Noose." The university administration protected the students' identities and refused to take any legal action against them or discipline them in any way.

But such student antics were just a warm-up. On Staten Island, New York, on Election Night, four young white men "decided to go after black people" in retaliation for Obama's election. First they drove to the mostly black Park Hill neighborhood and assaulted a Liberian immigrant, beating him with a metal pipe and a police baton, in addition to the usual blows from fists and feet. Then they drove to Port Richmond and assaulted another black man and verbally threatened a Latino man and a group of black people. They finished up the night by driving alongside a man walking home from his job as a Rite Aid manager and trying to club him with the police baton. Instead, they hit him with their car, throwing him off the windshield and into a coma for over a month. The last victim was a white man. All four men wound up convicted of hate crimes and spent the duration of Obama's first term in prison.

There were cross burnings and even arson. The morning after the election, in Hardwick Township, New Jersey, a black man taking his eight-year-old daughter to school emerged from his front door to discover that someone had burned a six-foot-tall cross on his lawn—right next to the man's banner declaring Obama president. That had been torched too.

Another cross was burned on the lawn of the only black man in tiny Apolacon Township, Pennsylvania, the night after the election. A black church in Springfield, Massachusetts, was burned to the ground the night of the election; eventually, three white men were arrested and charged with setting the fire as a hate crime. On election night, a black family in South Ogden, Utah, came home from volunteering at their local polling station to discover that their American flag had been torched.

Obama's inauguration on January 21, 2009, brought more haters out of the woodwork.

Two days before the big event, arsonists in Forsyth County, Georgia, set fire to the home of a woman who was known as a public supporter of Obama. Someone painted a racial slur on her fence, along with the warning "Your black boy will die."

On Inauguration Day, someone taped newspaper articles featuring Obama onto the apartment door of a woman in Jersey City, New Jersey, and set fire to it. Fortunately, the woman had stayed home to watch the inauguration on TV and smelled the burning, and she was able to extinguish the fire before it spread.

The next day, a large twenty-two-year-old skinhead named Keith Luke in Brockton, Massachusetts, decided it was time to fight the "extinction" of the white race. He bashed down the door of a Latino woman and her sister and shot them both; one died. Police apprehended and arrested Luke before he could pull off the next planned stage of his shooting rampage, at a local Jewish synagogue. According to the DA, Luke intended to "kill as many Jews, blacks, and Hispanics as humanly possible ... before killing himself." When he appeared in court a month later, Luke had carved a swastika into his forehead with a razor blade.

The Southern Poverty Law Center counted more than 200 "hate-related" incidents around the election and inauguration of Barack Obama as the nation's first African American president. The SPLC's Mark Potok stated: "I think we really are beginning to see a white backlash that may grow fairly large. The situation's worrying. Not only do we have continuing nonwhite immigration, not only is the economy in the tank and very likely to get worse, but we have a black man in the White House. That is driving a kind of rage in a certain sector of the white population that is very, very worrying to me.

"We are seeing literally hundreds of incidents around the country—from cross burnings to death threats to effigies hanging to confrontations in schoolyards."

The spike in racially motivated violence was accompanied by a sharp increase in business for white-supremacist websites such as the neo-Nazi forum *Stormfront*. It collected more than 2,000 new members the day after the election—so much traffic that the site crashed. One *Stormfront* poster, a North Las Vegas resident going by the moniker Dalderian Germanicus, reflected the consensus sentiment at the site: "I want the SOB laid out in a box to see how 'messiahs' come to rest. God has abandoned us, this country is doomed."

In Georgia, a middle-aged man expressed to an Associated Press reporter the typical view on the extremist right in the days and weeks after the election: "I believe our nation is ruined and has been for several decades, and the election of Obama is merely the culmination of the change."

The rise in right-wing media such as Fox News and other openly pro-conservative media and the spread of their dubious news values into the mainstream media played a powerful role in creating an epistemological bubble for the audience: for every news event, these outlets were able to provide a right-wing, anti-liberal spin on it. More often than not, that spin was not just factually dubious, it was outrageously false. Their audiences were able to create a Patriot-style alternative universe for themselves that they could confirm by turning on their TVs. They would disregard information that didn't fit in their universe.

The massive growth of the Internet, especially as it spread to the older and more rural American population, also played a significant role in the expansion of this alternative universe. Suddenly a vast ocean of dubious information was available to all, and it quickly filled with anonymous and phony smears, a floating island of garbage about Barack Obama that suddenly appeared, as if from the depths, and rapidly spread through what became known as the "viral email."

Everyone with an email account in America seemed to be receiving these emails containing "true" information revealing Obama to be an America-hating Muslim radical. There were dozens of permutations on this theme, everything from fake claims that Obama had the American flag removed from his jet and that he refused to wear flag lapel pins to theories that he was secretly raised a Muslim at a madrassa in Indonesia, and that in reality he was born not in Hawaii, but in Kenya. Another favorite was a Photoshopped Obama portrait that transformed him into a bearded bin Laden type, captioned "So America, you want change? … Just wait."

The viral anonymous email became such a fixture of the campaign to undermine the president's legitimacy that Obama's campaign was forced to create a website devoted specifically to debunking the false information the emails spread. In a story in the *Nation*, "The New Right-Wing Smear Machine," Chris Hayes detailed how movement conservatives—using far-right Web publications such as *NewsMax* and *WorldNetDaily* as bases of operations—spread rumors and wholly fabricated nonsense about Obama to millions of email readers, some of whom eagerly accepted it as gospel.

Thus was born the "Birther" meme, the conviction that Obama was not an American citizen.

No one's exactly certain where it originated, but somewhere in those forwarded emails appeared the suggestion that Obama was not really an American citizen because of the circumstances of his birth. Some claimed that Obama had been born in Kenya; others, that he had been born in Indonesia.

The Obama campaign responded to this and other disinformation by setting up a website, Fight the Smears, specifically to counter the wild rumors that were circulating. At the site was posted a copy of Obama's birth certificate showing he was born in Hawaii in 1961. Anyone born in Hawaii would present the same type of document when undergoing a security review or obtaining a passport.

For the conspiracy-mongers of the fringe right, though, that wasn't good enough.

Some of them noticed that the posted document was what the State of Hawaii calls a certification of live birth—which is basically the state's short-form version of a person's original birth certificate. It includes time of birth, city, parents, and so on, but lacks medical details and the name of the hospital. To get those details, you have to get the original certificate. Obtaining a copy of it requires making a special request to state officials.

Naturally, a fresh round of conspiracy theorizing erupted—the birth certificate on display had been digitally altered with Adobe Photoshop. It also lacked a stamped seal of the state, a certain sign of forgery. Jerome Corsi—the coauthor of the "Swift Boat" hoax that played a critical role in sinking John Kerry's presidential campaign in 2004, and more recently the author of *The Obama Nation: Leftist Politics and the Cult of Personality*—went on *Fox and Friends* and told Steve Doocy that "the campaign has a false, fake birth certificate posted on their website... It's been shown to have watermarks from Photoshop. It's a fake document that's on the website right now, and the original birth certificate, the campaign refuses to produce."

The Obama campaign invited FactCheck.org to come see the certificate for themselves, and it subsequently reported their definitive conclusion: "Obama was born in the USA. Just as he has always said."

Hawaii state officials subsequently confirmed that the state held Obama's original birth certificate on record, noting that "there have been numerous requests" for copies, but explaining that the state's records department was prohibited by state law from releasing it to "persons who do not have a tangible interest in the vital record."

Of course, there are always the births listed in local newspapers— and sure enough, both the *Honolulu Advertiser* and the *Honolulu Star-Bulletin* (on August 13 and August 14, 1961, respectively) published a birth notice for Barack Obama, listing the home address as 6085 Kalanianaole Highway in Honolulu. Contrary to later suggestions, these birth announcements were not paid announcements—a much later practice—but were collected by staff reporters assigned to make the rounds of area hospitals.

With all these dubious claims and theories floating about, the atmosphere was ripe for Alex Jones and his army of conspiracists to step up and make their presence felt.

Jones and his fellow "Truthers" had largely been consigned to the fringes of mainstream discourse for most of the Bush years, but that did not mean they had grown stagnant. Rather the contrary.

Even though right-wing media generally declined to even give their theories the time of day, the audience for Jones's always-expanding universe of conspiracies kept gaining steam throughout the first decade of the new century.

Jones's audience kept multiplying as 9/11 theories mushroomed, and as he churned out new "evidence" and claims in order to keep up. These included theories that Building 7, situated next to the Twin Towers and demolished when they fell, had actually been destroyed by hidden bombs, and that Flight 93, brought down in a field in Pennsylvania after passengers tried to invade the pilot's cabin to wrest control from the terrorists, was actually shot down by military jets, and that phone calls to family members by people on the airliner before it went down had been faked.

In addition to the *Zeitgeist* films produced by the far-right activist Peter Joseph, a number of other independent conspiracists kept offering their own takes on who and what was behind the terrorist attacks, including a British anarchist, Charlie Veitch, and a New York writer, Nico Haupt. The competition among the theories became fierce and internecine warfare soon broke out, with Jones accusing Haupt of being a secret FBI agent trying to undermine the movement. Veitch, promoted initially by Jones on his show, later announced he had become skeptical of certain core claims, causing Infowars fans to descend upon him viciously.

Infowars began drawing hundreds of thousands of daily hits, and his radio-show rants, uploaded to YouTube, began spreading quickly, especially as more people began sharing them on social media sites such as Facebook and Twitter. By 2009 Jones's YouTube channel had garnered over 60 million views.

By March 2009, Jones had produced one of his "documentaries" titled *The Obama Deception: The Mask Comes Off*, which portrayed the new president as a "corporate creation of the banking elite" who would enact the agenda of the military-industrial complex and eventually enslave Americans. Among other signs of the looming takeover, Jones pointed to Obama's early musings about the possibility of creating a public-oriented "national civilian service" to fill domestic needs, as military service fills our international needs, as proof that he intended to make young Americans into a compulsory army of brainwashed slaves, described on Jones's Prison Planet site as a "Stasi."

In August 2009 Jones got on the Birther bandwagon, which had already been joined up by a number of his fellow 9/11 conspiracists. Jones's Infowars site finally chimed in with a piece by Jones's contributor Paul Joseph Watson, headlined "Shocking New Birth Certificate Proof Obama Born in Kenya?" It soon emerged that *this* birth certificate was a hoax.

The convergence of old far-right conspiracists and the new anti-Obama fanatics gave birth, in the weeks after the election, to a campaign to prevent Obama from taking the oath of office in January, fueled in part by a pair of fringe right-wing lawyers named Leo Donofrio and Orly Taitz, who tried to take legal action to prevent Obama from being sworn in. The Supreme Court briefly considered Donofrio's lawsuit challenging Obama's US citizenship—a continuation of a New Jersey case embraced by the birth-certificate conspiracy theorists (or "Birthers," as they came to be known)—but peremptorily dismissed it.

Online campaigns arose: RallyCongress.com, which gathered over 125,000 signatures demanding Obama's birth certificate, and WeMustBeHeard.com, which organized sit-ins outside the Supreme Court building in Washington. The right-wing webzine *WorldNetDaily*, which has a long history of promoting right-wing conspiracy theories dating back to the 1990s, organized a similar petition drive. A longtime far-right tax protester named Bob Schultz—whose "We the People" organization later ran into serious legal problems for promoting a tax scheme predicated on old far-right "constitutionalist" theories that the federal income tax is illegal—purchased full-page ads in the *Chicago Tribune* asserting that Obama's birth certificate was forged, that his "grandmother is record[ed] on tape saying she attended your birth in Kenya," and that Obama had lost his citizenship by virtue of his mother's second marriage to an Indonesian man.

By the time of Obama's inauguration on January 20, 2009, however, all these efforts had come to naught. But that didn't mean they had subsided. Rather the opposite: the Birther theories continued to bubble and build, thanks in no small part to the mainstream media.

Orly Taitz filed a fresh lawsuit in July 2009 on behalf of Stefan Cook, an Army Reserve soldier, who claimed he could refuse deployment orders to Afghanistan because the president wasn't an American citizen. When the Army responded by simply rescinding Cook's orders, Sean Hannity reported about it on his Fox News program by describing Cook as a victim of crude political discrimination. Hannity shied away from any similar reports from then on.

Rush Limbaugh, too, briefly referenced it on his radio show: "God does not have a birth certificate, and neither does Obama—not that we've seen." Afterward, he made little mention of it. Eventually, though, the Birthers found an ardent supporter of their claims in the mainstream media: CNN's Lou Dobbs.

Dobbs kicked off his coverage of the birth-certificate controversy in mid-July on his syndicated radio show by hosting Orly Taitz and asserting repeatedly that Obama "needed to produce" his birth certificate. However, filling in for Dobbs on his own program a few days later, CNN's Kitty Pilgrim ran a report debunking the theories.

Dobbs shrugged it off, asserting on his CNN broadcast the next night that Obama's birth-certificate questions "won't go away." He featured a video clip of a town-hall attendee berating the Republican congressman Mike Castle of Delaware about Obama's birth certificate: "He is not an American citizen! He is a citizen of Kenya!" Dobbs commented: "A lot of anger in the audience, and a lot of questions remaining—seemingly, the questions won't go away because they haven't been dealt with, it seems possible, too straightforwardly and quickly."

The comments created an uproar. Chris Matthews, on MSNBC's *Hardball*, suggested that Dobbs was "appeasing the nutcases" by reporting the claims as if they had any credibility. Rather than back down, Dobbs doubled down, going on CNN and charging that

Obama could "make the whole ... controversy disappear ... by simply releasing his original birth certificate." On his radio show he similarly persisted: "Where is that birth certificate? Why hasn't it been forthcoming?"

When the resulting public firestorm produced calls from civil rights and Latino organizations to remove Dobbs from his anchor position, CNN's president, Jon Klein, defended his coverage as "legitimate"—but he sent an email to Dobbs's staff to inform them that the birth certificate story was "dead." That night, Dobbs reiterated that Obama could "make the story go away." As the controversy raged on other channels—Fox's Bill O'Reilly knocked Dobbs for his credulousness, but defended him against his attackers anyway—Dobbs claimed that he really didn't believe the theories: "All I said is the president is a citizen, but it would be simple to make all this noise go away with just simply producing the long-form birth certificate." Dobbs eventually lost his job at CNN, in part over the Birther controversy.

But the conspiracist alternative universe kept expanding into the mainstream media. That was mainly due to a fresh new face at Fox News: Glenn Beck.

By 2009, Limbaugh was the elder statesman of the incendiary pundit set. Yet as divisive and conspiracist as his rhetoric often became, he was overtaken that year in both those qualities by the hot new face on the right-wing scene, the boyish-looking Beck. Beck built on and amplified the central themes established during the 2008 campaign —that Obama was a foreigner, a leftist, an America-hating radical who wanted to destroy the American way of life. In the process, he opened up a whole new frontier in the transmission of right-wing extremist ideas into mainstream American discourse.

Beck already had an established reputation as a bomb thrower, first from his years as a radio "shock jock" at a number of stations around the country, and then from his tenure, beginning in 2006, at *CNN Headline News*, where he was noted for such antics as asking newly elected Representative Keith Ellison, the nation's first Muslim congressman, why he, Beck, shouldn't consider him to be working for the enemy. He also was open in his sympathy for right-wing extremists and their ideas; while credulously interviewing a John Birch Society official about a possible conspiracy to create a North American Union, Beck said, "Sam, I have to tell you, when I was growing up, the John Birch Society, I thought they were a bunch of nuts. However, you guys are starting to make more and more sense to me."

Beck announced he was making the leap to Fox News in October 2008, though his show did not begin running regularly until January 2009. Still, he gave the public a preview of where he was going with his new show in a mid-November appearance with Bill O'Reilly on *The O'Reilly Factor*, in which he ranted at length about the public's evident tolerance—judging by election results—of a presidential candidate who had "palled around" with terrorists like William Ayers. Beck explained away the election as the result of "cakes and circuses and too many dumb people. I mean, we should thin out the herd, you know what I mean?" He also set the table for what was to come:

> This is a total outrage, Bill. There is a disconnect in America. We are at the place where the Constitution hangs in the balance, and I think we're at a crossroads here. We're still about here [points to spot on hand], where the roads are just starting to split, but pretty soon, this side and this side are not gonna understand each other at all, because we're living in different universes.

It became clear early on that Beck was interested not in bridging this gap but in exploiting it. No sooner did his show, *Glenn Beck*, get started on Fox than he began focusing on the ideological aspects of Obama's supposed radicalism. The show also featured an unusually maudlin tone; in his Fox debut on January 19, Beck became teary-eyed talking about Sarah Palin's candidacy and how it made him feel like he "was not alone." A few nights later he featured a segment in which he had the camera zoom in around his eyes as he delivered his monologue. When Stephen Colbert parodied it hilariously with a zoom camera operated by a proctologist, Beck came on and explained that he had done it because "we don't look each other in the eyes" enough these days. A few weeks after this, in an hour-long program set up like a town-hall meeting, Beck again got choked up. "I just love my country—and I fear for it!" he blurted out.

Beck devoted most of his energy to the theme that President Obama was a far-left radical who intended to remake America into a totalitarian state. He had a problem, though, in figuring out just what kind of totalitarianism Obama was bringing: socialist, communist, or fascist. Over the course of the next several months, Beck began using all three terms to describe Obama's agenda, often interchangeably—terms which by anyone's lights but Beck's actually represent profoundly different and distinct ideologies.

Beck's show also featured an overarching apocalyptic sensibility. At various times, different dooms confronted the nation, according to Beck. He frequently fretted about the epidemic of violent crime by Mexican drug cartels south of the border, and hosted a hysterical discussion with the right-wing maven Michelle Malkin about the existential threat this posed to the United States. At other times he saw a global nuclear apocalypse looming in the form of a potential Middle East confrontation with Iran. But consistently the greatest threat to America was President Obama and his administration.

Soon Beck's paranoia began reaching a fever pitch—he even flirted with the conspiracy theories that Obama was using the Federal Emergency Management Administration to secretly prepare concentration camps into which conservatives were about to be rounded up. Beck announced he was investigating claims: he told his audience that "we can't disprove" the FEMA concentration camps story.

The FEMA camps claims dated back to the Militia of Montana and later gained traction under the auspices of Alex Jones's radio rants. Patriot-movement leaders had been claiming since the 1990s that black helicopters had been spotted—their mission unclear but much speculated on; such stories were based purely on fabricated "evidence." This, eventually, is what Glenn Beck reported back to his audience on his April 6, 2009, show, which featured a ten-minute segment with Jim Meigs, a *Popular Science* journalist, who looked into the claims and found them utterly spurious.

Beck was hardly chastened by the episode, and continued promoting beliefs held by militia groups in other arenas. On March 24 he had invited John Bolton, the former United Nations ambassador, on his show for a discussion of the globalist propensities of the Obama White House. During the discussion Beck lurched off on his own tangent: "I mean, I think these guys—these guys, they'll take away guns, they'll take away our sovereignty, they'll take away our, our, our currency, our money! They're already starting to put all the global framework in with this bullcrap called global warming! This is an effort to globalize and tie together everybody on the planet, is it not?"

Taking away guns—that was one of the militias' chief sources of paranoia in the 1990s, and now Beck was making the charge against Obama, too. Beck regularly warned his audience that "our rights are under attack," including "the right to keep and bear arms" guaranteed by the Second Amendment.

The notion that Obama and his administration intended to go on a gun-grabbing spree became a recurring theme on Beck's show. Twice he featured the president of the National Rifle Association, Wayne LaPierre, in segments with a large chyron titled "Constitution Under Attack." In April 2009 LaPierre suggested on Beck's show that administration support for international efforts to adopt strict gun-licensing standards amounted to a United Nations plot: "They're trying to pass, basically, a global gun ban on all individual possession of firearms ownership."

The paranoia whipped up by the NRA (as usual with the gun-rights crowd) had no known basis in reality. In the list of thirteen priorities for action in Obama's first year and beyond that was leaked to the *New York Times*, jobs and the economy completely predominated. Gun control was not on the list. Nor was there even a whisper of it from any Obama administration official in 2009.

Which, for the paranoid at heart, only proved once and for all that something nefarious was afoot.

Whether he was grounded in reality or not, Beck was tapping into something very real by promoting gun paranoia. In fact, one of the remarkable ways the fringe hysteria manifested itself in the real world after the election was in the astonishing surge in gun sales.

The initial spike occurred before the election, when firearms groups began noticing a surge in federal background checks for new gun purchases. In November alone, the number, 378,000 checks, was 42 percent greater than for the same month a year before. One gun-friendly outdoor news service named the new president its "Gun Salesman of the Year."

The only time gun rights really made their way into the news was during the confirmation hearings for Eric Holder, the nominee for attorney general, where one of the voices testifying against his confirmation was a "gun rights expert," Stephen Halbrook. Halbrook had authored a recent book about the Second Amendment. What upset the gun crowd about Holder was his support of the gun ban in DC, as well as an op-ed piece he had written in October 2001 for the *Washington Post*, "Keeping Guns Away from Terrorists." The article largely was an eminently sensible column about closing up gun-sales loopholes used by many terrorists to obtain weapons.

Nonetheless, the fears that Obama was a closet gun-grabber secretly plotting against them became widespread, particularly in the rural areas where the right to bear arms is traditionally prized. Obama's election produced a lightning bolt of fear among many, and they responded by a run on both guns and ammunition and even gunpowder.

"Barack Obama would be the most anti-gun president in history —bar none," the NRA's chief lobbyist, Chris Cox, wrote in a *Washington Post* op-ed. Warnings like that—as well as Glenn Beck's paranoid musings with Wayne LaPierre—produced predictable results among gun owners. "They're like, 'Hey, maybe I should buy one of these before they become illegal,'" one gun-shop owner told a reporter. "If you look in any NRA magazine or you're into guns, you see a lot of bills that are in the works."

At the NRA's big annual convention in Arizona that May, all the talk was about the spike in gun sales. The footage coming out of Arizona was striking for the level of paranoia. Michael Steele, chairman of the Republican National Committee, warned for the camera: "Whenever they can, wherever they can, the Democrats want to take away the rights of law-abiding citizens to own and purchase a gun, a right that is guaranteed under the United States Constitution."

Leonard Junker, a fifty-six-year-old trucker and Republican Party organizer from Tucson, told reporters, "Right now is a pivotal time in our history with a president and a total administration that is anti-gun. I truly believe that they want to disarm us."

People were driven to buy guns not just from fear of Obama but also fear of the social chaos they believed would result from his administration. Video footage from the NRA convention featured a number of white conservative women who were drawn to the organization via fearmongering. In one video, a woman talked about how women were buying guns partly out of a fear that society was about to fall apart. Glenn Beck's apocalyptic scenarios of a dog-eat-dog society obviously had struck a chord.

One year later in Arizona, that paranoia would strike home in a blizzard of bullets.

Mad Hatters and March Hares

E ven in its nascent form, Alt-America wanted Barack Obama to fail. Indeed, its earliest inhabitants were drawn to it out of their determination to make that happen.

Even before the inauguration, Sean Hannity had announced on his nationally syndicated radio show, *Hannity*, that he was organizing a force to attempt to stop Obama from enacting "radical" policies. He called his show the outpost of "the conservative underground." Another radio host, Mike Gallagher, promoted an effort by a far-right online group called Grassfire to present a petition announcing that signers were joining "the resistance" to Obama's presidency. That was soon followed by the campaign to prevent Obama from being sworn into office.

The message was clear: conservatives did not consider Barack Obama to be a legitimate president, a fact underscored by the growing Birther campaign. The right had set out to delegitimize Bill Clinton when he was elected president in 1992; now they intended to do the same to Obama. The effort to undermine and destroy Clinton had revolved around his alleged sexual proclivities; the campaign around Obama would focus on his foreignness, his name, his background, and, ultimately, his blackness.

Leading the charge after the election was Rush Limbaugh, who announced his hope that Obama would fail: "Based on what we've seen with General Motors and the banks, if he fails, America is saved. Barack Obama's policies and their failure is the only hope we've got to maintain the America of our founding."

Limbaugh's wish for Obama's failure stirred outrage among liberals and centrists alike, but he was defiant. At the Conservative Political Action Conference in February 2009, he justified his stance:

> Ladies and gentlemen, the Democrat Party has actively not just sought the failure of Republican presidents and policies and now wars, for the first time. The Democrat Party doesn't stop at failure. Talk to Judge Robert Bork, talk to Justice Clarence Thomas, about how they try to destroy lives, reputations, and character. And I'm supposed to say, I don't want the president to fail?

The rant was widely distributed and was discussed in several press reports. It became one of the definitive conservative responses to Obama's election: open political warfare, a defiance of the new president's every objective, was to be the right-wing political project for the ensuing eight years.

And within weeks, it had created the impetus for a new right-wing movement: the Tea Party.

Ron Paul, a GOP presidential hopeful who had been a Texas congressman from 1976 to 1985 and then again from 1997 to 2013, played a critical formative role in the gradual merging of the extremist right and mainstream conservatism in the years around Obama's election. He was also one of the fathers of the Tea Party.

Right-wing populism began surging to the fore in 2008 with Paul's insurgent Republican campaign. A longtime outsider generally considered to be a fringe candidate, Paul, who called himself a Libertarian, began surprising longtime political observers by attracting large, enthusiastic crowds to his rallies and drawing in substantial contributions.

Paul announced his candidacy in March 2007, and drew little notice at first. However, his presidential candidacy began picking up significant traction early on in the Republican primaries, in no small part because of his opposition to the Iraq War. He began using ingenious online fund-raising methods that quickly broke all kinds of records and won him the position of the GOP's top fund-raiser for the critical fourth quarter of 2007. Yet Paul tended to be ignored by both the mainstream media and mainstream Republicans: Fox News actually snubbed him by declining to invite him to one of its televised Republican presidential debates. The one exception was Glenn Beck, who invited Paul onto *CNN Headline News* for an entire hour, the first of many Paul appearances with Beck.

Paul also drew some of his most vocal support from a voting bloc whose presence in the Paul camp also went almost completely ignored by the mainstream media: the extremists of the radical right. It was striking to observe the unanimity with which the far right had coalesced behind Paul's candidacy.

Rather quietly and under the radar, Paul managed to unite nearly the entire radical right behind himself, more than any presidential candidate since George Wallace in 1968. The two main populist presidential candidates before Paul—Ross Perot in 1992 and 1996 and Pat Buchanan in 2000—had not achieved this level of unanimous and intense far-right support. Virtually every far-right grouping—neo-Nazis, white supremacists, militias, constitutionalists, Minutemen, nativists—in the American political landscape lined up behind Paul. White supremacists from the Nationalist Socialist Movement (NSM), the neo-Nazi website *Stormfront*, National Vanguard, White Aryan Resistance (WAR), and Hammerskins became outspoken supporters of Paul and turned out to rally for him at a number of different campaign appearances. At a Paul rally in August 2007 in New Jersey, a sizable number of Stormfronters showed up. Paul made no bones about welcoming this source of support. Paul made headlines by declining to return a donation from *Stormfront*'s proprietor, Don Black, and later posed with Black and his son Derek at a Paul event in Florida.

Paul's appeal to the extreme right was a natural outgrowth of his identity. Much of his popular image was predicated on the idea that he was a libertarian Republican—he was the 1988 presidential candidate of the Libertarian Party. The libertarian political label was

111

understood to revolve around the promotion of individual liberties in the mold of Ayn Rand and other philosophers. But a closer examination of Paul's brand of politics showed that he had a closer affinity to the John Birch Society than any genuinely libertarian entity. His declared goals of fighting the New World Order; eliminating the Federal Reserve, the IRS, and most other federal agencies; getting us out of the UN; ending all gun controls; reinstating the gold standard—all were classic elements of far-right populism. Even though Paul's candidacy received no institutional support from within the GOP, it reflected not just a resurgence of right-wing populism but a dramatic weaving of extremist beliefs into the national conversation. Paul's multiple appearances on Alex Jones's radio programs were the best evidence of his close relationship with the conspiracist right.

Paul's history as a right-wing extremist eventually caught up with him. It had been known among political researchers that, during the 1990s, Paul had produced a steady stream of newsletters filled with vile race-baiting, anti-Semitism, and Patriot-style conspiracy theories about the New World Order and its minions running the Federal Reserve. Finally, in January 2008, *The New Republic* got ahold of the newsletters and ran extensive excerpts from them, establishing clearly that Paul had sponsored the distribution of some genuinely vile material. His reputation never fully recovered.

But throughout 2007, that side of the candidate had largely remained hidden. Instead, Paul was seen as a genial if eccentric libertarian who wanted to reconfigure the monetary system and international political alignments, but otherwise seemed like an ordinary enough fellow. The people who called him an extremist seemed extreme themselves.

Political observers sat up and took notice after the first of Paul's fund-raising "money bombs"—a gimmick event that encouraged, through astute use of the Internet as an organizing tool, his supporters to donate small individual sums all within a short, twenty-hour time span. Paul supporters chose December 16, 2007, the 234th anniversary of the Boston Tea Party, to kick off the fund-raising campaign for their candidate. Michael Levenson, reporting for the *Boston Globe*, described how by 7 p.m., the campaign collected a one-day record of $4.3 million in contributions from some 33,000 donors. The kickoff also featured a march through the snowy streets of Boston that culminated with a reenactment of the Colonial rebels dumping tea into Boston Harbor. They replaced the crates of tea with banners reading "Tyranny" and "No Taxation Without Representation," which were tossed into boxes placed before an image of the harbor.

Conservative organizers watched these goings-on with keen interest, because, after eight years of conservative Bush rule and with the country in bad shape, they were expecting to be swept out of office. The question for many of them already was how to go about rebuilding afterward. And the Boston Tea Party protest set up by the Ron Paul supporters provided the perfect model of how to proceed.

In the wake of the global economic crisis that struck in mid-September 2008, Congress and the Bush administration began working in concert to pass a huge economic stimulus package needed to save the American economy from complete ruin. However, the legislation remained unfinished through the election. Shortly after Obama's inauguration, Congress set to work with the new president's team to craft a viable bill. Finally, on February 11, after two weeks of wrangling, Congress reached a deal on legislation bailing out the financial industry.

At around the same time, Keli Carender, a Seattle schoolteacher and member of the Young Republicans, began a blog, *Redistributing Knowledge*, for which she wrote under the nom de plume Liberty Belle. Liberty Belle wrote that conservatives needed to get busy and show real people what the GOP could do to solve the problems of the country, declaring, "We need something BOLD and DIFFERENT and REAL." Liberty Belle's second post put out a call to arms to conservatives across the land:

There are tens of millions of us, if not more. I think if we chose a day to show the world, scary coworkers be damned, that we exist and we are just as passionate about the direction of our country, that we could maybe finally find each other.

Liberty Belle announced a protest in Seattle on February 16, 2009. She was aided by another member of the Young Republicans, Kirby Wilbur, who put her on his local Fox Radio talk show. The conservative blogger Michelle Malkin saw an opportunity and jumped on Liberty Belle's blog posts, telling her readers to join the protests against Obama's "porkulus" bill, and then issued a call for the same kind of protest to be held in Denver. About 100 protesters showed up to hear Carender—who arrived dressed in an "Alice Wonderland" outfit—tell them, "We don't want this country to go down the path to socialism!"

A protest was held on the steps of the Colorado capitol the same day, drawing a modest crowd of about 200 who screamed in unison, "No more pork!" Malkin, who had moved to the state the year before, arrived in Denver to help stage the rally. She was fully funded by Americans for Prosperity, a right-wing think tank funded by the billionaire David Koch, and the Independence Institute, another conservative think tank funded by the Coors family's Castle Rock Foundation.

The spark that finally lit the Tea Party fuse came from a little-known Wall Street insider and CNBC analyst named Rick Santelli, a former trader and financial executive. The new Obama administration was preparing a housing plan as a stopgap measure after the mortgage collapse. On February 19, while discussing the Obama plan on CNBC, in a broadcast from the trading pit of the Chicago Stock Exchange, Santelli snapped.

Santelli claimed the "government is promoting bad behavior." He suggested the Obama administration "put up a website to have people vote on the Internet as a referendum to see if we really want to subsidize the losers' mortgages. Or would we like to at least buy cars and buy houses in foreclosure and give them to people that might have a chance to actually prosper down the road, and reward people that could carry the water instead of drink the water?" He then said, "We're thinking of having a Chicago Tea Party in July. All you capitalists that want to show up to Lake Michigan, I'm gonna start organizing."

Santelli's rant went viral when the video hit YouTube shortly afterward. And conservatives lapped it up. By the end of the day, a new website had gone online: officialchicagoteaparty.com. Soon, a Facebook page followed, administered by people affiliated with corporate-funded organizations such as FreedomWorks, one of the right's premier "astroturfing" oufits (a term describing fake "grass-roots" organizing that in reality is funded by large corporations and their CEOs), and Americans for Prosperity.

CNBC immediately ran a commercial starring Santelli, and his rant was the talk of cable TV for a week or so. Within days, the Chicago Tea Party organized for February 27 had morphed into a Nationwide Chicago Tea Party, with similar protests organized in some forty cities across the country. The blog *TalkingPointsMemo* interviewed the organizer of the event in Tampa, Florida, a local consultant named John Hendrix. He said he got the idea for the Tea Party from Tom Gaithens of FreedomWorks while in the same breath claiming that the protests were "completely spontaneous."

By February, the Tea Parties had become the focus of Freedom Works' operations. They were soon to get a boost beyond their wildest imaginings: the full-fledged support of a cable news network—namely, Fox News.

It costs advertisers thousands of dollars to air a single thirty-second commercial on a few cable stations for a week, even in relatively cheap rural markets. To advertise nationally on Fox News—the 2009 ratings leader in cable news—cost hundreds of thousands of dollars, even millions if the ads aired often enough and in prime time.

So what Fox News offered the organizers of the Tea Party events—and the conservative movement opposing Obama's pres-idency generally—was something you couldn't measure in dollars and cents, because not only did Fox air a steady onslaught of Tea

Party promotional ads, the network embraced the outright promotion of the events in their news broadcasts and on their opinion shows. Their on-air personalities as well as their websites took an active role day after day and night after night in promoting and urging the Fox audience to join in the Tea Party protests. Media Matters, a nonprofit organization that tracks the conservative media, documented sixty-three instances where Fox News anchors and guests openly promoted the Tea Parties and discussed them as newsworthy events, not as promotions.

Glenn Beck most avidly embraced the Tea Parties, making them his pet cause. Some of this had to do with the ease with which the Tea Party's anti-tax and pro-gun themes and small-government philosophy melded with themes Beck was already championing on his show.

On March 13, he hosted a special one-hour program, "You Are Not Alone," which broadcast some of Beck's most maudlin crying jags. The show featured live feeds from specially gathered audiences in locations around the country who wanted to join Beck's cause of "standing up to big government." Its purpose was to launch Beck's "9/12 Project"—named dually after Beck's wish to bring the country back to "where we all were on the day after 9/11" and the "9 Principles and 12 Values" Beck espoused, drawn from a 1972 book titled *The 5,000-Year Leap*, by the far-right conspiracy theorist W. Cleon Skousen. Beck, himself a member of the LDS Church, promoted Skousen's book and ideas, a mélange of Mormonism and Bircherite conspiracism (with a dash of the radical Posse Comitatus ideology) which had been promoted for years by people like Richard Mack, on his show and website.

Soon the Tea-Party themes began to meld seamlessly with Beck's 9/12 Project. On March 18, Beck remarked, "People are starting to get angry. These tea parties are starting to really take off." On March 20, Beck began making explicit the connection between the Tea Party and the extreme right wing—in other words, his coverage of the Tea Parties was a mechanism to mainstream the far right. Denouncing a report by a law-enforcement agency on right-wing extremism, he connected the "extremists" described therein to the Tea Partiers:

> But if you're concerned about the government, you're considered dangerous now in America … You know, are they militia members? Yes. Yes, sure they are, along with all the other people that are now on the Tea Parties nationwide. There is one here in Orlando, Florida. Tomorrow is supposed to be huge.

Beck turned out to be leading the way for the other Fox anchors. On April 6 he announced that not only would he be hosting his San Antonio "Tax Day Tea Party" on the fifteenth, but so would Neil Cavuto, Sean Hannity, and Greta Van Susteren, who planned to do similar broadcasts from respective Tea Parties taking place the same day in Sacramento, Atlanta, and Washington, DC. Fox was planning to flood the airwaves with Tea Party protests.

Beck's fellow Fox hosts did their best to keep pace. Sean Hannity featured segments on the Tea Parties a total of thirteen times between March 12 and April 14, while Neil Cavuto's afternoon business-oriented show featured a total of ten segments devoted to the protests during that same time. Nor were the "opinion shows" alone: another fifteen or so Tea Party promotional segments ran those weeks on such shows as *Fox and Friends*, *America's Newsroom*, and *Special Report with Bret Baier*.

Fairly typical was the March 25 edition of *Special Report*, when host Bret Baier described the Tea Parties as "protests of wasteful government spending in general and of President Obama's stimulus package and his budget in particular." Fox News also aired an on-screen headline: "Tea Parties Are Anti-Stimulus Demonstrations."

Despite the obvious anti-Obama bent of all these protests, Beck and other Fox hosts worked hard to present the Tea Parties as nonpartisan, bringing on guests who were either disappointed Democrats or conservatives still angry with the Republican Party, too. Yet the nonstop drumbeat supporting the protests made clear that they were primarily in response to Obama administration policies.

This is when the paranoid alternative universe of the conspiracist

Patriot movement began to meld with the world of Fox-watching conservatives. The first rough outline of Alt-America was appearing on the national horizon.

Until his dog peed on his mother's carpet, Richard Poplawski, twenty-three, was just another ordinary Pittsburgh guy living in his parents' home—albeit one who liked to spend his time hanging out on white-supremacist websites, fretting about the looming New World Order crackdown under Obama, posting Glenn Beck videos, and collecting guns. Lots of guns.

April 4, 2009, was supposed to be a typically quiet Saturday morning in the neighborhood. But when Margaret Poplawski awoke sometime around 7 a.m., she discovered that one of the two pit-bull puppies belonging to her son, Richard, had left a puddle on the floor. She woke him up and yelled at him to clean up the mess. A violent verbal shouting match erupted, and Margaret decided she'd had enough from her lay-about son, who'd washed out of the Marines the previous year after only a few weeks. So she called the cops to have him thrown out of the house.

She evidently forgot that her son had been stockpiling guns and ammunition "because he believed that as a result of economic collapse, the police were no longer able to protect society," she later told authorities.

So when two Pittsburgh police officers—Paul Sciullo III and Stephen Mayhle, both beat cops who had been on the force for two years—arrived at her front door, she invited them in and asked them to remove her son.

She didn't realize that Richard was standing directly behind her holding an AK-47 and wearing a bulletproof vest. And when the cops came in, he opened fire on them at point-blank range, killing Sciullo with a round to the skull and Mayhle with rounds to the body and head.

Margaret Poplawski ran from the room, shouting, "What the hell have you done?" She hid in the basement and remained there for the duration of the armed standoff that followed.

Another Pittsburgh cop, Eric Kelly, had cruised up to the Poplawski home on his own to act as backup for his two friends. When he heard the shots, he got out of the car and headed straight for the front door. But he only made it about halfway; Richard Poplawski mowed him down from the front window of the house with his AK-47. Kelly fell to the lawn, still alive, and was able to radio for help: "Shots fired! Officer down! Need assistance!"

When dozens more police arrived on the scene and surrounded the house, Kelly was still alive, but Poplawski opened fire on any officer trying to rescue him. One officer was wounded in the hand in the attempt. Kelly wound up bleeding to death on the lawn before he could be retrieved. Another officer broke his leg trying to enter the house by the backdoor.

Poplawski freely fired at the cops, and they returned the fire, riddling the house with bullets. Eventually, hunkered down and wounded himself, Poplawski surrendered, and was taken alive into custody by the tactical-unit cops who had negotiated with him. He was taken to a hospital and placed under police guard.

Outside the home, neighbors and other rubber-neckers mingled with news crews, everyone trying to figure out what had happened. A young man named Eddy Perkovic piped up that he was Poplawski's best friend, and explained that Poplawski feared "the Obama gun ban that's on the way" and "didn't like our rights being infringed upon."

Poplawski, it soon emerged, was a classic far-right conspiracist. He left an easily followed trail of postings on the Internet that gave the public a good deal of insight into his motives for gunning down three police officers. Many of these were on white-nationalist websites such as Don Black's *Stormfront*, where Poplawski had an account to which he regularly posted, especially in discussion forums. Many of his posts in the weeks leading up to the April 4 shootout indicated an increasing level of paranoia about a coming economic and political collapse under President Obama. Poplawski was also a fan of conspiracy-mongers Alex Jones and Glenn Beck.

Mark Pitcavage of the Anti-Defamation League surveyed Poplawski's postings and was able to reach some conclusions concerning his beliefs and their sources. Poplawski believed that the federal government, the media, and the banking system were all largely or completely controlled by Jews. He thought African Americans were "vile" and non-white races inferior to whites. He also believed that a conspiracy led by "evil Zionists" and "greedy traitorous goyim" was "ramping up" a police state in the United States for malign purposes. The neo-Nazi *Stormfront* forums and the antigovernment *Infowars* site fueled his racist, anti-Semitic, and conspiratorial mindset.

Poplawski appeared to have bought into SHTF/TEOTWAWKI (Shit Hits The Fan/The End Of The World As We Know It) conspiracy theories hook, line, and sinker. He had posted a link to *Stormfront* of a YouTube video featuring Glenn Beck talking about FEMA camps with Congressman Ron Paul. When the city of Pittsburgh got a Homeland Security grant to add surveillance cameras to protect downtown bridges, Poplawski told Stormfronters that it was "ramping up the police state." He said, too, that he gave warnings to grocery store customers he encountered (but only if they were white) to stock up on canned goods and other long-lasting foods.

However, an astonishing thing happened to the Poplawski case when it was picked up and reported on by the mainstream media: most of the information relating to his white-supremacist background and motives vanished.

Instead, the leads of the news stories around the country focused on Poplawski's dog peeing on his mother's carpet as the incident that sparked the killings. The *New York Times* at first completely ignored the white-supremacy aspect of the story, running an Associated Press story that only briefly alluded to Poplawski's paranoid fears and instead focused on the role of the peeing dog. The MSNBC.com headline was "Fight over Urinating Dog Got Police to Ambush"; CNN's was "Urinating Dog Triggered Argument Resulting in 3 Officers' Deaths." Only later, when a *Times* reporter filed a story, did any discussion of the killer's background appear.

Unlike the mainstream media, law-enforcement analysts who studied domestic terrorism were not blind to the reality of what was happening, for Poplawski's was not an isolated case. Moved to action in part by the Pittsburgh incident, the federal Department of Homeland Security on April 7, 2009, released an intelligence assessment by the Extremism and Radicalism Branch of the Homeland Environment Threat Analysis Division titled "Rightwing Extremism: Current Economic and Political Climate Fueling Resurgence in Radicalization and Recruitment."

This assessment had first been commissioned in 2008 by Bush administration officials and had just been completed when the Poplawski shootings occurred. Alarmed, DHS officials opted to hurriedly release it as a bulletin to "federal, state, local, and tribal counterterrorism and law enforcement officials," citing the Poplawski incident as "a recent example of the potential violence associated with a rise in rightwing extremism."

The DHS memo, like an earlier analysis by a Missouri law enforcement team, warned that conditions were ripe for a resurgence in right-wing extremism:

Paralleling the current national climate, rightwing extremists during the 1990s exploited a variety of social issues and political themes to increase group visibility and recruit new members. Prominent among these themes were the militia movement's opposition to gun control efforts, criticism of free trade agreements (particularly those with Mexico), and highlighting perceived government infringement on civil liberties as well as white supremacists' longstanding exploitation of social issues such as abortion, inter-racial crimes, and same-sex marriage. During the 1990s, these issues contributed to the growth in the number of domestic rightwing terrorist and extremist groups and an increase in violent acts targeting government facilities, law enforcement officers, banks, and infrastructure sectors ...

Historically, domestic rightwing extremists have feared, predicted, and anticipated a cataclysmic economic collapse in the United States. Prominent antigovernment conspiracy theorists have incorporated aspects of an impending economic collapse to intensify fear and paranoia among like-minded individuals and to attract recruits during times of economic uncertainty. Conspiracy theories involving declarations of martial law, impending civil strife or racial conflict, suspension of the US Constitution, and the creation of citizen detention camps often incorporate aspects of a failed economy. Antigovernment conspiracy theories and "end times" prophecies could motivate extremist individuals and groups to stockpile food, ammunition, and weapons. These teachings also have been linked with the radicalization of domestic extremist individuals and groups in the past, such as violent Christian Identity organizations and extremist members of the militia movement.

The report's unambiguous language may have reminded mainstream conservatives just how close to the radical fringe they had drifted—and that evidently freaked them out. Their immediate response was not merely to deny any such proximity, but to express outrage that anyone would point it out. A week later, a story in the right-wing *Washington Times* described certain aspects of the bulletin, namely, that it defined "rightwing extremism in the United States" as including not just racist or hate groups, but also "groups that reject federal authority in favor of state or local authority ... It may include groups and individuals that are dedicated to a single-issue, such as opposition to abortion or immigration."

The howls of wounded indignation from the mainstream right were immediate. Michelle Malkin, one of the most widely read right-wing bloggers, promptly ran a post headlined "The Obama DHS Hit Job on Conservatives Is Real" in which she called it a "piece-of-crap report" that "is a sweeping indictment of conservatives."

However, the report's authors couldn't have been more clear as to what it was about: it carefully delineated that the subject of its report was "rightwing extremists," "domestic rightwing terrorist and extremist groups," "terrorist groups or lone wolf extremists capable of carrying out violent attacks," "white supremacists," and similar, very real threats described in similar language. The people it described were so extreme in their views that they had the potential for violence.

The report said nothing about conservatives; the word never appeared in its text. Nonetheless, over the next few weeks, cable-news pundits and their guests repeated the narrative that the report had "smeared conservatives" as well as "our military veterans."

The claim that veterans were implicated in the extremism arose from a portion of the bulletin warning that returning veterans who have been radicalized, or were already right-wing extremists, pose a particular threat:

> DHS/I&A assesses that rightwing extremists will attempt to recruit and radicalize returning veterans in order to exploit their skills and knowledge derived from military training and combat. These skills and knowledge have the potential to boost the capabilities of extremists—including lone wolves or small terrorist cells—to carry out violence. The willingness of a small percentage of military personnel to join extremist groups during the 1990s because they were disgruntled, disillusioned, or suffering from the psychological effects of war is being replicated today.

The DHS report thus echoed an assessment made by the FBI a year before. In a July 2008 report titled "White Supremacist Recruitment of Military Personnel since 9/11," the FBI concluded that not only had neo-Nazis and other white supremacists successfully joined the ranks of American armed forces serving in Iraq—though it counted only about 200 of them—but that the hate groups from which they operated were also actively seeking to recruit military personnel already serving. As the FBI report explained:

> Military experience—ranging from failure at basic training to success in special operations forces—is found throughout the white supremacist extremist movement. FBI reporting indicates extremist leaders have historically favored recruiting active and former military personnel for their knowledge of firearms, explosives, and tactical skills and their access to weapons and intelligence in preparation for an anticipated war against the federal government, Jews, and people of color …
>
> The prestige which the extremist movement bestows upon members with military experience grants them the potential for influence beyond their numbers. Most extremist groups have some members with military experience, and those with military experience often hold positions of authority within the groups to which they belong …
>
> Military experience—often regardless of its length or type—

distinguishes one within the extremist movement. While those with military backgrounds constitute a small percentage of white supremacist extremists, FBI investigations indicate they frequently have higher profiles within the movement, including recruitment and leadership roles.

The DHS bulletin was not without its flaws, but these were largely analytical and methodological issues. For instance, the bulletin's analyst authors were criticized for drawing incorrect conclusions about economic effects on racist recruitment, based on old methodology, and the report also failed to distinguish between the blocs of the extremist right dedicated to radical and violent overthrow of the New World Order and those whose activities were focused more on mainstreaming extremist beliefs, which are overlapping but decidedly distinct segments. However, over time, both the DHS bulletin and the FBI report that preceded it proved prescient.

Mainstream conservatives ignored the report's real but relatively minor flaws and instead created a loud, fake controversy over issues drawn from an intentional misreading and distortion of the bulletin. Over the next few weeks a national chorus of conservative pundits erupted, not just at Fox News but also on CNN, MSNBC, and elsewhere. Conservative pundits, especially Lou Dobbs at CNN, pounced on the story and ran multiple segments devoted to exploring why Homeland Security wanted to demonize veterans and conservatives.

On Fox News, Bill O'Reilly speculated:

This is the bottom line on this: The federal government has changed from a conservative-oriented federal government under the Bush administration to a liberal-oriented federal government under Obama …

So, of course, these people, instead of saying, you know, we might have some Muslim problems, maybe there's a little cell somewhere talking to Pakistan and getting orders. No, it's the Glenn Beck guys, but we don't really have any evidence. But this is what's on their mind because that's the way they think.

On his nightly program on CNN, Dobbs ran a poll asking viewers if they thought "a person concerned about borders and ports that are unsecured, illegal immigration, Second Amendment rights or returning veterans from the wars in Iraq and Afghanistan is likely or even possibly probable, as the Department of Homeland Security suggests, to be a right-wing extremist?" The answers were overwhelmingly no.

Even the televangelist Pat Robertson got into the act. On the April 16 edition of *The 700 Club*, he and the cohost, Terry Meeuwsen, had a lively discussion of the report in which he called for the public to crash the DHS phone lines. He added, "It shows somebody down in the bowels of that organization is either a convinced left-winger or somebody whose sexual orientation is somewhat in question."

Soon there was a clamor for the head of Janet Napolitano, the DHS director, from Rick Santorum, Rush Limbaugh, and a number of other prominent conservatives. Veterans' groups—particularly the American Legion—jumped aboard the outrage bandwagon and began demanding that Napolitano apologize.

Initially Napolitano defended the report for its factual accuracy and purpose, which was to help give law enforcement officers the informational tools they needed to help survive in the field. However, the clamor and controversy finally grew so intense that she eventually met with the commander of the American Legion and offered her apologies, at least for the wording of the section on veterans, which, she understood, had offended a crowd of veterans eager to misread it. "I apologize for that offense," she said. "It was certainly not intended."

She later told Fox News: "If there's one part of that report I would rewrite, in the word-smithing, Washington-ese that goes on after the fact, it would be that footnote."

This apology never fully satisfied the right-wing pundits, who continued for years afterward to grouse that the DHS was "profiling conservatives as right-wing extremists." Nonetheless, the issue finally began to die down somewhat after Napolitano's mea culpa.

Fox hosts, though, continued to speculate that the DHS bulletin had really been intended to intimidate the Tea Party protesters, some of whom might fit the description of right-wing extremists in the bulletin. David Asram, filling in for Neil Cavuto on *Your World*, led off an April 14 segment by announcing, "Speak out, get shut down. What some say the government is doing to silence its critics," and went on to describe the DHS report as "ignoring liberal groups" (even though the DHS had previously issued a similar bulletin about left-wing groups) and invited contributor Andrea Tantaros onto the show. She described the DHS report as "an attempt to silence the right." Tantaros went on to assure Asram, "It's no coincidence this is happening right before these Tea Parties." Asram wondered if the government "was going to be sending spies to these Tea Parties."

Many others were thinking along similar lines. The day before the protests, Rush Limbaugh told his radio audience, "This speech of Obama's and the DHS report yesterday are timed for one reason, and that's the Tea Parties tomorrow ... The DHS report ... there is no proof here, no proof offered, no evidence offered, that anything they project is true."

Amid all this wild speculation, the DHS in short order proved prescient about the imminent likelihood of right-wing violence: On May 31, 2009, a radical "sovereign citizen" murdered an abortion provider, Dr. George Tiller, in Topeka, Kansas, as he attended church services. Then, on June 11, an elderly white-supremacist, James Von Brunn, walked into the Holocaust Museum in Washington, DC, and began shooting, killing a security guard before being shot himself. There were many more such incidents to come.

The April 15 Tax Day protests wound up being the largest of all the Tea Party events in 2009, with demonstrations occurring in more than 750 cities. The largest of these was Sean Hannity's Atlanta Tea Party, where the crowd estimates ran between 7,000 and 15,000 people. It was difficult to come up with an official number of actual participants, since estimates varied widely from city to city. The analyst Nate Silver reported 311,460 protesters in 346 cities.

Fox News's role in driving these crowd sizes cannot be overstated: without its open promotion of the Tea Parties, it's unlikely the movement would have attracted more than a quarter of these crowds, in a much smaller number of cities.

Fox's coverage of the protests was full-throated, including Glenn Beck's event in front of the Alamo in San Antonio, and in Sacramento, Neil Cavuto interviewing a costumed partier who told him, "I'm very angry. We don't want change. They can keep the change." In Atlanta, Sean Hannity featured guests such as "Joe the Plumber" Wurzelbacher and Dick Armey of FreedomWorks, who the night before had gone on Hannity's show and touted the "grassroots" nature of the event: "This is a bona fide American uprising of real people. Nobody is managing this. These are not paid political operatives. This is not a union-organized outfit ... It is not orchestrated by anybody."

Hannity also hooked up with a live telecast from the Tea Party in Birmingham, Alabama, featuring the radio talk-show hosts Rick Burgess and Bill "Bubba" Bussey, of the *Rick and Bubba Show*, who explained, "We've had enough," and announced, "It's time for a revolution!"

The slogans on signs held at Tax Day protests showed many of the protesters' preoccupations:

Marxism: Obama Embraces It / Reagan Defeated It

Obama = Socialist

Anatomy of a Liberal Fascist Coup / (Ninety Years in the Making)

Stop Obama's Marxist Agenda

Save the American Dream

OBAMA—Who Gave You Permission to Steal My Country? Not Me!

Even Hitler Was Elected—Once!

Obama's Socialism / Chains We Can Believe In

Government Control of Business Is Fascism

Where's the Birth Certificate?

The Tea Party events and coverage stirred up many who didn't actually attend one. In Oklahoma City, Daniel Knight Hayden, fifty-two, became so worked up that he posted a series of increasingly bizarre death threats and violent antigovernment rants on Twitter. FBI agents came to his home on the day of the protests and arrested him without incident a short time later.

Hayden appears to have been the first person ever arrested for making threats on Twitter—a somewhat newsworthy development. Oddly enough, amid all the voluminous airspace that Fox News journalists devoted to reporting on the Tea Party protests, they did not inform their audiences about the Hayden case.

Greta Van Susteren, the host of the Fox News show *On the Record with Greta Van Susteren*, was not the most ardent of Fox anchors in her support of the Tea Parties, but she played a critical role at key steps of the movement's development. Her February 27, 2009, show featured the first mention of the Tea Party movement on Fox News. Five months later, on her Tuesday, July 28, program, she played a major part in turning the Tea Parties into an anti-health-care-reform movement by reporting on the first Tea Party invasion of a public health-care forum.

It had occurred the day before, in St. Louis, when Democratic Senator Claire McCaskill's staff hastily assembled a town-hall forum to discuss health-care reform with local constituents. McCaskill didn't appear, but her staffers found themselves confronted by local Tea Party followers who shouted at them and jeered when they were told the senator supported reform. Van Susteren invited Dana Loesch, a St. Louis radio talk-show host and Tea Party organizer, onto the show to talk about the scene there. Van Susteren asked Loesch if McCaskill's absence was the reason her cohorts "sort of—I don't know if hijacked is the right word, morphed maybe, morphed it into a Tea Party." Loesch explained that the forum had come about because of a Tea Party protest two weeks before at the senator's St. Louis offices that had ended badly with police being called. The senator then arranged the forum "along with Carl

Bearden of Americans for Prosperity, and we at the Tea Party Coalition just kind of helped it out, and got some people together and got the word out."

Loesch also claimed that "it was open to everybody, because this health-care legislation is a concern, I think, to everyone, regardless of whether or not they're conservative or liberal or a member of any party."

This was artful spin: Like the April 15 Tea Parties, the town hall protest was clearly populated by anti-Obama voters focused on stopping yet another policy proposal by the new president. More disturbing was their behavior at the forum: video of the St. Louis event showed the Tea Partiers using their numbers to shout down their opposition and generally swamp the town hall nature of the forum. What was supposed to have been an open discussion of the issues instead became a confrontational shoutfest.

Within days of the St. Louis forum, Tea Party protests were disrupting health-care town hall forums around the country: in Florida, Virginia, Syracuse, New York City, Iowa, and Maryland. It soon emerged that the disruptions were being carefully planned and orchestrated by corporate Tea Party organizers, including Americans for Prosperity and FreedomWorks. A leaked memo from a volunteer with a Tea Party Patriots website run by FreedomWorks gave tips to members on how they could infiltrate town halls and harass Democratic members of Congress.

Some of the tips for Tea Partiers:

- Artificially inflate your numbers: "Spread out in the hall and try to be in the front half. The objective is to put the Rep on the defensive with your questions and follow-up. The Rep should be made to feel that a majority, and if not, a significant portion of at least the audience, opposes the socialist agenda of Washington."
- Be disruptive early and often: "You need to rock-the-boat early in the Rep's presentation. Watch for an opportunity to yell out and challenge the Rep's statements early."

- Try to rattle him, not have an intelligent debate: "The goal is to rattle him, get him off his prepared script and agenda. If he says something outrageous, stand up and shout out and sit right back down. Look for these opportunities before he even takes questions."

FreedomWorks and other Tea Party organizers later tried to downplay the significance of the memo, claiming that it was not widely read or distributed. However, regardless of whether it was an actual blueprint, it accurately described, or prescribed, the behavior that subsequently erupted at the Tea Parties around the country.

On August 1, visiting with constituents at an Austin town hall forum, Congressman Lloyd Doggett of Texas, a Democrat, encountered a disruptive mob of Tea Party protesters. When Doggett was asked whether he would support a public-option health-care plan even if he found his constituents opposed it, Doggett replied that he would. That sent the crowd into a frenzied chant of "Just say no," and they refused to stop. Doggett finally gave up, and was nearly overwhelmed as he moved through the crowd and into the parking lot. The congressman later issued a statement reaffirming his commitment to health-care reform and denouncing the protest.

On August 6, a crowd of jeering Tea Party protesters descended on a town hall meeting sponsored by the Democratic congresswoman Kathy Castor in Tampa, Florida, "banging on windows" until police and organizers were forced to end the event. The hall originally scheduled for the forum only held 250 people, and several hundred protesters showed up. Many of them—protesters who had arrived from outside Castor's district—were forced to remain outside, where they chanted anti-Obama slogans. Some of them pounded on windows, frustrated at being shut out.

It was worse inside. Castor and State Representative Betty Reed were scarcely able to make it through their opening remarks, since angry protesters began shouting at them and interrupting. Just outside the auditorium's main doors, scuffling broke out between a couple of the participants who were jammed into the hallway like sardines, so police closed off the meeting area. A man who could later be seen on video with a torn shirt was treated for minor injuries following the tussle. Things became so intense that police escorted Castor out of the building after an event organizer suggested she leave for her own safety.

It left an impression, but not a positive one. George Guthrie, who drove from Largo to attend the meeting, said to a local TV station: "They think they're exercising their right to free speech, but they're only exercising their right to disrupt civil discourse."

The health-care focus gave fresh life to the Tea Party movement, but as members of Congress began returning from their August recess, there were fewer town halls for Tea Partiers to disrupt. What they had to look forward to next was Glenn Beck's big 9/12 March on Washington, planned for September 12.

This event had been announced back in February, well before the Tea Parties had coalesced or become a Fox News cause célèbre. But in the intervening weeks and months, Beck's 9/12 Movement had become so seamlessly identified with the Tea Parties that they were now basically indistinguishable. And so the Tea Party organizers started marshaling their forces to make the march another big national media event, along the lines of the Tax Day protests.

In late August, ads started showing up on Fox News promoting the Tea Party Express: A 7,000-mile cross-country bus tour featuring Tea Party events in thirty-four cities, beginning in Sacramento on August 28 and culminating in Washington on September 12. This tour was sponsored by the Our Country Deserves Better PAC, an offshoot of Move America Forward, the right-wing answer to the progressive MoveOn.org. Move America Forward was chaired by Howard Kaloogian, a former Republican congressional candidate from California.

The Our Country Deserves Better PAC had been founded in August 2008 specifically to oppose Barack Obama and his policies. In October 2008, on a previous bus tour called the Stop Obama Express, radio host Mark Williams, one of the PAC's chief spokesmen and a vice chairman, had been out on the stump campaigning against Obama for being a socialist. In July 2009, the PAC had run ads comparing Obama to Hitler.

When September 12, Glenn Beck's big day on the National Mall in Washington, finally arrived, the media were in full frenzy mode, with camera crews from not just Fox but also CNN and MSNBC covering the event. District of Columbia authorities calculated that some 70,000 people showed up.

Afterward, Beck and his supporters, including Michelle Malkin, tried to claim that there had actually been as many as 2 million people at the event. On Monday after the march, Beck told his radio audience, "According to overseas reporting [it was] the "largest march on Washington ever." On *Fox and Friends* that day, he told Steve Doocy that the crowd had been estimated at 1.7 million, and adamantly denied that only 70,000 had showed.

The 9/12 event itself was actually rather uneventful. Most of the talks were standard rants about big government, too much taxation, and the evils of health-care reform. Out on the National Mall, though, there were all kinds of far more colorful expressions in the form of signs made by the protesters.

Some of the signs were simply in outrageously bad taste. Others were more openly racist, including one mash-up between racism and Marxism featuring a large picture of Obama as a witch doctor, with a bone through his nose. Its caption read "Obama Care: Coming soon to a clinic near you." The *C* was the sickle part of the hammer and sickle symbol.

Journalist Max Blumenthal strolled the National Mall with a camera and interviewed some of the sign carriers. A man with a sign saying "Obama and Nancy Pelosi Are Nazis" told Blumenthal he thought Obama was the biggest Nazi around: "Because I think he's trying to destroy the United States. Not only do I think he's trying, but I think he's gonna accomplish it. He's gonna do—I'm afraid he's gonna do what Hitler could never do, and that's destroy the United States of America."

A man carrying a sign reading, "If Al Qaeda Wants to Destroy

The America We Know And Love They Better Hurry Because Obama Is Beating Them To It" told him that Obama was a bigger threat to the country than terrorists. "Why? He's trying to change the country from within. We can fight Al Qaeda. We can't kill Obama." A friend chimed in, "He's the enemy within, that's why."

Perhaps the most prominent victim of the Tea Party ugliness was Arizona Congresswoman Gabrielle Giffords, a Democrat from Tucson in an otherwise deep-red state up for reelection in a tight race.

During one of Giffords's town hall gatherings to discuss healthcare reform, Tea Party protesters began making loud and angry remarks about the proposals. Somehow, during the minor fracas that ensued, one of the protesters dropped his handgun on the floor. Police were called, but no one was arrested.

The House gave the final approval to President Obama's healthcare reform plan, the Affordable Care Act, on March 21, 2009, bringing an impotent and unhappy end to months of organized outrage against it. Sometime in the early-morning hours after the vote, someone vandalized Giffords's offices in Tucson.

Giffords' health-care vote had literally put her in the cross-hairs: The morning after the vote was taken, former vice-presidential candidate Sarah Palin, a Tea Party darling, sent out a tweet, embellished with a cross-hairs graphic, urging her followers to target Democrats who had voted for the legislation.

"Don't retreat, instead, RELOAD!" Palin tweeted.

Later that summer, Pima County Republicans held a "Help Remove Gabrielle Giffords" event called "Get on Target for Victory in November" in support of Giffords's Republican Tea Party opponent, Jesse Kelly. There would be a shooting competition at a local gun range, and among the exciting opportunities was the chance to "shoot a fully automatic M16" with Kelly.

Giffords squeaked out a win that November over Kelly in a year in which House Democrats fell by the bushelful. In hopes of healing some of the political hard feelings in her district, she decided to begin spending more time with her constituents and planned a "Congress on Your Corner" event in front of a Tucson Safeway supermarket. On January 8, 2011, she was breezily chatting with voters in a friendly setting when a young man with a shaved head and a peculiar gleam in his eye stepped up to her to shake her hand. Then he pulled out a gun and shot her once in the forehead.

The young man then proceeded to turn and open fire on the rest of the crowd of twenty to thirty people who had gathered to meet the congresswoman. He shot eighteen more people, six of them fatally, before he was finally tackled and stopped.

The dead included a federal judge, John Roll, sixty-three; Gabriel "Gabe" Zimmerman, Giffords's community outreach director, thirty; Dorwan Stoddard, seventy-six, a retired construction worker; Phyllis Schenk, seventy-nine, a homemaker; and Dorothy "Dot" Morris, seventy-six, a retired secretary; and perhaps most heart-breaking, young Christina Taylor-Green, nine, who had come to the event with her neighbor so she could learn about politics. Green's tragic story reverberated for the next week and more on TV cable news networks.

Miraculously, Giffords was not among the dead. The bullet that penetrated her skull damaged only a small portion of her brain, and a young intern, Daniel Hernandez, who was there with her at the event gave her medical aid until ambulances arrived. He is credited with saving her life. Initial reports of her death were retracted as news came from the hospital where she had been rushed that she was still alive and doctors were operating to remove the bullet from her brain. Gradually, she would recover most of her health, though not her former life.

In the meantime, investigators were sizing up the young man who had gone on the rampage. Jared Lee Loughner, twenty-two, was a sometime student at the local community college who had few friends and a long-running reputation for strange behavior. Among the clues he left behind were a couple of hand-written letters that were mostly rambling disquisitions on strange conspiracy theories.

It shortly emerged that Loughner had a long history of mental illness and was likely suffering from something like an episode of paranoid schizophrenia (the diagnosis was later confirmed by a court psychiatrist). Pundits of all stripes were quick to pounce and claim that as proof that the assassinations were not political and that this was a case of mental illness, not terrorism.

"The killer, Jared Loughner, is a psychopath," intoned O'Reilly on Fox News. "Civilization has always had them and always will. There is no solution to the likes of Loughner."

However, it also soon emerged that Loughner was obsessed with the *Zeitgeist* films that had played such a prominent role in the 9/11 conspiracy scene. Friends described how the films had "a profound impact on Jared Loughner's mindset and how he views the world that he lives in." According to a family friend, Loughner was also influenced by the 9/11 documentary *Loose Change*.

There was no evidence that Loughner was influenced by Palin or her GOP cohorts, but it *was* evident he had actively indulged in, and had been influenced by, the deluge of hateful rhetoric directed at Giffords. Yet in the conspiracist alternative universe of Alex Jones and his Patriot cohort, the Loughner rampage was soon being portrayed as yet another false flag, whereby liberal media messages had inspired Loughner to commit an act that would then be falsely labeled as the result of right-wing motivation.

"The whole thing stinks to high heaven," he told his audience. "This kid Loughner disappeared for days at a time before the shooting? My gut tells me this was a staged mind-control operation. The government employs geometric psychological-warfare experts that know exactly how to indirectly manipulate unstable people through the media. They implanted the idea in his head by repeatedly asking, 'Is Giffords in danger?'"

It became a cornerstone trope of the alternative universe that would soon mature, fully formed, into Alt-America: any act of violence by any kind of right-wing extremists, including those of the Muslim variety, was instantly labeled a false flag operation. Any white Americans accused of terrorism had been mind-controlled into the act. It was an instant excuse and thus an invitation for more extremism.

Meanwhile, in the mainstream media the violence committed by white Americans was never described as terrorism, lest the wrath of conservative punditry descend upon any hapless journalist prone to describing it as such. They were henceforth described in the language of "isolated incidents."

The Return of the Militias

This did not seem to be your ordinary Tea Party gathering. Maybe it was the gun-making kits that were being raffled off as door prizes. Or maybe it was the fact that nearly everyone inside the chilly hall at the Ravalli County, Montana, fairground was packing heat. But most of all, it was the copy of *Mein Kampf* sitting there on the book table sandwiched between a survivalist book on food storage and a copy of Saul Alinsky's *Rules for Radicals*.

It was eyebrow-raising, perhaps, but not the wholesome image of the movement projected by the media. However, this was in fact what Tea Party gatherings were fast becoming.

Mind you, the event organizers didn't explicitly call themselves Tea Partiers. Their official name was Celebrating Conservatism. But their mission statement—"to restore our country, counties, and cities back to the Republic and the Constitution of the United States"— was classic Tea Party, and Celebrating Conservatism was listed as a member of the national Tea Party Patriots organization. Everyone in Hamilton, Montana—the whole of Montana's Bitterroot Valley, for that matter—knew them as the Tea Party's main presence in the area. Once a month or so the group held a potluck dinner at the county fairgrounds that typically attracted a couple hundred people, which in a place like the Bitterroot was a sizable presence.

This night's gathering was special because of a high-profile guest: Larry Pratt, leader of Gun Owners of America.

Lawrence D. Pratt, like a lot of Celebrating Conservatism's speakers, had a long history with the far right. He is considered a godfather of the militia movement, a network of conspiracy-minded, armed paramilitary groups that exploded in the 1990s. In October 1992, Pratt addressed a pivotal three-day meeting of neo-Nazis and Christian Identity adherents in Estes Park, Colorado, convened in the wake of the shootout in Ruby Ridge, Idaho, that had sent shock waves through the extreme right. That gathering is widely credited with birthing the movement's strategy of organizing citizen militias as a form of "leaderless resistance" to a looming New World Order.

Pratt was hardly the only controversial figure to address Celebrating Conservatism events. In May 2010, at its convention on the University of Montana's Missoula campus, Celebrating Conservatism hosted Red Backman, a tax protester notorious for his open anti-Semitism. In July 2009, likewise in Hamilton, Richard Mack of Arizona addressed the crowd; he had made a career in the 1990s out of organizing militias and speaking on the national anti-government Patriot circuit. The following month Mack's longtime Patriot movement confederate, Jack McLamb, spoke at the group's Hamilton potluck.

In December 2008 Mona Docteur, a Missoula housewife, had formed Celebrating Conservatism in reaction to the presidential election. It slowly gained members that spring by associating itself with a variety of Tea Party events in Bitterroot. But locals only took real notice in September 2009, when the group held a gun rights rally in downtown Hamilton at which participants brandished firearms. Organizers followed up with a Celebration of the Right to Bear Arms in March 2010, which featured a march of several hundred people along Hamilton's main drag. Anyone driving through town that day was greeted by a gauntlet of people packing weapons ranging from muzzle-loading muskets to a high-powered sniper-style .308 caliber rifle. Those events served notice that Celebrating Conservatism had embraced the Patriot movement cause.

The display of guns felt like a threat to some locals. Bill LaCroix, a Montana human rights activist, wrote an anxious op-ed in the *Bitterroot Star* after the September rally: "You have to wonder: If these teabaggers' views are so extreme that they have to carry guns to emphasize how much they can't tolerate your beliefs, what do they suggest be done with everyone who disagrees with them if they actually gained the power they demand?"

The obsession with all things gun was evident at the September 2010 potluck, from Larry Pratt's presence to a fund-raising raffle for registration-free gun kits. At one point Mona Docteur invited to the stage the owner of the Dillon-based company that sold the kits. He had a kit-made pistol strapped to his waist.

At the back of the room, alongside the bookseller and the gun kit merchant, were booths for a handful of local Tea Party political candidates—one running for sheriff, another for county commissioner—as well as a booth promoting two Patriot organizations: one was the Oath Keepers, a new group, founded by Stewart Rhodes in 2009, that was geared toward recruiting military and law enforcement veterans; the other was the Fully Informed Jury Association, a longtime far-right group dedicated to persuading juries to nullify federal tax and civil-rights laws. The latter group was closely associated for years with the Montana Freemen, which had engaged in an armed standoff with FBI agents in the mid-1990s.

Even before the speakers took the stage, it was manifestly clear that this was a gathering of old-style Patriot movement believers very similar to those who had made a splash in Montana back in the 1990s: militias, "constitutionalists," Freemen, survivalists, and other antigovernment extremists. But this time around they were riding the coattails of the Tea Party movement. References to "Tea Party principles" throughout the evening were almost as common as references to the Constitution.

The Tea Party had become a wholesale conduit for a revival of the Patriot movement and its militias.

Most observers of the movement had counted the Patriots largely extinct. The Southern Poverty Law Center (SPLC) continued to track the decline of the movement after the Y2K fiasco in 2000, from their 1996 high of 868 down to a mere 194 militia groups in 2000. For most of the next decade those numbers remained low, bottoming out at 131 in 2007.

But in 2009, there was a sharp spike upwards, to 512 militia groups. By 2010 they were back up to 824 groups, and the rise continued, easily surpassing their numbers in the 1990s: 1,274 in 2010, peaking at 1,360 in 2011.

According to Mark Potok, nearly all of this activity was closely associated with the rise of the Tea Party. An SPLC report stated: "The 'Tea Parties' and similar groups that have sprung up in recent months cannot fairly be considered extremist groups, but they are shot through with rich veins of radical ideas, conspiracy theories and racism."

Mark Pitcavage, intelligence director for the Anti-Defamation League (ADL), also tracked "a general growth of antigovernment rage and associated conspiracy theories." Its most mainstream expression was the Tea Party, he said, "but it has also manifested itself on the extremes by a resurgence of the militia movement, the sovereign citizen movement, [and] other Patriot-type groups like the Oath Keepers." The rise of the Tea Party and the resurgence of the Patriot movement were "two sides of the same coin."

David Barstow, in a widely read February 2010 *New York Times* article, wrote that "a significant undercurrent" within the Tea Party had more in common with the Patriot movement than with the Republican Party. But he failed to note a disturbing side-effect: the Patriot movement's affiliation with the Tea Party offered it a measure of mainstream validation. That validation energized the movement and enabled it to recruit a new generation to "constitutionalist" Patriot movement beliefs.

It did this in a number of ways. In some cases the Tea Party helped create a local organizing focus for newborn Patriot organizations such as Celebrating Conservatism, which effectively became the main Tea Party outfit in Ravalli County, even though it was clearly a Patriot group. In other instances, Tea Party organizing spun off Patriot groups that spread their own conspiracist and constitutionalist ideas while maintaining close Tea Party alliances. Often the most active and vocal Tea Party organizers were simultaneously leaders of local Patriot groups, especially in rural areas.

Travis McAdam, executive director of the Montana Human Rights Network, had seen this political hardening dynamic in Montana. Celebrating Conservatism's tone and message, he noted, had changed sharply over time. "Early on, they were portraying themselves very much as just this benign group that was educating the public about the Constitution and American history," he said. "Then months down the road, a year down the road, they're taking out an ad in the local paper where they're basically saying that if the government tries to restrict our access to firearms, it is our obligation to rise up and overthrow such a government. And then Mona starts to say things like, 'You know, we're not violent. But we could be.'"

Back in the nineties, he recalled, John Trochmann, the founder of the Militia of Montana, paid lip service to voting, but he always followed with a grim punch line: "When the ballot box doesn't work, we'll switch to the cartridge box."

After Obama's election, while gun paranoia was high within the mainstream NRA—particularly the fear that the new president would somehow set aside the Second Amendment and forcibly disarm ordinary Americans—it was at code red levels in the ranks of militias and the Patriot movement. On the fringes of right-wing thought, the fear became virulent, and the rhetoric threatening and violent.

By late February 2009, there were already signs that the militia movement was ratcheting itself back up for action after being largely dormant for most of the Bush years. Organized in the 1990s in response to Bill Clinton's gun-control measures (especially the 1994 assault-weapons ban) and law-enforcement fiascoes like Ruby Ridge and Waco, the newer militias had found new fears: President

Obama's supposedly socialist plans for stimulating the economy and reforming health-care insurance. They also drew on a different base: men who were younger, more militant, more paranoid, and more likely to have an actual military background.

A lot of this organizing occurred quietly, with a key role played by online social-networking platforms such as MySpace. Much of the networking occurred at private pages that required permission to access, but others were public. For instance, one site, run by an ex-Marine from Colorado, featured discussions such as "Training a Survival of Militia Group, Part 1."

A common organizational theme popping up among the new militiamen was *Μολών Λαβέ* ("Molon labe," pronounced MOH-lon lah-VAY), Greek for "Come and take [them]." This was largely inspired by its appearance in the 2006 film *300*, a recreation of the Battle of Thermopylae, in 480 BC, in which the Greek hero utters that phrase as a challenge to the invading Persian army. The general meaning is "Over my dead body." A couple of the would-be militiamen organized broadcasts of "Come and Take It Radio," hosted online at a MySpace page, where they published a rant decrying "the dark bleak abyss that will be the Obama Presidency" and vowed to "speak the truth that the true 'Conservative' will be so desperately seeking in this new age of world governance."

The revived militia movement had a disturbing component: military veterans voicing Patriot-movement beliefs, including threats of violent resistance to the Obama administration.

One of these veterans made the news in late February 2009. Kody Brittingham, a twenty-year-old Marine lance corporal based at Camp Lejeune, North Carolina, was arrested on charges that he had threatened the life of the president. He had first been arrested by civilian authorities in December 2008, on charges of breaking and entering. When Navy investigators searched his barracks after his arrest, they discovered a journal he wrote containing plans on how to kill the president. There was white-supremacist material in the journal as well.

◆

The bright yellow banner called the Gadsden Flag features a coiled rattlesnake and the inscription, "Don't Tread On Me." It has a colorful place in American history, having been designed by a colonel from South Carolina named Christopher Gadsden, who presented it as an honor to the commander-in-chief of the Continental Navy in 1775, who flew it as his personal standard on his flagship before its first mission of the war.

Over the ensuing two centuries, it had mostly been a curiosity and a historical relic. But it gained a new life as a popular symbol of antigovernment resistance by Patriot militiamen in the 1990s.

It was not unusual to see the Gadsden flag displayed on the stage behind the speakers at Patriot movement gatherings, and they were available as an item in John Trochmann's Militia of Montana catalogs for the militiamen who liked to display them.

In the new century, the Gadsden flag continued to pop up at Patriot events, even as the movement faded from view. It was flown when the Minutemen organized their media-circus border watch in Arizona in April 2005. It flew again when Minutemen mounted another watch the following summer near the Canadian border at Blaine, Washington.

So when the striking banners began appearing at the very earliest Tea Party gatherings in February 2009, it was a visible signal of the Patriot movement presence in the Tea Party. Soon they caught on wildly, and Gadsden flags were flying everywhere at Tea Party events broadcast nationally. The flag became the semi-official banner of the Tea Party movement.

The ease with which the Patriot symbol was swept up by the Tea Party was darkly symbolic of the ease with which it had incorporated and accommodated the Patriot ideology and thus had helped channel it into the mainstream of American politics. As time went on, the mainstream focus of the Tea Party movement lost its steam, while the Patriots began to assert their extremist presence within it more aggressively.

For a while after the April 15, 2009, protests, the Tea Party's energy began to dissipate somewhat, largely because there weren't any significant events on the horizon around which to organize, and the health-care fight had not yet shown up on the political horizon. The next "patriotic" holiday was July 4, and many Tea Partiers began planning for a fresh round of protests against Obama's "socialist" health-care plans then.

Although the Tea Party was unofficially seen as a branch of the GOP, mainstream Republicans weren't welcoming them to their July 4 celebrations. On July 4, 2009, Dave Weigel wrote in the *Washington Independent* that "the collaboration between the official Republican establishment and the Tea Parties has not lasted into June. The RNC has no plans to get involved with any Tea Parties. A spokesman for Rep. John Boehner (R-Ohio), who jaunted around northern California to attend several Tea Parties, said that his holiday plans were private but would probably not include Tea Parties. Gingrich will not attend any of the Tea Parties, although he recorded video messages for events in Birmingham and Nashville 'at the request of the respective organizers,' according to spokesman Dan Kotman."

Only Fox News remained loyal, and even then, its interest level was significantly lower for the July 4 Tea Parties than it had been in April. Glenn Beck, on his June 15 show, hosted first "a disenfranchised Democrat" and "a disenfranchised Republican" to promote the July 4 Tea Parties. But there were no Fox anchors doing live remotes from the parties this time.

The organizers of the July 4 events counted on local news coverage and on such right-wing websites as PajamasTV, which hosted an "American Tea Party" show and asked people who attended to send in their own videos from their rallies. But clearly there was a leadership vacuum, and it became an opportunity for far-right extremists to step in and take rhetorical charge of the Tea Parties.

Even before the July events, the Anti-Defamation League warned that "white supremacists and neo-Nazi hate groups" were planning to take advantage of the opportunity and make their presence felt at the gatherings. The ADL described the attempts by the racist right "to co-opt the anti-tax message of the events as a means to spread racism and anti-Semitism":

On Stormfront, the most popular white supremacist Internet forum, members have discussed becoming local organizers of the "Tea Parties" and finding ways to involve themselves in the events. Many racists have voiced their intent to attend these rallies for the purpose of cultivating an "organized grassroots White mass movement," with some suggesting that they would do so without openly identifying themselves as racists.

These warnings came largely true when the July 4 Tea Parties rolled around. Not only were the fringe elements out in force, distributing propaganda and recruiting, but the speakers used rhetoric taken straight from the conspiracist far right, including the Birthers, militiamen, and the theocratic religious right. In Duval County, Florida, people held signs comparing Obama to Hitler.

But the extremist ideas were not limited to signs. In Broken Arrow, Oklahoma, a young Marine sergeant named Charles Dyer stood up to advocate for the Oath Keepers, a national group of veterans who openly subscribe to Patriot movement conspiracy theories regarding the New World Order policies they believe President Obama intends to implement. But Dyer welcomed all comers: "Even if you're not current or former military, you too can be an Oath Keeper and spread the message."

Dyer read out a list of ten "orders that we refuse to obey," emphasizing the word "not" ten times:

1. We will not obey any order to disarm the American people.
2. We will not obey orders to conduct warrantless searches of the American people.
3. We will not obey orders to detain American citizens as "unlawful enemy combatants" or to subject them to military tribunal.
4. We will not obey orders to impose martial law or a "state of emergency" on a state.
5. We will not obey orders to invade and subjugate any state that asserts its sovereignty.
6. We will not obey any order to blockade American cities, thus turning them into giant concentration camps.

7. We will not obey any order to force American citizens into any form of detention camps under any pretext.

8. We will not obey orders to assist or support the use of any foreign troops on US soil against the American people to "keep the peace" or to "maintain control."

9. We will not obey any orders to confiscate the property of the American people, including food and other essential supplies.

10. We will not obey any orders which infringe on the right of the people to free speech, to peaceably assemble, and to petition their government for a redress of grievances.

Dyer then went on to warn that "urban warfare" drills were secretly being used to prepare American troops for rounding up and incarcerating American citizens. "The only logical reason for them to train going door to door in America, practicing disarming people, is to actually do that one day, here in America," he said.

The credo that Dyer read aloud came directly from the Oath Keepers website, the group's primary founding document, titled "Ten Orders We Will Not Obey." Given a cursory glance, it might have seemed innocuous and maybe even commonsensical: well, of course US soldiers should not be disarming people; after all, this is why there is a Posse Comitatus Act (of 1878; its provisions were substantially weakened in 2007) proscribing the use of military forces in domestic police work. Paying careful attention to the words, however, readily revealed the underlying paranoid conspiracist worldview—a naked fear that American civilians might be rounded up and disarmed by their own military forces.

Dyer himself had created a bit of a stir even before the Oklahoma appearance with a series of YouTube videos he had produced under the pseudonym July4Patriot. These videos consisted of Dyer, a Marine Corps veteran who had served in Iraq, holding forth on the rising "resistance" within the US military against the New World Order tyrants who were planning to disarm Americans, and urging active-duty military and veterans to join arms with the Patriots.

146

He recorded these videos while wearing a mask—a grinning skull that covered the lower half of his face; he explained that he had to hide his face in order to protect his family. In some of the videos he could be seen wearing his Marine Corps dress uniform.

These video rants spread widely among Patriots and became a recruitment tool targeting military veterans to get them to join their fast-expanding alternative universe (as the 2009 DHS bulletin had warned). The Oath Keepers soon emerged as the spearhead of that drive.

In one of the more ominous videos, Dyer, still masked, ranted to the accompaniment of a stirring Celtic soundtrack:

> We the American Patriots are tired of standing idly by. This is a call to arms. Support the sovereignty of your states, reclaim your freedoms, write your senators, write your congressmen, write your state representatives. For you American citizens that are asleep, there's something going on around here and you can't see it. It's only because you're so self-absorbed, with your trinkets and your cell phones and your video games, your corporate jobs. There's a revolution brewing under the surface of your country and you don't even know it …
>
> The time for you to make that choice is at hand. The enemies of the Constitution are not far away in some distant desert. They're found right here on our own soil. We have become complacent. We have allowed the tyrants to take over this country, and we have no one to blame but ourselves. The time is now. We must rise up together as one voice and resist while we still have the ability to resist.

In another video, Dyer, wearing his mask, warned his viewers: "With the DHS blatantly calling Patriots and veterans and constitutionalists a threat, all that I have to say is—You're damned right we're a threat!"

His fellow Patriots gobbled it up. The videos went viral with several hundred thousand views and also attracted thousands of comments, almost universally in praise. In a later video Dyer actually embraced the notion that he might be considered a terrorist: "Join the military?" he said. "Depends on what you want to do with it. Me? I'm going to use my training and become one of those domestic terrorists that you're so afraid of from the DHS reports."

Dyer finally revealed his face and his identity at an April 19 Tea Party gathering in Lexington, Massachusetts. He seemed to be a new rising star, one of the fresh new faces fronting the Oath Keepers concept. Until he was arrested for molesting his six-year-old daughter.

On January 21, 2010, sheriff's deputies in Stephens County, Oklahoma, arrested Dyer at his home and charged him with rape of a child and forcible sodomy. When his home was searched, investigators found a number of firearms and a 40 mm grenade launcher, leading to an additional count of possession of an unregistered military weapon.

Immediately, the Oath Keepers parent organization distanced itself from Dyer, claiming that he had never actually been a member. "Charles Dyer never became an actual member of Oath Keepers," the Oath Keepers founder Rhodes wrote on the website. "I met him when he attended our April 19, 2009, gathering at Lexington, and back then I considered him for a position as our liaison to the Marine Corps, but I decided against that when he made it clear he intended to train and help organize private militias across the country when he got out of the Marines. I considered such plans to be incompatible with the Oath Keepers mission and goals, and certainly incompatible with any leadership position within this org. He understood and agreed with my decision to not have him become officially involved with Oath Keepers. All of that was long before we even offered official memberships. So, he was never a member, and never in any leadership position."

Dyer skipped out on an August 15 court date and went on the run from authorities, hiding out in Texas until he was captured at a campground southwest of Houston ten days later. While on the lam, he sent a letter to his attorney, claiming he was the victim of a government conspiracy: "Our judicial system is nothing more than a system of liars and crooks, working under the color of the law, where the rich go free and the poor are made to suffer injustice," Dyer wrote. "Something MUST be done to expose it." Dyer was convicted of the rape of his daughter in April 2012 and sentenced to thirty years in prison. To this day, he claims that he was the innocent victim of a government frame-up job.

The Charles Dyer episode was just a brief bump in the Oath Keepers' steady climb in the Obama years. Over time they would be able to justifiably claim to be the nation's leading Patriot movement organization, bolstered in large part by their close associations with the Tea Party.

Like John Trochmann, James "Bo" Gritz, and Richard Mack before him, the Oath Keepers' Stewart Rhodes was less interested in organizing militias than in promoting the concepts and ideology behind them. Rhodes made a point of not using the term "militia" when describing his organization.

Elmer Stewart Rhodes, fifty-two, is a smart, well-educated man gifted with words and presenting a calm, normal demeanor. Raised in the Southwest, he served in the Army and then got a bachelor's degree in political science at University of Nevada, Las Vegas, in 1998. Deciding he was a libertarian, he landed a job supervising interns in the Washington offices of Congressman Ron Paul, whose conspiracist worldview Rhodes soon adopted.

He left the position with Paul to attend Yale Law School, graduated in 2004, and took a position as a clerk to a justice in the Arizona Supreme Court. He also took a volunteer position in Paul's 2008 presidential campaign, where he gradually became increasingly politically radicalized.

Angered by the story in *The New Republic* that outlined Ron Paul's history as a rabid right-wing extremist in the 1990s, Rhodes made one of his earliest public appearances in a blog post denouncing the story, in which he claimed that Paul had not really known what was in the newsletters that went out under his name. He labeled it a "lame attempt at guilt by association" and "stupid," adding, "This only tells me that Ron Paul is a real threat to the political establishment, and they are pulling out all the stops in an attempt to stop the Ron Paul Revolution."

About that time, Rhodes had become enamored of the idea that the German police and army could have saved their nation's populace if they had defied the Nazi government in the 1930s. In a 2008 letter to the pro-gun *SWAT Magazine* where Rhodes had a regular column, a retired colonel suggested that, with the Constitution and the Bill of Rights in peril, the ranks of soldiers, veterans, and police officers "is where they will be saved, if they are saved at all!" The ensuing discussion gave him the idea for the Oath Keepers.

Rhodes published the early Oath Keepers blog in early 2009 and soon attracted the support of fellow Tea Party participants, as well his old connections from the Ron Paul campaign.

Rhodes officially launched the Oath Keepers in Lexington, Massachusetts—the site of the "shot heard round the world" that started the American Revolution on the morning of April 19, 2009. He read aloud the "Ten Orders" as several hundred people listened. "You need to be alert and aware to the reality of how close we are to having our constitutional republic destroyed," he said. "Every dictatorship in the history of mankind, whether it is fascist, communist, or whatever, has always set aside normal procedures of due process under times of emergency … We can't let that happen here. We need to wake up!"

Many Patriots, eager for a new organizing strategy and a fresh brand (after the militias and Minutemen had seen their reputations permanently tainted), seized the opportunity and joined up. His speakers spread out and delivered the "10 Orders" gospel to Tea Party audiences around the nation for the July 4 nationwide events. That was followed by Oath Keepers rallies, often drawn through his aggressive recruitment via the website.

The idea spread like wildfire, especially as Rhodes began making media appearances and speaking before large audiences. Within a year of the Oath Keepers' founding Rhodes claimed to have members in every state, and by 2014 he claimed his organization had 30,000 people on its rolls ("an unverifiable and highly unlikely number," according to the Southern Poverty Law Center).

Rhodes has an affable media persona, which helped him when he made appearances with Chris Matthews on MSNBC and with Bill O'Reilly on Fox News. He presented a nonthreatening face of the organization, while anger seethed among the membership. Rhodes gave a crowd-pleasing speech to the crowd at the annual Conservative Political Action Committee convention in Washington in April 2010, and afterward schmoozed amiably with a reporter from the right-wing Pajamas Media TV network, reassuring viewers that the Oath Keepers were really just another community-watch organization. That became a favorite theme among the Oath Keepers, as it had been among a number of Patriot organizations over the years, including various 1990s militias and the Minutemen in the 1990s.

On Fox News with O'Reilly in March 2010, Rhodes justified the Oath Keepers' fear of a potential government disarmament of its citizens by pointing to the aftermath of the Hurricane Katrina disaster in New Orleans in 2006. Martial law had been briefly declared in the disaster zone, and some citizens had had their guns confiscated.

Rhodes put it this way: "So they disarmed Americans over some bad weather, as though the bad weather suspended the Second Amendment. So, that's the most recent example."

The previous day, March 8, O'Reilly had hosted the SPLC's Mark Potok, who put his finger on the deep and disturbing problem the Oath Keepers represented:

What [the group is] really about is the fear that martial law is about to be imposed, that Americans are about to be herded into concentration camps, that foreign troops are going to be put down on American soil. The Oath Keepers say specifically, we will not obey these orders, we will refuse orders to put Americans into concentration camps. Now, is that dangerous? It seems to me the danger is that these are men and women, in the case of police officers, who are given a real power over the rest of us, sometimes the power of life and death. They make very important decisions. And if these men and women are animated by the idea that, you know, foreign forces are about to come into this country and put us under martial law and throw us all into concentration camps, I think there is a certain danger associated with that ... They're operating on the basis of crazy theories that may cause one of them to draw a gun one day.

The Oath Keepers excelled at maintaining a friendly, mainstream-appearing public face. Rhodes in particular was gifted at presenting a reassuring manner in public, tamping down controversies when they arose, and keeping the association with the Tea Party movement strong and uncomplicated.

He described the relationship to O'Reilly: "Well, I've been to a lot of Tea Party events, we've spoken at quite a few of them, and I'm on the planning committee for the one on 9/11, this next September ... But, uh, we like the Tea Party movement a lot, we think it's great. It's a revitalization of our core Americanism and core constitutionalism."

In the meantime, the movement rank and file seethed with the kind of visceral anger and righteous paranoia that Charles Dyer voiced in his videos, and that the organization's rhetoric helped maintain with a steady patter of conspiratorial speculation and liberal baiting. Even though Rhodes kept insisting that his wasn't a militia organization, an inordinate number of Oath Keepers went about forming militias. Suddenly, as more veterans and people with serious training in the handling of arms came on board, these militia training exercises transformed from the often-bumbling comedies of errors that typified pre–Tea Party militia activities to serious training sessions with deadly intent.

In March 2010, Justine Sharrock, a *Mother Jones* reporter, spent time with a group of Oath Keepers in California who spent much of their time on such training exercises. Sharrock described the atmosphere and culture of the primarily male organization:

Oath Keepers is officially nonpartisan, in part to make it easier for active-duty soldiers to participate, but its rightward bent is undeniable, and liberals are viewed with suspicion. At lunch, when I questioned my table-mates about the Obama-Hitler comparisons I'd heard at the conference, I got a step-by-step tutorial on how the president's socialized medicine agenda would beget a Nazi-style regime.

I learned that bringing guns to Tea Party protests was a reminder of our constitutional rights, was introduced to the notion that the founding fathers modeled their governing documents on the Bible, and debated whether being Muslim meant an inability to believe in and abide by—and thus be protected by—the Constitution. I was schooled on the treachery of the Federal Reserve and why America needs a gold standard, and at dinner one night, Nighta Davis, national organizer for the National 912 Project, explained how abortion-rights advocates are part of a eugenics program targeting Christians.

Alt-America was taking shape. And that shape was heavily armed.

One of the participants in Stewart Rhodes's coming-out party in Lexington during that April 19, 2009, Patriot gathering was a long-time movement maven and one of its more colorful characters, Mike Vanderboegh.

Like Rhodes, Vanderboegh had an idea of how to encourage Patriots to organize militias to combat the New World Order. But instead of focusing on military and law-enforcement veterans, Vanderboegh had already concocted another scheme: enlist ordinary civilian gun owners into the Patriots' alternative universe and encourage them to form their own militia cells.

He called the concept the Three Percenters, an allusion to a myth that only 3 percent of the American colonists actually participated in the Revolutionary War as combatants. To these modern-day militia organizers, this suggested that a similarly tiny but sturdy faction of American Patriots—basically a cadre—would be called to under-take a second American Revolution, which their hyper-jingoistic rhetoric often led them to suggest they were now doing.

Vanderboegh explained that Three Percenters "are gun owners who will not disarm, will not compromise and will no longer back up at the passage of the next gun control act. Three Percenters say quite explicitly that we will not obey any further circumscription of our traditional liberties and will defend ourselves if attacked."

Though he and a handful of fellow movement ideologues had concocted the scheme in 2008, Vanderboegh was evidently also inspired by Rhodes's example and held a kind of coming-out party of his own exactly one year later, in 2010, with a "Restore the Con-stitution" rally. What made it stand out from dozens of similar

Patriot gatherings on April 19 commemorating the start of the first Revolutionary War was that not only was it planned for Washington, DC, where the open carry of weapons is not permitted by law, but Vanderboegh and other organizers made clear that they intended to bring their guns to the rally.

That news briefly made some national headlines, until organizers clarified that the event would actually be held at Gravelly Point Park in Arlington, Virginia, a national park property outside of the city. Ironically, this was only legal because of a law recently signed by President Obama permitting guns to be carried in some national parks.

Rally goers that April 19 nonetheless railed against the government tyranny that gun owners faced, Vanderboegh especially. "We are done backing up. Not one more inch," he told the crowd.

Yellow Gadsden flags were everywhere, as were protest signs such as "Which Part of 'Shall Not Be Infringed' Confuses You?" People handed out bright orange stickers reading "Guns Save Lives."

Vanderboegh had been something of a minor figure on the Patriot scene for a number of years. He first became involved in the movement in the 1990s with an Alabama outfit called the Sons of Liberty, and came to the attention of his fellow militiamen when he wrote a post-Waco call to arms titled "Strategy and Tactics for a Militia Civil War." He attracted further attention when, in 1996, he and a number of other militia leaders co-signed a statement denouncing the presence of any racists or white supremacists within their ranks and vowing to remove them if discovered.

For most of the following decade, Vanderboegh remained active on the Patriot organizing front, even as the movement's numbers went into a long-term tailspin. He briefly surfaced around the time of the Minuteman Project with his own Southern-fried version of the idea, the Alabama Minuteman Support Team, but it went out of business in relatively short order.

Fast-forward to 2008, when militia organizing began to stir again in rural America and Vanderboegh was poised to capitalize on it. Among his ventures that year was a novel he published online titled

Absolved that described a militia-led uprising against the federal government. The strategy it outlined involved small militia cells attacking federal officials and facilities in a guerrilla-terror campaign, not entirely dissimilar to the fantasy William Pierce had outlined decades before in *The Turner Diaries* in which a revolt against the federal government turns into a race war in which all undesirable groups are eliminated.

That year Vanderboegh came up with the Three Percent concept. One of his fellow Patriots and a onetime close associate, Chris Kerodin, also claimed at least conceptual ownership of the name. However, Kerodin and Vanderboegh soon had a falling-out over the direction of the organization. Kerodin, a onetime Maryland contractor, wanted to use the Three Percenters as a springboard for creating an off-the-grid, self-sustaining community built and operated by and for Patriot movement believers that would be totally independent of the federal government.

Vanderboegh thought that a separatist strategy was a bad idea, and the two parted company. Kerodin wound up pursuing his idea by setting up a backwoods Patriots-only community in northern Idaho, near the logging town of St. Maries, that he named The Citadel. He also claimed ownership of the Three Percent idea, setting up a website called III Percent Patriots that hawked the Citadel community as well as the gun-manufacturing operation, called III Arms, that Kerodin believed would be the community's main financial engine.

In early 2013, a few months after embarking on the Citadel project, it emerged that Kerodin was also a convicted felon: in 2004, he had been found guilty of extortion after he pretended to be an antiterrorism expert and tried to coerce shopping mall owners into buying his services. Vanderboegh and other fellow Patriots were quick to disassociate themselves from Kerodin. He still is trying to get The Citadel off the ground in Idaho but so far has failed.

The Three Percent meme has had more success and has spread widely to Patriot gatherings in every state as a new brand for creating independent armed militias capable of resisting the New World

Order. It especially appealed to paranoid gun owners who lacked the status of military or law-enforcement veterans, but felt compelled to do their part to "defend our freedoms."

The movement soon had a striking banner, based on a design made by a Patriot woman named Gayle Nyberg, and began selling it online and elsewhere. The design followed the usual arrangement of the American flag, with the standard red and white stripes. In place of the field of fifty stars was a large white Roman numeral III on a dark background, encircled with stars. Soon the design was simplified to just the III logo set on a black background. Big black "III" banners began appearing at Patriot events around the nation, and little black "III" stickers started appearing in the rear windows of people's pickups. And private Three Percenter units in various rural locales began organizing sessions for training in weapons use and military strategy.

They had a handy nickname for themselves, too: Threepers.

Richard Mack had a scheme for promoting the Patriots' "constitutionalist" belief system and the concomitant militia idea, although, like Stewart Rhodes, he never formed a militia of his own. His recruitment plan differed from Rhodes's and Vanderboegh's in that it targeted law-enforcement officers—specifically, the nation's county sheriff's and police officers.

Like Rhodes and Vanderboegh, he enjoyed a disturbing level of success. But then, he had been at this for a long, long time.

He called his organization the Constitutional Sheriffs and Peace Officers Association, and its entire purpose was to draw law officers into the radical "constitutionalist" belief system he had been promoting since the 1990s. Mack's core belief, based on an arcane interpretation of the Constitution, was that the county sheriff, and not the federal government, nor even the state government, was the supreme law of the land, and had the ability and legal power to override federal or state law enforcement authority. This interpretation of the Constitution has been tested in multiple legal cases and has been rejected by every court that has ruled on it.

Mack was a devotee of a far-right Mormon ideologue named W. Cleon Skousen, a John Birch Society leader who had a long career as a red-baiting conspiracist author in the 1960s and '70s. He wrote books in which he warned of the Communist threat to the United States, and the United Nations as the Trojan Horse of the Communist threat. Later in his career Skousen became a "constitutional" theorist. He lifted most of his ideas from previous "constitutionalists," especially the far-right Posse Comitatus movement of the 1970s and '80s, but stripped them of their original racism and anti-Semitism.

The Posse Comitatus movement had first organized in the late 1960s as a reaction to federal civil rights legislation. It was openly bigoted, and promoted conspiracy theories that Jews were a nefarious presence scheming to enslave white people. Its primary goal was to take away the government's ability to enforce civil rights laws. This led to its main focus being a kind of radical localism based on the power of a county sheriff, or other law officer, to conscript any able-bodied man to form a posse and assist him in keeping the peace or to pursue and arrest a felon. The group's founding document states,

> There is no legitimate form of government above that of the county level and no higher law authority than the county sheriff. If the sheriff refuses to carry out the will of the county's citizens, he shall be removed by the Posse to the most populated intersection of streets in the township and at high noon be hung by the neck, the body remaining until sundown as an example to those who would subvert the law.

In his magisterial *The Terrorist Next Door: The Militia Movement and the Radical Right* (2002) Daniel Levitas shows how the Posse ideology provided the basis for much of the Patriot movement ideology of the 1990s, including the militias in Montana and elsewhere, the "sovereign citizens" movement, and the Montana Freemen. Most of these movements' leaders filtered out the overtly racist and anti-Semitic component of Posse beliefs and presented the underlying "constitutional" framework as not only legitimate, but the *only* possible legitimate interpretation of the Constitution.

Skousen had done much the same thing in 1981 with his book *The 5,000 Year Leap*, which filtered the Posse interpretation of history and the Constitution into a more benign-seeming ideology that claimed that the American system was based not on the Enlightenment but on common Law and the Bible, and that the Framers believed in an extremely limited form of government. So limited, in fact, that the county was the highest level of law enforcement. This belief formed the core principle of Richard Mack's organization.

Mack had first come to national attention in the 1990s, when, as the sheriff of rural Graham County, Arizona, he defied President Clinton's ban on assault weapons. He was recruited by the NRA to join in filing a lawsuit against the federal government; the suit's claim was that a state law enforcement officer had the power to refuse to enforce federal laws. For his heroism, the National Rifle Association named him its Law Officer of the Year in 1994, and he gave a rousing speech at the NRA's annual convention.

The next year, Mack launched his long-running career as a Patriot "constitutionalist" speaker. I saw Mack in February 1995 at a Patriot gathering in Bellevue, Washington, where he displayed a knack for crowd-pleasing hyperbole: "Hitler was more moral than Clinton," he told the Bellevue audience. "He had fewer girlfriends."

He also promoted his book, *From My Cold Dead Hands: Why America Needs Guns*, and extolled the virtues of forming militias as a necessary defense against the coming New World Order tyranny. In the final chapter Mack concludes: "The US Constitution was written to protect honest Americans. Attempts to dilute its content and meaning must be met with fierce resistance in the polling places of America, in the Halls of Congress—and, if necessary, in the streets, the hills and dales of the Republic."

Mack's highest priority was recruiting sheriffs into the Patriot alternative universe, because, he argued, the sheriff stood as the ultimate bulwark against federal intrusion. Sheriffs' participation in standing up to the feds was essential in order for citizen militias to operate lawfully. Nonetheless, he spoke out against violence repeatedly, urging people to use the ballot box instead of armed rebellion.

He ran for reelection as sheriff in Graham County in 1996, but lost. By then, however, his career as a public speaker had taken off, and it remained fairly lucrative for Mack during most of the 1990s. He took a job as a chief lobbyist with Larry Pratt at the Gun Owners of America, in Washington, but quickly tired of the Beltway life. He moved up to Utah County, Utah, and ran for sheriff there in 1998, but lost in the primary. In 2006 Mack returned to Arizona, to rural Navajo County, and ran for Congress on the Libertarian Party ticket against the incumbent, Jon Kyl, a Republican. He got 3 percent of the vote.

Two years later, however, Mack began to find demand rising for his rousing speeches at Patriot and pro-gun-rights events. This was about the same time that the number of militia groups in the United States doubled. When 2009 and the Tea Party movement came around, he was suddenly being paid to travel around the country warning audiences of the impending tyranny of the Obama administration. Mack later claimed that he spoke to some 120 Tea Party gatherings.

In 2009 Mack also published a new book, *The County Sheriff: America's Last Hope*, depicting the county sheriff as the "last line of defense" against a tyrannical federal government. In looking for historical precedents he harked back—without a hint of irony—to the Civil Rights Movement, suggesting that if only a "constitutional sheriff" had been in charge back in 1955 in Montgomery, Alabama, Rosa Parks would have been freed and the local segregation ordinances defied.

All this ultimately led Mack, in 2011, to found the Constitutional Sheriffs and Peace Officers Association (CSPOA), which quickly attracted a bevy of sheriffs and police officers as supporters and members. "The greatest threat we face today is not terrorists," warned the CSPOA website. "It is our own federal government."

"The county sheriff is the one who can say to the feds, 'Beyond these bounds you shall not pass,'" Mack explained.

The key to Mack's recruitment efforts was, as always, guns: one of his first campaigns involved inviting sheriffs and police officers around the nation to sign a letter of protest to President Obama, suggesting they would not permit federal enforcement of the president's gun-control initiatives in the wake of the December 2012 massacre of twenty-six schoolchildren and their teachers at Sandy Hook Elementary in Newtown, Connecticut.

"We respect the office of the President of the United States," the letter read. "But make no mistake, as the duly-elected sheriffs of our respective counties, we will enforce the rights guaranteed to our citizens by the Constitution. No federal officials will be permitted to descend upon our constituents and take from them what the Bill of Rights—in particular Amendment II—has given them."

More than 200 sheriffs signed it. Some of them added their own letters, including one Colorado sheriff who wrote that "public safety professionals serving in the executive branch, do not have the constitutional authority, responsibility, and in most cases, the credentials to determine the constitutionality of any issue."

The recruitment scheme was a smashing success. Within a few years Mack would claim he had more than 500 members. Mack's annual CSPOA events drew large numbers of law enforcement officers—more than 100 attended the first such event in 2012, and the numbers grew steadily after that. Among the organization's honorees was the 2013 "Sheriff of the Year," Sheriff David Clarke of Milwaukee County, Wisconsin, a tough-talking African American.

In an interview with the SPLC, Daniel Levitas observed: "Ever since the notion of the supremacy of the county sheriff became popularized, it has continued to remain attractive—though when people hear it, they don't understand that what is behind it is violent lawlessness and vigilantism. That's what Richard Mack stands for when you strip all the window dressing away: lawlessness and vigilantism."

All the chickens—the gathering militias, the overheated and hateful rhetoric, the paranoid defiance of the Obama administration—came home to roost on a lonely stretch of sagebrush desert in southern Nevada in April 2014.

8

The Bundy Pandora's Box

Cliven Bundy was a colorful, cowboy-hat-bedecked sixty-eight-year-old Mormon rancher whose family had been grazing cattle on a sun-baked stretch of Bureau of Land Management sagebrush land in southern Nevada near the tiny town of Bunkerville, about an hour's drive north of Las Vegas, since 1954. He was known for pontificating at length about the Constitution and America. He also was an ardent devotee of Cleon Skousen.

Feeling that his arrangement with the federal government was becoming increasingly oppressive, he stopped paying his grazing fees to the BLM in 1993. The breaking point came, he later explained, when the BLM added restrictions to the permit designed to protect endangered desert tortoises, limiting him to grazing only 150 cattle. In most years, he grazed around 500.

The BLM canceled his permit in 1994, but he kept grazing his cattle on the tract. The agency attempted several times to get Bundy to renew his permit with the new restrictions, but by then he had become a full-fledged "sovereign citizen," and told federal authorities he no longer recognized their authority to regulate his grazing—he had "vested rights" to graze on BLM land, he claimed.

Bundy became a familiar figure in the Clark County Clerk's office in the 1990s as he began filing a blizzard of sovereign-citizen-style documents with the local court. In the documents (later obtained by the Southern Poverty Law Center) he acknowledged only a "sovereign state of Nevada," and declared the federal government illegitimate.

The BLM, determined to get his "trespass cattle" off their range, undertook a series of court actions against Bundy and his family demanding they remove their cows. Eventually, the courts gave BLM the authority to remove Bundy's cattle and dun him for damages. Over time Bundy's unpaid grazing fees and fines amounted to over $1 million.

In April 2012, when the BLM announced a roundup of Bundy's cattle, Bundy sent a threatening letter to the BLM contractor charged with removing the cattle: "There is a volatile situation currently taking place," Bundy wrote. "Cliven Bundy will do whatever it takes to protect his property and rights and liberty and freedoms of those of, We the People, of Clark County Nevada."

The letter unnerved the land managers at the BLM offices, so they canceled the roundup, citing "safety concerns." Further court actions led to a federal judge's court order issued in July 2013 permanently enjoining Bundy and his family from grazing cattle on the Bunkerville property, known as the Gold Butte, and another judge's order in October authorized the BLM to remove his cows permanently.

In late March 2014 Bundy sent communiqués to a number of county, state, and federal officials titled "Range War Emergency Notice and Demand for Protection." In subsequent interviews with reporters, he beckoned to the Oath Keepers, the White Mountain Militia, and the "Praetorian Guard" militia to come to his aid, deploying the "constitutionalist" language of the movement in his appeals.

On April 5, BLM rangers and cowboys contracted by the agency arrived and started rounding up Bundy's cattle. David Bundy, the family's eldest son, was filming the roundup when BLM officers arrested and charged him with failure to disperse. The next day Bundy responded with an angry call to arms: "They have my cattle and now they have one of my boys … Range War begins tomorrow at Bundy ranch," Bundy declared on his family's blog on April 6, 2014.

Alex Jones's *Infowars* picked up and avidly promoted the Bundy ranch story, as did the conspiracist host Pete Santilli on his Internet radio show. A "We Support Cliven Bundy" Facebook page had a similar tone. Santilli, in an interview with Bundy, called for militias to turn out and protect the rancher and his family.

Even the *Drudge Report* adopted the Bundy story, as updates from the "Standoff At Nevada Ranch" were featured on the site's front page—well before any actual standoff had taken place. Glenn Beck's *The Blaze* headlined it on the website's front page. All of these outlets depicted Bundy's "range war" as a last-gasp fight for American freedom against federal tyranny.

BLM officials, meanwhile, defended the crackdown on Bundy's activities by noting that he was the only rancher in the region who refused to acknowledge or heed the federal permit system for grazing rights. On the BLM website officials explained: "Cattle have been in trespass on public lands in southern Nevada for more than two decades. This is unfair to the thousands of other ranchers who graze livestock in compliance with federal laws and regulations throughout the West."

On April 9, a small collection of pro-Bundy protesters showed up at the roundup site. The confrontation escalated into a brief dustup between BLM officers and the protesters, who included Ammon Bundy, another of Cliven's sons. During the ruckus, caught on video, Ammon Bundy was shot with a stun gun that bloodied his shoulder. Eventually the officers retreated, amid much celebration by the protesters.

The scuffle appeared to follow efforts by the protesters to prevent vehicles involved in the roundup work from leaving the scene. At one point, officers began bringing in guard dogs and demanding that people get away from a truck whose exit had been blocked. At that point, some shoving and scuffling occurred, officers pulled out their Tasers, and Ammon Bundy was hit in the chest.

Eventually the truck moved on and the law enforcement officers all got into their vehicles and followed the roundup vehicles away from the scene. The protesters were jubilant, especially when Pete

Santilli's video of the confrontation went viral, mainly on anti-government websites and social media.

Almost overnight the Patriots started to arrive en masse: Oath Keepers, Three Percenters, independent militiamen, a scattering of independent gun owners and conspiracy fanatics. The scene of the roundup became an encampment of about a hundred Bundy supporters who parked along the roadside and harassed the roundup vehicles.

"Right now it looks like the movie *Red Dawn*," another of Bundy's sons, Ryan, told the crowd. "Right now we've got two hundred–plus federal agents up there in a military compound that they have put together and they've got snipers … Everybody's armed, and they've been monitoring our ranch with high-tech surveillance equipment … It was never about the grazing fees, it's about control."

Among those arriving was Ryan Payne, thirty, of Anaconda, Montana, an Iraq War veteran who now made his living as an electrician. Active in his local militia, the West Mountain Rangers, he was also the overseer of a nationwide Patriot organization called Operation Mutual Aid whose mission was to enable militias to respond to federal tyranny with a nationwide call to arms.

Before heading out from Montana and driving all night to get to Nevada, Payne first spoke with Cliven Bundy himself. "I said the type of help that I'm going to be bringing is militia units and Patriots from all over the country," Payne later told the SPLC's Ryan Lenz. Bundy, he said, told him: "I'm not going to tell you what to bring, I'm not going to tell you to bring guns or any of that type of stuff. All I'm going to say is we need help, and you use your own discernment and decide what needs to be brought."

After seeing the video of Ammon Bundy getting Tasered on April 9, Payne made that call to arms. He told everyone on the Operation Mutual Aid network to get themselves to Bunkerville if they could, and provided directions to the Bundy ranch. "At this time we have approximately 150 responding, but that number is growing by the hour," he wrote. "May God grant each and every one of you safety, wisdom and foresight, and courage to accomplish the mission we have strived for so long to bring to fruition."

Alex Jones made the trek out to the Bunkerville scene from Texas, and was joined by Richard Mack and Stewart Rhodes. The mainstream media also began showing up in large numbers, drawn by the exotic and violent nature of the story. But most of all, the Patriot foot soldiers came flocking in from around the country, heavily armed and itching for action. Estimates were that over 1,000 people traveled to Bunkerville that week.

Finally, on Saturday, April 12, all hell broke loose.

The pro-Bundy Patriots began that morning by holding a rally at the site of the main gathering along the highway, hoisting a banner reading "Liberty Freedom For God We Stand." There was a panoply of signs castigating "government thugs," the BLM, and President Obama.

Clark County Sheriff Doug Gillespie agreed to meet Bundy in front of the angry, heavily armed crowd. He gave them what should have been good news: the BLM had agreed to back down.

"The BLM is going to cease this operation," Gillespie told the protesters. "The Gold Butte allotment will be reopened to the public, and they will be removing their assets." He turned to Bundy and said, "What I would hope to sit down with you and talk about is, how to have this facilitated in a safe way."

But protesters screamed at him, "Where are the cows?" They wanted the cattle released. "Bring the cows back! You're holding them hostage to broker a deal," one of them shouted.

Surrender by the BLM wasn't enough; Bundy had his own demands. He gave the BLM one hour to release his cattle, remove their equipment, and disarms its agents. "You report back to these people, we the people, in one hour," he ordered.

Bundy addressed the crowd: "We definitely don't recognize [the BLM director's] jurisdiction or authority, his arresting power or policing power in any way," he said. "We're about ready to take the country over with force!"

Bundy suggested to the crowd that it block the freeway, and it did. Armed with both long rifles and handguns, protesters proceeded to block a portion of Interstate 15 for more than two hours, creating traffic backups for miles in both directions. Then the protesters, riding their horses and carrying banners and signs, headed down the draw and converged at the mouth of the Gold Butte preserve, where the cattle were corralled.

An excruciatingly tense, hour-long standoff ensued. Patriots took up sniper positions along the bluffs above the corral and along the freeway overlooking it. One Three Percenter, a veteran from Idaho named Eric "EJ" Parker, was photographed by a number of reporters prone on the freeway in a sniper position, aiming his scoped rifle directly at the site of the showdown.

At the end of the hour, the BLM cowboys began releasing the cattle, and the angry protesters at the gate drew away gradually. BLM rangers began dispersing the crowd blocking the freeway, warning over loudspeakers that they were prepared to use tear gas.

A week of endeavoring to enforce a federal court order had come to naught. "Based on information about conditions on the ground, and in consultation with law enforcement, we have made a decision to conclude the cattle gather because of our serious concern about the safety of employees and members of the public," the BLM's director, Neil Kornze, told ABC News.

With the desert sun high, about two dozen cowboys on horseback appeared in a cloud of dust on the hills above the protest area, ready to ride about three miles away to take Bundy's cattle back. "Until the cows come home!" the crowd cheered. Meanwhile, antigovernment Patriot groups such as the Oath Keepers grew only more excited. Wiley Drake, national chaplain for the Oath Keepers, said the time had come to no longer bow to President Obama, whom he called a half-breed.

Richard Mack later told a Fox reporter, William LaJeunesse, that the people who gathered there to stop law enforcement from rounding up the illegally grazing cattle—the crowd had grown to hundreds by the time the Bureau of Land Management caved in and returned many of the cattle—were prepared to lay their lives on the line to stand up to the government. Well, maybe not their lives, exactly—more like their wives' lives: "We were actually strategizing to put all the women up at the front. If they're going to start shooting, it's going to be women that are televised all across the world getting shot by these rogue federal officers."

The Patriot movement was ecstatic and immediately declared victory.

The blog *Bearing Arms* summed up the sentiment on the far right: "It is now a virtual certainty that Obamite acts of tyranny will be resisted, by hundreds, even thousands, and if necessary, by force."

Most Patriots believed the victory proved the legitimacy of their view that the federal government was a fraudulent entity with no legitimate power.

Leading the parade was Mike Vanderboegh, who wrote at his popular blog, *Sipsey Street Irregulars*, that the "feds were routed":

> It is impossible to overstate the importance of the victory won in the desert today. While the behind-the-scenes details are not clear yet, it is obvious that something unprecedented in the war on the west that has been waged by the imperial federal government has, against all odds, happened. The feds were routed—routed. There is no other word that applies. Courage is contagious, defiance is contagious, victory is contagious.

Vanderboegh, who spoke by phone with Ammon Bundy, saw the event—alongside most of his far-right brethren—as truly historic:

> I congratulated Ammon and told him that this was perhaps a pivotal moment in American history. He also agreed with me that it is impossible not to see the hand of God in all of this. I told him that it was my opinion that the empire would surely strike back, but that they would likely come at the Bundys and their supporters sideways next time. Still, it was a great victory, a pivotal moment, in the relationship between the federal government and the American people.

That was the sentiment at *Infowars*, where the headline proclaimed, "Historic! Feds Forced to Surrender to American Citizens." The site also featured an article from Ron Paul, who warned that federal agents might be planning a lethal raid against the Bundys as retaliation.

In the meantime, Richard Mack also weighed in at *Infowars* and similarly warned against a coming raid. Alex Jones himself warned that there would be many more such incidents.

> It's a very special time to be alive. And the victory that you saw at that event? There's going to be more of that as people push back, as they see victory. And the feds, if they miscalculate, and start shooting people, at another Lexington or Concord, are going to set a revolution off in our favor.

At the slightly more mainstream TownHall.com, the financial columnist John Ransom ran his story under the headline "War on Federal Bureaucrats Opens at the Bundy Ranch."

Meanwhile, Oath Keepers not only vowed to keep up its presence at the Bundy ranch but also sent out a national call to members, telling them to make their way to Nevada over the next week.

Oath Keepers' president, Stewart Rhodes, noted that they were "concerned that the domestic enemies of the Constitution that infest the federal government might try to take advantage of folks going home, and attempt to make a move on the Bundy family." So to prevent any raid, he was "calling on all Oath Keepers who can possibly get here to come to the Bundy ranch to serve as volunteers on an ongoing, rotating watch." Rhodes added, "We need boots on the ground. We want you here, standing watch, which is appropriate for us Oath Keepers since our motto is 'Not On Our Watch.'"

Rhodes also appeared on an Internet radio program at the website *North West Liberty News* and said that a number of leading far-right state legislators were lending their names to the cause, including representatives Matt Shea of Spokane, Washington, and Michele Fiore of Las Vegas. Also on the way was Pastor Chuck Baldwin, whose Montana-based Liberty Fellowship was a hotbed of Patriot radicalism.

In Nevada, local opinion makers were decidedly less enthusiastic. At the conservative *Las Vegas Review-Journal*, the columnist Steve Sebelius noted that the court orders and numerous rulings requiring the federal government to remove Bundy's cows remained intact:

> About the only thing that's different is that a bunch of armed would-be insurrectionists have gotten the message that if they show up with tough talk and loaded long guns, there's a good chance the government will back down. And that's not a very good message to send.

Even after the BLM officially backed down, the scene at the Bundy ranch carried on for a couple more weeks, before it all turned sour and fell apart.

Cliven Bundy continued to make demands. He went before reporters and demanded that Sheriff Gillespie disarm the National Park Service "at Lake Mead and Red Rock Park and all other parks where the federal government claims they have jurisdiction over," and that they do it within the hour. Bundy went on to insist that Clark County bulldozers and loaders be put to work tearing down "that entrance places where they ticket us and where they injure us and make us citizens pay their fees." He called the demands a "mandate from we the people."

The BLM ignored him. So Bundy went on national media to press his demands. Fox News's Sean Hannity hosted him for an interview in which he reiterated, "The demand on the sheriff was de-arm the Park Service rangers, and de-arm Red Rock rangers—that's two parks very close to the Lake Mead area. And then the demand was, tear down the toll booth shacks."

Bundy said he was disappointed by the federal response, the only solution to which was for "every county sheriff across the United States" to "disarm the federal bureaucrats."

Bundy had become, briefly, a bright TV star. Back at the Bundy ranch, the scene had become a complete media circus. The site of the protest attracted hundreds of journalists, who had no shortage of eager Patriots lining up to hold forth for the cameras about how they were fighting government oppression, heroically standing up for the nation's freedoms, and delivering the country from President Obama's tyranny.

The scene revolved around a stage—actually a flatbed trailer pulled onto the site and decorated—that had been set up and on which a number of speakers, including Bundy, held forth for the assembled press daily. Patriot and other right-wing luminaries crossed the stage and exhorted the crowd to keep fighting the federal government.

The media reports were generally hospitable to the alternative universe. On a Fox News segment hosted by Gretchen Carlson, the reporter William LaJeunesse's characterization of the situation seemed to report the Patriot ideology uncritically: "Bundy says that he doesn't recognize federal authority here, that his grazing rights predate and preclude federal authority in this area."

The speakers came from around the county. One of them was a CSPOA favorite, Brad Rogers, sheriff of Indiana's Elkhart County, who came to Nevada at the invitation of the Oath Keepers. Stewart Rhodes introduced Rogers onstage. Rogers's speech was aimed at encouraging other sheriffs to follow his example.

"I'm not here to judge Mr. Bundy," he said. "But even if he was wrong, two hundred armed federal agents to gather up cows? It should be the sheriff intervening so that we don't have a Waco or a Ruby Ridge all over again."

He lauded the crowd: "Basically it's a bunch of peace-loving Patriots like yourselves that are looking to have constitutional government and to not abide by any orders that are unconstitutional, like herding people into concentration camps or disarming the public or whatever the case may be," he said.

As the days wore on, the media became increasingly desperate to find a new story angle. Then Cliven Bundy gave them one. On April 23, while holding forth on his political philosophy, he decided to delve into the subject of race relations.

"I want to tell you one more thing I know about the Negro," Bundy told the reporters. He recalled how he once drove past a public-housing project in North Las Vegas, "and in front of that government house the door was usually open and the older people and the kids—and there is always at least a half a dozen people sitting on the porch—they didn't have nothing to do. They didn't have nothing for their kids to do. They didn't have nothing for their young girls to do.

"And because they were basically on government subsidy, so now what do they do?" he asked. "They abort their young children, they put their young men in jail, because they never learned how to pick cotton. And I've often wondered, are they better off as slaves, picking cotton and having a family life and doing things, or are they better off under government subsidy? They didn't get no more freedom. They got less freedom."

The *New York Times* published those remarks the next day on its front page, and every media outlet in the country—even Fox News—was leading with them. Bundy's support from mainstream conservatives and prominent Republicans basically vanished. Rather than registering this state of affairs with chagrin, Bundy doubled down, emphasizing at a press conference that he thought he was right to ask such questions:

> I've been wondering—Cliven Bundys are wondering about these people—now I'm talking about the black community. I've been wondering —are they better off with their young women aborting their children? Are they better off with their young men in prison? And are they better off with the older people on the sidewalks in front of their government-issued homes with a few children on them—are they better off, are they happier than they was when they was in the South, in front of their homes with their chickens and their gardens and their children around them, and their men having something to do?

He also went on CNN's *New Day* program and doubled down again, saying that Martin Luther King hadn't finished his job if black people were going to be offended by the things he said: "Maybe I sinned, maybe I need to ask forgiveness, and maybe I don't know what I actually said," he explained. "But when you talk about prejudice, we're talking about not being able to exercise what we think and our feelings—we don't have freedom to say what we want. If I say 'Negro' or 'black boy' or 'slave'—I'm not—if those people cannot take those kinda words and not be offensive, then Martin Luther King hasn't got his job done yet."

The flight from Bundy became a stampede, as Republican politicians and party officials repeated that they had nothing to do with the Nevada rancher. But the militiamen who showed up with weapons at Bundy's ranch in Nevada continued to support him—they saw the negative news stories as just another conspiracy.

"It's part of misinformation to maintain the divide," one militiaman told the *Las Vegas Sun*. "Things like this will be put out there to discredit Bundy."

Alan Keyes, a conservative black pundit, defended the remarks, finding grist in them for his anti-socialism message. The comments weren't racist—"He wasn't talking so much about black folks, but about the harm and damage that the leftist socialism has done to blacks."

But most of Bundy's mainstream backers made it clear that they preferred to talk about other cases of "government abuse," not about Bundy's racist theories or even putative abuse of Bundy. At Fox News, Sean Hannity, Bundy's biggest on-air champion, while not defending the rancher, seemed to blame it all on the liberal media:

All right, allow me to make myself abundantly clear. I believe those comments are downright racist … And it's beyond disturbing … I think it's extremely unfortunate that Cliven Bundy holds those views.

Now, while I supported the Bundy ranch as they took a stand against the Bureau of Land Management, I was absolutely dismayed … after reading the article and then hearing the commentary. However … the ranch standoff … was not about a man named Cliven Bundy. At the heart of this issue was my belief that our government is simply out of control … This was about a federal agency's dangerous response to a situation that could have resulted in a catastrophe … people dying and people being shot, kind of comparable to what we saw in Waco, Texas.

Hannity then rambled through a number of other supposed examples of out-of-control government and then concluded by throwing the 2012 Benghazi, Libya, incident and Obamacare into the mix.

On April 24, 2014, the *New Yorker*'s Andy Borowitz satirized the Bundy dust-up online: "Cliven Bundy's outrageous racist remarks undermine decades of progress in our effort to come up with cleverer ways of saying the same thing."

Ryan Payne, who had been in charge of coordinating the military positions of the gunmen around the April 12 standoff scene, later told a Montana newspaper: "We had counter-sniper positions on their sniper positions. We had at least one guy—sometimes two guys—per BLM agent in there. If they made one wrong move, every single BLM agent in that camp would've died."

A couple of weeks afterward, KLAS-TV of Las Vegas aired a broadcast that exposed just how fragile the situation had been on April 12, and how narrowly an all-out gun battle had been averted—a battle the Patriots gathered to defend Bundy seemed determined, if not outright eager, to have.

When the BLM realized it was badly outnumbered that sunny day, it had called on Las Vegas police officers for help in bolstering the outmanned local law enforcement ranks at the scene. Several of the Las Vegas Metro officers were African American, and the foot soldiers on the Bundy side were anything but civilized.

One of the Las Vegas Metro officers, Tom Jenkins, told a reporter, "We were told, we're going to go down there and we're going to get between the BLM and the protesters. We were going, 'Okay, we've been there before,' but as we were driving up, it was like a movie set. It didn't look real; people in the back of pickup trucks with rifles and shotguns. It was hard to grasp."

About 30 Las Vegas Metro officers were placed between an estimated 400 militiamen, bristling with weaponry, and the fearful BLM workers, whose job was gathering cattle. The crowd became nasty and began hurling taunts and every kind of insults at the officers: "Everything that you can think of to call a human being, animals ...

They had no respect for authority," said Jenkins. One of the protesters asked him if he was ready to die. "I don't know his name. He was wearing a Pittsburgh Steelers jersey," he said.

Militiamen also vandalized vehicles of KLAS-TV reporters.

Clark County Assistant Sheriff Joe Lombardo confirmed that officers were gathering intelligence on the people who brandished guns at the scene, and said that people who aimed their guns at officers would be dealt with: "Yes, there will be consequences, definitely. That is unacceptable behavior. If we let it go, it will continue into the future." Such behavior typically constitutes assault against an officer and is a federal crime that can carry a sentence of up to twenty years in prison when a deadly weapon is involved. FBI agents were also investigating verbal threats that were made that day.

By late April, however, the drama had withered, and there were less than a hundred protesters still at the camp. Paranoid rumors are not only common at gatherings of antigovernment Patriots, they're practically the entire raison d'être for the get-togethers in the first place. Sometime around April 25, a rumor began circulating that Attorney General Eric Holder was preparing a drone strike on the armed militiamen. It unleashed a rift within the camp, which was already brimming with fear, rage, testosterone, and firearms. Stewart Rhodes of the Oath Keepers claimed he had obtained the information from a "reliable source," and responded by pulling his people out of what they called "the kill zone," the area they thought the drone would be striking. When the other militiamen learned that the Oath Keepers had pulled out, they were outraged.

Infighting broke out among those remaining at the camp, who had vowed to stay on and protect Bundy. It kind of resembled a sand-box squabble, except for the adult viciousness of the threats and taunts exchanged between the Oath Keepers and their critics, particularly members of independent militias. Led by Ryan Payne, who had been acting as the spokesman for the militiamen at the ranch, this faction held an impromptu gathering at the camp to discuss the situation. It was captured on video.

They openly talked about shooting Rhodes and other Oath Keepers leaders for "desertion" and "cowardice" and described how "the whole thing is falling apart over there." At the end, they voted unanimously to oust the Oath Keepers, or at least its leadership, from the Bundy ranch camp. Payne was caught on the video saying, "We are open to gentlemanly conversation. But this man and the people that obeyed that order have violated my personal creed. You don't fucking walk in and say, 'I'm sorry,' and you're back in, brother. You can walk in and say you're sorry, and you're lucky that you're not getting shot in the back. Because that's what happens to deserters on the battlefield."

Initially, Rhodes and his fellow Oath Keepers glossed over Payne's threats. Oath Keepers organizer Elias Alias described the incident on the group's website as an effort "to sabotage the Bundy stand against the government," and reported that other Patriot movement leaders, including Mike Vanderboegh and Richard Mack, remained firmly within their camp.

Alias also tried to explain the drone rumor: "Yes, it is true: Oath Keepers received a bizarre bit of leaked info which could not be verified but which also could not be ignored. Our contact is connected with the Department of Defense—or was. The info we received stated that Eric Holder of the Department of Justice had okayed a drone strike on the Bundy ranch near Bunkerville, Nevada, within a forty-eight-hour period over the weekend of April 26–27, 2014."

In the ensuing panic at the camp, Alias said, "Oath Keepers advised people there to consider evacuation." He referred to the angry reaction of the militiamen as "backwash."

Another YouTube video revealed the depths of the militiamen's animus toward Rhodes and his organization. One of them—the head of "security" for the Bundy family, a man nicknamed Booda Bear—ranted angrily:

> My guys sleep in the dirt out here, we're on shifts for fourteen hours a day and trying to make sure that this family stays safe and secure … and just so everybody knows, as Booda, head of security for the Bundy Family I

can swear on the white skin that covers my ass there will not be an Oath Keeper—there *will not be an oath keeper* allowed to set foot on the internal ranch property.

Alias responded by insinuating that Booda and his pals were actually FBI plants: "Some of the purported 'leaders' of the militia at the ranch are doing exactly what any agent provocateur would do after having infiltrated the militia and claimed a role in leadership," he wrote. Then Rhodes teamed up with fellow Oath Keepers Steve Homan, Robert Casillas and Brandon Ropolla in a video they made to attack the "nutcases" that Rhodes said had assumed control of the militia camp at the Bundy ranch. He painted an unflattering portrait of volatile "crazies" at the camp. Rhodes also revealed that the Bundy Patriots had actually brandished weapons at each other:

> Now, when [John] Bidler was dropped on his butt ... another guy—some Mountain Man militia guy, put his hand on his gun and said, "I dare ya to draw—draw motherfucker, I'm gonna kill ya." I'm sorry to cuss but that's what he said. So they were being threatened. Guys with hands on their guns threatening them. That's why we told [our people] to get out of there. We knew the situation was this close from being a gunfight, right there inside the camp ...
>
> And this is the tip of the iceberg of the cluster out there. One of our guys from Montana, Rick Delap, who was there from the beginning—he's been out there for two weeks in the dirt—the day of this confrontation, I come to find out he had to draw on somebody. Two of the Mountain Men guys came up to him—were aggressing on him. Then one of them ran back to his vehicle and grabbed an AR and came back with an AR in his hand and Rick had to draw on him. And those two ran off. That was this close from Rick having to shoot that ding-a-ling. If that guy had raised his barrel, Rick would have had no choice but to shoot him.

This kind of macho radicalism proved fatally toxic to the environment at the Bundy ranch. Over the next week after the blowup, people began leaving the scene and returning to their homes in a steady stream. The stage/trailer next to the freeway was pulled away.

A week and a half later, only a handful of defenders and the Bundy family remained at their ranch. But the damage had been done.

One of the people who had been eagerly spreading the paranoid rumors about the imminent drone attack was Jerad Miller, a thin young man from Indiana, now living in Las Vegas. Miller, thirty-one, a sometime construction worker and ex-convict, had driven out to Nevada with his young wife, Amanda, in tow, determined to take part in the events at Bunkerville. It's not clear when they actually arrived at the scene, but they were present for at least the last couple of weeks of April.

That's mainly because Jerad Miller was happy to give TV journalists interviews from the Patriot perspective during that time period. He told the reporter for KRNV-TV that Minutemen were ringing the scene of the standoff and said, "So, you know, I feel sorry for any federal agents that want to come in here and try to push us around, or anything like that. I really don't want violence toward them, but if they're gonna come bring violence to us, well, if that's the language they want to speak, we'll learn it."

The reporter was shocked: "Well, that sounds kind of like a menacing statement, I have to tell you," she said.

Miller responded, "You know, the people here, that have come here to support Bundy, we're not afraid. You know, we know that in the past the government has used force against civilians, like Waco, Ruby Ridge ... We're not afraid of that."

When Melissa Chan of Al-Jazeera interviewed him on April 17, he was dressed in full combat gear and a Kevlar jacket, with yellow shooting glasses protecting his eyes. He told her his "call name" was Joker, saying, "I figure if the government is going to label me a terrorist, why not, you know, be the call sign 'Joker' for the most notorious 'terrorist' in the D.C. [Comics] universe?"

Miller expanded on one of his earlier remarks, that he was "willing to die," saying, "I'm not afraid of death, I'm afraid of being a slave. I'm afraid of living under tyranny. I'm afraid of my nieces and nephews having to grow up with, you know, the day they're born they have fifty thousand in tax debt over their heads already … It's so hard to explain. You know, after 9/11, despite what you might think about it, the police state has grown exponentially, okay? The abuses of police have just grown out of control, with no repercussions."

Chan recalled later that she had spent time off-camera with Miller and his pretty young wife, Amanda. Chan had snapped a photo of Miller getting a hot sandwich from the food table, served up by Ammon Bundy, on cooking duty that day. She was struck by how attentive Miller was to Amanda, and how *normal* they seemed.

"He was very nice to his wife," Chan recalled. "There was this kindness and they were just kind of this cute couple—in this crazy context that we were in."

In the KRNV-TV interview, Miller mentioned that even more violence-prone friends of his had nearly came out to Nevada to join him: "I know personally a couple people that wanted to come out here, um, and join up, but they [protest organizers] were afraid they might get a little trigger-happy, you know, and wouldn't wait for them to fire the first shot. So they were advised to stay home, we only need cool-headed people here that aren't going to antagonize them, you know, and—pretty much make it to look like we fired the first shot, or had anything involved in any of that kind of thinking."

Miller insisted that he and his fellow Patriots were not "instigating anything. We are here in response to their criminal activity, as we see it."

Another camp participant said that Miller ran afoul of the people running the show when it emerged that he had been telling a large number of people about the imminent drone attack.

Howard Scheff, a onetime Nevada legislative candidate under the banner of the far-right American Independent Party, was also at the ranch. He said he befriended the Millers, but was disconcerted when he discovered that Miller had a criminal background. Then he received a worrying text from Miller after he had made a trip home to Las Vegas.

"You need to get back here, it's going down," it read. "They've got drones in the sky, they've got guys coming in to attack us."

Scheff put in a quick call to the Bundys, who told him that everything was normal. When Scheff got back to the ranch, Miller was even more "amped up."

"I'm going over to the (BLM) base camp to get this started," Jerad Miller told him.

Scheff alerted militia members that Miller might be unstable and shouldn't be carrying a gun. The Bundys' "security chief," Booda Bear, ran a criminal background check on Miller. He found that Miller had a long rap sheet, including a felony, and was at that moment under investigation for threatening a police officer in Indiana. Yet there he was appearing fully armed for the television cameras. Booda Bear told Miller and his wife they had to leave, apparently none too gently.

"They just told them to leave, and he cried—hysterically cried, so emotional my heart broke," Scheff said. "He wanted to do the right thing, but he didn't know how to do that."

Scheff and others at the camp who had befriended the couple offered to put the Millers up in a hotel in the nearby town of Mesquite, ostensibly to act as their "eyes and ears" there. But the Millers chose to go to Las Vegas.

"I believe Jerad was looking for a place," Scheff said. "He wanted to make a difference, he wanted to leave a mark. He was looking for someplace to belong."

Melissa Chan later reflected on how much Miller was a creature of the universe that existed in the minds of the Bundy ranch standoff participants: "They all said stuff similar to what Jerad Miller said," she told me. "So, how do you differentiate the ones who are just the talkers from the ones who actually pull the trigger? It's unclear to me."

Miller was bitterly disappointed about being ousted from the Bundy ranch, and complained at length to his friends about it. His posts on his Facebook page became increasingly volatile and the paranoia mounted. On March 25, he wrote: "I stand firm in my convictions and stand prepared to die for them. Come for me, free me from your slavery. Give me the death a hero deserves."

On May 2 he wrote, "There is no greater cause to die for than liberty." On June 2 he wrote that in order to restore "freedom" to the United States, the "best men" would strike for "a free and just world with our blood, sweat and tears as pavement ... I will willingly die for liberty."

Later that day he wrote: "We must prepare for war. We face an enemy that is not only well funded, but who believe they fight for freedom and justice. Those of us who know the truth and dare speak it, know that the enemy we face are indeed our brothers. Even though they share the same masters as we all do. They fail to recognize the chains that bind them. To stop this oppression, I fear, can only be accomplished with bloodshed."

On Saturday, June 7, he wrote on his Facebook page: "The dawn of a new day. May all our coming sacrifices be worth it."

The next morning was a sunny and clear Sunday in Las Vegas, a day like any other in the Nevada summers. At a small Cicis pizza shop in a suburban strip mall in the northern part of the city, two Las Vegas Metro Police officers, Igor Soldo and Alyn Beck, sat down for lunch. They probably paid little attention when Jerad Miller walked in, spoke briefly to an employee behind the counter, and then walked out—or when he walked back in with Amanda Miller and strolled past their table toward the counter.

Just as Jerad walked past Soldo, he turned back toward him, pulled out a handgun, and shot him in the back of the head, killing him instantly. Seconds later he pointed the gun at Beck and shot him in the throat as Beck reached for his gun. Beck remained alive long enough to try to return fire, at which point both Jerad and Amanda both opened fire on him and riddled him with bullets.

They strolled out of the Cicis, crossed a parking lot, and walked up a long sidewalk to a nearby Wal-Mart, long guns and packs strapped over their shoulders and handguns holstered on their hips. Jerad fired a round and began shouting, "This is a revolution!" as he entered the store.

Inside the store, the Millers continued their rampage, killing a man who attempted to pull a gun on them. Trapped, both Millers died in a hail of police bullets near the back of the store.

At the Millers' little apartment in Las Vegas, investigators found a manifesto filled with classic anti–New World Order rants. They also found a carefully laid out plan to storm an unidentified courthouse building in Las Vegas by force and then, once in control, to begin executing the public officials inside.

At the Cicis pizza shop, investigators found Jerad and Amanda Miller's calling cards. On Officer Soldo's slumped-over body the Millers had pinned a note reading: "This is the beginning of the revolution."

On Officer Beck's body, lying on the floor, they had placed a bright red-white-and-black Nazi swastika. And over that, they had covered his corpse with a flag. A bright yellow Gadsden flag: "Don't Tread On Me."

9

Bad Days on the Malheur

Donald Trump had appeared on Sean Hannity's Fox News show on April 17, several days before Cliven Bundy began holding forth on race relations, but just before the Nevada rancher was about to come on the air behind him. Trump offered his two cents on the standoff and on Bundy himself.

"I do like him. I respect him," Trump said. "He ought to go and cut a good deal right now. That's the best thing that could happen for everybody. It's really vicious. I'm not involved very much in it. I see it a little bit by watching you. But he ought to go out and cut a great deal."

Bundy's media stardom came to an abrupt end about a week later in the wake of his remarks about "Negroes." And the Millers' murderous rampage cast an even darker cloud over the whole Bundy ranch affair. But among his fellow Patriots, he had achieved a kind of godhood. And even after people packed up their guns and went home, the sense of victory in the Bundy confrontation became entrenched.

"This was a watershed moment, there's no question," said Jerry Bruckhart of the Idaho-based Operation Mutual Aid, a coalition of state militia groups he cofounded with Ryan Payne. "It's going to be recorded in history—assuming we can keep up the pressure—as the beginning of the counterrevolution."

Larry Pratt of the Gun Owners of America also hailed the Bundy ranch standoff as a historic moment for the nation. "I think that this is a very positive development that came out of the confrontation out on that ranch," said Pratt, speaking outside the NRA's annual meeting in Washington, DC. "And hopefully we will look back on what happened there as a turning point in modern American history. The American people are saying, 'Enough, no farther.'"

Bundy began making political appearances. He announced that he was leaving the Republican Party and becoming a member of the far-right Independent American Party. Later that fall, he filmed a TV ad promoting the candidacy of the Independent American Party's candidate, Kamau Bakari, an African American running for Congress in Nevada's First Congressional District.

Speaking at a gathering billed as "An Evening with Cliven Bundy" in Nevada that October, the garrulous rancher again expounded on his disdain for the federal government.

"I was really surprised that they would go this far to put their guns down we the people's throat and try to show the public, the world, the federal government has unlimited power over we the people of the state of Nevada. That isn't right, and that's not ever going to happen again in America or in the state of Nevada," Bundy said.

Emboldened by what they interpreted as the government's tepid law enforcement response at the Bundy ranch, antigovernment radicals around the country began creating confrontational situations in which they challenged the federal government's right to manage federally owned lands. The protesters thought their rights to use the land—for example for grazing their cattle—granted by the government took precedence over the government's right to manage the lands, for environmental and other concerns.

Just one month after the Bundy standoff, a parade of some fifty motorized ATVs decorated with Gadsden flags and protest signs, led by a San Juan County, Utah, county commissioner named Phil Lyman, drove into Bureau of Land Management property called Recapture Canyon that had been closed to vehicles in order to protect Native American artifacts contained therein. Members of the Bundy family were among the protesters who denounced the BLM vociferously.

"If things don't change, it's not long before shots will be fired,"

Lyman warned BLM managers. "We can avoid it. But it's not going to be by the people changing their attitudes and accepting more intrusion." Lyman was charged with misdemeanor conspiracy in organizing the ride and convicted, eventually serving a ten-day stint in jail; he continues to appeal his conviction.

While driving along rural Interstate 15 in Utah near the Nevada border, two men (one of them wearing a mask) pointed a handgun at a BLM worker in a marked federal vehicle while holding up a sign that said, "You Need To Die."

At about the same time, there was another tense confrontation between state and federal officials in Otero County, New Mexico. US Forest Service officials had been demonized by conspiracists for steps they had taken to protect the habitat of the endangered jumping mouse, which included closing gates that cut off water for grazing. On May 8 the Forest Service capitulated to the protesters and opened the gates, ending the confrontation.

A few weeks later, in May, in Burkburnett, Texas, a number of militiamen and other Patriots arrived to protest a BLM survey along a stretch of the Red River, which serves as the border between Texas and Oklahoma. The survey had been occasioned by changes over time in the location of the actual riverbed.

In mid-June, outside Nevada City, California, a self-declared sovereign citizen named Brent Douglas Cole got into a gunfight and wounded a BLM ranger and a California Highway Patrol officer near his campsite.

That July, the Department of Homeland Security reported a spike in antigovernment violence, citing these events and the Millers' rampage in particular. The "perceived success" of militias at the Bundy ranch, it stated, "likely will embolden other militia extremists and like-minded lone offenders to attempt to replicate these confrontational tactics and force future armed standoffs."

It was an accurate assessment. The Patriot militiamen were now eager for another showdown with the federal government, and they began looking for opportunities to create one.

◆

In early April 2015, just under a year after the Bundy ranch standoff, Rick Barclay, the co-owner of a mining operation deep in a BLM property called the Sugar Pine Mine, near the southwestern Oregon town of Grants Pass, began complaining among his Patriot friends that the feds were trying to force him off his claim, mainly because of a court hearing he faced over renewing his permit. The feds had a history of doing it to other backcountry miners, he claimed, and now they were harassing his operation with letters of noncompliance and demands that he improve the site and his operations.

Barclay was a friend of Joseph Rice, a local man who headed up the Josephine County Oath Keepers, based in nearby Medford. Rice and his crew offered to organize a "security operation" to keep Barclay's property safe from federal arsonists. Pretty soon the word spread among the Oath Keepers that a standoff might be brewing in Oregon. The message went up on the Oath Keepers' national website—a call for Oath Keepers to come to Barclay's rescue. And in no time at all, they began pouring in.

A protest rally on April 23 became the chief focal point. A couple hundred Patriots, including a contingent of black-clad Three Per-centers from Idaho, showed up in the parking lot of the building that housed offices of the joint BLM–Forest Service in Medford and waved signs and gave speeches over a PA system. The BLM and Forest Service opted to close the door to their building as a safety measure.

The action was led by Rice, a bearded veteran and helicopter pilot. "I took an oath to uphold the Constitution against enemies foreign and domestic, and a domestic enemy is anyone who will abuse some-one's rights within that Constitution," Rice told the crowd. "Today it is the BLM, because they did not allow the due process to occur. They need to seriously look at their administrative process and pro-cedures and address that. It's a cultural issue. We saw it a year ago. Here we are again today. It doesn't seem to be willing to change or improve that."

The Oath Keepers and assorted militiamen created an encamp-ment just outside Grants Pass in the town of Merlin, in an open space next to the freeway. Rows of Gadsden and American flags fluttered in the breeze. Over the next couple of weeks, several hundred Patriots drifted in from around the country to take part in the new standoff. Although it wasn't an official standoff.

"This is *not* a standoff with BLM," Barclay insisted. "We are *not* promoting any confrontation with BLM. This is a security operation for the protection of constitutional rights."

People in Grants Pass were dismayed by the militiamen's presence, and an array of local community leaders held a press conference on April 24 at the Josephine County courthouse at which the locals asked the militiamen to leave and go back to their homes. Rice and several other Oath Keepers and Three Percenters showed up and stood in the back and heckled them.

Finally, on May 25, a federal administrative judge in Washington, DC, granted Barclay his request that the BLM be restrained from enforcing its mining codes on his claim until his case could be adjudicated. Actually, the BLM never contested Barclay's right to his day in court, saying it had no intention of trying to burn Barclay out or take any other action until they had a court ruling. Barclay and the Oath Keepers declared victory, and the gathering of militiamen scattered back to their homes.

The Patriots' next attempt at re-creating a Bundy-like standoff occurred near the tiny western Montana logging town of Lincoln, where a couple of mine owners operating on US Forest Service property were raising the alarm about pending federal oppression in the form of a Justice Department lawsuit requiring them to follow federal mining regulations.

Operators of the White Hope Mine, a few miles outside Lincoln, had been building roads and constructing buildings at the site without following the usual permitting process. They too believed the feds were planning to burn them out.

On August 5, the Oath Keepers issued another call for "all American patriots" to join their planned "Operation Big Sky." The sponsors of the action included the Idaho Three Percenters, who had been in Medford, and a new Oregon-based Patriot organization run by a man named B. J. Soper called the Pacific Patriot Network. Once again, armed militiamen came flooding into the small town, though this time in much smaller numbers. At its peak, the White Hope Mine "security operation" attracted only around a hundred participants.

The hoped-for standoff never materialized, in part because the Forest Service that summer was feverishly focused on dealing with a wave of forest fires that were sweeping the region, leaving western Montanans in a cloudy thick haze of smoke that settled over every valley and left people wheezing. The local support for the Oath Keepers and Three Percenters was especially thin, since they were protesting against the very agency that was hard at work trying to save people's homes and communities.

After the Justice Department filed its lawsuit against the miners on August 11, and they began having their hearings in court, the Oath Keepers again declared themselves largely satisfied—but also promised to continue their vigilance in the weeks ahead. And indeed, the Idaho-based Three Percenters continued to maintain "security operations" at the mine site for a couple more weeks, but that action, too, eventually fizzled out. Especially because they had found bigger fish to fry.

People always recognized Eric "EJ" Parker at these events. He was the young man from Hailey, Idaho, who had been photographed at the scene of the Bundy ranch standoff as tensions reached their peak, prone on the asphalt, aiming his rifle through the freeway jersey barrier. Tall, slender, bearded, and always sporting shades, the thirty-one-year-old was a hero among the Patriot set, and as he helped lead the black-clad Three Percent of Idaho, as they officially named themselves, at the Grants Pass and Lincoln events, people treated him like a celebrity.

Not so well known was the founder and real leader of the group, a Meridian, Idaho, property manager named Brandon Curtiss. Curtiss was somewhat shorter and less physically imposing, but he was a dynamic group leader who was eager to engage his militiamen in issues well beyond land-use disputes. Parker was officially vice president of Three Percent of Idaho; Curtiss was the president and chief organizer.

After the fizzled standoff attempts in Grants Pass and Lincoln in the spring and summer of 2015, Curtiss turned his attention to other issues in which the militiamen could assert their presence. In August, some of his Threepers showed up at Boise-area military-recruiting stations in the wake of an Islamist terror attack on a station in Tennessee, vowing to defend local recruiters who were prohibited by military rule from carrying arms. In short order, their focus became what they called "the Islamic threat."

The object of the militiamen's ire was the College of Southern Idaho's refugee resettlement program, which had been helping people fleeing war- and conflict-torn countries resettle in the Twin Falls, Idaho, area since 1980. In the fall of 2015, as word spread that the program planned to take in several hundred refugees from Syria's civil war, resistance to the program had become a hot political topic in the Magic Valley, as this portion of the Snake River was called, much of it reflective of the recent nationwide tide of Islamophobia.

The Three Percenters first made their presence felt in the controversy over the refugee program when they organized a march in Twin Falls on October 17, which drew several dozen participants. At that march, Brandon Curtiss explained the group's rationale for becoming involved in the issue in an interview with an antigovernment website, the *Voice of Idaho*: "What we want to do, we want to take care of Idahoans first, and we are tired of them taking the dwindling resources we already have for the state of Idaho, and funneling that over to refugee programs to help these guys coming in here, and ignoring our Idaho citizens—our homeless, our veterans, our students that need help here first. We're not against refugees, what we're saying is, we need a better process," he told the *Voice of Idaho*'s Michael Emry. "They're draining our dwindling resources that's already in place and not looking out for Idahoans first, or US citizens for that matter," he added.

On November 1, Three Percent of Idaho led a contingent of marchers to the steps of the Idaho statehouse and held a rally denouncing the refugee program. "Now, refugees coming from Islamic hotbeds of terrorism, don't you think that poses a threat to Idaho communities?" shouted a Three Percent of Idaho spokesman, Chris McIntire, into a bullhorn.

"YEAH!!!!" shouted the gathered protesters.

Three weeks later, on November 22, interfaith leaders around Idaho organized a rally of their own in defense of the refugees and the assistance program on the statehouse steps. Over 1,000 people showed up to voice their support, waving signs with messages such as "Idaho Is Too Great to Hate" and "Refugees Welcome." Curtiss and his Threepers, accompanied by people waving signs with anti-Muslim messages ("Ban Islam! Deport All Muslims," read one; "Raghead Retreads From The Islamic Plant In The White House—Just Say No! To BHO," read another) organized their own counterprotest across the street, but only a hundred or so showed. They were badly outnumbered. But the anti-refugee crowd was undeterred by the meager showing, chanting "Veterans first! Veterans first!" and "USA! USA! USA!" One man shouted, "Hey, while you're teaching your kids to play with everybody else, they're teaching their kids to kill yours! Remember that!"

Near the end, some pro-refugee demonstrators crossed the street and attempted to engage the Patriots in civil conversation. It did not work out so well.

One man wearing a US Army jacket, who had been flipping off the pro-refugee side throughout the rally, began screaming at the people who approached him to talk, and at one point reached over to grab the head of a woman speaking to him, whereupon police intervened and separated them.

The man continued shouting at the refugees' defenders. "Hey, go back to your candy-cane, candy clowns, unicorn, kumbayah world, where you've got no life experience!"

Nearby, a woman shouted through a bullhorn, "We don't want to shake hands with people who are selling America out. Don't you get it? We love our country!"

◆

Despite the addition of Islamophobia to the menu of themes, the standoff at Bundy ranch, and the tussle over the right to use federal lands that it was about was never far from the minds of the Idaho Three Percenters and the rest of the Patriot Nation. Ammon Bundy moved from Nevada to Idaho that summer, taking up residence near Emmett, about an hour's drive from Brandon Curtiss's place, and just a hop, skip, and jump from the Oregon line. The two men began talking. A fresh opportunity was arising in Burns, Oregon, south of the Malheur National Forest.

Two Burns-area ranchers—Dwight Hammond, seventy-three, and his son, Steven, forty-six—had set a couple of backfires on federal land near their property and had been charged and convicted in 2012 of two counts of arson. They accepted a plea bargain and the prosecutor intended to seek the mandatory minimum sentence of five years. But for reasons never fully explained, the judge agreed with the Hammonds' lawyer that the required sentences were unconstitutional and handed them lighter sentences: three months for Dwight Hammond and a year for Steven Hammond.

The US Attorney for Oregon appealed the case, arguing that the sentences had been shortened inappropriately. Both men had been long released when, in October 2015, a federal appeals court restored the original five-year minimum sentence and ordered the men back to prison to serve out their time. Many ranchers in the area thought the new sentence was deeply unfair, and the Hammonds' case began to attract the attention of the Patriots.

The Hammond family had been warring with the federal government, and the BLM in particular, for years, and in fact had been leading figures in the so-called Sagebrush Revolt in Western states in the 1990s. Dwight and Steven Hammond had first been arrested by federal agents in 1994, the culmination of a simmering dispute over public lands and cattle grazing on the Malheur National Wildlife Refuge, a national bird sanctuary that was adjacent to their ranch. The two men were charged with obstructing and threatening federal workers who had been building a fence designed to keep the Hammonds' cattle from wandering into the refuge.

In its coverage of the case the *High Country Times* described Dwight Hammond as "a hot-tempered eastern Oregon cattle rancher [who had] galvanized a nasty campaign of retribution against the US Fish and Wildlife Service" and had "made death threats against federal land agency managers."

The Hammonds later paid some fines, after federal prosecutors reduced them to misdemeanors, and walked free. But that was not the end of the story.

In 2001, despite having received a warning from the BLM that they couldn't burn public lands without prior approval, the Hammonds once again lit a backfire (a blaze set intentionally to prevent the spread of a larger fire) on their property that soon spread to BLM land.

The Ninth Circuit Court of Appeals later heard evidence that "although the Hammonds claimed that the fire was designed to burn off invasive species on their property, a teenage relative of theirs testified that Steven had instructed him to drop lit matches on the ground so as to 'light up the whole country on fire.'" Soon the flames were up to ten feet high. The fire wound up burning 139 acres of BLM land and took the acreage out of production for two growing seasons.

That did not seem to teach the Hammonds a lesson. In 2006 they lit another backfire that once again spread to BLM land. This time there was less damage, because BLM firefighters spotted the blaze early and extinguished it. After several years' investigation, the Justice Department filed arson charges against the Hammonds in 2010, but in the aforementioned trial, which took place in 2012, their sentences were inexplicably lightened, which the appeals court corrected three years later.

The case caught the attention of Ammon Bundy, who was outraged that the men had been convicted under an antiterrorism statute. He began posting about it on social media in November 2015, getting the attention of his Idaho Three Percenter friends. He also contacted Ryan Payne—the Montanan who had become the camp overseer at the Bundy ranch and who still operated the Operation

Mutual Defense network that connected militiamen ready for action nationally—and asked him to become involved. Bundy, Payne, and a contingent of about twelve other Patriots from Oregon and Idaho met with the Hammond family in mid-November to figure out what they could do to help.

It was an emotional, daylong meeting. Bundy and the militiamen wanted to lead another Bunkerville-style standoff, with a ring of armed Patriots surrounding the Hammond ranch and refusing federal marshals any entry. But the Hammonds wanted nothing like that; they pleaded for a simple community rally in their support in Burns.

Bundy and Payne apparently were not satisfied with that. The two men found a place to rent in Burns and by early December 2015 had taken up residence there. Payne later told the *Oregonian* that he had moved there to take up surveillance with a possible occupation in mind. Such an occupation, Payne said, would allow the Patriots to simultaneously highlight the Hammonds' story and address what he called the "economic warfare" inflicted on American citizens through federal ownership of massive public land tracts such as the Malheur refuge. Payne told the *Oregonian* that he realized in November, "You can't do that work from a rally. It takes more time. Luckily," he added, "we the people have been provided the means to do that because the federal government has provided facilities through legal plunder."

Bundy tried to persuade both the local citizens and the local sheriff to come to the Hammonds' aid. He and Payne organized a December 16 gathering at the local Memorial Building, which was attended by about seventy people who listened to Bundy expound on constitutional theory and why the community should create a refuge for the Hammond family. The group organized a "committee of safety" designed to take action to protect local residents.

BLM officials became aware that Bundy and Payne were in the area and circulated their photos among their staff, telling them to "be on the outlook" for them. Sure enough, Payne and a few others showed up for several days near a construction project on the refuge, and were observed surveilling the area with binoculars.

In the meantime, some of the Patriots who had been involved in the original meeting with the Hammond family were proceeding with the plan the Hammonds had requested—holding a public rally in Burns protesting the government's treatment of the Hammonds and generally supporting their cause. B. J. Soper of the new Pacific Patriots Network took the lead role in putting this rally together, while Brandon Curtiss rallied all of his Idaho Three Percenters behind the protest and pitched in with logistics. Joseph Rice, the Oath Keepers leader from Josephine County, also pitched in.

The event, announced in mid-December, was scheduled for January 2, 2016, the Saturday after New Year's Day, to be held in the Safeway Stores parking lot. Excitement for the event in the weeks preceding it grew intense in Patriot circles on the Internet. An Arizona militiaman named Jon Ritzheimer posted a video on Facebook explaining tearfully to his young daughters why he had driven all the way to Oregon: "Your daddy swore an oath—he swore an oath to protect and defend the Constitution, against all enemies, foreign and domestic, and that's why he couldn't be with you on Christmas. It's why I can't be with you on New Year's.

"The oppression and the tyranny that has taken place here in Oregon—we know it's taken place all across the US. The Bundy ranch was a prime example. And we the people need to take a stand. And I am 100 percent willing to lay my life down to fight against tyranny in this country," he said.

Ritzheimer had already attracted a national following with his Islamophobic rants and gun-oriented protests, which had led him to try to organize a nationwide armed protest of various mosques around the country in the summer and autumn of 2015, but these events had mostly fizzled out.

On December 28, Ritzheimer and a couple of other Patriot leaders, a video raconteur named Blaine Cooper and an Arizona militiaman, Joseph O'Shaughnessy, issued a YouTube video featuring a "call to arms" to Patriots around the country in which O'Shaughnessy announced, "This is a call-out to all Patriots, constitutionalists, militias, and good Americans who believe in the Constitution." Cooper chimed in: "This is a call to action in Burns, Oregon, and we all will be present."

Tensions had been building in the community. Some locals, mostly federal employees and their families, reported that they had been harassed by strange men from out of town who followed them home in their cars from school and work. On Thursday, December 30, the BLM locked up all of its offices early and told its employees to just stay home, away from work, through the weekend. There was hope that things would settle down.

Saturday was a frigid, crystal-clear day. About 300 Patriots showed up, and none seemed to mind the crisp, single-digit cold and layer of snow. Soper, of the Pacific Patriots Network, and Curtiss were ecstatic at the turnout at the staging area in the Safeway parking lot. They pulled a flatbed trailer into one of the parking spots and converted it into a stage with a PA system, and an array of speakers kept coming up to speak through the bullhorn: members of Oath Keepers and Three Percenters, and assorted camo-clad and gun-toting militiamen. No sheriff's deputies or Oregon State Police officers or their vehicles were anywhere to be seen.

Local residents watching the rally told the Southern Poverty Law Center's reporter Bill Morlin they didn't see any Burns residents— not even the extended Hammond family—participating in the rally.

"They're just using this issue to push their own agendas," one longtime Burns resident, Beebee Stiz, said as she watched the demonstrators gather in the supermarket lot. "I want them to go home. We take care of ourselves here."

Richard Mack was in the crowd, according to a Constitutional Sheriffs and Peace Officers Association (CSPOA) official, as was the extremist radio host Pete Santilli.

Waving a colorful array of flags, especially the bright yellow Gadsden banner, and signs denouncing the federal government, the demonstrators joined to sing "God Bless America," and then marched down Burns's main street to the Harney County sheriff's office. The front door was locked. Ammon Bundy handed out rolls of pennies for the crowd to toss out in front of the sheriff's office, to mock Sheriff Dave Ward for "[selling] out to the feds."

The march continued on to the county courthouse, where speakers again demanded that county officials step up to protect the Hammonds, and further denunciations of federal "tyranny" were heard. Eventually, people began getting in their cars to head to the county fairgrounds for a closing event featuring more speeches.

As they were departing, though, Ammon Bundy stood up on a large snow bank and began exhorting demonstrators to take "a harder stand" with him. He told them he was headed for the Malheur refuge, and urged people to come with him. As he walked to his car, he talked to a TV reporter and explained what he meant by a "harder stand":

"As you can see, Dwight and Steven Hammond are salt-of-the-earth people, and that's what this country is about. It's about defending individuals from exactly what is happening to them. Some good American men are going to prison ... It's time to make a stand and to do what is right. And if that takes an effort like this protest, or if it takes an effort—a hard stand, which is happening today, to reverse these things, then I am willing to do it."

Bundy went on to repeat the point that "this was not just about [the Hammonds], this was about America." The reporter asked him if they really thought they could make a difference in this case.

"Absolutely. We can enforce the Constitution in Harney County. And that's what we intend to do."

Asked what he meant by that, he demurred: "We have a lot of plans, but as far as going into any details with you, I can't do that right now."

Then he and several carfuls of fellow Patriots, including his brother Ryan Bundy, headed out in their cars to their real destination that day, a little over thirty miles away down Highway 205: the Malheur National Wildlife Refuge.

◆

Walter Eaton was an elderly local Burns Patriot and ardent supporter of the Hammonds who had at first been skeptical about Bundy, Payne, and their crew of outsiders. But after talking with them he had become a wholehearted believer in their protest plans. He later testified that he wasn't really sure what they meant when they talked about an "occupation" of the refuge, though.

When he got into the car with Ryan Payne that afternoon, he thought they were headed to the fairgrounds with everyone else. Instead, Payne turned and headed south out of town, and drove directly to the refuge.

When they arrived, a cadre of armed men were already there, fanning out from building to building to see if any of them were occupied by any federal workers. Some of the buildings were open, he said, and some weren't. The main central building at the refuge complex was apparently still locked, so no one had entered it at that point.

Fearful that he was breaking federal laws, Eaton said he watched the operation for about a half hour and then took off on foot down the road, back toward the highway, where he eventually hitched a ride back into Burns.

At some point, the men taking over the refuge found a ring of keys and gained entry to the main building, as well as all the other buildings at the facility and the locked gates around it. They unlocked the gates and let in a number of fellow occupiers. By morning, their occupation of the refuge was complete, and the Patriots were all over the national news.

National, state, and regional media came flooding to the scene at the refuge, and were mostly welcomed eagerly at the site by the two dozen or so occupiers, who gave copious interviews to the gathered reporters.

Ammon Bundy told the *Oregonian* that he and others occupying the US Fish and Wildlife headquarters were "planning on staying here for years, absolutely. This is not a decision we've made at the last minute." Ryan Bundy told the paper that he and the assembled Patriots were "willing to kill and be killed if necessary."

Soon the occupiers were scheduling daily press conferences.

One of the more colorful occupiers was a skinny little man in a cowboy hat and wire-rim glasses who had parked himself in a rocking chair under a blue tarp along the perimeter of the refuge so that he could help keep an armed watch on the place. Robert LaVoy Finicum, fifty-four, was a Mormon rancher from Utah, and he was ready to become a martyr.

"I have been raised in the country all my life," Finicum told his interviewer, sheltered under his tarp, a rifle on his lap. "I love dearly to feel the wind on my face. To see the sun rise, to see the moon. I have no intention of spending any of my days in a concrete box."

Sheriff Ward ordered the occupiers, "Go home"—a message underscored by hundreds of county residents who showed up for a community meeting three days after the occupation began. In the meantime, behind the media army, Burns began to fill with federal and state law enforcement officers.

But the Bundy brothers refused to decamp until, they said, the federal refuge lands were in local control and the Hammonds were released. At one point, Ward met with Bundy and told him, "I am here to escort you safely out of town. I'm willing to get you an escort all the way out of the state." Bundy declined, and conversations with law enforcement ceased for the next two weeks or so. However, three weeks into the standoff, video surfaced showing FBI negotiators apparently once again engaging Bundy in a conversation.

In the meantime, media outlets reported that those involved in the takeover appeared to be well supplied and armed. On social media, the occupiers informed their followers that they were short on some home-comfort supplies, and posted a mailing address in case anyone wanted to send them some care packages, listing "cold weather socks, snacks, energy drinks … anything you think will help."

The plea went viral on Facebook and elsewhere, on all sides of the political landscape. Critics of the standoff created the mocking hashtag #YAllQaeda for the Malheur occupiers, and the plea gained huge play there. Soon the mailing address was flooded with donations from all over the country, mainly items that expressed ridicule of the occupiers: glitter, nail polish, pedicure socks, perfume, dildoes, and penis-shaped candies.

Jon Ritzheimer was furious, and posted a video that showed him emptying out a boxful of the mock donations, mostly sex toys, onto a table, while fuming, "They spend and waste their money on all this hateful stuff to send out here to us and buy this ridiculous stuff. It's really ridiculous, even the—this one was really funny, a bag of dicks. So rather than going out and doing good ... they just spend all their money on hate, and hate, and hate, and hate. So we're gonna clear the table and we're gonna continue to do work and do good for our country. We're not gonna be deterred." And he swept all the goodies off the table and onto the floor with his arm.

Indeed, the occupation was not greeted with open arms by the Bundys' usual allies in the Patriot movement. B. J. Soper of the Pacific Patriots Network, who had largely organized that day's rally, was one of those who expressed dismay at the takeover and told reporters he felt "betrayed" by Bundy's actions.

Brandon Curtiss and most of his Three Percent of Idaho militiamen turned around and headed home that Saturday, refusing to participate.

The next day a group of organizations issued a press release that stated:

> The 3 percent of Idaho, 3 percent of Oregon, The Oregon Constitutional Guard, and PPN [Patriot Pacific Network] organizations in no way condone nor support these actions. They do not mirror our vision, mission statement, or views in regards to upholding the Constitution, The Rule of Law, or Due Process.

Richard Mack of CSPOA also issued a statement denouncing the action:

> CSPOA does not support or condone the occupation by those individuals who have taken over the Federal Wildlife building just outside Burns, OR. With all our hearts we appeal to all those occupying the federal facility to immediately vacate the building and to go home to their families!

Stewart Rhodes, president of the Oath Keepers, the antigovernment group that was a major participant in the Bundy ranch standoff in 2014, backed away from any involvement in the takeover and released a statement:

> By doing this, they have given Obama the best New Years present he could hope for—an example of militia movement/patriot aggression, which gives up the high ground while also having the least credibility and support from the locals possible, after lying to them, and also the least support from the patriot community, who were also blind-sided by Ammon and Ryan Payne.

Alex Jones took that speculation to the next level, claiming on his daily show that the Oregon standoff was actually the work of agents provocateur who had swindled the Bundys into taking their course of action: "Guaranteed provocateurs are showing up and other things are happening, the whole Soros group is saying, 'Here are our white terrorists, here are our cowboy-hat wearing terrorists,' it gives them the backdrop they need, they want to start a civil war," he told his national audience.

He elaborated the circumstances into a new conspiracy theory: "Ladies and gentlemen, don't let Obama be successful when it comes to starting civil unrest and riots in this country. They will use that as a civil emergency to bring in a type of soft martial law."

Mike Vanderboegh, the national cofounder of the Three Percent movement, was equally conspiratorial and vociferous at his blog: "My initial reaction was to observe that at least afterward we'll know who the federal snitches are because they will be the only ones who survive the raid to take back the building," he wrote.

> There is nothing on the talking heads channels as yet, but by Monday, when Obama meets with his Attorney General on the subject of citizen disarmament, you can bet the farm that this will play right into that narrative. Perfect timing. You've got to give the federal handlers of these pukes credit. This is precisely the sort of offensive action on the part of the "militia terrorists" that they needed.

For their part, the Bundys and their militia cohort were defiant, insisting that the cause of the Hammond family was worth "taking a stand" over.

Ammon Bundy also issued a videotaped response to Rhodes and other critics, claiming that he had been called by God to stand up on behalf of the Hammonds. "I have respect for Stewart Rhodes," Bundy said. "But he does not understand what is truly transpiring, or he has chosen to be in opposition."

Bundy went on to explain that he had come to envision the plan to take over the wildlife refuge because God led him there. "And so I am asking you to come to Harney County—to make the decision right now, of whether this is a righteous cause or not, whether I am some crazy person—or whether the Lord truly works through individuals to get his purposes accomplished. I know that we are to stand now, and that we are to do these things now, or we will not have anything to pass on to our children."

Over the next several weeks, as the standoff dragged along, sentiments within the larger Patriot movement began to shift. The standoff began to take on a veneer of legitimacy, of historicity, and gradually more and more Patriots were drawn to its defense, but still, internecine tensions surfaced.

Brandon Curtiss and his Three Percent of Idaho militiamen returned to Burns on January 9, offering to serve as a buffer between federal agents and the occupiers. Bundy and the militants inside the refuge sent out an attorney to deliver their reply: thanks, but no thanks. The Idaho contingent packed up and went back home that afternoon.

Over the next couple of weeks, LaVoy Finicum, who had a sprightly knack for dishing out media-friendly sound bites, became one of the occupiers' chief spokesmen, giving dozens of interviews. In an exchange with a *Washington Post* reporter, he said, "It needs to be very clear that these buildings will never, ever return to the federal government."

◆

For the most part, the occupiers came and went from the refuge at will, frequently traveling out of town altogether. Some Bundy supporters claimed on social media they were rotating in and out of the headquarters to return home for rest or to watch the NFL playoffs before returning to the Malheur refuge.

Several of them—it's unclear who, exactly—drove north around January 10 to neighboring Grant County and met at a restaurant there with Sheriff Glenn Palmer, a CSPOA-affiliated "constitutional sheriff" who had been the organization's "lawman of the year" in its first year of existence, 2012.

The men pleaded with Palmer to become involved in the standoff by taking Sheriff Ward's place as the chief law officer in the region. Palmer declined, but that wasn't the end of his involvement.

Others seemed to travel freely as well. Ammon Bundy returned to his home in Idaho at least once, and LaVoy Finicum also made a brief return to Utah. It looked as though government officials were hesitant to act. The only exception occurred January 15, when one occupier, Kenneth Medenbach, sixty-two, of Crescent, Oregon, drove a government truck he took from the refuge into town and was arrested for driving stolen property.

In the meantime the occupiers were trashing the refuge in full public view. On January 20, they bulldozed and excavated two large trenches and a new road through an area near the center that had been set aside as an archaeological dig for ancient Native American artifacts. One of the trenches became converted into a latrine for the entire encampment to use. Soon the trench was filled with raw sewage that covered the artifacts. The occupiers also rifled through a warehouse filled with native artifacts, and LaVoy Finicum made a video in which he rifled through the boxes and carelessly tossed the items about, promising to return them to their "rightful owners."

Media accounts documented that some of the occupiers were illegally using federal computers, and accessing employees' personal information. They also made illegal use of federal land-moving equipment and damaged or destroyed BLM fencing by cutting it down.

Law enforcement officials were watching closely. Oregon's US attorney, Billy J. Williams, and his assistant prosecutors remained mum, but it became clear that they were doing research in preparation for senior Justice Department officials to bring criminal charges.

Two weeks into the standoff, the SPLC reported that prosecutors had likely already obtained "secret grand jury indictments and warrants that FBI agents would use when they deem the time is right to make arrests, likely avoiding any violent confrontation."

Earlier that week, in a letter addressed to law enforcement and military forces and framed as a "warning," Stewart Rhodes cautioned law enforcement to "tread lightly" in dealing with the occupiers.

"This is not an emergency situation, unless you turn it into one," Rhodes said, laying preemptive blame on federal authorities for any escalation that might come. "These ranchers, cowboys, and veterans just happen to be armed, as westerners tend to be. Get over it. There are no hostages, there are no close-by neighbors at risk, there is nobody there except those who want to be."

The Bundys had remained in contact with Sheriff Glenn Palmer up in Grant County, and he had agreed to host a public gathering there, in the county seat of John Day, at which Ammon and Ryan Bundy would address local residents and recruit their support. It was to be held at 6 p.m. at the local senior center on January 26.

But the speakers never showed.

Around 4 p.m. that afternoon, a black Jeep SUV and a large white Dodge four-door pickup with a full cab pulled out of the refuge. Ammon Bundy was driving the Jeep, and LaVoy Finicum was driving the pickup. They were headed for John Day, 100 miles and two hours' drive to the north of the refuge.

The trip was uneventful for the first forty-five minutes or so. They passed through Burns quickly and headed up Highway 395 toward Grant County, Finicum in the lead. When they had gotten about seventy miles out of town, all hell broke loose in a blizzard of red and blue lights and, eventually, bullets.

Oregon State Police officers sprung the trap, with FBI and other federal agents on the scene to act as backup and support. Two OSP vehicles came up behind Ammon Bundy's Jeep and pulled it over. Bundy and his passengers surrendered peacefully there.

LaVoy Finicum continued driving, until he encountered a large police SUV blocking his path on the highway, and two more OSP vehicles came up behind him with lights blazing. He stopped and opened his window. Ryan Payne, sitting in the passenger seat, opened his window and stuck out a rifle in warning. Ryan Bundy was in the back seat, along with Shawna Cox, one of the few female occupiers, and an eighteen-year-old supporter from Montana named Victoria Sharp, who had come with her Patriot family out to Oregon to sing as a chorus for the occupiers at one of their public gatherings in Burns.

Officers got out of their vehicles and opened their doors, taking up firing positions; others approached the pickup cautiously from both the front and the rear. Ryan Payne promptly opened the passenger-side door, got out, and surrendered.

LaVoy Finicum began yelling at the police from his window, "If you're gonna shoot me, do it now. Just put the bullet right through my head. Because we going to see the sheriff."

The shouting continued for several minutes, with Ryan Bundy joining in the exchange. Bundy got out his cell phone and tried calling Joseph Rice, but they were out of cell-phone range.

"You've got to realize, we've got people on the way. If you want a bloodbath, it's going to be on your hands. We're going to go see the sheriff."

Ryan Bundy began sounding panicked. "We should never have stopped. We should never have stopped," he said. "Where's the guns?"

Everyone else inside the pickup, anticipating they would be shot at, agreed to duck down low in their seats and let LaVoy just drive on. Finicum put his foot on the gas and the pickup took off at high speed. The OSP officers clambered back into their vehicles and took off in pursuit.

At first, it seemed to the truck's occupants as though Finicum's gambit might work. Careering up the winding roads, they managed to get about a mile away from where they had been pulled over. But when they came around a curve, three vehicles blocked the roadway. More OSP officers were positioned in the woods off to the sides. Inside the pickup, occupants heard a bullet strike their vehicle.

Still hurtling along at high speed, Finicum—shouting "Hang on!"—tried steering the pickup around the roadblock and into the snowy roadside. Narrowly missing an FBI agent who had jumped out to flag them down, the truck quickly became bogged down and came to a sudden stop.

LaVoy Finicum leapt out of the driver's seat and into the deep snow, even as two more shots rang out, fired by an FBI agent. "Go ahead and shoot me!" he shouted. "Go ahead and shoot me!"

He staggered in the snow a bit as two OSP officers approached him, ordering him, "Get down on the ground! Get down on the ground!"

"You're gonna have to shoot me!" he shouted repeatedly. Then he reached inside his jacket for his gun. The two officers fired three shots into Finicum—in the shoulder, the chest, and the abdomen. Ten minutes later he was pronounced dead at the scene.

Ryan Bundy surrendered peacefully. He had gotten a minor shrapnel wound when one FBI agent fired two shots at the pickup's cab. The two women in the back seat surrendered with him, after police shot tear-gas rounds into the vehicle.

The next day, Victoria Sharp, the eighteen-year-old from Montana, told reporter Kyung Lah from CNN that Finicum had been murdered in cold blood: "He had his hands up," Sharp said. "He was shouting that if they were going to shoot, then just shoot him. I remember him saying that if they shoot him, it's an innocent man's blood on their hands … I was just a few feet away." Sharp had heard Finicum, but video shot inside the cab showed that she had not seen him.

Thus was a new Patriot martyr born.

◆

Michele Fiore, the Nevada legislator who had participated in the media festivities at the Bundy ranch, was actually the first to spread the "LaVoy was murdered" meme. Only a few hours after the shooting, as the word spread like wildfire on the Internet and social media, she sent out a tweet: "My heart & prays [*sic*] go out to LaVoy Finicum's family he was just murdered with his hands up in Burns OR."

Fiore told the *Oregonian*'s Les Zaitz that she had spoken with Finicum's widow, Jeanette, by phone, and had been informed that Bundy told his wife that Finicum was cooperating with officials and was lying on the ground with his hands up when he was shot three times.

"America was fired upon by our government and one of liberty's finest patriots is fallen," the Bundy ranch posted on Facebook shortly after the shooting. "He will not go silent into eternity. Our appeal is to heaven."

"Tonight peaceful Americans were attacked on a remote road for supporting the Constitution," read a graphic meme accompanying the post. "One was killed. Who are the terrorists?"

Within a few days, Oregon State Police had released complete video files of the shooting, which showed from multiples angles exactly what happened. They showed Finicum shouting at the officers to shoot him. They showed him reaching inside his jacket. They showed him tumbling on his back into the snow.

A few weeks later, the state's independent investigation, by the Deschutes County Sheriff's Office, in Bend, vindicated the officers, although the FBI agent who had fired off the two rounds as Finicum was exiting the truck tried to hide that fact during the investigation and wound up being disciplined.

None of this information quieted the Patriots. In fact, it seemed to fuel their anger even more, especially as the Finicum family continued to insist, video evidence notwithstanding, that LaVoy had been shot with his hands in the air. They also claimed he had been shot nine times, not the three that his autopsy showed.

Alex Jones's conspiracy mill weighed in promptly as well. "Was LaVoy Finicum Murdered By the FBI?" shouted the headline at *Infowars*. Reporter Paul Joseph Watson's conclusion: probably. Ten months later, Watson and Jones were still peddling "Finicum Was Murdered" conspiracy theories.

In no time at all, the threats began rolling in.

Oregon Public Broadcasting reported that a post on social media urged other extremists to "kill cops because they are cops, if for no other reason. Just walk up asking for directions and shoot them in the [expletive] face."

The Deschutes County Sheriff's Office later released redacted samples of threats received by various public officials and law enforcement. Some of the threats came from people who appeared to use their real names, but many threats were anonymous.

Oregon's governor, Kate Brown, was one of the targets. One anonymous caller left the message "We're going to shoot to kill" at the governor's office the day Finicum was shot. "Yeah, Kate Brown authorizing federal agents to use deadly force," the caller continued. "Fuck you. You'd better watch your back, bitch."

The FBI moved swiftly. Others arrested on January 26 included the surviving members of the brief highway confrontation: Ammon and Ryan Bundy; Ryan Payne; Shawna Cox, fifty-six, from Kanab, Utah; and Brian Cavalier, forty-four, from Bunkerville. Later that evening, in Burns, Oregon State Police arrested Joseph O'Shaughnessy, the Arizona militiaman who had joined Jon Ritzheimer in making the national "call-out" in late December. They all faced federal felony charges of conspiracy to impede officers of the United States from discharging their official duties through the use of force, intimidation, or threats. Pete Santilli was also picked up and charged with conspiracy counts. The next day Jon Ritzheimer surrendered to authorities in Mesa, Arizona, where he had returned to visit his family.

After the arrests and the death of Finicum, most of the assembled occupiers at the refuge scattered back to their homes. When the snow had settled, only twelve occupiers remained. This group, some of whom faced arrest when they left, adamantly insisted they would not leave. But the next day, after brief negotiations, eight of them walked out. Three were taken into custody and charged, and five walked free.

Four holdouts would not budge: David Fry, Jeff Banta, and Sean and Sandy Anderson, a middle-aged married couple from Riggins, Idaho. After talking things over with federal agents for a couple of days, the four announced on January 29 they would remain inside the center until their supplies ran out. But talks resumed the next day, and continued for the next two weeks.

The foursome did not remain inside the refuge's administrative building the entire time. They often ventured outside, tinkering with the land-moving equipment and making videos that they shared on social media. Posted on the occupiers' YouTube channel, the videos provide a glimpse inside the straggling remnant of Patriots. Sean and Sally Anderson posted a video titled "Husband and Wife—Maybe Last Dance?" in which they danced, outside the building, to a sad-sounding country-and-western tune.

Several of the holdouts' videos showed that they believed they had the feds surrounded and that it was just a matter of time before good, God-fearing, red-blooded American patriots stood up and said, "Enough is enough" and sent the FBI and the Oregon State Patrol packing.

Another video showed Sean Anderson freaking out:

> The media has been ordered to leave—that means they're coming to kill us, and they don't [want] them to see that. They're gonna murder all of us! And the medias are cowards! ...
>
> The media's been waiting for a bloodbath, this whole time we been here. Now there's gonna be one, and they're running! They're told to run, because the feds don't want anyone to know who's murdering us?!
>
> American people better wake up, get here, and fight for your country! Right now! It is on! ...
>
> There are no laws in this United States now! This is free-for-all Armageddon! Any military, or law enforcement, or feds that stand up and fuck their oath, don't abide by their oath, are the enemy! If they try to stop you, kill them!

A few days later, on February 10, David Fry went on a high-speed romp in an all-terrain vehicle, wheeling past the police barricades before returning to the center in a hurry. The police saw the provocation as an escalation and began drawing in their perimeter around the refuge center. The holdouts observed the shift and began reporting on the escalation on a live Internet feed, begging for Representative Michele Fiore, the Nevada legislator, to come and negotiate for them. Fiore had flown into Portland anyway and was on her way to Burns when she got the message.

Fiore spent much of that evening negotiating inside with the four holdouts and then came out. The next morning she met with the Reverend Franklin Graham, who had flown from his North Carolina home to Burns in his private plane, and the FBI transported them in an armored truck to the refuge. Fiore and Graham took turns talking to the militants over a loudspeaker on the truck, urging them not to waste their lives and to come on out. They also played a tape with a message from Ammon Bundy, urging them to give themselves up.

Finally, at about 11 a.m. on February 9, all four of the holdouts came out, and were arrested.

The day before, on February 10, Cliven Bundy had flown into Portland. FBI agents greeted him at the arrival gate and arrested him. They informed him of the raft of charges against him, for crimes associated with the April 2014 standoff in Bunkerville.

The wave of arrests and indictments continued. One week later, the FBI informed Ammon and Ryan Bundy that they and their brothers David and Melvin were also being charged in connection with the Bunkerville confrontation. Two weeks after that, more indictments were handed down, and thirteen other men were arrested at their homes in various locales around the nation, including some already well-known movement leaders—Ryan Payne, Pete Santilli, Brian Cavalier, and Joseph O'Shaughnessy, already in prison for their roles in the Malheur standoff, and Eric "EJ" Parker, thirty-two, of Hailey, Idaho, who had gained notoriety as the man spread-eagled on the asphalt aiming his rifle at federal agents—and a host of the rank-and-file, from the Western states of Arizona, Idaho, and Colorado, with one from New Hampshire.

The flow of hate mail and intimidating messages increased, with much of the venom directed at the BLM. On February 26, the agency's regional office in Salt Lake City spotted a posting on Facebook demanding the release of Nevada rancher Cliven Bundy and his sons. That poster demanded the issuance of "arrest warrants for FBI agents and ... the nastiest whore in Oregon, Kate Brown, for the murder of LaVoy Finicum and false arrests of all the other protesters." If those demands weren't met, the poster threatened, "I am going to begin returning fire!!!!!! I cannot site [sic] quietly when war and lies are being levied against the United States!!!!!!"

On February 1, the Patriots had held a last rally in Burns. Their signs and slogans reflected their white-hot anger: "FBI Go Home— LaVoy Can't"; "LaVoy's Voice Lives On"; "Federal Supremacists Murdered An Innocent Man"; "YOU Murdered LaVoy!"

They came, a couple hundred strong, from around the interior West—from Idaho, Washington, Montana, and Utah—to protest on behalf of their new martyr.

Finicum's face—skinny, bespectacled, pale, wearing a cowboy hat—adorned some of the signs the protesters carried, mixed in with American flags and a yellow "Don't Tread On Me" Gadsden flag or two.

"Cold-blooded murder! Cold-blooded murder!" chanted the protesters. "He was executed!" shouted one. After a while, a new chant arose: "FBI killed LaVoy! FBI killed LaVoy!"

Right-wing websites began running wild with rumors and conspiracy theories, and social media bubbled with memes denouncing the federal government and decrying Finicum's martyrdom.

No doubt the FBI was hoping to prevent Finicum from being viewed as a martyred victim when, two days after the shooting, the agency released video of the shooting and the circumstances before and after it happened. Officials knew all too well that a toxic concoction of conspiracy theories and wild speculation—calling out federal authorities as murderers and out-of-control bullies—was brewing.

Probably the agency should have known better than to imagine that releasing the videos could contain the bile: the Patriot movement would never let an opportunity to create a good martyr go to waste. Embracing martyrdom and the idea of martyrdom is a key—an essential—element of what makes such extremist belief systems tick. The movement has a long history of attracting violent actors who are willing to both kill and be killed in the name of their extreme worldview.

Finicum had not only embraced his own martyrdom, he had foreshadowed it to reporters when he said, "I'm not going to end up in prison. I would rather die than be caged. And I've lived a good life." That kind of talk had been heard in the camp of the Malheur occupiers. A number of the militants asserted that they were "willing to die and "to kill or be killed" to defend their position. Becoming a martyr for the movement was clearly on their minds.

So when Finicum was shot, the Patriots were eager to make a martyr of him. At the site of his death, alongside Interstate 395 in a lonely, wooded stretch of rural Oregon, they erected a makeshift memorial in his honor, replete with a cross, voluminous flowers, and handmade signs: "RIP LaVoy Finicum, A True American Hero," and "The Fight Isn't Over." Someone attached a cowboy hat to the cross emblazoned with the words, "An American Hero." The memorial was later torn down by locals, and then rebuilt by indignant Patriots. Eventually, a small band of Oregon Patriots kept watch at the site for several months to prevent it from being taken down.

At the rally in Burns, the belief that Finicum had been foully murdered by out-of-control federal agents was rampant. One protester showed up with red holes in a flannel shirt she wore to demonstrate how Finicum had been "shot in the back."

"He had his hands in the air!" she insisted.

"LaVoy's blood is on your hands," another told a large group of counterdemonstrators, mostly residents of Burns and the surrounding area, while squirting out blood-colored liquid into the snow in front of them.

The following Saturday, an event was held in Boise, Idaho, to protest Finicum's death. The rally's flier warned: "In today's society, our citizens are being gunned down by our law enforcement unjustly." Participants were asked to bring signs saying, "Hands Up Don't Shoot." Similar commemorations were held around the country, from nearby John Day, Oregon, to Arizona, Kentucky, West Virginia, Florida, Ohio, Washington State, Ohio, Colorado, South Carolina, and even Massachusetts.

Overnight, it became a bedrock axiom in the Patriots' belief system that LaVoy Finicum had been murdered by federal agents. Conspiracy theories linking the Oval Office with the plot and a dozen other variations on the events all began circulating in the alt-right.

A dark cloud lingers over the affair at the Malheur, beyond the deaths and injuries that came about because of the Bundys' quixotic quest to prove the legitimacy of their "constitutionalist" fantasia. Finicum's martyrdom meant that somewhere, someday, someone would be seeking retribution—someone must pay.

The story was far from over. But then it never really is.

The Alt-Right Reinvention

The anti-Semite has chosen hate because hate is a faith; at the outset he has chosen to devaluate words and reasons ... Never believe that anti-Semites are completely unaware of the absurdity of their replies. They know that their remarks are frivolous, open to challenge. But they are amusing themselves, for it is their adversary who is obliged to use words responsibly, since he believes in words. The anti-Semites have the right to play. They even like to play with discourse for, by giving ridiculous reasons, they discredit the seriousness of their interlocutors. They delight in acting in bad faith, since they seek not to persuade by sound argument but to intimidate and disconcert.

—Jean-Paul Sartre, "Anti-Semite and Jew," 1944

On October 10, 2014, Brianna Wu, a computer-game developer who lived in Massachusetts, began receiving a series of tweets on her Twitter account from someone using the nom de plume DeathToBrianna, hostile messages such as these:

You just made a shitty game no one liked. That's it. No one will care when you die.

I hope you enjoy your last moments alive on this earth. You did nothing worthwhile with your life.

I've got a K-Bar and I'm coming to your house so I can shove it up your ugly feminist cunt.

Guess what bitch? I now know where you live. You and Frank live at [her real address].

Wu, the development chief at a game company, Giant Spacekat, and her husband called the police and that evening moved out of their home for several days; eventually they hired a bodyguard. The number of sources of the hostile tweets multiplied. Within days, they were accusing Wu of having "manufactured" the threats; they advised their readers to "incite as much butthurt as possible, so don't engage in civil reasoned debate. Flame anyone who disagrees." Two years later, Wu continued to receive such a volume of threats that she hired a staff member to track them all.

The threats directed at Wu arose from her involvement in the so-called Gamergate controversy, which revolved around the internal politics of the video-gaming community. On one side were feminists and other liberals who believe the gaming world was dominated by males, both as game developers and as members of the target audience. This group, to which Brianna Wu belonged, argued for greater inclusion of games appealing to female audiences. On the other side were males who found such talk not merely threatening but a declaration of a "culture war" against white males by a nefarious leftist conspiracy. They called the conspirators' ideology "cultural Marxism" and believed that under this banner "social justice warriors," wielding the cudgel of "political correctness," were waging a cultural war to impose the values of multiculturalism and feminism on American society.

Most of those making these arguments were white males. A whole army of them swung into action on social media and in Internet chat rooms to harass and threaten the feminists and liberals they perceived as their enemies. Brianna Wu—who, the day before the first threat arrived, had tweeted out a message mocking the Gamergaters—was one of several women who were victimized by the flood of threats.

One of the feminists' chief online assailants was a young gay man living in London named Milo Yiannopoulos, who wrote a widely read column for *Breitbart News*. In a September 2014 piece Yiannopoulos described the anti-Gamergate faction as "an army of sociopathic feminist programmers and campaigners, [who] abetted by achingly politically correct American tech bloggers, are terrorizing the entire community—lying, bullying and manipulating their way around the internet for profit and attention."

Yiannopoulos, who would later parlay his Gamergate activism into the role of *Breitbart*'s tech editor and as a leader of the emerging "alt-right" phenomenon, responded to the threats against Wu in a typically "not-my-fault-she-deserved-it" tweet: "Whoever sent those tweets deserves to be charged and punished. It was vile. But I cannot be alone in finding the response distasteful."

The controversy heralded the rise of the alt-right and provided an early sketch of its primary features: an Internet presence beset by digital trolls, unbridled conspiracism, angry-white-male-identity victimization culture, and, ultimately, open racism, anti-Semitism, ethnic hatred, misogyny, and sexual and gender paranoia. A place where human decency and ethics are considered antiquarian jokes, and empathy is only an invitation to assault.

The most earth-shaking aspect of the rise of the Internet, starting in the 1990s, may have been the liberation of information from its previous constraints in the mainstream media and the halls of officialdom. Initially, this was widely heralded as an important advancement for the democratization of our emerging globalized economy. After all, the more information that people had at their fingertips, the more they might be liberated by the truth.

Within a few years, however, it also became self-evident that there was a serious downside to all this liberation. While the constraints on information imposed by the top-down mass media pyramid that had developed in the postwar years—often to the public's long-term detriment—had seemingly been lifted, one of their important by-functions had vanished as well: the ability to filter out bad information, false or badly distorted "facts," or outrageous claims designed not just to titillate but to smear whole groups of people and to radicalize audiences against them.

The Internet made possible alternative universes such as the one inhabited by the adherents of the Patriot movement, or Alex Jones's conspiracy milieu: constructed of fabrications based on fragments, interacting with others' shared realities but operating almost entirely within its own framework. It began as a relatively small world limited largely to a fringe in the 1990s, but was resilient and grew steadily as the new century advanced. In the end, it gave birth not just to the alt-right but also to the much larger universe of Alt-America.

Traditional journalism had been largely constrained for most of the postwar period by a kind of "do no harm" ethos that prevented members of their reading and television community from the harm that could be inflicted by the thoughtless and malicious release of this kind of information—the threat of libel lawsuits being one of the chief constraints. That ethos began to vanish with the rise of the Internet, with its easy anonymity, its wanton disregard of the rules of evidence and factuality, and the loss of basic interpersonal regard required for a civil society to function. By the early 2000s, it had already become host to a swamp of conspiracy theories, false smears, and wild speculation. Extremist movements such as the Patriots found that it was an eminently hospitable place to organize.

Soon an "anything goes" attitude applied not only to the information on the Internet but also to the ruling behavioral ethos in many of its ever-expanding niches and nooks. Enter the digital troll.

Anyone who's spent much time on the Web, especially in the comments sections of articles and news stories, as well as on social media such as Facebook and Twitter, has encountered a troll. Most likely many of them.

They are the usually anonymous creatures who lurk under the bridges of our discourse on the Internet, and whose entire reason for being is to disrupt and destroy that discourse by anyone crossing those bridges: lobbing insults, non sequiturs, off-topic remarks, and racial or religious incendiary grenades. Their chief tactic is called flaming, merciless abuse of their target. They are not interested in debate, only in the destruction of your viewpoint through aggressive abuse.

The term "trolling" originally referred to the act of fishing with a long line, dropping your lure out deep behind you and slowly chugging around whatever lake or sea you might be on until some nice, not-so-smart fish took your bait and you hooked him, then slowly reeled him in. That more or less describes the behavior of digital trolls, too, as they cruise blogs and chat rooms and forums and Twitter accounts in search of fresh gullible suckers to reel in.

Initially, trolling was considered a relatively harmless activity undertaken by juveniles, and there was even a kind of "positive" trolling in which the person trolling would present their target with a series of fact-based questions intended to lead them to a logical conclusion. However, as these flaming behaviors grew and spread, the troll became someone whose deportment closely resembled the dreaded creatures who dwelt under bridges and snagged unwary travelers of legend.

The media-sciences expert Judith Donath described how trolls operate in her 1999 study, "Identity and Deception in the Virtual Community":

> Trolling is a game about identity deception, albeit one that is played without the consent of most of the players. The troll attempts to pass as a legitimate participant, sharing the group's common interests and concerns; the newsgroups members, if they are cognizant of trolls and other identity deceptions, attempt to both distinguish real from trolling postings, and upon judging a poster a troll, make the offending poster leave the group.

What makes trolls matter, and gives their ugly behavior traction inside people's real-world, everyday lives is a third kind of consequence of the rise of the Internet: the ability of people in the digital age to construct their entire social lives online, with only a nominal interaction with the reality of the physical world.

Increasingly, many people, especially those employed in technology-driven fields, are employed in corporate bubbles, consigned to cubicles and disconnected work partnerships, or they work from home and network with other people through the Web. For their social lives, they turn increasingly to chat rooms, email listservs, and political and special-interest forums. As social media platforms such as Facebook and Twitter took off toward the latter part of the new century's first decade, this phenomenon became not only widespread but profoundly consequential, because what happened in people's online lives began affecting them in the material world—even though that digitized version of reality was only, at best, a simulacrum of real human interaction.

As Donath explains:

> In the physical world there is an inherent unity to the self, for the body provides a compelling and convenient definition of identity. The norm is: one body, one identity ... The virtual world is different. It is composed of information rather than matter.

This is part of why conversations on the Internet so frequently dissolve into misunderstanding and readily traded insults: the other person is only there as an abstraction. There is no exchange of body or facial language, none of the nuance of vocal expression, none of the physical presence to enforce the reality that this is a living, breathing person with whom you are conversing. Without these things, what's left, really, is a digitized, relatively crude version of conversation and human company: a pure exchange of information and little more. We can't read a person's intentions online the way we can in real life, and so obscure motives and agendas can become a breeding ground for anger and paranoia.

It also explains why the introduction of bad information so profoundly pollutes and toxifies people's worldviews, their interpretations and understandings of news and events as they occur, as well as their interactions with others, when they are predicated on these ephemeral constructs. Facts can be falsified or distorted or spun in order to support a constructed reality that, as more false information is accreted, spins an epistemological bubble that both resembles the real world but is also largely detached from it, except insofar as the people inside it are able to share their illusions with like-minded others.

The culture of trolling, by its very nature, quickly attracted some of society's most poisonous elements: sociopaths, psychopaths, and sadists. And that has had a powerful political effect, because it turns out that the same personality traits that generate trolling behavior are also closely associated with the worldviews that fuel right-wing extremism.

The personality profile of trolls was revealed in a broad study of Internet users by a team of psychologists led by Erin E. Buckels of the University of Manitoba, who focused particularly on the people attracted to antisocial uses of the Web. Buckels released a disturbing article in 2014 based on the results of the study that found that trolls share what psychologists call the "dark tetrad" of psychological traits: Machiavellianism (willingly deceptive and manipulative), narcissism (self-obsessed and egotistic), psychopathy (an absence of empathy or remorse), and sadism (enjoys the suffering of others). The correlation with the last of these traits was particularly powerful, and in fact provided the greatest overlap with the other traits.

"Both trolls and sadists feel sadistic glee at the distress of others," Buckels wrote. "Sadists just want to have fun ... and the Internet is their playground!"

"Frequency of activity is an important correlate of antisocial uses of technology," the authors reported.

Buckels's study also found that even though trolls have an outsize influence on Internet discourse, they make up only a small percentage of Web users: only 5.6 percent of the survey's respondents said they enjoyed trolling, while some 41 percent reported they don't engage interactively online at all.

Buckels explained in an email that there is a high correlation of these "dark tetrad" traits with another important mass-psychological phenomenon known as "social dominance orientation," or SDO. It's based on the recognition that people orient themselves socially according to a kind of fundamental view: Do they believe people are inherently equal or unequal? Psychologists have tested people accordingly, devising an "SDO scale" that measures a person's preference (or lack thereof) for hierarchy based on inherent inequalities within any social system, as well as the concurring desire for domination over lower-status groups.

The original 1994 study, whose authors designed the SDO scale, asked participants whether they favored such ideas as "increased social equality," "increased economic equality," or simply "equality" itself. Subjects were also asked whether they agreed that "some people are just more worthy than others" and that "this country would be better off if we cared less about how equal all people were."

The psychologist Robert Altemeyer summarizes: "In social dominators' way of thinking, equality should not be a central value of our society or a goal toward which we should strive. To high SDOs, 'equality' is a sucker-word in which only fools believe."

If any movements could be said to describe the manifestation of SDO in the political realm, they are those associated with right-wing extremism in its various manifestations. In the twenty-first century, that has become increasingly embodied by white nationalism.

White nationalism had been lurking on the fringes of the American political right for a couple of decades before the alt-right came along to give it a fresh new life, rewired for the twenty-first century.

Of course the new white nationalism was a natural outgrowth of the old ideology of white supremacy, a worldview that had dominated much of American discourse for nearly all of the nineteenth and much of the first half of the twentieth centuries, but that had been repudiated widely after World War II and relegated to a tiny and much-reviled political nonentity during the postwar period. By the 1990s, it still lurked on the fringes in the forms of small Klan groups and neo-Nazi skinhead organizations such as the Aryan Nations and the National Alliance. All along, though, its ideologues harbored dreams of returning to the political mainstream.

White nationalism essentially became the favored vehicle for white supremacists' return to the mainstream in the 1990s, a way to reshape their image by emphasizing their advocacy for white people as a distinct ethnic entity similar to groups that advocate for blacks or Latinos. This, they claimed, distinguished their views from white supremacists, whose primary concerns revolved around their own racial superiority and, concomitantly, the degradation and demonization of nonwhite races, as the Klan and the Aryan Nations were inclined to do.

However, a deeper look always revealed that this fine distinction didn't lead to different outcomes: white nationalists not only advocated for whites' civil rights, they also actively promoted the concept of a white ethno-state—a nation run by and for white people, in the manner of Israel's role as a homeland for Jews. Moreover, even if they made fewer displays of racial animus, they also made abundantly clear in their writings their views that most if not all other races were inferior to whites, and their belief in fundamental inequalities among races was undiminished. Their reasons for desiring to live only among "their own kind," as they liked to put it, ultimately came down to their prejudice against minorities of various kinds. The separatist state and the authoritarian system they favored was precisely the same as that long envisioned by Klansmen and neo-Nazis.

Most of the white nationalists of the 1990s cultivated buttondowned suit-and-tie images of professionalism and academic credibility to go along with their pseudo-reasonable rhetoric. Among the movement's most prominent figures were such "academic racists" as Jared Taylor, Peter Brimelow, and Kevin MacDonald.

Jared Taylor epitomized the image: a thin man given to wearing tweed suits and speaking quietly, Taylor was well educated, having graduated from Yale and studied in Paris, and fluent in several languages. He became active in the white-nationalist scene around 1990, when he founded his think tank, the New Century Foundation, and shortly thereafter began publishing its house-organ magazine, *American Renaissance*, dedicated to Taylor's belief that America is "a self-consciously European, majority-white nation," which he claims was "the original conception of [the US], and one that was almost universally accepted until the 1960s."

221

"Blacks and whites are different," Taylor wrote in 2005, as part of his interpretation of the lessons of the Hurricane Katrina disaster. "When blacks are left entirely to their own devices, Western civilization—any kind of civilization—disappears."

In the late 1990s Taylor published a booklet, *The Color of Crime*, which "proved" that blacks are more prone to criminality than whites by presenting a set of manipulated national, regional, and local crime statistics. By deliberately conflating interracial crimes with bias-motivated crimes, Taylor argued that hate crimes committed by black people against whites exponentially outnumbered the reverse. Taylor's booklet was soon widely distributed by other white-nationalist groups such as the Council of Conservative Citizens. That is where Dylann Roof found and read it and was thus inspired to commence his murderous rampage at a Charleston, South Carolina, church in June 2015.

Peter Brimelow also fit the suit-and-tie image that white nationalists aimed to project. A onetime editor at *Forbes* magazine, Brimelow became a proponent of white nationalism in the 1990s after publishing a book titled *Alien Nation*, which argued that the United States was historically a white nation and should remain that way. The text described foreign immigrants as "weird aliens with dubious habits" and argued that American immigration policy should encourage whites to enter the country.

He founded his flagship enterprise, the website *VDare* in 1998, and it promptly became a home for a variety of white-nationalist and nativist views. Brimelow was particularly enraged by the Immigration Act of 1965, which eliminated racial quotas that had been in place since 1924, giving strong preference to immigrants from nations with primarily white ethnic majorities. On August 22, 2006, Brimelow wrote at *VDare*:

> The mass immigration so thoughtlessly triggered in 1965 risks making America an alien nation—not merely in the sense that the numbers of aliens in the nation are rising to levels last seen in the 19th century; not merely in the sense that America will become a freak among the world's

nations because of the unprecedented demographic mutation it is inflicting on itself; [and] not merely in the sense that Americans themselves will become alien to each other, requiring an increasingly strained government to arbitrate between them.

Brimelow's longtime mainstream media credentials meant that his website was able to traffic in ideas from both the extremist right and mainstream conservatism: *VDare* published articles from contributors ranging from racist border-militia organizer Glenn Spencer to the popular conservative pundit Michelle Malkin. Other white nationalists such as Taylor and Kevin MacDonald were also contributors.

Kevin MacDonald is a white nationalist who used to be a psychology professor at California State University, Long Beach. In the 1990s he became obsessed with what he saw as the special psychological and social profile of Jews as a group. In 1994 he published *A People That Shall Dwell Alone: Judaism as a Group Evolutionary Strategy*. MacDonald's thesis is that Jewish culture enhances Jews' ability to outcompete non-Jews for resources. The core of MacDonald's argument, which he explored in greater detail in two more books, both published in 1998, is that this group behavior of Jews produced "understandable" hatred for Jews because it brought them so much material success over the years. Thus, he claimed, anti-Semitism is a logical reaction to Jews, not an irrational hatred. MacDonald called for systematic discrimination against Jews in college admissions and in hiring, as well as special taxes "to counter the Jewish advantage in the possession of wealth."

MacDonald's open anti-Semitism won him a fan base among white nationalists, but it also created an uproar at Cal State–Long Beach that led to student protests and attempts to have him removed from the faculty. In 2008, the CSULB psychology faculty voted to formally dissociate itself from MacDonald's work. He announced his retirement in 2014, and began to devote himself full-time to promoting the white-nationalist movement.

MacDonald was one of the earliest proponents of the concept of "cultural Marxism." In *The Culture of Critique: An Evolutionary*

Analysis of Jewish Involvement in Twentieth-Century Intellectual and Social Movements (1998), he argued that Jews criticize non-Jews' desire to form "cohesive, nationalistic, corporate gentile groups based on conformity to group norms" while hypocritically pursuing their own cohesiveness. Jews, in other words, foist multiculturalism on the rest of us while maintaining their own ethnic enclaves.

The phrase "cultural Marxism" had first appeared in right-wing circles only a few months before, in July 1998, when William Lind, leader of the far-right Free Congress Foundation, gave a speech he titled "The Origins of Political Correctness." Lind described political correctness and cultural Marxism as totalitarian ideologies that were transforming American college campuses into "small ivy-covered North Koreas, where the student or faculty member who dares to cross any of the lines set up by the gender feminist or the homosexual-rights activists, or the local black or Hispanic group, or any of the other sainted 'victims' groups that revolves around, quickly find themselves in judicial trouble." One of the subscribers to this theory was the right-wing Norwegian terrorist, Anders Breivik, who in 2011 slaughtered seventy children at a Norway school because he believed they had been "polluted" by cultural Marxism.

The phrase quickly became popular not just among white nationalists but also among paleoconservatives such as Patrick Buchanan, who, while campaigning for the presidency in 2000 on the Reform Party ticket, said, "America's history and heroes and Western civilization itself are under relentless attack. The violence of this political correctness is nothing less than cultural Marxism."

The Council of Conservative Citizens warned in one of its videos: "Racism, sexism and chauvinism are powerful weapons in the Marxist psychological warfare against traditional American values. Political correctness, the product of critical theory, is really treason against the US Constitution and against America."

After finishing the race with a mere 0.4 percent of the popular vote, Buchanan returned to punditry the following year with a book titled *The Death of the West: How Dying Populations and Immigrant Invasions Imperil Our Country and Civilization*. The book describes cultural Marxism as a "regime to punish dissent and to stigmatize social heresy as the Inquisition punished religious heresy. Its trademark is intolerance."

The concept was similarly popular with the lingering remnant of white supremacists, Klansmen and neo-Nazis who remained active on the political fringes well into the twenty-first century. Indeed, many of these people and entities also embraced white nationalism through the 1990s and beyond in an effort to downplay their overt hostility to minorities and in hopes of making inroads into the political mainstream.

David Duke is a former Ku Klux Klan leader and the inventor of the border militia. Duke enjoyed some success in his long campaign to mainstream himself in the late 1980s, beginning with his 1988 campaign for the presidency under the banner of the Populist Party, appearing on the ballots of eleven states. In 1989 he won a seat in the Louisiana Legislature and used that position as a springboard in 1990 to run for a seat in the US Senate. This was followed by his 1991 candidacy for the Louisiana governorship; he won the Republican nomination but was denounced by the national party, and lost the election. Several more unsuccessful campaigns followed the 1991 loss.

Throughout this period Duke claimed he was renouncing his former racism and anti-Semitism, and was now solely interested in representing the interests and civil rights of ethnic whites, in the manner of the white nationalists. But after his electoral defeats he began sounding more and more like the old David Duke. *My Awakening* (1998) was a popular white-nationalist tract that described Duke's reasoning for believing in the superiority of whites. By 2001, with the publication of his book *Jewish Supremacism*, he had reverted back to his former neo-Nazi ways, denouncing the Holocaust as a hoax and touting old conspiracy theories.

In 2002 Duke ran into trouble with the law when he was arrested and convicted of wire fraud, having spent large sums of donors' funds on his own gambling habit, and he spent fifteen months in prison. When he got out, he began spending long periods of time spreading the white-supremacist gospel abroad, particularly in Russia and a number of states that were former Soviet republics.

Stormfront is the nation's leading neo-Nazi website—motto: "White Pride Worldwide"—operated by a longtime associate of Duke's, a former Alabama Klansman named Don Black, now based in Florida. Founded in March 1995, the site had remained mostly an obscure if deeply vile corner of the Internet for most of the first few years of its operation, but began gaining visitors as the decade wore on.

For most of its history, *Stormfront* has primarily featured extended in-house chats among members over the day's news events or articles posted to the site. Predictably, the comments have been unrestrained in their bigotry. A typical comment: "Beating down a mud [a non-white person] when they try to poisen [*sic*] one of our own or when they try to seduce one of our girls may not be God inspired, but rather a righteous act of collective preservation."

In 2002, the site began encouraging prominent white nationalists and supremacists to begin filing posts there, and within the year, its membership had grown from 5,000 to 11,000. It kept expanding from there, to 23,000 members in 2004, to 133,000 registered users in 2008. By 2015, it boasted 300,000 members, and showed no sign of slowing down.

The Knights Party is an organization built on the bones of David Duke's former organization in the 1970s and early '80s, the Knights of the Ku Klux Klan, by his successor, Thomas Robb. A longtime Arkansas pastor who preached the white-supremacist Christian Identity belief system, Robb maintained the group as one of the nation's leading Klan organizations well into the new century.

Although the group was renamed, the Knights Party's rhetoric stayed pretty much the same. After Barack Obama's election in 2008, Robb remarked on what he saw as a "race war ... between our people, who I see as the rightful owners and leaders of this great country, and their people, the blacks."

Robb is quite elderly now, and as the new century wore on, the Knights Party was increasingly run by his daughter, Rachel Pendergraft, who had for years been a presence on the scene as a white-robed Klan TV host on the organization's public-access broadcasts. Pendergraft specializes in outreach to potential female recruits, and runs pages on the Knights Party's website devoted to appeals to conservative-minded women.

The Council of Conservative Citizens (CCC) is a new avatar of the supremacist White Citizens Council, which was a prominent actor in the South during the civil rights struggle of the 1950s and '60s. The CCC was founded in 1985 by Gordon L. Baum, a Missouri organizer who wanted to reshape and rebrand the group for the current era.

Its meetings attracted the participation of a number of elected Republicans, including former Representative Bob Barr of Georgia and Mississippi senator Trent Lott. In 2002, Lott had to resign his Senate seat amid an uproar over racially charged remarks he had made, his image further tarnished by this earlier association.

Despite the "conservative" moniker, there is little doubt that the group's approach to race is still very much that of the "uptown Klan" of old. On its website the CCC states: "God is the author of racism. God is the One who divided mankind into different types … Mixing the races is rebelliousness against God." It has prominently featured Jared Taylor's *The Color of Crime* screed, and routinely denigrates blacks as "genetically inferior," labels LGBT people "perverted sodomites," and claims immigrants are turning America into a "slimy brown mass of glop." Naturally, it also frequently complains about "Jewish power brokers."

Yet it still managed to attract the participation of elected officials: In 2004, a review by the Southern Poverty Law Center found that thirty-eight federal, state, and local elected officials had attended CCC events since 2000. Much of that mainstream interest began to wane as the decade wore on, but the group's website remains a powerful and popular gathering place for white nationalists and other bigots.

Vanguard News Network (VNN) is one of the last remnants of the old neo-Nazi organization of the 1970s and '80s called the National Alliance, which had been founded in the 1970s by a white supremacist, William Pierce—the author of *The Turner Diaries*, the book that inspired the murderous 1980s neo-Nazi gang The Order and the 1995 Oklahoma City bombing (see Chapter 3). VNN was founded in 2000 by a young National Alliance activist, Alex Linder, to function as the Web branch of the group's magazine, *National Vanguard*. Linder envisioned the site as "an integrated global media and services company getting out the White message and serving the White market in a thousand forms."

Much like *Stormfront*, VNN soon became an open sewer for bigotry and violent rhetoric, as well as open misogyny: Linder once opined that women should "make everything happy and smooth running by providing offspring and sex and cookies and iced tea."

Linder is especially fond of promoting the idea of multicultural-ism as "white genocide." "Katrina flashed whites an eternal truth: 'African-American' is pretty for 'jungle savage,'" he wrote in 2005.

> The question is: Why do we pretend it is otherwise? The answer is: we don't. We normal whites move away from these jungle creatures when-ever we can. But the murderous hands of government, guided by Big Jew, again and again and again push us back in with the savages. And that, my friend, is genocide by integration—a man-made disaster far worse than any natural.

The National Alliance largely vanished as an organization after Pierce's death in 2002; Linder's website, which remains relatively popular among skinheads and other neo-Nazis, is its only lingering remnant.

The main idea underlying white nationalism was that it supported a hierarchy produced by what were presumed to be inherent racial inequalities. But by the late 1990s it had evolved from its origi-nal claims to be simply promoting the interests of ethnic whites to pursuing the typical activities and rhetoric of the far right, dehu-manizing and demonizing nonwhites and LGBT people, and swimming in the common undercurrents of anti-Semitism and con-spiracism. And indeed, many of the movement's leaders displayed the kind of personality characteristics—the utter lack of empathy, the manipulativeness and aggression, the hostility to femininity and equality—associated with people who score highly on the SDO scale.

During the years of the Bush administration, white national-ists focused less on attacking liberalism and grew largely into an anti-mainstream conservative movement, directing their attacks to those Republicans who they believed were failing to "stand up for white interests." The antagonism created a gulf in which the move-ment struggled to reach new followers, at least in the early part of the decade.

But the white nationalists' predilection for conspiracism soon brought them the audience they sought. The growing network of conspiracy theorists first generated by the antigovernment Patriot movement of the 1990s had similarly broken away from mainstream conservatism after the terrorist attacks of September 11, 2001, which had given birth to a whole new industry of "9/11 Truther" theories predicated on the idea that the attacks were an inside job perpe-trated with the willing assistance of Bush administration operatives and their New World Order. As the decade wore on, the far-right conspiracist and white-nationalist ideologies started to meld. Far-right conspiracists began picking up and promoting theories that originated with white nationalists (such as political correctness as a form of what they called "cultural Marxism"), and white national-ists began picking up and promoting fresh material generated by the conspiracy mills. In the twenty-first century, the Internet began to prove an increasingly hospitable meeting ground as their respective followings began to grow.

However, it took an infusion of fresh blood from a new genera-tion of white nationalists not only to make them culturally relevant again, but also to realize their long-held dream of returning to the mainstream of American politics.

The audience for conspiracy theories, as the psychologist Robert Altemeyer observes, often comprises right-wing authoritari-ans: people who are inclined to insist on a world in which strong

authorities produce order and peace, often through the iron imposition of law and order. Highly ethnocentric, fearful of a dangerous
world, prone to extreme self-righteousness, aggressive, highly dogmatic, with poor reasoning abilities, they are, Altemeyer explains,
"very dependent on social reinforcement of their beliefs. They think
they are right because almost everyone they know, almost every
news broadcast they see, almost every radio commentator they
listen to, tells them they are. That is, they screen out the sources that
will suggest that they are wrong."

Altemeyer, whose groundbreaking work on authoritarian personalities accurately describes the psychological makeup of right-wing
authoritarian (RWA) followers, explains that even though their
underlying beliefs in inequality create a powerful common interest,
people with high SDO scores in fact correlate poorly with people
who score highly on the RWA scale. Among other differences is
that authoritarian followers lack dominators' lust for power; they
are much more religious; their hostility is rooted in fear and self-
righteousness in the name of authority, whereas dominators are
hostile as an act of intimidation and control; followers' compart-
mentalized thinking leads them to have mixed ideas about inequality,
and their logic is often littered with contradictions and hypocrisies,
whereas dominators often seem much more intellectually sound—
they simply believe inequality is a natural state of being, and that
some people are just innately more valuable and gifted than others.
Especially them, of course.

However, authoritarian leaders and RWA followers have a great
deal in common. They share an overpowering tendency toward
prejudice against racial and ethnic minorities, women, gays and lesbians, and religious minorities. They also share deeply conservative
politics, and consequently favor right-wing parties.

Altemeyer's 2006 study in which he warned about the rise of
authoritarianism focused especially on the special kind of chemistry
that happens when right-wing authoritarians and social dominators
(especially those of the latter who also score highly on the RWA
scale) come together. He called it the "lethal union":

When social dominators are in the driver's seat, and right-wing authoritarians stand at their beck and call, unethical things appear much more likely to happen. True, sufficiently skilled social dominators served by dedicated followers can make the trains run on time. But you have to worry about what the trains may be hauling when dominators call the shots and high RWAs do the shooting. The trains may be loaded with people crammed into boxcars heading for death camps.

And of course this lethal union is likely to develop in the real world. Authoritarian followers don't usually try to become leaders. Instead they happily play subservient roles, and can be expected to especially enjoy working for social dominators, who will (you can bet your bottom dollar) take firm control of things, and who share many of the followers' values and attitudes. The "connection" connects between these two opposites because they attract each other like the north and south poles of two magnets. The two can then become locked in a cyclonic death spiral that can take a whole nation down with them.

The gradual coalescence of the alternative-universe worldviews of conspiracists, Patriots, white supremacists, Tea Partiers, and nativists occurred after the election of the first black president, in 2008. Fueled in no small part by racial animus toward Obama, the Internet and social media became the grounds on which this "lethal union" could finally occur, after decades of internecine bickering among far-right factions and their relegation to the political fringes. The same chat rooms and political forums and Facebook threads where trolls gathered and took over whole communities became the places where far-right-wing social dominators—many of them espousing openly transgressive worldviews such as neo-Nazism and misogyny—could come together with the right-wing authoritarians whose ranks grew with every Alex Jones convert and wannabe Oath Keeper militiaman.

That "lethal union" ultimately gave birth to the twenty-first century's new baby: the alt-right.

It all began, really, with people talking online about Japanese anime, the animated cartoons featuring everything from ultra-cute kittens to horrifying monsters, and pretty much everything in between, produced for the massive Asian markets by studios based largely in Tokyo.

The website's owner—a then-fifteen-year-old student named Christopher Poole—called it 4Chan when he launched it out of his bedroom in 2003. His idea was to create an open forum where anyone could post images and chat about anime, as well as its associated manga comic-book culture. And it was an immediate success, drawing over a million hits in his first six days of operation, reflecting the immense online popularity of Japanese anime generally. Soon it had expanded into a massive operation, one of the Internet's most influential referral sites.

Much of its original success was built on Internet memes—those little social media messages featuring a single (though sometimes combination) photo with words scripted over it. One of the earliest and most popular social media memes, "LOLcats," featured humorous scripts and photos of cats in various facial poses, the most famous of which—"I Can Haz Cheezburger"—went on to spawn a million-dollar company; it was hosted at 4Chan.

4Chan trolls were inventive, too. They devised the act of "Rick-Rolling"—tricking a friend into viewing a video of Rick Astley's uber-sweet 1987 pop hit, "Never Gonna Give You Up," usually by sharing a link with them they expect to go elsewhere—that became one of those things many people on social media tried as a prank at one time or another.

4Chan meant what it said about being an open forum. People could register without entering an email address, so most commenters posted anonymously. The "anything goes" ethos meant that 4Chan's boards not only were host to gamers and hobbyists but also were soon crawling with neo-Nazis, white supremacists, gay bashers, and a flood of pornographic material. Pedophiles opened their own boards. Trolling soon became not just the ruling ethos, but a competition among peers at 4Chan.

The "manosphere" too, was a major presence at 4Chan. This online community comprised a collection of blogs, chat forums, and websites with subcommunities such as Reddit, all dedicated to the "men's rights" movement. The "movement" quickly became an open sewer of rampant misogyny and rape culture, particularly at the "men's rights activists" (or MRA) discussion boards at 4Chan.

MRA websites are like wildlife refuges for misogynist ideas. They call feminists "a social cancer," and assert, "Feminism is a hate movement designed to disenfranchise and dehumanize men." They complain that women cry "rape" too easily. "Just as the Nazis had to create a Jewish conspiracy as a way to justify mass slaughter," declared one post at a "manosphere" blog called *Alcuin*, "so feminists have to create patriarchy as a way to justify mass slaughter of innocent unborn, and the destruction of men and masculinity. Rape is now a political crime, not a crime of sex or violence." Another MRA site named Boycott American Women described US women as "generally immature, selfish, extremely arrogant and self-centered, mentally unstable, irresponsible and highly unchaste. The behavior of most American women is utterly disgusting."

So it was unsurprising when, in early 2013, all these forces converged at 4Chan to create the "Gamergate" controversy that subsequently blew up in the media when the online threats began creeping over into the real world—for a year or so, at least.

Gamergate began when a feminist game designer named Zoe Quinn came up with a woman-friendly online game, Depression Quest, that attracted a good deal of media attention for its unique purpose: by guiding the user through the trials and tribulations of a person suffering from clinical depression, it helped inform even non-sufferers about some of the hidden dimensions of the disease. One reviewer, Adam Smith, wrote that it transformed computer gaming from a mere exercise in conflict to "'game' as communication, comfort and tool of understanding."

Quinn's media fame and the nonviolent conflict resolution the game's architecture created, which was seen as a direct challenge to the male-oriented first-person-shooter architecture that still dominates gaming, attracted the ire of anti-feminist gamers, and Quinn soon found herself inundated with hate mail and threatening social media messages. Someone mailed a detailed rape threat to her home address. Then, in August 2014, shortly after Depression Quest was released to the general public on the Steam platform, a former boyfriend of Quinn's published a nasty tell-all post about their relationship, complaining that her new boyfriend was the videogame journalist Nathan Grayson. At 4Chan's boards this story quickly took a new twist as Quinn's critics began to claim that Grayson had written a positive review of Depression Quest as a result of their relationship—although Grayson had never reviewed the game.

That did not matter, of course: the 4Chan trolls were off and running, claiming they had uncovered an ethical scandal within the world of gaming journalism. Grayson's supposed breach of standards reflected what they claimed was a pro-feminist, pro-liberal, anti-white-male bias growing within the computer-game industry. Soon anyone who questioned their interpretation of events was part of the conspiracy.

The actor Adam Baldwin, highly active in right-wing circles though never a participant in the trolling, dubbed the controversy #Gamergate on Twitter, and it quickly spread like wildfire within the gaming community and on social media as the claims grew increasingly heated.

Quinn's previous flood of hate mail was dwarfed by the incoming tide of vitriol and bile that descended on her. She was "doxxed"— her home address and personal contact information published online—and she was forced to flee her home.

"Long story short," she later wrote in an account of the experience, "the Internet spent the last month spreading my personal information around, sending me threats, hacking anyone suspected of being friends with me, calling my dad and telling him I'm a whore, sending nude photos of me to colleagues, and basically giving me the 'burn the witch' treatment."

The harassment didn't end with Quinn. After she became a public critic of the Gamergaters, Anita Sarkeesian, a well-regarded feminist cultural critic, endured death and rape threats, as well as a phoned-in bomb threat that forced the cancellation of a speaking appearance. That was followed shortly by the online threats against Brianna Wu.

Appalled by the wave of harassment emanating from their boards, the owners of 4Chan, including Christopher Poole, announced in September 2014 that they would ban any further Gamergate discussions. However, a longtime 4Chan user named Fredrick Brennan had, that previous October, already created a similar, competing website called 8Chan that was even more wide open, because he believed 4Chan had become too censorious. In short order, the entire Gamergate discussion moved over to the 8Chan site, and trolls began organizing their coordinated attacks against Brianna Wu there.

The Gamergaters on 8Chan, Steam, Twitter, Reddit, and other forums created a lingo of their own, mainly a range of pernicious rhetorical devices designed to create a buffer between themselves and the threats that were flooding out to women and minorities in the industry. It was a language of dismissal and belittlement. They called them "special snowflakes" and "cry bullies," derided their websites as "safe spaces" and their hopes for civil discourse as "unicorns." They claimed that the targets of the abuse were lying or exaggerating, and even when the abuse was factually substantiated, Gamergaters' usual response was that people on their side were being abused, too.

Conspiracy theories were part of the attack: feminists and women generally were portrayed as a subset of the nefarious plot to oppress white males by a much larger left-wing conspiracy to destroy Western civilization by "cultural Marxists."

The cultural Marxism theory, which had spread from the cloistered circles of white nationalists to wider circulation through the world of Alex Jones and a range of other conspiracy theorists and their audiences, became the focal point of many of the Gamergate discussions, as well as the ensuing political discussions over other news events that ensued at the 4Chan and 8Chan boards. A panoply of other conspiracy theories began floating around, ostensibly proving that white men were being systematically oppressed by dark left-wing forces. They also contended that mainstream conservatives, through their "weak" response to multiculturalism, had "sold them out," and so also came in for their cutting critiques.

Eventually the Gamergate controversy subsided, but far more important was what had transpired in the process. Aggrieved MRAs from the "manosphere," white nationalists who shared their virulent hatred of feminists and adoration for what they called "traditional values," gamers, and online trolls all came together during Gamergate to form their own online movement. They began chatting about politics, and conspiracies, and how much they hated "sellout" mainstream conservatives, but they reserved their most bilious outbursts for liberals and multiculturalism and gays and lesbians and blacks and Hispanics and Jews. Especially Jews.

Pretty soon, they came up with a name for their growing community of like-minded defenders of the white race and "traditional values": the alt-right.

Richard Spencer, an editor at the paleoconservative *Taki's Magazine*, coined the term "alternative right" in 2009 while writing a headline for an article by a white nationalist, Kevin DeAnna, describing the rise of a new kind of conservatism, one hostile to neo-conservatism and open to "racialist" politics. Less than a year later, in early 2010, Spencer founded his own webzine and named it *The Alternative Right*. In short order, the nature of Internet discourse at the site shortened the name of the movement it promoted to "alt-right." The name stuck.

Spencer grew up in Dallas, Texas, the son of an ophthalmologist, and earned humanities degrees at the University of Virginia in 2001 and the University of Chicago in 2003. He did doctoral studies at Duke University from 2005 to 2007, where he first became active in politics as a member of the Duke Conservative Union. He left Duke, he later wrote, to "pursue a life of thought crime."

He first landed a job as an assistant at *The American Conservative* magazine, where he shortly ran into trouble because of his increasingly radical beliefs, which got him fired ten months into the job.

He later explained that his experience at the magazine led to his disillusion with mainstream conservatism, which, he wrote, "can't or won't represent explicitly white interests."

But Spencer quickly landed on his feet at *Taki's*, where he was executive editor for two years. The magazine's far-right outlook was an ideal fit for the budding radical, and while there he came under the mentorship of Paul Gottfried, a Jewish paleoconservative who taught humanities at Elizabethtown College in Pennsylvania.

Gottfried, like most paleoconservatives, ardently believed that inequality is the natural state of things, and that efforts to overcome it amounted to a kind of tyranny. Gottfried theorized that the United States had ceased to be either a republic or a liberal democracy, the meanings of which had been lost in the postindustrial period, when bureaucracies had exploded and transformed the nation into a "therapeutic managerial state." This state, he argued, was ruled by a managerial class that justified its status by foisting liberal precepts, such as multiculturalism and political correctness, on the populace, pitting various groups against each other.

By 2010 Spencer had come to fully embrace white nationalism as his guiding philosophy, including its conspiracism, its underlying racism, and its anti-Semitism. Separating himself from his Jewish mentor, he left *Taki's* to found *The Alternative Right*, with backing from Peter Brimelow and the VDare Foundation, where he was free to expound on his increasing radicalism at will.

Unlike many younger white nationalists, however, Spencer gravitated to the suit-and-tie image of the "academic racists" he had now befriended. Handsome, with an all-American look, he was fond of projecting a sense of calm rationality even while discussing overt anti-Semitism, and he became a popular speaker on the white-nationalist circuit.

"We have to look good," he told a reporter. After all, he said, nobody wants to join a movement that is "crazed or ugly or vicious or just stupid."

"As long as whites continue to avoid and deny their own racial identity, at a time when almost every other racial and ethnic category is rediscovering and asserting its own, whites will have no chance to resist their dispossession," was one of Spencer's standard recruitment pitches. This focus on white identity was then associated with a set of ideas originating in Europe known as "identitarianism," which included specific national identities in movements in France, Italy, Germany, and elsewhere, but shared a loathing of immigrants and nonwhites and a longing for "traditional values" as well as ethnic separatism.

In 2011, Spencer took over the reins of the National Policy Institute (NPI), a smallish white-nationalist organization based in Virginia, and promptly made it into one of the leading centers of the budding alt-right movement. Eventually giving up the reins at his old webzine, he created a new online and biannual publication called *Radix Journal*, which shortly came to specialize in articles connecting IQ to race and crime.

Spencer moved his end of NPI's operations to Whitefish, Montana, in 2012 to join a growing "white homeland" movement in the Flathead Lake region; he maintains a part-time residence there with his parents. And he continually honed his political message, believing that white Americans would soon listen to his simultaneously soothing and radicalizing philosophy.

The core concept he promotes is "sort of white Zionism," he says: "Our dream is a new society, an ethno-state that would be a gathering point for all Europeans. It would be a new society based on very different ideals than, say, the Declaration of Independence," he told a *Vice* reporter.

The alt-right community that he hoped would extend outward from his website included growing alliances with other white nationalists, including two from his own generation, Brad Griffin and Matthew Heimbach.

Brad Griffin, a thirtysomething born-and-bred Southerner, has said that his upbringing in rural Eufala, Alabama, wired him to think in racial terms: "I knew that race existed and that racial differences were real from growing up in the Alabama Black Belt. It wasn't something that I thought much about. I had arrived at that conclusion from observation and experience. I found it strange that anyone could believe otherwise given the sheer weight of the evidence."

He attended Auburn University, which is where he says he became politically active, mainly upon reading Patrick Buchanan's white-nationalist screed, *The Death of the West*. "I was 'red-pilled,'" Griffin later explained. He grasped that "Western civilization as a whole was dying and that a great historical event was unfolding within my lifetime." He quickly found racist forums like *Stormfront* and a variety of online message boards.

As much as he despises liberals, Griffin hates mainstream conservatives almost as deeply: "From the beginning, I hated everything about George W. Bush," he writes. "In fact, I disliked W. so much that I voted for Al Gore and John Kerry out of spite."

In 2008, Griffin founded the white-nationalist blog *Occidental Dissent* under his nom de plume, Hunter Wallace. The blog quickly grew a wide audience through its exposure on 4Chan, *Stormfront*, and other forums. Griffin quickly communicated his alt-right philosophy even before the term had been coined, writing, "How would White Nationalists react if they were engaged in an open dialogue about race, given economic opportunity, allowed to celebrate their own identity, and lobby on behalf of their own genetic interests like other groups?"

Griffin later explained in a post at *Occidental Dissent* how the alt-right had come together, and outlined its basic strategy for achieving broader acceptance: "Alt Right is presenting itself as a sleek new challenger to mainstream conservatism and libertarianism ... Alt Right was designed to appeal to a younger audience who reject the Left, but who don't fit in on the stuffy or banal Right either."

Occidental Dissent became one of the fonts of white-nationalist ideology. Unlike Spencer's, Griffin's blog specialized in linking to and promoting a broad range of articles by other white nationalist writers. Griffin also promoted a cleaned-up image, but more in the vein of a middle- or working-class father who cleans up well, minus the suits and ties.

Notwithstanding the congenial image, Griffin's rhetoric was incendiary, both racially and politically. In commenting on the civil unrest that came in the wake of the high-profile shootings of Trayvon Martin in Sanford, Florida, and Mike Brown in Ferguson, Missouri, Griffin called for Americans to brace for a race war:

> In Black Run America, White Americans should expect the most violent criminals to return to the streets in the near future, the Mainstream Media to continue to ignore, incite, cheer on, excuse, apologize for and rationalize black mob violence against Whites, politicians continue to cave to pressure from black mobs, and the President and the Justice Department to take the side of the black mobs.
>
> We're not the only ones expecting to see violent black mobs of noble looters, incited and glamorized by the Mainstream Media, burning down our cities in the name of "social justice." Most of our neighbors are expecting to see it too. It says a lot about the state of race relations in Obama's "post-racial" America when almost no one would be surprised to see the race war land on their doorstep.

Now a resident of rural Midway, Alabama, Griffin also embraces the neo-Confederate movement—what he calls "Southern nationalism"—an ideology based on unabashed defense of the Confederacy and slavery, and open promotion of modern secession for Southern states, often associated with the white-supremacist Council of Conservative Citizens. In 2013, the movement's leading organization, the League of the South, called Griffin one of its leading youthful organizers.

Griffin is also married to the daughter of the CCC's founder, Gordon L. Baum, and his pieces have often appeared on the organization's website. When Baum died in March 2015, Griffin wound up in charge of the group's website, and it was widely assumed that he was also the heir-apparent to take the reins of the organization going forward.

In the alt-right's formative years leading up to 2014, both Griffin and Spencer formed an alliance with another youthful white-nationalist organizer, Matthew Heimbach. Born in 1991, Heimbach had become involved in white nationalism when he was nineteen.

As a student at Towson State in Maryland, he organized a campus chapter of the far-right Youth for Western Civilization, where he promoted activities such as chalking campus sidewalks with the words "White Pride" and "White Guilt Is Over".

Like Griffin, Heimbach was heavily involved in the League of the South and often promoted that neo-Confederate flavor of white nationalism. He attended the LoS's annual conferences in 2011, 2012, and 2013, and became friends with the league's president, Michael Hill.

He also held forth on his racial views in the Youth for Western Civilization (YWC) newsletter, writing in 2013:

> This is our home and our kith and kin. Borders matter, identity matters, blood matters, libertarians and their capitalism can move to Somalia if they want to live without rules, in the West we must have standards and enforce them. The "freedom" for other races to move freely into white nations is nonexistent. Stay in your own nations, we don't want you here. Those who promote miscegenation, usury, or any other forms of racial suicide should be sent to re-education centers, not tolerated.

When YWC dissolved as a national organization in 2013, Heimbach simply formed his own outfit at Towson, which he called the White Students Union. He also organized student night patrols to combat what he called a "black crime wave."

Heimbach explained his white-nationalist beliefs to Wes Enzinna, a documentary filmmaker from *Vice* magazine:

> I think that especially the black community will find areas in the South, areas like Detroit, where they can have their own homelands, we don't have to be antagonistic towards them. And if you want to sell yourself and your children down the river of multiculturalism, you can do that. But we deserve the right to exist, deserve the right to defend our culture, and deserve the right to have a future for our culture.

After graduating from college, with his father-in-law, Matthew Parrot, Heimbach cofounded a new group he called the Traditionalist Youth Network, and soon found himself in demand as a speaker on the white-nationalist circuit; he addressed a CCC gathering with a pistol on his hip. As the summer of 2013 wore on, he also became increasingly involved with neo-Nazi groups, attending a *Stormfront* gathering in Tennessee at which he praised David Duke fulsomely, as well as a gathering of skinheads in rural Kentucky, cohosted by the Imperial Klans of America and the National Socialist Movement.

Those associations turned Heimbach's reputation toxic among some other white nationalists, at least for a while: Michael Hill barred him from a League of the South rally and kicked him out of the organization that summer, though the ban wound up only lasting a few months; by 2014 he had been reinstated and named the league's "training director." Evidently such associations ceased to be an issue for LoS: when, in October 2016, Heimbach addressed a gathering of skinheads in Georgia, no one paid any mind.

In 2015, again working in concert with his father-in-law, Heimbach announced he was forming a political wing of the Traditionalist Youth Party called the Traditionalist Workers Party. In addition to being white nationalist, the Traditionalist Workers Party was also fervently anti-LGBT.

"Homosexuality is universally taboo because it's dangerous, dysfunctional, and degenerate," wrote Parrot at the Traditionalist Workers Party website. "It's not a healthy part of a balanced civilization. Homosexuality's like shingles, always lingering in the background but only flaring up into a real problem when a civilization's somehow weakened or decrepit."

Anti-Semitism was another of Heimbach's central themes. At his blog he wrote, "All nationalists, regardless of ethnicity, should stand united against our common foes, the rootless international clique of globalists and bankers that wish to dominate all free peoples on the Earth."

These young white nationalists not only forged alliances with more established movement ideologues, they also massively expanded the movement's recruitment base by making the alt-right into something entirely new—largely organized online, openly transgressive and anti-liberal, deeply conspiracist, and capable of adapting its appeal to a wide range of audiences. The name "alt-right" was developed with public relations well in mind: it permitted the white nationalists who coined the term to soften their image while drawing in recruits from mainstream conservatism.

Which is where the Breitbart News Network came in.

Andrew Breitbart built his career, and his online news agency, by being a self-proclaimed gadfly for right-wing causes. A onetime tech worker for the right-wing news aggregator the *Drudge Report*, Breitbart had launched his own website, Breitbart.com, on the side, and originally bolstered it by getting links to his posts listed at *Drudge*. He also worked with Arianna Huffington to help her set up her liberal news website, the *Huffington Post*.

He launched Breitbart News Network in 2007 with "the aim of starting a site that would be unapologetically pro-freedom and pro-Israel." For its first few years it specialized in fairly mainstream conservative, Fox News–type fare, with an occasional nod to Glenn Beck–style conspiracism, especially anti-Muslim and immigration-related theories.

Breitbart.com launched itself into the national limelight in 2010 when it published a series of undercover videos generated by a right-wing provocateur, James O'Keefe, that seemed to demonstrate that officials at the Association of Community Organizations for Reform Now (ACORN) were giving advice to a pimp on how to run an illegal business employing underage girls in the sex trade. It eventually emerged that the videos had been heavily edited in order to create a misleading impression of the conversations. Subsequent investigations cleared the officials of any kind of wrongdoing, but the damage had been done. The uproar, fueled especially by Fox News and other right-wing media coverage who repeated the most outlandish disinformation about O'Keefe's caper, was enough to cause Congress to cut ACORN's funding, and the organization soon went belly up. Breitbart also was able to claim another liberal scalp when his website caught Congressman Anthony Weiner, a

Democrat, texting sexual messages to his admirers. Weiner eventually resigned his congressional seat.

Despite its mainstream position, the Breitbart website always included the work of a number of far-right figures, particularly those with anti-Muslim preoccupations, and Islamophobia became a steady feature of the organization's coverage. Articles commonly appeared by Frank Gaffney, an anti-Muslim conspiracist whose organization, the Center for Security Policy, was designated a hate group by the Southern Poverty Law Center. Breitbart also frequently promoted the work of the extremist Pamela Geller, whose group Stop Islamization of America also earned the SPLC's hate-group designation.

In fact, there was often an ugly racial undertone to all of the stories Breitbart promoted. His video about ACORN was premised on stereotypes about blacks and criminality in its underlying claims. Similarly, when Andrew Breitbart published excerpted videos of a speech given at a National Association for the Advancement of Colored People convention by a Georgia agriculture official named Shirley Sherrod that seemed to encourage anti-white racism, she was fired from her job and condemned by the NAACP. Later, unedited videos of the speech were released and it became clear that her speech in reality had been about racial reconciliation. The NAACP apologized to Sherrod, and she was offered her old job back (which she declined). Breitbart, however, never corrected the misleading reportage and never apologized to Sherrod.

Building on his burgeoning audience at Breitbart.com, Breitbart soon launched a series of associated websites aimed at different components of the conservative agenda, all named "Big" Something: Big Government, Big Hollywood, Big Journalism, and Big Peace. But on March 1, 2012, he suffered a massive heart failure while out for a walk and died. He was forty-three.

After a couple of weeks the board at Breitbart News Network announced that it would replace the founder with a longtime conservative operative named Stephen Bannon as executive chairman, while Breitbart's former CEO role would be filled by Laurence

Solov, a childhood friend of the founder and a litigation specialist who had been the company's chief counsel. Bannon was a former Goldman Sachs investment banker who had moved into the entertainment industry, financing and acting as executive producer on a number of films. He eventually parlayed that into a career creating conservative "documentaries" such as *In the Face of Evil*, a 2004 encomium to Ronald Reagan, as well as a 2010 Tea Party promotional titled *Battle for America*; another 2010 film blaming the recession on minority lending programs titled *Generation Zero*; and a laudatory portrait of Sarah Palin titled *The Undefeated* in 2011. Bannon had been one of the founding board members of the Breitbart News Network in 2007.

Bannon reportedly became a very hands-on executive, sitting in on budget meetings and guiding the website's daily coverage. Under his guidance, Breitbart.com unified all of the previous "Big" websites beneath its banner; initially they continued the programming agenda of their founder, including his pattern of running racially incendiary material.

More and more, however, Breitbart began specializing in coverage that supported white-nationalist narratives about black criminality and the supposed "threat" of immigration. After a white journalist and her cameraman were murdered live on air in August 2015 by a disgruntled former co-worker who was African American, Breitbart published the race-baiting headline "Race Murder in Virginia: Black Reporter Suspected of Executing White Colleagues—on Live Television!" Breitbart also portrayed Trayvon Martin as a young black criminal, "a full-grown young man with a history of violence" whose shooting was fully justified. Per Breitbart, Michael Brown and the protesters in Ferguson were reflective of a black "crime wave ... part of the Left's plan. You paralyze the cops with persecution, justify riots and looting, and by extension empower the criminals. The result is city-wide chaos, despair, and hopelessness."

Breitbart's headline over a piece by the nativist former congressman Ted Tancredo: "Political Correctness Protects Muslim Rape

Culture." Over a Milo Yiannopoulos piece: "Silicon Valley's Startup Culture Explains Why Mass Muslim Immigration Must Stop." A Yiannopoulos anti-feminist rant was headlined "The Solution to Online 'Harassment' Is Simple: Women Should Log Off."

When the uproar over the Confederate flag erupted in the summer of 2015 in the wake of Dylann Roof's murderous rampage in Charleston, Breitbart came out in stout defense of the symbols and monuments of the Old South: "Hoist It High and Proud: The Confederate Flag Proclaims a Glorious Heritage." A London-based Breitbart staffer, Gerald Warner, wrote:

> The liberals feel they are on a roll, having trashed states' rights by railroading compulsory acceptance of homosexual marriage through the Supreme Court. Now, they feel, is the time to airbrush out of history every tradition that is an obstacle to their new, rootless, alien society based on intolerant political correctness.

Breitbart.com rarely promoted white-nationalist ideology openly. But the site's readers consumed the material as fodder with which they fed their own racially charged narratives. This could especially be seen in the comments sections of the site's various articles, where readers were permitted to say anything they pleased, resulting in an open sewer of racial, ethnic, religious, sexual, and gender bigotry. A fairly typical example, from August 24, 2015, could be found in a Breitbart piece about the film director Quentin Tarantino remarking that "the issue of white supremacy is being talked about and dealt with" in the wake of the Ferguson, Missouri, civil unrest. One commenter wrote: "Would Tarantino know that Black supremacy is on the rise in the USA? No, no he would not, now, would he, because he is a hollyweird libturd." Another wrote: "Tarantino is going to win Goyim of the Year award with this film. Someone kill this race traitor. He is exploiting whites for shekels."

The website's staff also reflected an increasing extremism. One of Breitbart's fresh hires in 2014 was a young woman named Katie McHugh, formerly a staff member at the conservative webzine *The Daily Caller*. McHugh, it soon emerged, had a taste for trolling

Twitter with outright white-supremacist and racist tweets, such as "The only way to strike a balance between vigilance, discrimination, (& terror) is to end Muslim immigration" and "Mexicans wrecked Mexico & think invading the USA will magically cure them of their retarded dysfunction. LOL." McHugh also followed a neo-Nazi hacker and several anti-Muslim extremists on her Twitter feed. She was eventually fired in May 2017.

However, Breitbart's primary connection to the alt-right was Milo Yiannopoulos, who parlayed his Gamergate notoriety into the position of technology editor for the website and began running pieces extolling the virtues of the new alt-right movement. He more or less cemented the website's relationship with mainstream conservatives with a March 2016 piece co-written with Allum Bakhari, "An Establishment Conservative's Guide to the Alt-Right."

"For decades, the concerns of those who cherish western culture have been openly ridiculed and dismissed as racist," they wrote. "The alt-right is the inevitable result."

The piece was primarily an attempt to give the movement a kind of academic veneer by suggesting that intellectual forebears for the alt-right included Oswald Spengler and H. L. Mencken, and led to figures such as Richard Spencer, Peter Brimelow, Jared Taylor (their white nationalism was not mentioned), a eugenicist named Steve Sailer, and the social psychologist Jonathan Haidt.

Yiannopoulos and Bokhari concluded by conceding the ongoing presence of actual white supremacists as players in the alt-right. They labeled this element by one of their own names: "the 1488ers," or neo-Nazis. The name is a portmanteau referencing two arcane neo-Nazi neologisms. According to Yiannopoulos and Bokhari, "For all [alt-righters'] talk of there being 'no enemies to the right,' it's clear from the many conversations we've had with [them] that many would rather the 1488ers didn't exist." They went on to make a bizarre comparison:

> 1488ers are the equivalent of the Black Lives Matter supporters who call for the deaths of policemen, or feminists who unironically want to

#KillAllMen. Of course, the difference is that while the media pretend the latter are either non-existent, or a tiny extremist minority, they consider 1488ers to constitute the whole of the alt-right.

Those looking for Nazis under the bed can rest assured that they do exist. On the other hand, there's just not very many of them, no-one really likes them, and they're unlikely to achieve anything significant in the alt-right.

The 1488ers took a very different view.

Andrew Anglin, like a lot of neo-Nazis, has a tattoo on his chest. An Ohio native who still lives there, not far from his parents' place in Worthington, Anglin traveled widely in Asia, Europe, and elsewhere in his early twenties. His tattoo is fairly exotic and obscure: a black sun, a sort of wheel design that incorporates three swastikas. The symbol is heavily associated with Nazi mysticism, which is the kind of thing that would appeal to a neo-Nazi.

Anglin announced his arrival on the Internet in 2012 with a short-lived website called *Total Fascism*. Since then he has been clear and unrestrained in his ardent promotion of fascist ideology. Around 2010, Anglin wrote, he "went full Nazi" while trolling the boards at 4Chan, "and so I got into Hitler, and realized that through this type of nationalist system, alienation could be replaced with community in a real sense, while the authoritarianism would allow for technology to develop in a direction that was beneficial rather than destructive to the people."

At first Anglin used *Total Fascism* as an outlet for long essays about fascism, but he soon realized that shorter, punchier, more graphics-laden posts were far more effective in getting his point across. After several months, in July 2013, he abandoned the first website and founded the *Daily Stormer*.

The new site was named after the Nazi newspaper *Der Stürmer*, a virulently anti-Semitic weekly newspaper in tabloid format published by Julius Streicher, a prominent Nazi Party official. True to its heritage, Anglin's website featured overt racism and anti-Semitism, as well as the full phalanx of neo-Nazi imagery retooled for Hitler admirers. Racist headlines were commonplace, such as "All Intelligent People in History Disliked the Jews"; "Infant and Grandma Raped: Two Instances of Black Sexual Behavior Expose the Fact That These People are Operating on a Totally Variant Psychological Framework."

Anglin wrote in February 2014: "My problem with blacks is that I have come to understand that their biological nature is incompatible with White society … and that we will never have peace as long as they are among us, given that irrational outbursts of brutal violence are a part of their nature."

Anglin particularly embraced the alt-right movement and promoted it at every opportunity. Within a year of founding the *Daily Stormer*, Anglin was reeling in readers by the tens of thousands, many of them drawn from his longtime haunts as a commenter at 4Chan and other forums such as *Stormfront* and 8Chan. By the spring of 2016, he was advertising his site as "the world's most visited alt-right website." One of the website's regular visitors was Dylann Roof, using the handle "AryanBlood1488."

What set the *Daily Stormer* apart from other alt-right sites was Anglin's open activism and eagerness to engage "the enemy" on social media and elsewhere, particularly with the trolling techniques he had mastered in previous forums. Among his most ardent participants at the site were his "Stormer Troll Army," followers who perpetrated various forms of online harassment against targets named by Anglin in his *Daily Stormer* posts. The site also maintained a bulletin board–style system for its internal forum, which permitted the organizing—and the undiluted racism—to proceed "in private."

Largely owing to the example of the *Daily Stormer*, trolling became the alt-right's reigning ethos, and Andrew Anglin was the movement's troll king. He targeted some of his supposed allies.

Most important, he targeted *Breitbart News*. He attacked *Breitbart News* for being too friendly toward Israel; he attacked Alex Jones for being married to a Jewish woman and launched a campaign titled Operation: Jew Wife. He leveraged a number of racist hashtags—#GasTheKikes, #RaceWarNow, #WhiteGenocide—both to spread his ideology and to harass Jews, journalists, and minorities.

But Anglin's agenda was more than just details. He felt utter contempt for Breitbart's attempt to align itself with mainstream conservatism. This contempt broke out into the open after Milo Yiannopoulos and Allum Bakhari posted "An Establishment Conservative's Guide to the Alt-Right." Anglin published his own lengthy manifesto of sorts, titled "A Normie's Guide to the Alt-Right," in which he set out to correct the record, as it were. He dismissed the Yiannopoulos-Bakhari piece as an "alternate history of the movement" that was "contrived and largely nonsensical." He tore into "forced leaders who had little or nothing to do with the ideological and spiritual journeys of most people who make up the movement."

Anglin was clear about the role of white nationalists such as Spencer, Taylor, Brimelow, Heimbach, and Griffin in the alt-right's origins and unapologetic about their ideologies. He also detailed the importance of conspiracism and the "manosphere." He explained that the core ideology of the alt-right was composed of anti-Semitism, "white countries for white people"; "scientific racism"; "opposition to feminism and 'gender equality'"; " support for "traditional families"; the endorsement of "white history"; "common sense economics"; and the view of "the white struggle as a global battle." He wrote: "The core concept of the movement, upon which all else is based, is that Whites are undergoing an extermination, via mass immigration into White countries which was enabled by a corrosive liberal ideology of White self-hatred, and that the Jews are at the center of this agenda."

Anglin also correctly pointed out that the alt-right in reality was made up of a broad network of websites, Internet media figures, and social-media activists, well beyond the handful of relatively obscure players named in the Breitbart piece. And even beyond Anglin's list, there were other key contributors as well:

The Right Stuff is a website founded anonymously by someone who calls himself "Mike Enoch" in 2012 with the intent, according to its mission statement, of "reinvigorating dialogue among a disparate and edgy right-wing" and "severely rustling jimmies among the childish and regressive left-wing … We're white and we're not sorry." The site engages in the open promotion of ethnic cleansing ("Genocide is just a word invented by a Jew to demonize the Nazis") and anti-Semitism. It reached its greatest notoriety so far in the summer of 2016, when an Internet meme it created on its "Daily Shoah" podcast, involving a novelty "echo" sound whenever a Jewish name was used, spread to social media as three sets of parentheses around the name: (((Cohen))). The meme was used to harass Jewish journalists on social media and elsewhere.

Danger and Play, a "manosphere" website, was created by Mike Cernovich in 2011 after his first wife divorced him. He claimed that the marriage had been "ruined by feminist indoctrination." The site specializes in anti-feminist rants, but also ardently embraces the tenets and conspiracism of white nationalists. Cernovich makes use of the lingo and social-media tirades common to the alt-right, attacking "cucks," "cuckservatives," "cultural Marxists," and Muslims. "The only rape culture is Muslim rape culture," he tweeted March 9, 2016.

RamZPaul is the YouTube pseudonym of Paul Ramsay, a fifty-something father of two from suburban Tulsa, Oklahoma. He established the pseudonym in 2009 when he first began posting his thoughts in the form of often humorous video rants. His viewership began picking up steam and by 2013 his videos had racked up 5 million views. His comedic if openly transgressive self-presentation sometimes made his intent unclear; it usually took viewers awhile to realize that he was in fact a dedicated racist, someone who also posted regularly at Stormfront and Vanguard News Network. As he became increasingly associated with the alt-right, Ramsay's viewer numbers began climbing exponentially. His rants primarily revolved around his mockery of "the establishment's religion of Cultural Marxism," and he was known to call feminism "a disease … What is the cause? It is the delusion that the sexes are equal. It is the mother of all delusions." He also told a gathering of white nationalists: "We need to Balkanize and create our own homeland. We have a right to exist."

The Political Cesspool is a white nationalist podcast and radio show owned by James Edwards, a dedicated neo-Confederate and white nationalist. Edwards began broadcasting his three-hour weekly show in 2004, based out of WLRM-AM in Millington, Tennessee, sponsored by the Council of Conservative Citizens, on whose board Edwards sat. The show began raising a substantial following during Barack Obama's presidency, featuring such white-nationalist guests as the CCC's Gordon Baum, Jared Taylor, Michael Hill, president of the League of the South, and David Duke. The show's mission statement claims it "stands for the Dispossessed Majority," rejects "homosexuality, vulgarity, loveless sex, and masochism," and believes that "secession is a right of all people and individuals." Its tenth-anniversary celebration featured the alt-right luminaries Matthew Heimbach and Brad Griffin.

@RickyVaughn is the nom de plume of a wildly popular alt-right Twitter personality about whom little is known except that the real person behind it borrowed the name of a character in the Charlie Sheen movies *Major League* and *Major League II*. Establishing the account in 2014, @RickyVaughn labeled himself a "right-wing nativist" and launched into a series of tirades against "cuckservatives" and Muslim immigrants. He told Richard Spencer in an interview that he had been attracted to the alt-right after several years as a libertarian working for the Ron Paul campaign, and had become engaged in the anti-feminist "manosphere" blogs during the Gamergate controversy. But what fully radicalized him was the debate over the killing of Trayvon Martin, of which he said: "At that time I realized what a con job the media was playing on all of us, and how the mainstream race propaganda was all bullshit. So from there I began to explore the different facets of cultural Marxism. The Jewish role in subversion, homosexuality, et cetera."

Roosh V stands for Roosh Vörek, which is the pseudonym of a self-proclaimed "pickup artist" from Maryland named Daryuth

Valizadeh. Roosh V has published some twenty books instructing readers on how to "bang" the women of various nations; Icelandic officials described his book about that country's women as "a rape guide." He also sneered at "American cunts who I want to hate fuck." Valizadeh described his philosophy as "neomasculinity," which he said "aims to aid men living in Westernized nations that lack qualities such as classical virtue, masculinity in males, femininity in females, and objectivity, especially concerning beauty ideals and human behavior. It also serves as an antidote for males who are being programmed to accept Western degeneracy, mindless consumerism, and immoral state authority." His speaking tour of Canada in 2015 drew numerous protests and calls for officials to ban him from entering the country.

weev—actually, Andrew "weev" Aurenheimer—was at one time a well-regarded "black hat" hacker (a hacker with malicious intent) who became a hero in hacker circles when he poked a hole in the security of Apple's iPad devices and exposed the information of 114,000 users. Aurenheimer apparently became radicalized in 2013 while serving a year in prison for the crime. When he emerged, with a large swastika now tattooed on his chest, he went to work for Anglin, providing tech support for the *Daily Stormer*. Among the lessons he had gained in prison: "A hostile government whose agents are not confronted with the deaths of their agents and their families on a regular basis will consider our Constitution as nothing more than toilet paper." In 2016, he began targeting printers at college-campus offices around the country with faxed fliers containing violently racist rants. One of them read:

> I unequivocally support the killing of children. I believe that our enemies need such a level of atrocity inflicted upon them and their homes that they are afraid to ever threaten the white race with genocide again ... We will not relent until far after their daughters are raped in front of them. We will not relent until far after the eyes of their sons are gouged out before them. We will not relent until the cries of their infants are silenced by boots stomping on their brains out onto payment.

Given such a diverse array of worldviews and interests, not to mention the inherent contentiousness of each of their social-dominance-driven voices, it was inevitable that ideological and personality-driven fissures would begin appearing in the new movement as its leaders jockeyed to lead it and also define its outlines and political thrust. Many of them revolved around Andrew Anglin and the "1488ers."

Anglin was especially vicious in attacking not only the ideas in the Yiannopoulos-Bakhtari essay but Yiannopoulos personally. Anglin denounced Yiannopoulos as "a subversive and a disease, ... a homosexual Jew [who] jumped on the movement a few months ago and was promoted by the entire media, propelled as the representative of the 'official movement.'" Yiannopoulos had "a history of engaging in sneaky Jewish tricks ... Clearly, the man seeks to undermine right-wing movements for Jewish purposes."

In August 23, 2016, a *Washington Post* profile of the alt-right largely succumbed to the whitewashed version of the movement peddled by Breitbart.com, concluding, "The goal is often offensiveness for the sake of offensiveness in the way that many young white men embrace." Anglin retorted: "No it isn't. The goal is to ethnically cleanse White nations of non-Whites and establish an authoritarian government. Many people also believe that the Jews should be exterminated."

The troll king's quarrel was not just with *Breitbart* and mainstream conservatives. RamZPaul had begun claiming that the *Daily Stormer* was actually a subversive operation funded by the Anti-Defamation League to make the alt-right look bad. Anglin shot back: "Ram's apparent assertion (again, the obscure style of humor creates this plausible deniability angle for him) is that the *Daily Stormer* is a Jewish-run Neo-Nazi organization."

More feuds broke out. Richard Spencer became involved in a dispute among white nationalists over some of his organizing tactics abroad and tangled with a longtime ally, Greg Johnson of the white-nationalist site *Counter-Currents*. RamZPaul came in for more attacks after he began criticizing other white nationalists for supporting the candidacy of a neo-Nazi candidate in Kentucky named Robert Ransdell.

After recounting all the white-nationalist internecine "beefs," Brad Griffin advised his *Occidental Dissent* readers to "get your popcorn." He later joined Anglin in deriding *Breitbart News* as part of "the Alt-Lite."

The new movement's leaders often spoke of their ambitions to replace establishment mainstream conservatism with a new vision of a white-identity-driven American right. However, it was looking as though it would share the fate of previous far-right populist movements in the United States: after a burst of initial organizing energy, it would dissolve in fractious disputes over ideology and strategy.

The movement needed something to make it cohere, something big enough to make the players forget their differences.

Pepe the Frog did not begin life as the mascot of the alt-right. His cartoonist creator, Matt Furie, a liberal Democrat, drew the smiling little green-faced fellow one day in 2005 as a character in an absurdist comic book called *Boys' Club*. Pepe's panel featured him peeing with his pants down around his ankles, saying, "Feels good, man."

Pepe's highly expressive features, the simplicity of the drawing, and the ease of altering his expressions made him a popular choice for Internet memes. By 2014, his visage had become one of the most popular memes on all of social media.

And then he was hijacked by the alt-right. Pepe was already wildly popular among the far-right trolls at 4Chan, and as they began spreading out to other forums, Pepe's image came increasingly to be featured in alt-right Internet memes. Andrew Anglin featured Pepe's visage prominently at the *Daily Stormer*. Other alt-right activists began claiming him as their own. Soon other users stopped using Pepe for their memes out of fear that they would be presumed to be racist white nationalists.

In September 2016, Furie voiced his dismay to an interviewer from *Esquire*: "It sucks, but I can't control it more than anyone can control frogs on the Internet," he said.

It was only a dumb cartoon, but what Pepe really represented to the alt-right was something much deeper and more powerful: irony. The leaders and followers of the alt-right are much smarter than their forebears in the Ku Klux Klan and Aryan Nations. Their rhetoric is driven by humor—undergirded by vile racism, violence, and open eliminationism, such as the memes portraying President Obama being hung, or Pepe the frog raping Hillary Clinton.

As Anglin explained it at the *Stormer*, "A movement which meets all of the SPLC's definitions of Neo-Nazi White Supremacism using a cartoon frog to represent itself takes on a subversive power to bypass historical stereotypes of such movements, and thus present the ideas themselves in a fun way without the baggage of *Schindler's List*."

Pepe is hardly the only cartoon figure deployed by the alt-right. The alt-right's roots in 4Chan are on display in its many anime-inspired memes, most of them showing cute cartoon girls wearing various kinds of Nazi regalia or sporting openly misogynist, racist, and anti-Semitic texts. Comic characters of various kinds are deployed to ironically promote white-nationalist ideas.

The alt-right established itself primarily through its cultural agility—its ability to stay at the forefront of events, themes, ideas, and names in the media by adapting them to their own uses and then running wild with them. Richard Spencer explains that these memes have "power" and are "a way of communicating immediately."

The alt-right's memes and other cultural markers—from anti-Semitic "echo," now also used by Jews and others pushing back on the meme, to the use of "Shitlord" as an honorific to describe alt-right true believers—can be inscrutable to outsiders, and have served as a kind of secret handshake for alt-right cognoscenti. The most prominent of these is the #WhiteGenocide hashtag that spread throughout social media, a handy reduction of the white-nationalist mantra, "Diversity Is a Code Word for White Genocide." Alt-rightists also spread the slogan through highway billboards and on fliers.

Many alt-right memes are not original: instead alt-righters hijack images from popular culture, for example, using Taylor Swift's image to promote "Aryan" beauty, or attacking the new *Star Wars* films for including major black and female characters. Others express a fixation on masculinity, such as "cuck" or "cuckservative," terms used to suggest that mainstream conservatives are spineless cuckolds. Others tap into deep veins of American racism, such as the term "dindu nuffin," a linguistic caricature of "I didn't do nothing," used to describe African Americans, especially Black Lives Matter protesters. These and other such terms are deployed as social media hashtags—#Cuckservative, #Dindu—that spread the ideas behind them readily to a mostly young and impressionable audience.

Frequently, alt-right activists describe the conversion to their point of view as getting "red pilled," for the red pill in the 1999 science fiction film *The Matrix* that enables Keanu Reeves to see reality. Alt-righters see it as a metaphor for what they consider to be the revelatory power of their ideology, which cuts through the lies of "social justice warriors" (SJWs), cultural Marxists," and the mainstream media they insist are actively suppressing their views.

"The Alt-Right is a 'mass movement' in the truest possible sense of the term, a type of mass-movement that could only exist on the Internet, where everyone's voice is as loud as they are able to make it," explained Anglin. "In the world of the Internet, top-down hierarchy can only be based on the value, or perceived value, of someone's ideas. The Alt-Right is an online mob of disenfranchised and mostly anonymous, mostly young White men … *The mob is the movement.*"

But the alt-right was much more. It had effectively become a massive mechanism for the online radicalization of young white Americans.

Domestic terrorism attacks in Chattanooga, Tennessee, and San Bernardino, California, in the fall of 2015 and the massacre of forty-nine people at a gay nightclub in Orlando, Florida, were all committed by nonwhites ostensibly motivated by Islamist extremism.

In their wake various experts on terrorism and media pundits and government officials began raising concerns about the role of the Internet in radicalizing Muslims and fueling such violence.

But the massive media and public attention to these incidents also underscored how disproportionate this response was compared to the response to acts of terrorism committed by those influenced by white supremacism or other kinds of far-right extremism. Both media accounts and law enforcement officials were reluctant to identify Dylann Roof's rampage as domestic terrorism, despite the fact that it easily fit the FBI definition of terrorism: politically motivated acts of violence intended to influence policy and/or terrorize the public.

Similarly, when an anti-abortion extremist shot up a Planned Parenthood clinic in Colorado Springs, Colorado, in November 2015, and killed three people, and when a militia gang was arrested for plotting to bomb a Kansas Muslim community in October 2016, not only were the crimes not identified as domestic terrorism, but the cases received relatively little media and public attention. All of these incidents had one thing in common: their perpetrators had been radicalized online. Dylann Roof spent most of his days reading alt-right websites.

It was little noted, despite plenty of evidence, that the same phenomenon believed to be fueling terrorist acts by Muslim radicals was occurring simultaneously on a large scale in a complete separate region of the Internet: among radical white male nationalists of the alt-right. The people being radicalized were not brown-skinned foreigners who subscribed to a different religion, but the young white men and women in white America's neighborhoods and churches and colleges, white America's sons and daughters.

How does online radicalization happen? The phenomenon has been studied for years, and there are a number of different models that have been developed for understanding it. Most of them have been geared toward examining Islamist radicals, but their findings fit remarkably well in explaining how the same process works with white nationalism.

One of these theories, "identity demarginalization," articulated by Katelyn McKenna and John Bargh in a 1998 study, attempts to explain why some social groups are more drawn to the Internet than others. People with "concealable and culturally devalued identities" were found to be more likely than people with ordinary mainstream identities to participate in and value online communities. McKenna and Bargh's study found that people who posted in online forums dedicated to concealable identities valued the feedback and opinions of other group members much more powerfully than people who belonged to forums focusing on easily perceivable marginalized identities, such as obesity and stuttering.

McKenna and Barge wrote that because of the Internet, it was now possible for an individual exploring his or her marginalized identity to "reap the benefits of joining a group of similar others: feeling less isolated and different, disclosing a long secret part of oneself, sharing one's own experiences and learning from those of others, and gaining emotional and motivational support."

A 2012 study by Neal Caren, Kay Jowers, and Sarah Gaby that examined subscribers to the neo-Nazi website *Stormfront* and the white-nationalist movement observed that the Internet's elimination of spatial boundaries allows online communities "to draw in otherwise isolated movement participants." McKenna and Bargh found that a kind of self-reinforcing called "demarginalization" also occurs in online communities, whereby individuals who actively participated in online discussions not only came to "consider the group identity more important than did those who did not actively participate" but also intensified their own marginalized behaviors based on the positive reinforcement from other group members.

According to J. M. Berger, a fellow with the George Washington University Program on Extremism, there are four stages of online recruitment:

1. First contact with a potential recruit.
2. Creation of a "micro-community" in which recruiters generate an echo chamber of radical ideas around the target.

3. A shift to private communications.
4. Determination of which type of action the recruit should perform.

Within that framework, there are an infinite number of variables, all dependent on the interests and personal psychological needs of the recruit and the ideology of the radicalizing movement. On the alt-right, the psychological profile often seems to be a powerful sense of aggrieved entitlement.

The process of radicalization also occurs in steps. The journalist Abi Wilkinson examined the course of various alt-right adherents as they became increasingly extreme and even violent in their views, writing in 2016:

> Reading through the posting history of individual aliases, it's possible to chart their progress from vague dissatisfaction, and desire for social status and sexual success, to full-blown adherence to a cohesive ideology of white supremacy and misogyny. Neofascists treat these websites as recruitment grounds. They find angry, frustrated young men and groom them in their own image. Yet there's no Prevent [a UK program for identifying extremists] equivalent to try to stamp this out.

Keegan Hankes, an analyst with the Southern Poverty Law Center who specializes in monitoring the alt-right, explained that the very shape of the alt-right's discourse plays an important role in its recruitment: people are first exposed to alt-right ideas via wildly over-the-top jokes that celebrate Nazis or other kinds of ugly behavior designed to attract attention by their craziness.

"You know, people will laugh at these things, just because they're so transgressive," says Hankes. "And who is most susceptible to that? Young minds. The idea is to attract young minds, and of course, they are targeting the people who spend the most time in these environments. This movement is very immersive, and people wind up building their whole lives around it."

The targeting of a young, impressionable white audience was made manifest in the summer of 2015. It was during the height of the Pokémon Go craze, when young people everywhere could be seen walking about in public and congregating in "gyms," online battle areas, while searching for Pokémon to capture on their phone. Swooping in on the idea was Andrew Anglin at the *Daily Stormer*, who publicized a campaign to target Pokémon Go "gyms" for distribution of white-supremacist recruitment fliers.

Hankes explains that the alt-right's recruitment process doesn't merely entail the ongoing contact with fresh recruits, but also takes in the bigger picture. The strategy is "to change what's acceptable to talk about" in public and in the media.

Hankes notes that Anglin is especially keen on this idea, which is why the discourse at the *Daily Stormer* is so wildly and crudely racist and pro-Nazi; such talk makes more intellectual-sounding white-nationalist ideas, such as forming a separate white nation, sound eminently reasonable in comparison. And it inures the public to the existence of hateful rhetoric. Anglin's idea, says Hankes, "is that when you change what you can talk about, … [when] that slight change about what's acceptable to see in discourse, what's not being censored out, occurs, it's enough to awaken all these people they think are sympathetic to these ideas."

Berger, whose focus for most of his career has been on Islamist radicalism, writes that he sees the potential for white-nationalist radicalism to spread even wider and faster than Islamist radicalism:

> After decades of being silenced, white nationalists could suddenly organize into significant audiences. Functional anonymity insulated many adherents from the professional and social consequences of professing overt racism in the real world. And they could project their message to audiences who had not sought them out—hundreds of thousands more.

By the summer of 2015, the alt-right was gaining significant momentum as an online movement. But it lacked a real leader—a charismatic political figure around whom it could finally coalesce, whom its members could devote their energies to electing to office.

It was the perfect time for Donald Trump to come along.

11

"Hail Emperor Trump!"

D onald Trump had expressed his interest in possibly running for president someday on numerous occasions. It took a personal humiliation, borne of his ardent adoption of a far-right conspiracy theory, to make him get serious about it.

A Trump candidacy had first been mooted in 1992, when he was briefly considered as a replacement running mate for George H. W. Bush, but was passed over when Bush retained the incumbent, Dan Quayle. Then in 1999, he flirted with running for president on the Reform Party ticket; he won a couple of that party's primaries, then dropped out.

He started taking the idea seriously in 2011, publicly speculating about the possibility of running against the incumbent president, Barack Obama, in his frequent TV appearances in the wake of his stint as host of the popular reality TV show *The Apprentice*. A poll released in March 2011 found him leading among potential GOP contenders, a point ahead of the eventual nominee, Mitt Romney. Another poll a month later gave him a nine-point lead in the field.

Trump began making headlines that spring by becoming a Birther. After their initial appearance in 2008 and 2009, the Birther theories had come to be widely rejected in mainstream media. Soon, believing the theories came to be considered a certain sign of nutty extremism, if not outright racism. "Here is what the Republican party needs to do: we have to say that's crazy," South Carolina's Senator Lindsey

Graham, a Republican, told reporters in October 2009. "So I'm here to tell you that those who think the president was born somewhere other than Hawaii, you're crazy ... Let's knock this crap off and talk about the real differences we have."

None of this deterred Donald Trump. On April 5, 2011, he told reporters he'd been asked about it a few weeks before in an interview and replied that he didn't really know, but said that since then he'd looked into it and now believed "there is a big possibility" that Obama's presidency might be in violation of the Constitution.

"I'd like to have him show his birth certificate," Trump said. "And to be honest with you, I hope he can."

There was an immediate backlash, but instead of backing away, Trump doubled down. "Three weeks ago when I started, I thought he was probably born in this country," Trump told Meredith Vieira on the *Today* show. "Right now, I have some real doubts." He also doubted that Obama's college grades had been good enough to get him into Harvard Law School. Trump soon announced that he had commissioned a team of investigators to fly to Hawaii to look into the matter. Later he said on *Today*, "They cannot believe what they're finding."

Joseph Farah, the publisher of the conspiracist online newspaper *World Net Daily*, told *Politico* reporter Kendra Marr that he was in daily contact with Trump that month. "We have been speaking quite a bit," he said, exulting in what he saw as a positive response. "It's irresistible theater, but he's actually winning support."

According to *Politico*, Trump was contacted by *World Net Daily* when he first began talking about the Birther theories. Farah offered Trump a Birther primer: "His people were very quick to respond," he said.

Farah said he advised Trump to simply ask, "Where is the birth certificate?" and to skip talking about such particulars as what Obama's grandmother had said.

The controversy kept swirling as Trump called on Obama to lay the citizenship issue to rest by releasing the long form of his birth certificate, which had been kept private by records officials in

Hawaii. Two days later, on April 27, Obama did so, releasing the entire long form along with a statement hoping that the issue was finally done with.

If only. The release actually set off a fresh round of theorizing by amateur document experts who claimed that the form was a fake. Trump joined in the next day, saying he was proud of his role in forcing the document's release, but added that he hoped it "checks out," concluding: "We have to see, is it real?"

Three days later, on May 1, Obama had his revenge. It was the annual White House Correspondents Dinner, a black-tie affair at which political satire and humor is the primary fare, with the president typically among the participants in spreading the levity. Donald Trump was in the audience, and had been seen gregariously shaking hands and chatting up politicians before the event got under way. Obama opened the night by diving right into the birth-certificate affair: "My fellow Americans ... It is wonderful to be here at the White House Correspondents' Dinner ... As some of you heard, the state of Hawaii released my official long-form birth certificate. Hopefully this puts all doubts to rest. But just in case there are any lingering questions, tonight I'm prepared to go a step further. Tonight, for the first time, I am releasing my official birth video."

A cartoon version of a "secret birth video" then played to much laughter. Obama continued with the joking patter, skewering a number of his critics and rivals, including Romney, who Obama noted had actually passed health-care reform as governor of Massachusetts—"Somebody should look into that! And I know just the guy to do it—Donald Trump is here tonight!" he joked.

Obama continued: "Now, I know that he's taken some flak lately, but no one is happier, no one is prouder to put this birth certificate matter to rest than The Donald. And that's because he can finally get back to focusing on the issues that matter—like, did we fake the moon landing? What really happened in Roswell?"

Some of those present reported that Trump spent most of the dinner hunched over his plate, and departed swiftly when the event was over. A *New York Times* account several days later noted that he was "incredibly gracious and engaged on the way in [but departed] with maximum efficiency."

Few people among the pundit class took any of this very seriously. It was widely assumed that Trump was actually just trying to pump up the ratings for *The Apprentice* with his Birther flirtation. In mid-May 2011, he announced he wouldn't be running for president and instead endorsed Romney.

But Trump did not relent in promoting the Birther theories, nor did the theories fade away. In August 2011 Arizona's notoriously nativist Sheriff Joe Arpaio announced that—at the request of the local Tea Party Patriots in the retirement community of Surprise—he would launch a full-scale investigation of Obama's birth. He sent a couple of detectives to Hawaii to sniff around, initially at the expense of private donors.

Arpaio held a press conference on March 31, 2012, to inform reporters that he was now completely convinced that Obama's long-form birth certificate was a forgery. That May, he dispatched a Maricopa County "threats detective" to Hawaii to aid in the investigation "for security reasons" (county taxpayers footed the bill).

Trump wrote a personal letter of congratulation to Arpaio: "Joe—Great going—You are the only one with the 'guts' to do this—Keep up the good fight—Donald Trump," he scribbled on a printout of news coverage of Arpaio's March 31 press conference.

Trump also continued to tweet out Birther theories. On May 12, 2012, he posted: "Let's take a closer look at that birth certificate. @BarackObama was described in 2003 as being 'born in Kenya.'" A few months later, in August, he tweeted: "An 'extremely credible source' has called my office and told me that @BarackObama's birth certificate is a fraud." He began reaching deep into the conspiracist mindset the next year when a Hawaii health official was killed in a December aviation accident, inspiring him to tweet: "How amazing, the State Health Director who verified copies of Obama's 'birth certificate' died in plane crash today. All others lived."

Trump, intentionally or not, had become the nation's most prominent promoter of the Birther theory, and in doing so immediately established a firm level of credibility in the conspiracist universe. That credibility, however, did not extend into every corner of the far right. Alex Jones had become a fan of Senator Rand Paul of Kentucky, the son of Ron Paul, and ardently supported his candidacy through most of 2015. Indeed, in July he called Trump part of a New World Order conspiracy to stop Paul.

Andrew Anglin was also a Trump skeptic early on, telling a commenter at his forum that Trump was "interesting," but concluded that he also clearly was "not one of us."

However, Trump began gaining fans among other far-right conspiracists. The radio talk-show host Michael Savage, probably the most popular and widely heard anti-liberal ranter after Rush Limbaugh and Alex Jones, hosted Trump on his show on February 20, 2014, and begged him to run for president: "We don't have a candidate who could beat Hillary, other than you. I'll go out on a limb and say it right now: whoever the conservatives are thinking of putting up there, they can't beat Hillary, and you could. I think you should run."

Throughout 2014, Savage ratcheted up attacks on President Obama, claiming that he was trying to wipe out Americans by allowing migrant children to bring disease across the border; that he was trying to bring an Ebola epidemic to the United States; and that soldiers with post-traumatic stress disorder—whom he called "a bunch of losers"—were weaklings symptomatic of the forces destroying the country. He also wanted the new Republican Congress to promptly arrest the president.

Savage and Trump formed a mutual-admiration society. "I love your show, you're a special guy," Trump told Savage in their February interview. "I've known over the years what a great show you have."

Soon enough, support for Trump in the extremist universe began spreading. At the white-nationalist website *VDare*, the columnist Matthew Richer devoted an April 12, 2015, piece to the rich possibilities of a Trump candidacy: "Maybe Donald Trump will run and maybe Donald Trump is an immigration patriot ... Given ...

Trump's public criticisms of GOP squeamishness on immigration over the last few years, Trump certainly deserves a closer look."

When Trump made his candidacy official two months later, on June 16, he earned more than a "closer look" from the American far right—he got the support not just of the conspiracists like Savage, but of all its other sectors: the white nationalists, Patriot movement militiamen, neo-Nazis, Klansmen and other white supremacists, and the budding white-male-power trolls of the alt-right.

Thus it was that the interrelated but often disputatious spheres occupied by the followers of these ideologies were united by Donald Trump. Combined, they converged to form a massive new alternative universe they all shared: Alt-America.

The initial coverage of Trump's announcement of his presidential candidacy scarcely mentioned the remarks that would become the focus of a raging controversy about his candidacy within the week—his description of Mexican immigrants: "They're bringing drugs. They're bringing crime. They're rapists. And some, I assume, are good people."

It wasn't until later in the week that the media began reporting that those remarks had created an uproar both within the Hispanic American community and abroad, in Latino nations. "This is a man who has a pathological need for attention," said Lisa Navarrete, a spokeswoman for the National Council of La Raza (now known as UndidosUS), a Hispanic civil rights and advocacy organization. "I look at him as a two-year-old who will say a naughty word to get their parents' attention. That's what he's doing."

Officials in Mexico were outraged: "The remarks by Donald Trump seem prejudicial and absurd," said Miguel Ángel Osorio Chong, Mexico's interior minister. "He surely doesn't know the contributions made by migrants from practically every nation in the world, who have supported the development of the United States." In Mexico, piñatas featuring images of Donald Trump began appearing at markets and sold wildly.

Trump shortly responded, issuing a statement:

I am personally offended by the mainstream media's attempt to distort my comments regarding Mexico and its great people. I have many successful business relationships with Mexican companies and employ and am close friends with many Mexican people. I also have tremendous respect for the leaders of Mexico, who, frankly, are much smarter and tougher than our politicians here in the United States.

Pressed to clarify his position a few days later in an interview, he explained: "Some are good and some are rapists and some are killers. We don't even know what we're getting."

Even if Trump really had not implied that all Mexican immigrants were criminals—as a strictly literal reading of his comments would interpret them—they were, even at their most benign, a smear of those immigrants. The *Washington Post* awarded Trump four "Pinocchios" for dishonesty:

Trump's repeated statements about immigrants and crime underscore a common public perception that crime is correlated with immigration, especially illegal immigration. But that is a misperception; no solid data support it, and the data that do exist negate it. Trump can defend himself all he wants, but the facts just are not there.

But none of that mattered to the Republican base, the voters Trump wanted to reach. What mattered to them was Trump's vow to construct a wall along the entire border with Mexico: "I will build a great, great wall on our southern border. And I will have Mexico pay for that wall," Trump told his audience.

Within days, the chant was heard at Trump's rallies: "Build that wall! Build that wall!" Soon, "the Wall" became the chief symbol of Trump's candidacy.

The seemingly open display of anti-Latino bigotry that erupted disgusted many observers and pundits, who predicted that Trump would pay a price among voters. Instead, Trump began rising in the polls, easily leading the Republican field when polls were released in early July. Emboldened, Trump doubled down on the remarks about Mexicans.

"I can never apologize for the truth," Trump said in a Fox News interview on July 5. "I don't mind apologizing for things. But I can't apologize for the truth. I said tremendous crime is coming across. Everybody knows that's true. And it's happening all the time. So ... all of a sudden I'm a racist. I'm not a racist. I don't have a racist bone in my body."

The next day he issued a statement to clarify what he meant: "What can be simpler or more accurately stated? The Mexican Government is forcing their most unwanted people into the United States. They are, in many cases, criminals, drug dealers, rapists, etc."

This talk was certainly popular with Republican voters—but its effect on the extremist right was downright electric.

"I urge all readers of this site to do whatever they can to make Donald Trump president," gushed Andrew Anglin, officially endorsing Trump twelve days after the announcement. Anglin hailed Trump as "the only candidate who is even talking about any-thing at all that matters."

"His announcement contained many important statements, but the most important were about Mexicans ... I agree with this entirely. Even the part about some being 'good people.' I also assume that some of them are 'good,' in the sense that all they want to do is work, but that is not in any way the point. The point is: Why are they here?"

The godfather of the "culture wars," Patrick Buchanan, hailed Trump's candidacy the day after the announcement: "A vote for Trump is a vote to say that both parties have failed America and none of the current crop of candidates offers real hope of a better future," he wrote in his syndicated column. "Politically incorrect and socially insensitive certainly, but is he entirely wrong?"

Peter Brimelow's white-nationalist website, *VDare*, on July 9 published a piece titled, "We Are All Donald Trump Now":

Case in point: The unprecedented political and economic terror campaign being waged against Republican presidential candidate Donald Trump for stating the facts about immigrant crime ... And this characteristically totalitarian Cultural Marxist drive reveals an American political and economic system increasingly defined by increasingly blatant hatred of the historic American nation in general and of white males in particular.

Trump is important because he represents the first figure with the financial, cultural, and economic resources to openly defy elite consensus. If he can mobilize Republicans behind him and make a credible run for the Presidency, he can create a whole new media environment for patriots to openly speak their mind without fear of losing their jobs.

Other white nationalists were attracted by the controversy, but were not quite convinced yet. At Richard Spencer's white-nationalist *Radix Journal*, Gregory Hood posted "Why We Need a Troll as President" on July 22:

Trump is worth supporting ... because we need a troll. We need someone who can expose the system that rules us as the malevolent and worthless entity it is. We need someone who can break open public debate. We need someone who can expose and heighten the contradictions within the system. And we need someone who can call out the press, the politicians, and the pseudo-intellectuals as the empty shells they are. The fact that Trump himself is part of this same farce is utterly irrelevant.

Writers at the alt-right website *Occidental Dissent* were also lukewarm but intrigued: "After the eye glazing rollout of ¡Jeb! 2016, I thought the 2016 Republican presidential race was going to be a complete snorefest, but now with The Donald officially in the race, we will at least see some fireworks in the debates," wrote the site's editor-publisher, Brad Griffin.

Trump chased away any lingering doubts on August 16, when he put out a three-point, 1,900-word immigration plan. Of course it included construction of that border wall with Mexico, but more pointedly, he called for the mass deportation of all undocumented immigrants (an estimated 12 million people).

Trump's position paper convinced Jared Taylor of the white-nationalist *American Renaissance*, who published an August 20 piece titled "Is Trump Our Last Chance?":

> He is easily the best presidential candidate on border security and immigration since Pat Buchanan … And we can be sure he is not a bait-and-switch politician who excites supporters with a few sensible ideas and then betrays them. Mr. Trump has single-handedly made immigration the key issue of this election. His heart is in it when he says we need to build a wall, deport illegals, and have an immigration "pause" until every American who wants a job gets one.

David Duke enthused about the plan on his radio show, but stopped short of endorsing Trump. "I praise the fact that he's come out on the immigration issue. I'm beginning to get the idea that he's a good salesman. That he's an entrepreneur and he has a good sense of what people want to hear, what they want to buy," said Duke, noting that he had previously been critical of Trump's run.

Brad Griffin promptly jumped on the Trump bandwagon at *Occidental Dissent*: "I think a comparable moment just happened in American politics with marginalized and disaffected voters," he wrote.

> All those people, long laughed at and excluded from the "mainstream," who were cast out beyond the wall of "respectability," are now in the tank for Donald Trump. The signal has gone out to join the Trump campaign and to openly organize in the mainstream under the banner of the Republican frontrunner to take down the hated cuckservative establishment.

Peter Brimelow's *VDare*, on August 19, published a full-throated endorsement of Trump as a "wrecking ball" against Jewish influence, writing that "objectively, Trump's historical function is clearly to break the Washington Cartel and to bring the immigration issue into politics."

Trump fever quickly spread. Other extremists new to presidential politics who openly endorsed Trump included Don Black; Rocky Suhayda, chair of the American Nazi Party; and Rachel Pendergraft.

Richard Spencer's *Radix Journal* came aboard fully in September, writing in "Our Big, Fat, Beautiful Dog Whistle":

Looking at the question from another perspective, Trump is expressing the deeply symbolic nature of the immigration issue. By "symbolic," I don't mean that immigration is not a real issue with palpable and often immediate effects. What I mean is that when we talk about immigration, we're really talking about something else.

Concern over "illegal" immigration really means concern over White displacement by Hispanics and other non-Whites. In other words, when a conservative says "illegal immigrant," he or she is thinking of a dangerous Mexican gang member. Support for "legal" immigration, on the other hand, means that people have a hard time actively opposing the immigration of smart White people (and, to a less extent, Asians). When people talk about how great legal immigration is, they are imagining a Norwegian PhD in biochemistry. Leftists are thus entirely correct when they claim that the immigration debate is filled with racial "dog whistles."

Another leading white nationalist, the "academic racist" Kevin Mac-Donald, also saw the release of the immigration plan as "a game changer as far as I was concerned. I thought that was just terrific, and then I really started taking him seriously." MacDonald, writing at *Occidental Observer*, called Trump's plan a "breakthrough": "Trump is saying what White Americans have been actually thinking for a very long time."

Matthew Heimbach, a leading white nationalist, made his embrace of Trump official in October, in a piece headlined "The Trump Train and the Southern Strategy: The Only Hope for the GOP" at his website *Traditional Youth*:

> While Donald Trump is neither a Traditionalist nor a White nationalist, he is a threat to the economic and social powers of the international Jew. For this reason alone as long as Trump stands strong on deportation and immigration enforcement we should support his candidacy insofar as we can use it to push more hardcore positions on immigration and Identity. Donald Trump is not the savior of Whites in America. He is however a booming salvo across the bow of the Left and Jewish power to tell them that White America is awakening, and we are tired of business as usual.

◆

273

Donald Trump loves to portray himself as a man of the people, so throwing the microphone open to his supporters at a September 17 town hall gathering in Rochester, New Hampshire, seemed like a natural gesture. The first questioner at the town's Republican presidential primary event identified himself as someone "from White Plains" and came out with the kind of blunt talk that Trump himself reveres.

"We have a problem in this country," the man said. "It's called Muslims. You know our current president is one."

"Right," Trump answered, an unsurprising reply, perhaps, given that polls then showed that 66 percent of his supporters believed President Obama was secretly a Muslim.

"You know he's not even an American," the man continued.

Trump gestured to the audience: "We need this question. This is the first question."

"Anyway, we have training camps growing where they want to kill us," the man said. "That's my question: When can we get rid of them?"

"We're going to be looking at a lot of different things," Trump replied. "You know, a lot of people are saying that and a lot of people are saying that bad things are happening. We're going to be looking at that and many other things." And then he moved on.

In the days that followed, Trump was questioned about his response to the man. Why hadn't he corrected the man's claim that Obama is Muslim? Or his claims about training camps?

Trump answered the first question by saying that he didn't feel "morally obligated" to defend President Obama. Muslim-rights groups wanted to know why he seemed to condone the man's rabid hatred of Muslims and his plans to "look at" rounding them up. Trump ignored these issues.

Then another Republican presidential candidate, the conservative Ben Carson, added fuel to the fire. Asked by the host, Chuck Todd, on NBC's *Meet the Press* about Trump's response, Carson said that he didn't believe Islam was consistent with the US Constitution: "I would not advocate that we put a Muslim in charge of this nation. I absolutely would not agree with that," he said.

That, too, provoked an outcry, with Muslim civil-rights groups calling for Carson to "withdraw from the presidential race because he is unfit to lead, because his views are inconsistent with the United States Constitution." Indeed, Article VI, Paragraph 3, of the Constitution specifically prohibits any religious test for persons to hold office.

Moreover, many Muslim Americans saw the candidates' rhetoric as a sign that a fresh wave of the visceral, irrational ethnic loathing of all things Muslim was about to descend upon them. Bias against Muslims had been part of the American landscape since at least September 11, 2001, and now Islamophobia suddenly began reaching a fever pitch—a perfect storm of electoral politics, conspiracy theorizing, and nativist fearmongering.

Islamophobia had gradually infected small-town America, too, from Duncan, South Carolina, to Twin Falls, Idaho, to Irving, Texas—places where longtime operations that had carefully placed refugees from around the world in jobs and new lives in America were suddenly under siege from their own neighbors. These citizens, whipped up by anti-Muslim activists and right-wing media, were deeply fearful about Muslims—notably, those from Syria— destroying their communities.

One incident that caught national attention involved a Muslim teenager named Ahmed Mohamed, whom Irving, Texas, police arrested after he brought an electronic clock of his own making to school to show his teacher, who mistook it for a bomb. It soon emerged that Irving's mayor was well known nationally for her role as a right-wing activist against the (nonexistent) threat that "sharia law" was about to be imposed. She continued to defend her police force's actions in arresting the teen.

Though the teen's trauma was ameliorated somewhat by becoming a national celebrity toasted by President Obama and various tech companies for his bravery, the incident also clearly demonstrated the dangers of succumbing to ethnic fearmongering. Eventually, the conspiracists got around to fabricating a conspiracy theory about Mohamed and his clock: he was a tool of Islamist radicals and had carefully planned the whole stunt from the start. Within the month, Mohamed and his family had fled to Qatar, where the boy continued his education in peace at a prestigious academy.

Local media fueled these flames of fear. In Twin Falls, local talk-radio hosts encouraged an anti-Muslim discourse with discussions of refugees "changing our culture" and "bringing a threat to the community." One caller on Bill Colley's KLIX-AM radio show was especially upset about the criticism of Ben Carson: "This makes me mad, and also scared to death. We've got a Muslim, a Muzzie leader in this country, telling a presidential candidate that he should resign because of what he said? I mean—it is against the Constitution! They have Sharia law, we do not!"

Colley did nothing to discourage this kind of talk, but instead blandly folded it in with his own discussion.

The day after Trump's town hall broadcast, Alex Jones hosted Larry Klayman of Judicial Watch, a onetime respected Beltway insider who in recent years had gone off the rails in claiming that President Obama was secretly a Muslim conspiring to destroy America. That very theory was the primary subject of his interview with Jones.

The twist in this discussion was Klayman's belief that some generals might take out the president in a coup to prevent him from turning America into a subject nation of the Caliphate. "Maybe Obama is pushing them to the point that maybe someday will wage a coup in this country," Klayman speculated. "I'm not advocating that, but I know that some of these retired generals and admirals have talked about it. I know that, it's been in the public domain, because Obama, and I'll say it straight up because no one else is, … Obama is a Muslim through and through. Obama sympathizes with a Muslim Caliphate, Obama sympathizes with the mullahs in Tehran, he sympathizes with the radicals in the Far East."

The spread of Islamophobia into the conservative mainstream extended well beyond Trump and Carson. Most of the GOP's candidates indulged in Muslim bashing of some kind or another during the 2015 campaign:

Mike Huckabee, the former Arkansas governor turned TV show host, called Muslims departing mosques "uncorked animals," and said that Islam was "a religion that promotes the most murderous mayhem on the planet."

Governor Bobby Jindal of Louisiana refused to back down from his groundless claim that certain areas of Europe were "no go zones" dominated by Muslims using sharia law.

Former governor Jeb Bush of Florida hired as his political adviser Jordan Sekulow, who has a long background of anti-Muslim activism and is noted for calling supporters of the so-called Ground Zero mosque terrorists.

Senator Ted Cruz of Texas hired Kevin Kookogey as his Tennessee campaign chairman; Kookogey has a history of anti-Muslim activism.

Rick Santorum, too, had a long history of making anti-Muslim comments, including a speech at the 2014 Values Voters Summit in Washington, DC, in which he claimed that "the West" was in an existential struggle with the forces of "radical Islam" and commented that "you don't have Baptist ministers going on jihad." Santorum has also endorsed profiling Muslims by security and law enforcement officers.

But it was Trump, now the front-runner, who was the chief catalyst for some of the most overheated Muslim-bashing. In September he had told Bill O'Reilly on Fox News that the United States should take in more refugees from the Syrian crisis. On October 1, at a rally in New Hampshire, he abruptly changed his mind. Trump's rationale could have come straight out of an Alex Jones radio show: Syrian refugees could form a kind of fifth column military force within the United States. "This could be one of the great tactical ploys of all time—a two-hundred-thousand-man army, maybe!" Trump ranted. "Or if you sent fifty thousand, or eighty thousand, or one hundred thousand—we got problems! And that could be possible! I don't know that it is. But it could be possible. So they're going back. They're going back. I'm telling you."

This was met with loud applause.

"So if they come, that's great. And if I lose, I guess they stay," Trump continued, somewhat confusingly, but then he got back on track: "But if I win, they're going back. A lot of people will say, oh, that's not nice. We can't afford to be nice! We're taking care of the whole world, we're losing our shirts on everything we do! Everything we do!"

Trump was united with the aggrieved of Alt-America.

On November 22, 2015, Donald Trump sent out a retweet that impressed even Richard Spencer: "Wow. Just wow," he tweeted. Other white nationalists soon joined the chorus of tweets.

Trump had retweeted a graphic about crime statistics suggesting that black people were responsible for most crime in America—including the false claim that black people were responsible for the deaths of 81 percent of white homicide victims. The most remarkable aspect of Trump's retweet was not the spurious claim, but its source: #WhiteGenocide, an alt-right social-media hashtag for the white nationalist "mantra" that "multiculturalism is synonymous with white genocide." The tweet originated with a British white nationalist using the nom de plume "Non Dildo'd Goyim," who believes that and who, in addition to a profile featuring a swastika, has also tweeted out his admiration for Hitler.

The alt-right video blogging star RamZPaul rejoiced over the retweet with the comment "Trump watches and is influenced by the Alt Right." James Edwards, the white-nationalist host of the radio show the *Political Cesspool*, wrote on his blog that "Teflon Don," like " a masterful conductor," likely "knew the media would blast him for this retweet which would only solidify his growing base of support even more."

This new controversy followed the pattern of the Birther uproar: Trump makes a statement showing sympathy with an extremist point of view, he responds to the uproar by temporarily backing away, at least in his press appearances, and then declines further comment.

At times Trump issued official disavowals of the extremists who endorsed him, but this had little effect on his approval among the swelling ranks of alt-right supporters, who dismissed the disavowals as Trump's concessions to political realities. What mattered to them was the original signal.

At other times, Trump would actually double down, insist he was right and had done nothing wrong, and refuse to apologize or walk back his positions. This is what he did with the black-crime retweet: he declined to delete it, and shortly afterward followed up by telling Bill O'Reilly at Fox News, "Am I gonna check every statistic? I get millions and millions of people @realDonaldTrump by the way ... all it was was a retweet." Two months later he retweeted another #WhiteGenocide comment, this time about Jeb Bush. Over time, he would continue to retweet material from a range of white supremacists.

Among the white nationalists of the alt-right, this was all further confirmation that Trump was their champion. Andrew Anglin of the *Daily Stormer* explained after the January retweet: "Our Glorious Leader and ULTIMATE SAVIOR has gone full-wink-wink-wink to his most aggressive supporters ... Whereas the odd White genocide tweet could be a random occurrence, it isn't statistically possible that two of them back to back could be a random occurrence. It could only be deliberate."

The account @TheNordicNation celebrated too, posting, "You can say #WhiteGenocide now, Trump has brought it into the mainstream" and "Trump is the only one willing to stop white genocide by stopping non-white immigration." At the white-supremacist forum *Stormfront*, one user observed, "This is a GOOD thing. [Trump] willingly retweeted the name. The name was chosen to raise awareness of our plight. Helped propagate it. We should be grateful."

Earlier in January, when the white-nationalist American Freedom Party ran robocalls in support of Trump in Iowa, Spencer had worried on his blog, "This robocall could force him to distance himself from the American Freedom Party and American Renaissance, which wouldn't be good." But Jared Taylor and William Johnson, who voiced the calls, were thrilled by Trump's response.

Taylor wrote on *Political Cesspool*: "For days everybody was calling him up, calling up his campaign saying, 'What do you think of these horrible people? Denounce them, denounce them.' And he didn't, he maintained a dignified silence."

Though CNN's Erin Burnett got Trump to "disavow" them, Taylor read it as merely pro-forma, since Trump went on "to explain why people are so angry. In effect, he's saying, 'Yeah, yeah, if you want me to denounce it I will, but I understand exactly what these guys are saying, they're furious, and they're right to be furious.' So if he disavowed us, he did it, I thought, in the nicest possible way." Johnson, on *Political Cesspool*, called Trump's response "wonderful": "He disavowed us [American Freedom Party] but he explained why there is so much anger in America. I couldn't ask for a better approach from him."

This tango between Trump and his alt-right supporters in which Trump continued to lead and then back off continued until February 2016, when David Duke, after saying for months that he liked what Trump was saying, explicitly endorsed him. He told listeners to his radio show that voting against Trump was "really treason to your heritage."

When asked about Duke's endorsement by CNN's Jake Tapper, Trump demurred: "Well, just so you understand, I don't know anything about David Duke. OK? I don't know anything about what you're even talking about with white supremacy or white supremacists." Tapper pressed him, saying he simply wanted to know if Trump rejected Duke or the KKK. Trump continued to demur: "I don't know any—honestly, I don't know David Duke. I don't believe I have ever met him. I'm pretty sure I didn't meet him. And I just don't know anything about him."

The Monday after the interview aired, Trump went on MSNBC's *Morning Joe* and denounced Duke, saying, "David Duke is a bad person, who I disavowed on numerous occasions over the years." When the subject arose later, Trump referred back to this disavowal.

At *Occidental Dissent*, Brad Griffin hailed "Trump's 'disavowal' of David Duke and [his] refusal to cuck and condemn 'white supremacists.'" "Cuck" is derogatory alt-right-speak for a weakling of any kind. When RamZPaul hosted a Twitter discussion on the question of whether Trump was a "cuck" for disavowing, most participants concluded that it was a "quick short and smart answer" in order to avoid "media games." RamZPaul commended Trump for giving the best response he could, once forced into a "compliance test."

Duke himself was not fazed by the disavowal: "I'll laugh it off. It's fine. Look, Donald Trump, do whatever you need to do to get elected to this country, because we need a change," he said. In July, when he announced he was running for the Senate seat in Louisiana, he credited Trump with inspiring the bid: "I'm overjoyed to see Donald Trump and most Americans embrace most of the issues I've championed for years."

This pattern continued throughout the spring and summer and into the fall: when Trump disparaged the Mexican heritage of a judge overseeing the case involving a lawsuit for his now-defunct Trump University; when he refused to condemn anti-Semitic social media trolls who attacked the journalist Julia Ioffe after she wrote an unflattering portrait of his wife, Melania Trump; when he claimed that "some people" wanted a moment of silence for the black man who killed five and wounded nine police officers in Dallas; when his son and campaign officer, Donald Trump Jr., retweeted a comment from a notorious anti-Semite, and refused to delete it. Throughout the Trump campaign his tango with extremists continued.

And it worked: extremists were encouraged to continue supporting him—and to believe that they were building their own ranks because of him. As Jared Taylor put it, "People are being empowered through individuals such as Donald Trump who are unashamed of the truth."

Although he did not bring up the Birther issue at his rallies, Trump remained a firm, if not particularly vocal, defender of the theories. He let proxies bring it up.

On July 9, 2015, he appeared at a campaign rally in Phoenix with

Joe Arpaio where the "Nation's Toughest Sheriff" reminded voters, "We have a couple things in common, I won't talk much about them. One is the birth certificate. You don't have to be interested, but I am."

The next day, CNN's Anderson Cooper asked Trump about the birth-certificate business, and he used the same technique, saying, "Honestly, I don't want to get into it."

But Cooper was disinclined to let Trump off the hook so easily and asked him whether he really thought the president was born in the United States. Trump replied: "I don't know. I really don't know. I don't know why he wouldn't release his records."

Then he launched into a kind of diversionary defense, making the groundless claim that Hillary Clinton had originated the theory. "Do you know that Hillary Clinton was a Birther?" he said. "She wanted those records and fought like hell. People forgot. You know that John McCain was a Birther, wanted those records. They couldn't get the records. Hillary failed. John McCain failed.

"Trump was able to get something," he concluded. "I don't know what the hell it was, but it doesn't matter. Because I'm off that subject. I'm about jobs, I'm about the military, I'm about doing the right thing for this country."

Such conspiracy theories have been the mother's milk of right-wing extremism for most of the past century, and by mid-2015 had become the fuel for the massive expansion of the Alt-America universe. Trump's open embrace of the claims naturally made him a favorite among those conspiracists.

Now leading the parade was Alex Jones, after Trump's adviser Roger Stone appeared on Jones's show on November 9, 2015, and assured Jones and his listeners that "Trump is for real." On December 2, 2015, Trump himself came on Jones's *Infowars* for a full interview.

Trump warmly endorsed Jones, and the interview shortly became a mutual admiration society. "I know now, from top people, that you are for real, and you understand you're in danger, and you understand what you're doing, is epic—it's George Washington level," Jones gushed to Trump.

Trump gladly gushed back, "Your reputation's amazing. I will not let you down."

Jones ended by warning Trump, "You will be attacked for coming on. We know you know that. Thank you." They were now partners in understanding.

In the weeks and months that followed, Jones's conspiracy mill continued to churn out outlandish theories, including the suspicion that the election was going to be rigged in Clinton's favor: "If she stole the primary, she's going to steal the general," Jones intoned on his show and pleaded with Trump to make it a campaign issue. Two days later, Trump obliged, voicing his fears at a rally in Columbus, Ohio, that the election "is going to be rigged."

Jones later claimed that he was advising Trump personally and boasted that Trump was bringing his followers' views into the mainstream. For his part, Trump promoted many of Jones's conspiracy theories on his Twitter feed. This continued all through the 2016 election.

In August 2016, Jones marveled at his influence with Trump, saying, "And I'll tell you it is surreal to talk about issues here on air and then word for word hear Trump say it two days later … And it just shows how dialed in this guy is and that's why they're so scared of him."

Trump and Jones particularly bonded over their hatred of Hillary Clinton—it was not unusual to see a large number of Jones's "Hillary For Prison" T-shirts bedecking rallygoers at Trump events. It was one way the kind of ugliness that both Jones and Trump embraced spread to the crowds of ordinary voters who came to join what Trump called "my movement."

The real issue raised by Trump's embrace of Jones and his ideas was that the ideas often made themselves manifest in the real world. The key role played by conspiracy mongers like Jones and others in fueling violent talk and eventually violent behavior in their followers has been well documented.

"The kind of conspiracism pushed by Alex Jones and his ilk is not harmless," said Mark Potok, of the Southern Poverty Law Center.

"It names specific enemies and, in effect, promotes violence against those enemies. When rhetoric gets this extreme, it's a recipe and also an excuse for violence. The fact that a major-party nominee like Trump would essentially endorse the furious tirades of his friend Jones is just astounding."

As the weeks went on, and mainstream candidates continued to drop out of the race, it became increasingly clear that the real-estate tycoon was likely to become the official nominee of the Grand Old Party.

February 2016 had already seen the withdrawal of a slew of candidates: former Arkansas governor Mike Huckabee, senator Rand Paul of Kentucky, former senator Rick Santorum of Pennsylvania, former Hewlett-Packard CEO Carly Fiorina, Governor Chris Christie of New Jersey, and Jeb Bush. They were followed by Ben Carson and Marco Rubio in March. The only remaining candidate, Senator Ted Cruz of Texas—who had his own history of indulging in and encouraging far-right extremism and conspiracism—managed to remain in the race for several more weeks, primarily by gathering support from Christian evangelicals who were turned off by Trump's well-documented "amoral lifestyle" in the 1980s and '90s.

When Cruz finally folded his tent on May 3, unofficially handing Trump the Republican Party nomination, the extremist right celebrated in unison. The Internet buzzed all that week with the celebratory boasts of a broad range of right-wing extremists, from the ranks of neo-Nazi haters, Klansmen and other white supremacists to the hunkered-down conspiracy-spinning paranoids of the antigovernment movement—all of them cheering on their new hero, Donald Trump. Most of them made it clear that he was perhaps the first presidential candidate most of them could get behind unreservedly.

"White men in America and across the planet are partying like it's 1999 following Trump's decisive victory over the evil enemies of our race," exulted Andrew Anglin at the neo-Nazi website the *Daily Stormer*.

"He is getting white people excited for the first time in my memory," said a *Stormfront* participant. "Look at the crowds when he gets the cameras to pan out. They're huge (or should I say YUGE?) and almost one hundred percent white. It is fantastic to see."

Conspiracy-meister Alex Jones embraced Trump as being "basically like a Patriot sleeper cell," but warned him darkly against betraying their movement and its commitment to fighting the New World Order.

"Why not take a chance on him?" asked one *Stormfront* participant. "The choice of Clinton vs cuckservative isn't particularly good. Trump, by contrast, has said/proposed many things that are more implicitly pro-white than anything offered by an American politician in my lifetime."

Anglin, posting at the *Daily Stormer*, was downright giddy: "This is a buzz that won't soon wear off. Sort of like an IV drip of pure cocaine. Or perhaps like having a computer chip implanted in your brain which electronically stimulates continual dopamine release."

Other white supremacists weighed in on the Trump candidacy. Former Klan leader David Duke declared that Trump had scored a great victory for the cause of whites simply by becoming the GOP nominee:

> The Trump campaign at a whole series of levels is a great opportunity for us to expose the people who really run the Republican Party, who run the Democratic Party, who run the political establishment and who are leading us all to disaster. Even though Trump is not explicitly talking about European-Americans, he is implicitly talking about the interests of European-Americans.

Duke went on to explain how the Trump victory was guaranteed to help spread their ideology and to discredit the Jewish neo-conservatives he said had long claimed control of the Republican Party:

> I think that these Jewish extremists have made a terribly crazy miscalculation, because all they're really going to be doing by doing a "Never

Trump" movement is exposing their alien, anti-American, anti-American-majority position to all the Republicans and they're going to push people more into awareness that the neocons are the problem, that these Jewish supremacists who control our country are the real problem and the reason why America is not great.

"Jewish chutzpah knows no bounds," he observed, with no hint of irony.

Trump rebuked Duke's endorsement and his remarks, publishing a statement saying he "totally disavows" Duke's views. "Anti-Semitism has no place in our society, which needs to be united, not divided," Trump said.

But the flow of pro-Trump proselytizing continued to flow forth from the extremist right.

James Kirkpatrick of *VDare* chimed in with an encomium for the candidate:

Trump is taking the nationalist impulses the Republican Party has used for years and putting them at the forefront of his new political movement. He's downplaying some of the hardcore social issues which conservatives have already lost on anyway. He's abandoning rhetoric about slashing programs which actually benefit the Republican Party's core constituents. And he's tapping into a narrative of national redemption which is deeply felt all over the country.

Kirkpatrick concluded that "the Republican base has caught on. They have chosen to displace the Beltway Right entirely. And they don't want the same old goofy slogans—but a nationalist movement that will actually fight for them."

Matthew Heimbach of the pro-Trump Traditionalist Worker Party and his radio cohost, Sven Longshanks, on their daily radio show, *The Daily Traditionalist*, declared:

Trump has changed the face of politics around the world with his refusal to bow down to the monied interests and by doing so he has encouraged others to do the same.

The fires of nationalism, the fires of identity, the fires of anger against the corrupt establishment are arising all around Europe, all around America, all around the entire world ... Hail, Emperor Trump! And hail, victory!

It all came swirling to a climax in July, at the Republican National Convention in Cleveland.

Donald Trump's imminent coronation as the GOP nominee brought a floodtide of far-right groups to Ohio the week of July 18–21, who created something of a media circus outside the convention hall. Matthew Heimbach told reporters that he actually was encouraging delegates to write in the name of the long-dead neo-Nazi figure George Lincoln Rockwell as the nominee, since he thought that "Trump doesn't go far enough."

A contingent of Oath Keepers showed up. They eschewed their usual open-carry weapons, but still vowed to protect Trump supporters from the supposed threat of Black Lives Matter protesters. A handful of extremist black nationalists from the New Black Panther Party did show up, but there were no confrontations. Alex Jones was also outside, leading chants of "Hillary for prison! Hillary for prison!"

A contingent of armed militiamen, calling themselves the West Ohio Minutemen, walked around the convention perimeter and made sure everyone saw their AK-47s and G3s. They said they were there to "protect" their community.

Inside the convention hall, far-right figures mixed with a larger general parade of mainstream-conservative politicians, including the extremist anti-LGBT evangelical leader Rev. Jerry Falwell Jr. and the so-called "prosperity preacher" Mark Burns. The most noteworthy of these extremist speakers was the "constitutionalist" sheriff David Clarke, of Milwaukee County, who had somehow parlayed his fame with Richard Mack's far-right Constitutional Sheriffs and Peace Officers Association into a media career as a frequent guest on Fox News. There he weighed in on racial issues with incendiary language, accused President Obama of waging a "war on cops," and particularly smeared Black Lives Matter, describing them as "scum" and "subhuman" and calling for their eradication.

Spurred in part by the convention crowd's chants of "Lock her up!," Clarke said:

> You see, Donald Trump understands that what can make our nation safe again is a recommitment to a system of justice in which no government official, not even those who have fought their way to the marble and granite halls of Washington; no private citizen, not even Hillary Clinton; and no group of people, despite the fervor with which they press forward their grievances, can claim privilege above the law. It cannot happen in the United States.

Sarah Posner of *Mother Jones* spent the week talking to white-nationalist movement leaders, the type who preferred business suits to bullhorns—who were there to participate in the week's events, as well as network and hobnob.

Posner chatted with Peter Brimelow, at a party hosted by Milo Yiannopoulos. He told her the atmosphere at the convention reminded him of a rally he had attended in 1964 by the far-right Young Americans for Freedom and told her it was "phenomenal to see young people here."

Richard Spencer was there, too. He readily explained to Posner his support for Trump:

> It's not so much about policy, it's more about the emotions that he evokes. And emotions are more important than policy, emotions are more important than facts. Trump sincerely and genuinely cares about Americans, and white Americans in particular. And he expresses such nationalism and togetherness that no other candidate has expressed ... That is a complete change.

Posner asked Spencer about Trump's early-July retweet of the #WhiteGenocide "Star of David" meme, an attack on Hillary Clinton. Spencer explained, "Our emotions are more important than facts and policies ... I think that Trump really does love the American people, and he loves white people."

Spencer was especially bullish on the future prospects of the alt-right, thanks to Trump's ascendancy. "We're going to replace conservatives, who are losers and dorks and dumb," he said. "The alt-right is an intellectual movement. In the future, we're going to be thinking for conservatives.

"You need a think tank, you need a brain, for the ethno-state," he continued, alluding to the white-nationalist "homeland" he and other movement ideologues envision. "We're going to be the ones who are going to do that for conservatives. The conservative movement has been around since the 1950s, and they're saying the same nonsense since the foundation of *National Review*. And that's over. It just can't go on. We're the future. And we're smarter than they are."

For Spencer, Trump was not the logical outcome of a radicalized Republican Party, but an entirely new phenomenon born of the alt-right's growing prominence and mainstream conservatism's collapse. "I've met lots of conservatives," he said. "They're usually dumb. They're really sub-mediocre people. I don't think I've ever met an intelligent movement conservative."

At a screening later that week of a right-wing propaganda film, Posner caught up with Stephen Bannon, the film's director and the chairman of Breitbart News Network. Bannon had been one of the earliest and most consistently enthusiastic backers of Trump's candidacy on the alt-right.

Bannon took credit for fomenting "this populist nationalist movement" long before Trump came on the scene. He told Posner that Senator Jeff Sessions of Alabama, by then a Trump adviser, should get the most credit for laying the movement's groundwork. Trump, Bannon told her, "is very late to this party." Bannon also pointed to his other films, including a hagiographic Sarah Palin documentary, *The Undefeated*, and an exposé titled *Occupy Unmasked* as "very nationalistic films."

Three weeks later, on August 17, following some brief mid-campaign turmoil, Donald Trump held a press conference to announce who would lead his campaign: Stephen Bannon.

The Id Unleashed

I n the summer of 2016 until the election in November, drivers on Interstate 5 were treated to an occasional sighting of a large utility truck bedecked with bright signs, roaming up and down the Northwest corridor between Washington and Oregon on a regular basis.

The signs read, "Trump: Do The White Thing"; "Jew Lies Matter"; "Truth Dispels Darkness" (inscribed over a large swastika); and "'Holocaust' Is Hokum." The truck's owner was a well-known Oregon white supremacist named Jimmy Marr.

State police responded to complaints by explaining that Marr was not threatening anyone with his signs and it was well within his free-speech rights for him to drive on the I-5 with the signs. Marr exulted in the effect Donald Trump's campaign was having on his recruitment efforts. "Steamrolled 6 million miles of semitical correctness this Labor Day weekend. Resistance is feeble," he tweeted.

He described for his many admirers at the neo-Nazi Vanguard News Network website how he had driven to a book club meeting affiliated with Andrew Anglin's alt-right website, the *Daily Stormer*: "The young man who arranged the meeting was the newest convert to white nationalism and testified that Donald Trump had been his red pill. He told me that as a result of Internet searches for articles about Trump, he had stumbled across the *Daily Stormer*, and as a result of researching links there, things quickly spiraled out of the controlled narrative and he found himself carried away by the flood of truth."

That was pretty much how it all worked, in a nutshell: Trump was the gateway drug for the alt-right.

Right-wing extremism has always been woven into the American political and social landscape: the nativists, the paranoid conspiracists, the white supremacists, white nationalists, xenophobes, and misogynists. Donald Trump had the charisma to become a national-level coalescing figure for these many threads, and for the first time united them under one banner—his banner. He drew all those elements out of the fringe and into the mainstream of American politics.

Time and again the alt-right read Trump's winks and nods in their direction as confirmation that he was "on their side." For instance, after reporting critically on the Trump campaign, Jewish journalists were besieged by a flood of anti-Semitic hate messages on social media and elsewhere. Trump largely chose to remain silent on the matter.

"We interpret that as an endorsement," Andrew Anglin emailed the *Huffington Post*. "We support Trump because he is the savior of the White race, sent by God to free us from the shackles of the Jew occupation and establish a 1000 [*sic*] Reich." At the *Daily Stormer*, Anglin headlined one post "Glorious Leader Donald Trump Refuses to Denounce Stormer Troll Army."

The mainstreaming of alt-right ideology by the Trump campaign also had an invigorating effect on an older generation of white nationalists: David Duke, who used the impetus from the Trump campaign to launch a campaign for the US Senate in Louisiana; Jared Taylor; Peter Brimelow, who now reigned over *VDare*, a central address of the alt-right; and Rachel Pendergraft, Duke's successor at the helm of the Knights of the Ku Klux Klan (now the Knights Party) who specialized in white supremacist appeals to women.

Pendergraft endorsed Trump in December 2015. Via email she told me she attributed an increase in her organization's membership to Trump. "White people are realizing they are becoming strangers in their own country and they do not have a major political voice speaking for them," she wrote. "Trump is one example of the alternative-right candidate [whom] Knights Party members and supporters have been looking for. And we feel that through continued grassroots mobilization, more candidates will arise who will speak out for white Christian America."

In late August, *Occidental Dissent*'s Brad Griffin mused about the possibility of a Trump win: "Can you imagine a world in which white nationalists have come out of the closet, the charge of 'racism' elicits only a 'meh' and shrugged shoulders, and we have begun to openly organize?

"Don't underestimate the power of the presidency to legitimize marginalized people and deviant movements," he wrote. If Barack Obama can legitimize gay marriage and transsexuals, Donald Trump can legitimize the alt-right."

Trump's effect on the radical right went well beyond a mere recruitment boost. His rhetoric empowered extremists not just to angrily revive open expressions of bigotry, such as Jimmy Marr's truck rolling up and down I-5, but also to open the floodgates of violence inherent in the far right's ideology and unleash the nation's dark id.

All the long-suppressed hatreds and resentments, all the deep anger and black fears about the nation and the changing shape of American society, came bubbling up and burst into public view in predictably ugly ways. Trump's rhetoric seemingly gave permission for the unleashing of an eliminationist flood.

An increasing number of Trump followers seemed to feel empowered by his rhetoric and disdain for "political correctness" to freely express their own bigotry and racial or religious hatred, as well as freely professing the bizarre conspiracy theories concocted by Jones and his "Patriot movement" cohort. Sometimes, they also began acting out violently.

At Trump rallies, violence directed at protesters became so common that some incidents received relatively light media coverage. The violent trend began in the fall of 2015 with incidents in the South, where Trump supporters grabbed protesters' signs and assaulted them (first, on October 14, in Richmond, Virginia, and then on October 23 in Miami). The violence increased over time, leading his alt-right fans to ardently defend him on social media and dismiss the protesters as worthy of violence. After a March 9, 2016, rally in Fayetteville, North Carolina, Trump disparaged protesters from the stage and a black protester was hit. The alt-right social media maven @RickyVaughn tweeted: "Black militants preemptively kicked out of Trump rally. We wuznt gonna do nuffins, honest! we wuznt gonna protess."

Trump seemed to encourage the violence, directed both at protesters at his rallies and at minorities generally, by expressly suggesting the use of assaults and threats against them in his fiery rally speeches. When challenged by reporters he then danced around the issue.

In other words, he hewed to the same pattern he had already established in connection with controversial statements. In Cedar Rapids, Iowa, on February 1, 2016, Trump told rally participants to "beat the hell out of" protesters, said he'd like to "punch [a protester] in the face," and described the violent fate that "back in the old days" was expected for such protesters. But when Jake Tapper confronted him about it at the March 10, 2016, GOP presidential debate, he briefly decried the violence, and then rationalized it:

> We have twenty-five, thirty thousand people—you've seen it yourself. People come with tremendous passion and love for the country, and when they see protest—in some cases—you know, you're mentioning one case, which I haven't seen, I heard about it, which I don't like. But when they see what's going on in this country, they have anger …
>
> They love this country. They don't like seeing bad trade deals, they don't like seeing higher taxes, they don't like seeing a loss of their jobs where our jobs have just been devastated. And I know—I mean, I see it. There is some anger. There's also great love for the country. It's a beautiful thing in many respects. But I certainly do not condone that at all, Jake.

There were many other indications that increasing numbers of unrepentant racists were now openly advertising their ideology. A video of a flag-waving pro-Trump pickup truck and motorcycle convoy in Wrentham, Massachusetts, in July 2016 has voice-overs exchanging racial slurs on the CB channel: "Lynch the niggers by their dicks!" shouts one. Another says: "Burn every single nigger!" A third chimes in: "All I know is we got plenty of trees to hang niggers from."

Such vicious ideas were soon expressed in a nationwide surge of hate crimes, particularly against Hispanics, Muslims, and African Americans. Shortly after Trump opened his campaign with his speech denouncing Mexican immigrants, Latino organizations warned that his rhetoric could inspire hate crimes against people perceived to be undocumented immigrants. Those fears were realized in August 2015, when two white men in Boston beat up a Latino man and said they had been inspired by Trump: "Donald Trump was right. All these illegals need to be deported." Later, in May of 2016, a motorcyclist began beating a Latino man and a Muslim man outside a Wichita convenience store while shouting "Trump! Trump! Trump!" In Olympia, Washington, a white supremacist stabbed an interracial couple after seeing them kiss; a police officer investigating the case said the man began "talking about Donald Trump rallies and attacking people at the Black Lives Matter protest." On July 23, a video captured a white Trump supporter verbally assaulting a black woman on the New York subway and shouting, "Worthless stupid fucking stupid cunt. Donald Trump 2016! Put them back in the fucking fields where they belong."

Trump responded to these incidents with his now-familiar tango. About the Boston incident, at first he tweeted out a civic-minded response: "Boston incident is terrible. We need energy and passion, but we must treat each other with respect. I would never condone violence." But the next day he responded to reporters' questions with the same "love of country" rationalization: "I will say that people who are following me are very passionate. They love this country and they want this country to be great again."

Muslims were a special target for Trump supporters. On May 3, 2016, outside a DC Starbucks, a woman verbally assaulted another woman wearing a hijab (head scarf), telling her, "If Donald Trump wins the nomination, I'm going to vote for him so he can send all of you all back to where you came from." In October in Brooklyn, a frenetic Trump supporter attacked two women wearing hijabs as they walked their babies in strollers, knocking them down and screaming, "Get the fuck out of America, bitches!" She was charged with a hate crime.

The evidence was not merely anecdotal. A May 2016 study by the Bridge Initiative and Georgetown University found a sharp spike in anti-Muslim hate crimes nationally in 2015, especially in the wake of terrorist attacks, presumably by Islamist extremists, in Paris and San Bernardino, California. The study's authors found a correlation between the elevated level of attacks and the presidential election season, noting that after

> the first candidate announced his bid for the White House in March 2015, there have been approximately 180 reported incidents of anti-Muslim violence, including: 12 murders; 34 physical assaults; 49 verbal assaults or threats against persons and institutions; 56 acts of vandalism or destruction of property; 9 arsons; and 8 shootings or bombings, among other incidents.

The study also placed the blame on Trump, noting that he had "escalated anti-Muslim vitriol in the wake of the terrorist attacks in Paris, France in November 2015 rather than urge calm or international unity." It went on: "Mr. Trump made many anti-Muslim statements during televised appearances on mainstream news media outlets, impacting millions of viewers across the US and around the world."

The San Bernardino attacks became a frequent Muslim-bashing point for Trump. During the murderous rampage on December 2, 2015, two apparently radicalized Muslims, Syed Farook and Tashfeen Malik, massacred fourteen people and wounded twenty-two more at a holiday gathering for Farook's co-workers at the county public health department. The Monday after the tragedy, Trump created a national uproar by declaring that he wanted to see all Muslim immigration into the United States shut off—temporarily, he claimed, "until our country's representatives can figure out what is going on."

It's impossible to establish a clear cause-and-effect relationship between Trump's announcement and subsequent events, but within days there was a series of ugly incidents: phoned-in and social-media threats, vandalizing attacks on mosques, and arsons of Muslim businesses, in locations all around the United States.

- December 4, St. Louis, Missouri. A man phoned in a threat to the local offices of the Council on American-Islamic Relations, vowing to kill any Muslims who dared show up on his property. He is unlikely to be charged with any crime.
- December 4, Manassas, Virginia. The local mosque was threatened with a phoned-in threat from a man claiming to be a member of the extremist Jewish Defense League and vowing that his group "will do to your people what you did to them." "We are checking now to see if one Jew has been shot or killed in California," he said. "You all will be sorry. You all will be killed."
- December 4, Palm Beach, Florida. A lone vandal attacked a local Islamic center, breaking windows and wreaking property damage inside. The man who was later arrested for the crime is the son of a well-known local educator.
- December 8, Philadelphia. Someone in a red pickup truck rolled up next to a neighborhood mosque and hurled a severed pig's head onto the steps. Security cameras caught images of the perpetrators, but so far, investigators have had no luck tracking them down.
- December 10, Grand Forks, North Dakota. Someone scrawled graffiti featuring a Nazi symbol and the words "Go home" on the walls of a Somali restaurant owned by a Muslim family. Two nights later, someone deliberately set fire to the restaurant, causing an estimated $90,000 in damage.
- December 10, Twin Falls, Idaho. Someone spray-painted boards that covered the windows of the local Islamic center

with the words "Hunt Camp?" The graffiti referred to the old Minidoka Relocation Center in nearby Hunt, the site of the massive Japanese American internment erected during World War II, apparently suggesting internment for local Muslims.

Mark Potok, the Southern Poverty Law Center's Senior Fellow and *Intelligence Report* editor, observed to *Hatewatch*: "Although the hateful comments of Trump ... are protected by the First Amendment, there is little doubt that they will ultimately lead to more violence directed at minorities ... Words have consequences."

Trump's wink-wink suggestions to use violence against undesirables and opponents were not limited to minorities. Trump also deployed similar innuendo to attack Hillary Clinton.

In August 2016 he said at a rally audience that Clinton's election would doom Americans' gun rights: "If she gets to pick her judges, nothing you can do, folks." The crowd began to boo. Then he quickly added: "Although the Second Amendment people ... maybe there is, ... I don't know ..." As the *New York Times* reported, the remark seemed "to raise the possibility that gun rights supporters could take matters into their own hands if Hillary Clinton is elected president." Trump quickly danced away from the suggestion that he was encouraging gun advocates to shoot her, insisting instead that he was simply out to unify gun owners against Clinton in the voting booth.

"This is a political movement. This is a strong political movement, the Second Amendment," Trump told Fox News's Sean Hannity. "And there can be no other interpretation ... I mean, give me a break."

Unchastened, Trump made his rhetoric more pointed when he later told a crowd: "I think that her bodyguards should drop all weapons ...Take their guns away. She doesn't want guns ... Let's see what happens to her ... It'd be very dangerous."

He understood the importance of the issue to his supporters. A woman participating in a question-and-answer session at an Albuquerque, New Mexico, rally for Trump's running mate, Mike Pence, told him, "If Hillary Clinton wins the election ... and she's on that Second Amendment, taking your guns away, there is going to be a civil war in this state." The crowd applauded.

"But, if President Trump would win," the woman continued, "there's also going to be a war, because Obama is going to pull that martial law on the United States."

Hillary Clinton was not taking the right-wing onslaught lying down. She began speaking out against the rising tide of right-wing extremism her opponent was empowering. On August 25, at a campaign appearance in Reno, she went on the offensive. First, she called out Trump for hiring the self-described alt-right leader Stephen Bannon as his campaign CEO. Then she connected the dots on the central issue of Trump's empowerment of the far right, now the alt-right:

> It's truly hard to believe, but according to the Southern Poverty Law Center, which tracks hate groups, Breitbart embraces "ideas on the extremist fringe of the conservative right."
>
> This is not conservatism as we have known it. This is not Republicanism as we have know it. These are race-baiting ideas, anti-Muslim and anti-immigrant ideas, anti-woman—all key tenets making up an emerging racist ideology known as the 'Alt-Right' ...
>
> Now Alt-Right is short for "Alternative Right" ...
>
> The de facto merger between Breitbart and the Trump Campaign represents a landmark achievement for the "Alt-Right." A fringe element has effectively taken over the Republican Party.

Far from being upset, members of the alt-right claimed that Clinton had actually "legitimized" them with the speech.

"The alt-right as a moniker of resistance is here to stay," Richard Spencer said. "Hillary just ensured that; there will be more and more people, with various perspectives, adopting it. At this point in history, the 'alt' is just as important as the 'right.' Hillary aligned herself with George W. Bush and John McCain. The alt-right is the real opposition. We've made it, I never thought this would happen so quickly."

However, the speech also led some journalists to begin reporting more proactively on what the alt-right was really about: a "rebranding of white supremacy for the twenty-first century," as Mark Potok put it.

On September 9, Clinton gave a private talk to the LGBT for Hillary Gala in New York City, at which she expanded on the subject. A video of the talk was leaked to the press. Clinton's remarks raised a firestorm of protest from the right:

> I know there are only sixty days left to make our case—and don't get complacent, don't see the latest outrageous, offensive, inappropriate comment and think, well, he's done this time. We are living in a volatile political environment. *You know, to just be grossly generalistic, you could put half of Trump's supporters into what I call the basket of deplorables. Right? The racist, sexist, homophobic, xenophobic, Islamophobic—you name it. And unfortunately there are people like that.* And he has lifted them up. He has given voice to their websites that used to only have eleven thousand people—now eleven million. He tweets and retweets their offensive hateful mean-spirited rhetoric. Now, some of those folks—they are irredeemable, but thankfully they are not America.
>
> But the other basket—and I know this because I see friends from all over America here—I see friends from Florida and Georgia and South Carolina and Texas—as well as, you know, New York and California—but that other basket of people are people who feel that the government has let them down, the economy has let them down, nobody cares about them, nobody worries about what happens to their lives and their futures, and they're just desperate for change. It doesn't really even matter where it comes from. They don't buy everything he says, but he seems to hold out some hope that their lives will be different. They won't wake up and see their jobs disappear, lose a kid to heroin, feel like they're in a dead-end. Those are people we have to understand and empathize with as well. [Emphasis added]

Suddenly, the press became focused on Clinton's "gaffe" in calling some of Trump's supporters "deplorables"—while the latter part of Clinton's remarks were utterly dismissed and ignored. Seeing an opportunity, the Trump campaign leapt into action, characterizing Clinton as having dismissed *all* of his supporters as a "basket of deplorables." Trump remarked that Clinton had revealed "her true contempt for everyday Americans."

On CNN with Wolf Blitzer, vice-presidential candidate Mike Pence did say of David Duke that "we don't want his support and we don't want the support of people who think like him," but still declined to say that Duke might be someone he'd call "deplorable," saying, "No, I'm not in the name-calling business, Wolf. You know me better than that."

Clinton soon apologized for saying that "half" of Trump's supporters fitted that description, and added, "But let's be clear, what's really 'deplorable' is that Donald Trump hired a major advocate for the so-called 'alt-right' movement to run his campaign and that David Duke and other white supremacists see him as a champion of their values." The political analyst Nate Silver examined the poll results of the often-racist and xenophobic views of Trump supporters: Clinton's statement wasn't much of an exaggeration. Nonetheless, the whole "deplorables" episode became settled in the media narrative as a "gaffe" by Clinton.

Trump's army of followers embraced the "deplorables" label. Soon "Deplorable," or "I'm Deplorable," or "Proud Member of the Basket of Deplorables" T-shirts started to be seen at Trump rallies.

The alt-right cooked up their usual menu of memes. One of the most popular was a play on the poster for the Sylvester Stallone film *The Expendables*, renamed *The Deplorables*, that featured an array of faces from the campaign Photoshopped onto the bodies of the film's armed characters. Lined up behind Donald Trump as the leading figure were Roger Stone, Ben Carson, Chris Christie, and Gary Busey to the left, and Milo Yiannopoulos, Alex Jones, Donald Trump Jr., Rudolph Giuliani, and Pepe the Frog to the right.

Donald Trump Jr. liked the meme so much he shared it on Instagram. Roger Stone retweeted it.

Trump's dance with Birtherism seemingly ground to a halt in mid-September when, pressed by a rising chorus of press inquiries seeking an explanation of his position, he held a press conference–

cum–promotional event at his new hotel in Washington, DC. After a long buildup touting the setting, he read a brief statement acknowledging that President Obama was an American citizen, but blamed the whole mess on Hillary Clinton.

"President Barack Obama was born in the United States, period. Now we all want to get back to making America strong and great again," Trump told the reporters. "Hillary Clinton and her campaign of 2008 started the Birther controversy. I finished it."

With that, he urged the reporters to check out the new hotel, and his handlers then announced that reporters could film him giving tours of the hotel, but could not ask any more questions.

By the time the two candidates finally met face-to-face ten days later for the first nationally televised debate on September 26, their respective armies of supporters were in full roar, and the nation at large was captivated: the event wound up being the most-watched presidential debate in history, with 84 million viewers.

Trump fared reasonably well for the first half hour or so, but he fell apart in the final hour, barking answers, talking over Clinton, and throwing out word salads to avoid answering questions. He seemed unprepared and easily flustered.

Alt-righters groused about Trump's debating style. "Trump doesn't always get his message across, he pulls punches regarding race," wrote Patrick Slattery at the *Stormer;* at *Occidental Dissent*, Brad Griffin complained, "He struck me as nervous, irritable, and thin skinned" and blamed the "Jew media" for its supposed bias. One commenter on the *Stormer*'s debate comment thread was angry: "I nominate him for the firing squad for what he has done." But Andrew Anglin posted the results of online polls as proof that Trump had actually won the debate.

Clinton eventually brought the Birther conspiracy theories back to the table in their second debate on October 9, demanding once again that Trump apologize to President Obama and to the American public for having promoted the plainly racist claims. Trump responded with his previous litany—Clinton had actually invented the theory, it was all her fault, and all he had done was get Obama to produce the birth certificate.

Then he went on the offensive:

> TRUMP: But when you talk about apology, I think the one that you should really be apologizing for and the thing that you should be apologizing for are the 33,000 e-mails that you deleted, and that you acid washed, and then the two boxes of e-mails and other things last week that were taken from an office and are now missing.
>
> And I'll tell you what. I didn't think I'd say this, but I'm going to say it, and I hate to say it. But if I win, I am going to instruct my attorney general to get a special prosecutor to look into your situation, because there has never been so many lies, so much deception. There has never been anything like it, and we're going to have a special prosecutor.
>
> When I speak, I go out and speak, the people of this country are furious. In my opinion, the people that have been long-term workers at the FBI are furious. There has never been anything like this, where e-mails—and you get a subpoena, you get a subpoena, and after getting the subpoena, you delete 33,000 e-mails, and then you acid wash them or bleach them, as you would say, very expensive process.
>
> So we're going to get a special prosecutor, and we're going to look into it, because you know what? People have been—their lives have been destroyed for doing one-fifth of what you've done. And it's a disgrace. And honestly, you ought to be ashamed of yourself.

Clinton interjected that "everything he just said was false," though she was "not surprised":

> CLINTON: I told people that it would be impossible to be fact-checking Donald all the time. I'd never get to talk about anything I want to do and how we're going to really make lives better for people.
>
> So, once again, go to HillaryClinton.com. We have literally Trump— you can fact-check him in real time. Last time at the first debate, we had millions of people fact-checking, so I expect we'll have millions more fact-checking, because, you know, it is—it's just awfully good that someone with the temperament of Donald Trump is not in charge of the law in our country.
>
> TRUMP: Because you'd be in jail.

It didn't matter what else Trump or Clinton said the rest of that night. In the minds of Trump's supporters, he won the debate hands down with that single comment.

When it was all over, polls again seemed to show that Clinton had won the debate, though by less of a margin than the first debate, while this time Trump at least had exceeded expectations. But there was no doubt in the minds of his supporters, especially those on the alt-right: the moment Trump vowed to throw Clinton in jail, he was the winner.

That moment deeply disturbed most mainstream legal observers. "It's a chilling thought," said Michael Chertoff, the former Homeland Security chief and federal appeals court judge. He added, "It smacks of what we read about tin-pot dictators in other parts of the world, where when they win an election their first move is to imprison opponents."

But his supporters were thrilled. Andrew Anglin proclaimed Trump the runaway winner of the second debate: "The people believe Trump won the debate. It's really just an objective fact. Not sure how even liberal kikes could claim otherwise," he wrote.

A commenter chimed in: "ANYBODY speaking the Truth knows GL [Great Leader] kicked the shit out of the hag tonight!!"

Most national polls of the presidential race had shown Hillary Clinton leading Trump fairly widely ever since early August, after the conclusion of the Democratic National Convention in Philadelphia. Trump had been suggesting for months that there might be something hinky with the American election system. As the gap in their poll numbers widened he started explicitly suggesting that Democrats were planning to rig the vote.

"November 8, we'd better be careful, because that election is going to be rigged," he said at an August 1 rally in Columbus, Ohio. "People are going to walk in and they're going to vote ten times, maybe, who knows?"

That same evening, he went on Fox News with Sean Hannity and said: "I know last time, you had precincts where there were practically nobody voting for the Republican ... I'm telling you, November 8, we better be careful because that election is going to be rigged and I hope the Republicans are watching closely, or it's going to be taken away from us."

After the second debate, in October, he returned to that theme, and began turning up the volume. "Remember, we are competing in a rigged election," Trump said at a Wisconsin rally. "They even want to try and rig the election at the polling booths, where so many cities are corrupt and voter fraud is all too common."

He told the *New York Times* in an interview that, even though he had begrudgingly said in the first debate that he'd "absolutely" support her should she win the election, he was now reconsidering that: "We're going to have to see. We're going to see what happens."

This kind of talk had a profound effect on his followers. Eagerly following the lead of their chieftain, they blew the scenario up into a conspiracy and talked of "revolution." At a campaign rally in Green Bay, Wisconsin, *Washington Post* reporter Jenna Johnson talked to the supporters who flocked to hear the candidate. Dave Radtke, sixty-six, told Johnson he feared that Democrats would bring busloads of people from Chicago to Wisconsin to load the ballot boxes, since Wisconsin law allowed same-day voter registration.

One voter sensed that "something seems off" about early-voter programs in large cities, while another warned that Democrats would use "any means necessary" to win. He said he feared "the stealth thing that they can do electronically or some other way to really either erase somebody's valid vote or get a bunch of people in secretly voting to load it up for the other side."

Every Trump supporter with whom Johnson spoke was insistent that not only was such fraud pervasive, but that the "liberal media" were conspiring to hide it. Johnson also noted that most of the rally attendees told her they preferred information from such sources as Fox News, the *Drudge Report* and Rush Limbaugh's radio show, while others said they obtained most of their news from their Facebook or other social media feeds.

Trump took a wildly conspiracist turn on October 13 at a rally in West Palm Beach in a speech that, it later emerged, had been cowritten by Stephen Bannon and Stephen Miller, a campaign adviser. It featured some classic Breitbartesque themes rich with anti-Semitic undertones, as Trump assailed Clinton and her associates.

"We've seen this firsthand in the WikiLeaks documents in which Hillary Clinton meets in secret with international banks to plot the destruction of US sovereignty in order to enrich these global financial powers, special-interest friends, and her donors," he told the crowd.

This charge was greeted with chants of "Lock her up! Lock her up!"

Trump responded: "Honestly, she should be locked up. Should be. Should be locked up."

By the time the third debate rolled around, on October 19, the campaign chatter again revolved around whether Trump would accept the outcome of the election.

So the subject turned up fairly early in the debate, which was moderated by Chris Wallace of Fox News. It was a shocking and electric moment when, on national television, Trump bluntly refused to say whether he'd accept the final vote count:

WALLACE: Mr. Trump, I want to ask you about one last question in this topic. You've been warning at rallies recently that this election is rigged and that Hillary Clinton is in the process of trying to steal it from you. Your running mate Governor Pence pledged on Sunday that he and you, his words, will absolutely accept the result of this election. Today your daughter Ivanka said the same thing. I want to ask you here on the stage tonight, do you make the same commitment that you'll absolutely accept the result of the election.

TRUMP: I will look at it at the time. I'm not looking at anything now … What I've seen … is so bad. First of all, the media is so dishonest and so corrupt and the pile-on is so amazing. The *New York Times* actually wrote an article about it, but they don't even care. It is so dishonest, and they have poisoned the minds of the voters. But unfortunately for them, I think the voters are seeing through it … We'll find out on November 8 … If you look—

WALLACE: But, but—

TRUMP: Excuse me, Chris. If you look at your voter rolls, you will see millions of people that are registered to vote. Millions. This isn't coming from me. This is coming from Pew report and other places. Millions of people that are registered to vote that shouldn't be registered to vote. So let me just give you one other thing. I talk about the corrupt media. I talk about the millions of people. I'll tell you one other thing … She's guilty of a very, very serious crime. She should not be allowed to run, and just in that respect I say it's rigged because she should never—

WALLACE: But, but—

TRUMP: Chris. She should never have been allowed to run for the presidency based on what she did with e-mails and so many other things.

WALLACE: But, sir, there is a tradition in this country, in fact, one of the prides of this country is the peaceful transition of power and no matter how hard fought a campaign is that at the end of the campaign, that the loser concedes to the winner. Not saying you're necessarily going to be the loser or the winner, but that the loser concedes to the winner and the country comes together in part for the good of the country. Are you saying you're not prepared now to commit to that principle?

TRUMP: What I'm saying is that I will tell you at the time. I'll keep you in suspense, okay?

Clinton promptly responded by saying, "That's horrifying"; she then described Trump's claiming that the system was "rigged against him" when *The Apprentice* lost in the Emmy Awards competition. ("Shoulda won," Trump quipped.)

"This is a mind-set," Clinton said. "This is how Donald thinks, and it's funny, but it's also really troubling. That is not the way our democracy works. We've been around for two hundred and forty years. We've had free and fair elections. We've accepted the outcomes when we may not have liked them, and that is what must be expected of anyone standing on a debate stage during a general election."

Once again, polls found that most people who watched the debate thought Clinton won handily, with numbers resembling that of the first debate. A couple of Trump gaffes—at one point, he described Mexican immigrant criminals as "bad hombres," and then tossed a verbal grenade at Clinton by interrupting her as she jabbed him about his taxes: "What a nasty woman!"—became the subject of viral social media conversations as Clinton supporters seized on them as opportunities to mock Trump.

Among his fans on the extremist and conspiracist right, the debate postmortem focused on whether or not Trump should have said he'd accept the outcome. Actually, the latter wasn't really an issue; the question it raised was whether they, too, would accept Clinton as their legitimately elected president. In the end, the question was what they intended to do about it.

SPLC's Ryan Lenz and the *Hatewatch* staff monitored far-right websites in the wake of the debate and found "a chorus of racists and angry voters echo Trump's allegations of a rigged election with warnings of civil war and promises of violence should Clinton win."

At the neo-Nazi chat forum *Stormfront*, a poll asked: "Will you accept Hillary as President?" Exactly one of the ninety-four respondents said yes.

"You have 1.8 million people who are dead, who are registered to vote, and some of them absolutely vote. Now, tell me how they do that," Trump said to Sean Hannity on Fox News on October 19, after the third debate. He also now claimed that Clinton would win because of the 2.5 million people in the country registered to vote in two different states. "That means they're voting twice," he declared, though as *Politico* noted, there was "no evidence that either of the two problems he's flagging happen at any size or scale."

"Help Me Stop Crooked Hillary From Rigging This Election!" shouted the headline at Trump's website. The piece sought volunteers to fan out to local polling places around the nation and spot any signs of voter fraud.

At the same time, Trump's adviser Roger Stone devised an "independent" nonprofit campaign called "Stop the Steal" that he hoped would sign up some 1,300 volunteers who would conduct exit polls at voting locations in ten selected urban areas around the country. Stone said he wanted to see how much the exit polls varied from the final results, in order to obtain "solid evidence" the election was rigged, should Trump lose and seek to overturn the outcome in court.

"If there's real evidence of electoral fraud then it'd be un-American of him to not challenge the results," Stone said.

Trump's followers came fervently to believe that democracy itself was in the balance. In short order they were being joined in the cause of "election integrity" by none other than those self-styled militia-man defenders of democracy, the Oath Keepers.

So far, Patriot leaders such as Rhodes and Richard Mack had kept a low profile in the election, declining to issue an endorsement for Trump, though the men's virulent anti-Clinton sentiments were well established. However, a number of midlevel figures in the Patriot hierarchy were deeply enmeshed in the Trump campaign.

- Milwaukee County Sheriff David Clarke, the "constitution-alist" lawman who had carved out a blossoming career as a Fox News pundit, was one of Trump's most visible and avid supporters.
- Gerald DeLemus, the New Hampshire militiaman who had been arrested for his role in the Bundy ranch standoff, was the head of his home state's "Veterans for Trump" campaign.
- David Riden, a Tennessee militia member, had been a Trump delegate at the Republican National Convention (RNC). He told *Mother Jones*'s Sarah Posner that any government official in violation of the Constitution should be, "the polite word is, eliminated. The harsh word is killed. And they're killed by American citizens with weapons."
- Michele Fiore, a Nevada legislator, had played a role in the Malheur refuge standoff. She had lost her bid in the Republican primary for a Nevada congressional seat and had campaigned hard for Trump in Nevada.
- Joseph Rice was the Josephine County, Oregon, Oath Keepers leader who played a role in the Malheur standoff. He attended the RNC as an at-large GOP delegate and cast his vote for Trump.

Furthermore, among the regular foot soldiers of the Patriot movement the support for Trump was both deep and highly energized.

Many of the people who thronged to see Trump had been earlier participants in Tea Party and Patriot events, and so Gadsden flags and *Infowars* shirts were almost as common at his rallies as red "Make America Great Again" baseball caps and "Hillary For Prison" T-shirts. It was the first grand convening of all the parts of Alt-America.

Stewart Rhodes had a sensitive finger-tip feel for the sentiments of rank-and-file Patriots in his organization. As the days before the election counted down, Rhodes issued a call to all members to join the effort to combat "voter fraud." He named it "Operation Sabot 2016," and boasted of his militiamen's "significant capabilities" to conduct covert intelligence operations in order to prevent the theft of the election. On October 25 the call went out to his members "to form up incognito intelligence gathering and crime spotting teams, and go out into public on Election Day, dressed to blend in with the public … with video, still camera, and notepad in hand, to look for and document suspected criminal vote fraud or intimidation activities."

Rhodes did not specify where the Oath Keepers would monitor polls, but was clear about the nature of the enemy: "We are, indeed, most concerned about expected attempts at voter fraud by leftists, but we will spot, document, and report any apparent attempt at vote fraud or voter intimidation … as is our duty."

Another group of militiamen had their own plans for election 2016. They were going to blow up a Muslim community with Timothy McVeigh–style truck bombs the day after the election.

On October 14, federal authorities arrested three Kansas men, members of the Crusaders militia group, for plotting to attack a housing complex and a mosque, in the small, rural town of Garden City. The Crusaders were also known as an antigovernment group called the Kansas Security Force, which in turn was part of a much larger Patriot coalition called the Three Percent Security Force.

Curtis Allen, Gavin Wright, and Patrick Stein had stockpiled guns and bombs and planned to use cars laden with fertilizer bombs to attack the complex, home to several hundred Somali immigrants, and create a "bloodbath" on November 9.

A confidential source who infiltrated the group had provided the FBI with information about the defendants' plans. The criminal complaint stated, "They chose the target location based on their hatred of these groups, their perception that these groups represent a threat to American society, a desire to inspire other militia groups, and a desire to 'wake people up.'" The men had conducted surveillance to identify potential targets. After searching for targets for several months, the group's focus had settled in the Somali housing complex.

The plan was to position a car loaded with fertilizer and fuel at each of the exits to the complex at around prayer time, when the largest number of people would be gathered in one place. Curtis Allen began learning how to make explosives by watching YouTube videos.

The militiamen had described the Somali immigrants as cockroaches. The men had been recorded saying things such as "Unless a lot more people in this country wake up and smell the fucking coffee and decide they want this country back ... I think we can get it done. But it ain't going to be nothing nice about it."

In the meantime, militiaman Chris Hill, overseer of the Three Percent Security Force organization, was busy down in Georgia preparing for the aftermath of an election win by Clinton.

Hill began organizing his own local Three Percent unit, the Georgia Security Force, in weapons training exercises in order to be ready if federal agents came to take the weapons away. "We thought it was bad under eight years of Obama, but the gun-grabbing is going to get a whole lot worse if Hillary gets elected," Hill told the *New York Times*, which described him as wearing "combat fatigues and ... a .40-caliber Smith & Wesson pistol on his hip."

Also interviewed for the *Times*'s story was Teresa Bueter, forty-one and a mother of three who had worked for twenty-six years at a local Waffle House. An active member of Hill's outfit, she was the proud owner of a German-made sniper rifle and a .32-caliber handgun and wielded them handily throughout the day.

The issue most on Bueter's mind, she told the *Times*, was Syrian refugees, who "scare the crap out of me. Donald Trump would fit right in with our little group," she said. "He wants America the way we want it, back like it used to be."

These sentiments were widespread throughout the ranks of militiamen. "If she wins ... it's over, time for a revolution," one of them wrote on Facebook. "Enough of being tough on the blogs, be tough in real life."

"I will be there to render assistance to my fellow countrymen, and prevent them from being disarmed, and I will fight and I will kill and I may die in the process," Hill told a Reuters reporter.

The federal conspiracy trial of the first seven key defendants in the Malheur National Wildlife Refuge standoff case—Ammon and Ryan Bundy, Shawna Cox, Kenneth Medenbach, Jeff Banta, David Fry and Neil Wampler—had been quietly proceeding for five weeks in Portland with relatively little coverage from the national press. That ended suddenly on October 27, when the verdict came in: acquitted on all counts.

The announcement shocked most legal observers, who had believed there was abundant evidence to demonstrate that the Bundys and their cohort had carefully planned the takeover with the full intention of interfering with the performance of a federal officer in the line of duty, the crime with which they had been charged. The jury, clearly, had decided otherwise.

The Bundy brothers were not released, since they still faced a string of federal charges in Nevada stemming from the April 2014 standoff in Bunkerville. Still, outside the courtroom the Bundys' supporters whooped and waved flags, especially yellow Gadsden flags. Shawna Cox issued a call to action: "Wake up, America, and help us restore the Constitution. Don't sleep with your head in the sand."

Mainstream observers, however, feared what the verdict might produce. "The government took them to court, they played the government's game and they won," Bob Harris, a specialist in training law enforcement officers to identify and handle militant extremists, told the *Kansas City Star*. "I think it's a spark that could lead to some real potential problems. And it's going to spread not only through the West but all throughout the anti-government groups across the country."

"I fear this ruling will embolden other militants to use the threat of violence and I worry for the safety of employees at our public land-management agencies," said John Horning, executive director of WildEarth Guardians, in a statement.

Jessica Campbell, chief organizer for the Oregon-based Rural Organizing Project, saw a different threat—to the majority of rural dwellers who were not participants in the Patriots' Alt-America universe. In small Oregon towns, bullying, threats, and intimidation had increased dramatically with the movement's increasing presence, she said. "In rural communities, a lot of folks are pretty scared—scared of an occupation happening in their communities, scared that vigilante violence will go completely unchecked."

Trump ignored the polls and kept relentlessly pounding home to his crowd the warnings that the election was rigged, and America's fate lay in the balance. At times his tone veered toward the apocalyptic.

"This is it, folks," he told a crowd in Wisconsin on the eve of the election, November 7. "We will never have another opportunity, not in four years, not in eight years, it will be over. With Supreme Court justices, with people pouring into our country—this is it! This is it! Good luck—get out there! ... If she gets in? It's a disaster! She's not gonna get in, folks. I don't see it, I tell you."

He also kept refusing to say whether he would concede the election if he lost. He told Fox News, in a phoned-in interview, that he would "have to see under the circumstances" what he would do if he lost.

"It's largely a rigged system. And you see it at the polling booths, too," Trump said, citing unverified "reports" that electronic machines switched Republican votes to Democratic votes.

A Sky News reporter, covering a Trump rally in Florida, caught the essence of his supporters' sentiments while interviewing an elderly man in a white "Make America Great Again" baseball cap.

"Are you worried about these latest polls?" the reporter asked. "He's slipping a bit. "

"No, I don't care because we are going to take this country back no matter what," the man answered. "She's going to prison. Even if they pull off the fake campaign with all the voter fraud, and she wins with voter fraud—"

"We have no evidence of voter fraud, sir."

"There's evidence of it. You say there's no evidence of it, there is. This is a rigged system."

"What will you do if Donald Trump does not win?"

"We're going to rebellion. We're overthrowing this country! We're getting rid of this clown act. It's over! Clinton, the Marxists, it's over!"

After the polls began closing on Election Day and the returns began pouring in, at first it looked as though the pollsters' predictions of a Clinton win were largely holding true: both Clinton and Trump did well in the states where they were expected to win.

The election's outcome would be settled in swing states that were officially too close to call—but where Clinton held polling leads in most cases. And then, as the night wore on, they began falling in Trump's favor: first Ohio. Then Florida. North Carolina. Two states where Clinton was not expected to win, Iowa and Georgia, went to Trump.

Then the roof caved in on Clinton as the vote counts from critical Rust Belt states began accumulating, and Trump began winning them all: Wisconsin. Michigan (which later went to Trump) hung in the balance. At 3:04 a.m. Eastern Standard Time, Pennsylvania's twenty Electoral College votes put Trump over the 270 hump required for victory.

Clinton had already called Trump to concede the race at about 2:40 a.m. Shortly after the Pennsylvania results were in, Trump took the stage at his campaign headquarters in his hotel in New York City.

"I've just received a call from Secretary Clinton," Trump said, to uproarious applause. "She congratulated us—it's about us—on our victory, and I congratulated her and her family on a very, very hard-fought campaign ... Hillary has worked very long and very hard over a long period of time, and we owe her a major debt of gratitude for her service to our country. I mean that very sincerely."

He continued: "Now it's time for America to bind the wounds of division ... To all Republicans and Democrats and independents across this nation, I say it is time for us to come together as one united people ... I pledge to every citizen of our land that I will be president for all Americans, and this is so important to me ... And I can only say that while the campaign is over, our work on this movement is now really just beginning."

The crowd roared, and the celebrating began. Even if less than half the nation's voters were celebrating. Even if many of the celebrations that followed were of a violent, hate-filled, and threatening nature. As he told his crowd that night, Donald Trump was not alone in the victory. For his supporters on the alt-right, their oft-reviled, long-discredited alternative universe was now real. And it held the reins of power.

Alt-America had won.

13

The Aftermath

To the Children of Satan,

You Muslims are a vile and filthy people. Your mothers are whores and yours fathers are dogs. You are evil. You worship the devil. But, your day of reckoning has arrived.

There's a new sheriff in town—President Donald Trump. He's going to cleanse America and make it shine again. And, he's going to start with you Muslims. He's going to do to you Muslims what Hitler did to the Jews. You Muslims would be wise to pack your bags and get out of Dodge.

This is a great time for Patriot Americans. Long live President Donald Trump and God Bless the USA!!!

—Americans For a Better Way, handwritten letter
sent to over twenty US mosques, November 2016

Heidi Beirich did not expect the day after Election Day to be anything out of the ordinary.

Beirich, the director of the Southern Poverty Law Center's Intelligence Project, which gathers and distributes information about right-wing extremism around the United States, arrived at her desk in Montgomery, Alabama, that Wednesday still a little in shock from the election results, but otherwise not anticipating a busy day. It did not work out that way.

"Early on the day after the election, I came into the office to find a flood of voice-mail and emails from people who had been victims of hate incidents or had witnessed them," she told me. "The phones were ringing off the hook and it was hard to keep up. The calls came from all over the country and seemed to represent every population Trump had attacked during the campaign—Latinos, immigrants, Muslims, women, gays and lesbians. Some of them involved vicious assaults or unhinged rants."

The calls and emails were flooding into the SPLC because the organization is known as the nation's premier anti-hate organization. "Here at SPLC, we very quickly realized that a wave of hate was breaking over the country and we started to collect as much information as we could," says Beirich. "Within ten days, we had data on more than seven hundred such incidents, many of which involved attackers who self-identified as Trump supporters or committed their acts in his name. A month later we were over a thousand such incidents."

Every day they poured in from around the country:

In Richmond, Virginia, at an Amtrak train station a white man approached a half-Filipino man and shouted, "Drumpf! Drumpf! Build a wall!" in his face. When asked to stop, the Trump supporter punched the Filipino man in the face and a fight ensued. No bystanders stepped in, though there were many. No police report was filed, as the victim feared prosecution for fighting back.

In Anaheim, California, white males in a black Ford truck pulled up next to a black family in a vehicle at a stop light and started shouting at them, calling them niggers and yelling that it was "Trump's country now." The truck sped off before the victims or witnesses could get license info.

In Aurora, Colorado, a twelve-year-old African American girl was approached by a white male classmate who told her: "Now that Trump is president, I'm going to shoot you and all the blacks I can find." Parents reported it to the school, who followed up with both the girl and bully appropriately.

In Port St. Lucie, Florida, at a convenience story off Interstate 95, a shirtless, white, tattooed young man started yelling, "Trump, Trump, Trump!" at minorities standing in line, then said to the cashier that she and other "niggers" would be "thrown out of the country" and that "Trump would make America white again."

Police were called. Even though the man challenged witnesses to "do something about it," the police decided he hadn't made a direct threat that would place the cashier in imminent danger and left the scene.

In Hillsdale, Illinois, two high-school freshman girls who were Hillary Clinton supporters, one of them black, were harassed daily by three white boys in their class. The boys taunted them with "Black people are poor and ugly" and "Now that Trump is in office, we can stop giving black people money to buy fried chicken and give it to white people instead."

In Marquette, Michigan, a black woman bumped into a man in a Wal-Mart parking lot. She tried to apologize, but the man turned and shoved her to the ground, saying, "I hope President Trump does what he says he's gonna do! He should send all you niggers back to Africa!"

In Bartlesville, Oklahoma, white men in a pickup truck threatened a black woman in a Wal-Mart parking lot, shouting, "Hey, nigger bitch! Get back on the boat back to Africa, and get the fuck out of America! This is the white man's land! Make America *white* again!" The men threw two cups full of their spittle from chewing tobacco at the woman, hitting her and soaking her dress, before driving off.

The most striking pattern in this wave of hatefulness was the frequency with which the perpetrators referenced Donald Trump or his campaign rhetoric as justification for their acts. Among the incidents recorded in that first month, in nearly half the attacker referenced Trump and his campaign directly or indirectly. Dozens more of the incidents' perpetrators mentioned the election outcome.

Trump's response was consistent with his campaign tango: he deflected questions for as long as he could, and then generally ignored the issue when asked about it.

When asked in a November 14 sit-down interview for *60 Minutes* with Lesley Stahl whether he had heard such reports, he replied, "I am very surprised to hear that. I hate to hear that."

"Do you want to say anything to those people?" Stahl asked.

"I would say don't do it, that's terrible, 'cause I'm gonna bring this country together," Trump said.

"They're harassing Latinos, Muslims . . ." Stahl added.

"I am so saddened to hear that. And I say: stop it," Trump told her. "If it, if it helps. I will say this, and I will say right to the cameras: stop it."

That was the last anyone heard on the subject from the new president for the next two months.

"It was clear the election had unleashed a massive wave of celebratory violence that the president-elect took little interest in, even though he could have tamped it down with a forceful denouncement," Beirich observed. "To this day, he hasn't exhibited the kind of leadership that could quell a fire like his campaign unleashed."

The celebratory response to Trump's victory from the far-right contingent of his supporters was triumphalist and self-congratulatory.

Most Trump supporters in militias—especially those who had been gearing up to challenge a Clinton win—were ecstatic. "To pull victory from the jaws of defeat, it's amazing," said Chris Hill of the Georgia Security Forces. "I'm sick and tired of the Department of Homeland Security or the Southern Poverty Law Center or FBI or all these law enforcement agencies brainwashing people to say that anybody who believes they need to hang on to their guns to protect their own security are the bad guys and they're the terrorists. I hope that Donald Trump plays an instrumental part in getting the government off our backs."

Shortly after Trump was declared the winner on national television, the website Modern Militia Movement proclaimed, "Tonight we claim a victor, thank God, now the hard work begins, holding their feet to the fire to make sure that they do all in their power to help us restore our country back to what it should be, a constitutional republic!"

However, some of the Patriots were more typically cautious and paranoid. Mike Morris of a Colorado-based Three Percent Militia told a *Mother Jones* reporter that although he found the election results encouraging—"I think the American people have woken up"—he worried that his fellow militiamen might "still find conflicts with a Trump administration, particularly when it comes to attempts to implement a nationwide stop-and-frisk program or block people on the no-fly list from buying guns. The Patriot movement cannot be a mouthpiece for the incoming administration. We have to be just as vigilant in January as we are today."

Several of Trump's alt-right and white-supremacist backers took credit for the victory. Richard Spencer tweeted, "The Alt-Right has been declared the winner. The Alt-Right is more deeply connected to Trumpian populism than the 'conservative movement.' We're the establishment now."

Andrew Anglin, at the *Daily Stormer*, trilled, "Our Glorious Leader has ascended to God Emperor. Make no mistake about it: we did this. If it were not for us, it wouldn't have been possible ... The White race is back in the game. And if we're playing, no one can beat us. The winning is not going to stop."

David Duke agreed, tweeting, "Make no mistake about it, our people played a HUGE role in electing Trump!"

However, very few political analysts agreed with their claims. Most of the post-election assessments revolved around the effects of external patterns that had shifted the electoral tide in the last few weeks:

- FBI Director James Comey's letter to Congress in late October warning that the Clinton campaign's emails were being investigated again, which exit polls suggested had depressed the Clinton vote in key states.
- The news that Russian intelligence services had been involved in efforts to shape the outcome of the election, primarily through the hacking of the Democratic National Committee's emails and the subsequent release of embarrassing internal discussions that angered a large number of Bernie Sanders supporters and other Democrats, who perhaps had not voted.
- A flood of fake news—Internet posts created for wide dissemination on social media conveying made-up information,

primarily aimed at smearing Clinton. It soon emerged that many of these operations were also Russian propaganda operations, many of them well-financed outlets in Macedonia and the Baltic states.

Infighting broke out among Democrats about whom to blame for the stunning loss. Mainstream Clinton supporters pointed to lukewarm support by Sanders backers, some of whom wound up voting for third-party candidates and diluting support for Democrats. The progressive faction claimed that Sanders would have won the election and that Democrats only lost because of the Clinton campaign's incompetence, especially in failing to appeal to the working class and failing to campaign in Midwestern swing states.

Analysts gleaned some meaning from the raw numbers in the election, beginning with the reality that Clinton won the popular vote by nearly 2.86 million. Trump only assumed the presidency by winning unexpectedly by a total of 80,000 votes in three key swing states: Pennsylvania, Michigan, and Wisconsin. Had Clinton performed only 1 percent better in each of those three states she would have won the presidency. So what happened in those key states?

Primarily, analysts were content to surmise that Trump rode to the presidency on a wave of blue-collar economic anxiety resulting from persistent unemployment and lagging wages amid a recovering economy, especially in the swing states. They pointed to Trump's promises to bring back jobs to those areas and his frequent attacks on "bad trade deals" as being the primary inducement for blue-collar Democrats to switch tickets.

However, that analysis papered over a much more powerful dimension of the unrest in the nation's political landscape: racial and ethnic demographic shifts that had been occurring in these areas. Well before the election, the *Wall Street Journal* had reported that Trump was attracting a wave of support from areas where there had been a powerful demographic change in recent years in the form of a large influx of Latino labor. These areas had previously been predominantly homogenous and white, especially in the Midwest and

Rust Belt regions, which were simultaneously dealing with gutted local economies and lagging unemployment.

Don Leibl, a fifty-one-year-old computer systems analyst, saw the dairy farming hamlet of Arcadia, Wisconsin, where he lived, being transformed from nearly all white to more than one-third Latino as Mexican immigrants streamed in for jobs. It was a main reason, he said, he was voting for Trump.

"If you'd seen the way things have changed in this town, you'd say, 'Something needs to be done about it,'" Leibl told the *Wall Street Journal*. He and others interviewed by the reporters said Trump's wall-building pledge and vows to prioritize white workers had struck a chord. They believed that undocumented immigrants were crowding their schools and taking unfair advantage of public assistance, and felt Trump could solve that.

The *WSJ* study relied on a tool often used by social scientists and economists called the diversity index, which measures the likelihood that any two people in a county will differ by race or ethnicity. "In 244 counties, that diversity index at least doubled between 2000 and 2015, and more than half those counties were in the cluster of five Midwestern states," the *WSJ* reported.

It noted that even though traditional immigrant gateways in California, Florida, and New York attract far larger numbers of minority immigrants, they have been melting pots for so long that their diversity levels have changed little over the past generation or so.

"In 88 percent of the rapidly diversifying counties, Latino population growth was the main driver. In about two-thirds of counties, newcomers helped expand the overall population. In the remaining third, the population fell despite an influx of new arrivals, which magnified the shift for locals as their peers died or moved away."

The study found that Trump had won the Republican presidential primaries in these counties by large margins, winning 73 percent of counties where the diversity index value had risen by at least 100 percent since 2000, and 80 percent of counties where the diversity index rose by at least 150 percent.

The support in the primaries for Trump in areas experiencing sharp demographic shifts clearly carried over into the general election: not only did he handily win in most of the Midwestern states experiencing such shifts, he also eked out narrow margins in three key states—Wisconsin, Michigan, and Pennsylvania—where they were known to be a campaign issue. Overall, Trump won among white voters in nearly every demographic category.

Such demographic shifts related to race and ethnicity have a long history of also being powerful predictors of interracial violence and hate crimes. One of the persistent myths about hate crimes is that they are associated with economic turmoil and joblessness. Actual statistics over the years have not borne out that correlation; periods of hate-crime upticks have occurred during economically prosperous times, as well. Instead, social scientists have found that the incidence of hate crimes most often correlates with changes in the diversity index, driven by immigration and other demographic and accompanying social shifts. This was particularly illustrated this past decade by the sharp increase in anti-Hispanic crimes.

"There are a couple of things going on," explains Heidi Beirich. "There was a backlash brewing against Obama among people who harbor white-supremacist ideas. That backlash started in 2000 when the census said that white folks will become a minority in the 2040s. We know from social science research that as communities change, there are these tipping points where white people get very, very upset. When a neighborhood is less than five percent minority, they are fine. It gets up to fifteen [percent], and there's ... racial panic.

"So I think we have to think about demographics here because the country is going through a major demographic shift. In fact, the last time that the United States had these levels of a foreign-born population was in the late 1910s, early 1920s, when we had the largest Klan ever."

The contemporary Klan members had their own view of this. Rachel Pendergraft of the Knights Party reported that she attributed the "record numbers" in membership in her group largely to Trump's influence. She, too, was exultant in his victory: "America's white voting majority, men and women, have spoken by electing Donald J. Trump to the presidency. They have recognized that this was a last chance election ... They are beginning to feel like a stranger in their own country. They are saying to the establishment, 'Keep your hands off our families, Second Amendment, and Christian faith.' And, 'No, to a globalist agenda!'"

Donald Trump's connections to the extreme right became an issue not long into the transition process. One of his first hires was Stephen Bannon as his "chief strategist."

"Critics See Stephen Bannon, Trump's Pick for Strategist, as Voice of Racism," read a *New York Times* headline. The Anti-Defamation League called Bannon's appointment a "sad day," and the SPLC urged Trump to "rescind this hire."

Again, white nationalists were ecstatic. David Duke told CNN, "I think that anyone that helps complete the program and the policies that president-elect Trump has developed during the campaign is a very good thing, obviously. So it's good to see that he's sticking to the issues and the ideas that he proposed as a candidate."

American Renaissance's Jared Taylor said he thought Bannon would hold Trump to his campaign promises. "There has been some waffling on some of candidate Trump's signature positions. Build the wall, deport illegals, end birth-right citizenship, take a hard look at Muslim immigrants, etc.," he said. "I suspect one of Steve Bannon's important functions will be as an anti-waffler, who will encourage President Trump to keep his campaign promises."

Richard Spencer agreed with this assessment, telling CNN, "Steve Bannon might even push Trump in the right direction. So that would be a wonderful thing." He hoped the alt-right generally would push Trump in "an increasingly radical direction."

Bannon rode out the controversy surrounding his appointment by generally keeping a low profile while Trump defenders on cable TV dismissed the claims that he was any kind of racist or white supremacist. Bannon helped defuse those claims by giving an interview in which he claimed he had no racist inclinations at all: "I'm an economic nationalist. I am an America-first guy. And I have admired nationalist movements throughout the world, have said repeatedly strong nations make great neighbors. I've also said repeatedly that the ethno-nationalist movement, prominent in Europe, will change over time. I've never been a supporter of ethno-nationalism."

Trump's cabinet and administration selections, announced over the next few weeks, demonstrated a similar inclination toward extremism:

- Michael Flynn, Trump's first selection as national security adviser, had a long history of associations with extremist anti-Muslim groups. It also soon emerged that he had extensive connections to the Russian regime of Vladimir Putin. He also praised Milo Yiannopoulos as a "phenomenal individual" and "one of the most different, one of the most brave people that I've ever met."
- Senator Jeff Sessions was appointed attorney general. He has deep connections with Islamophobic and anti-immigrant organizations and a long legislative history of opposing civil-rights advances, for both the African American and the LGBT community.
- Rex Tillerson, an Exxon-Mobil oil executive with extensive connections to the Putin regime in Russia as a result of Exxon's Arctic oil interests, was appointed secretary of state.
- Betsy DeVos was chosen to be education secretary despite having no educational or administrative experience. She is the sister of Eric Prince, the founder of Blackwater USA (now called Academi), mercenary subcontractor. She promotes a far-right education agenda aimed at gutting the public education system and replacing it with charter schools. She also has multiple associations with extremist evangelical groups that attack LGBT rights and promote the notion of a Christian state. DeVos has claimed that a system of vouchers to promote private Christian schools will help build "God's kingdom."

- Scott Pruitt, a committed climate-change denier who as Oklahoma's attorney general built a record attacking environmental regulations, was chosen to head up the Environmental Protection Agency.
- Sonny Perdue, a former Georgia governor, was appointed agriculture secretary. He is also a known climate-change denier, who has derided environmentalists concerned about global warming as "disconnected from reality."

All these developments generally pleased the alt-right contingent. Richard Spencer spoke approvingly of Sessions. "It's getting what is realistically possible," he said, meaning what was realistically possible for the alt-right: "Jeff Sessions, again, is ... not alt-right but ... seems to see eye to eye with us on the immigration question. I think Jeff Sessions might very well resonate with something like a long-term dramatic slowdown of immigration."

With everything seemingly going their way, the alt-right's white nationalists decided it was time to grab their share of their credit and the limelight. Spencer and his cohorts decided to hold a press conference in Washington on November 19 to do just that.

"Donald Trump's campaign was the first step towards identity politics in the United States," Spencer told the assembled press. "I do think we have a psychic connection, a deeper connection with Donald Trump, in a way we simply do not have with most Republicans."

The room was filled with alt-right supporters, and took on the feel of a rally as Spencer spoke, calling the media "leftists" and "cucks," as well as the "Lügenpresse"—"lying press"—a term originally coined by Hitler.

"We [white people] don't exploit other groups," he said. "We don't gain anything from their presence. The press has clearly decided to double down and wage war against the legitimacy of Trump and the continued existence of white America," he said. "But they are really opening up the door for us ... America was, until this past generation, a white country, designed for ourselves and our posterity. It is our creation, it is our inheritance, and it belongs to us."

Eventually, Spencer got carried away and raised his right arm in a Nazi-style salute. "Hail Trump!" he shouted. "Hail our people! Hail victory!"

Some of his fellow alt-righters in the crowd raised their arms in salute and shouting too.

Video of the moment soon spread across social media and was picked up by mainstream media, and within a day mainstream news anchors and columnists around the country were running it and warning of the dangers posed by the rise of the alt-right.

Spencer shrugged off the media frenzy. "I guess I forgot to apologize," he tweeted. "My bad."

However, it created enough of a stir that the issue finally bubbled up during Trump's discussions with the press. On November 23, he was asked about his support from the alt-right during a sit-down interview with *New York Times* staffers. He replied:

> I don't want to energize the group, and I disavow the group … I don't know where they were four years ago, and where they were for Romney and McCain and all of the other people that ran, so I just don't know, I had nothing to compare it to … If they are energized I want to look into it and find out why.

A little later in the interview, the subject of the alt-right came up again with respect to Stephen Bannon, and Trump answered, "If I thought he was a racist or alt-right or any of the things, the terms we could use, I wouldn't even think about hiring him." He added, "A lot of people coming to his defense right now."

Among Bannon's defenders was Alex Jones. On his video channel, Jones posted a plea to liberals to stop attacking Bannon and Trump. He claimed they had been brainwashed by globalists and said that Trump offered the best chance for ordinary Americans to take on the "global elite."

Jones also defended Trump's electoral victory—which was under attack by both Democratic and Green Party leaders and various left-wing NGOs. Jones hypothesized that Trump had actually won the popular vote as well as the Electoral College votes, due to the illegal participation of millions of undocumented immigrants. *Infowars* ran a story headlined "Report: Three Million Votes in Presidential Election Cast by Illegal Aliens," in which Jones cited a tweet from Greg Phillips of the VoteFraud.org organization, in which Phillips claimed, "We have verified more than three million votes cast by non-citizens."

Infowars reporter Paul Joseph Watson then ran an article based on Phillips's tweet claiming, "Virtually all of the votes cast by 3 million illegal immigrants are likely to have been for Hillary Clinton, meaning Trump might have won the popular vote when this number is taken into account."

The president-elect himself then promoted this claim on Twitter. "In addition to winning the Electoral College in a landslide, I won the popular vote if you deduct the millions of people who voted illegally," Trump tweeted.

Trump cited Phillips, whose shoddy work had been previously debunked, in other tweets. The national media picked up on the story, reporting that the president was once again citing groundless claims promoted by conspiracy theorists.

Trump's attraction to conspiracy theories briefly became a topic of conversation on cable TV news. Trump's spokesperson Scottie Nell Hughes went on Diane Rehm's public radio show to explain it all away, saying, "There's no such thing, unfortunately, anymore of facts." It seemed like a shocking claim, unless you had been paying attention. "One thing that has been interesting this entire campaign season to watch is that people that say facts are facts, they're not really facts," she explained. "Everybody has a way, it's kind of like looking at ratings or looking at a glass of half-full water. Everybody has a way of interpreting them to be the truth or not true.

"And so Mr. Trump's tweet amongst a certain crowd, a large—a large part of the population, are truth. When he says that millions of people illegally voted, he has some—in his—amongst him and his supporters, and people believe they have facts to back that up. Those that do not like Mr. Trump, they say that those are lies, and there's no facts to back it up. So ..."

Alt-America had become the new normal.

In November, just before the election, James Alefantis noticed a sudden uptick in followers for the Instagram feed of Comet Ping Pong, his Washington, DC, pizzeria.

A month later, on December 4, a spiral of conspiracist-driven lunacy culminated in a North Carolina man entering the business and firing off a round from his AR-15 assault-style rifle.

The gunman was arrested by Metro police in the street outside the pizzeria shortly afterward. He was identified as Edgar Maddison Welch of Salisbury, North Carolina. Welch told investigators he was there to "self-investigate" the sordid claims about the restaurant that he had been reading online.

The "Pizzagate" conspiracy theories, as they came to be known, arose as a result of a series of emails from Clinton campaign chief John Podesta that were released by WikiLeaks late in October, in the election's waning days. Ambiguous language they contained was interpreted to mean that Podesta and Clinton were part of a child-sex-abuse ring who selected their victims for sex acts in secret rooms at the pizzeria. One of the theories' chief promoters was Alex Jones, who claimed the emails contained pedophile code words, and that the whole affair was more deeply connected to a global child-abuse conspiracy.

The theories originated on the anything-goes Internet forum 4Chan, and soon articles began circulating on Facebook and Twitter with headlines such as "Pizzagate: How 4Chan Uncovered the Sick World of Washington's Occult Elite."

Alefantis told the *New York Times* he first became aware of the conspiracists' claims about his pizzeria when his Instagram account showed an unusual spike in followers in the days before the election. Within the week he began receiving hundreds of threatening and hateful messages on social media and through texts, including one reading, "I will kill you personally." One Instagram message read, "This place should be burned to the ground!"

Alefantis stated that he has never met either Clinton or Podesta (though Podesta's brother is one of his customers), has no secret rooms at his pizzeria, and otherwise quietly employs forty people in his family-oriented business.

"From this insane, fabricated conspiracy theory, we've come under constant assault," Alefantis told the *Times*. "I've done nothing for days but try to clean this up and protect my staff and friends from being terrorized."

One Pizzagate theorist came into the restaurant and shot a live video of its interior that he posted on Facebook. Police told the man to leave.

The claims kept ratcheting up, especially as Jones began stoking them to a nationwide audience on his *Infowars* site. One such post, published the day of Welch's assault on the pizzeria, claimed that Clinton was secretly behind the death of a sex-worker activist in Haiti.

Soon, even nearby businesses were targeted for harassment on social media and in their shops.

On his Facebook page, Welch indicated that he was a fan of Jones's *Infowars* program. He also posed for several photos that he posted there with the AR-15 he carried into the restaurant. In his car, he had left behind a shotgun and a handgun as well. Soon it came out that in October, Welch had run over a thirteen-year-old black teenager who was walking along a road in Salisbury.

What was especially remarkable about the Pizzagate conspiracy theories was the extent to which the bizarre claims were embraced by people close to the new Trump administration. The theories also were promoted on Twitter by a member of Trump's transition team, Michael Flynn Jr., the son of Lieutenant General Michael Flynn, Trump's national security adviser pick.

Earlier in November the elder Flynn had tweeted out a comment that supported claims that Clinton was involved in child sex abuse, though not at Comet Ping Pong specifically. "U decide—NYPD

Blows Whistle on New Hillary Emails: Money Laundering, Sex Crimes w Children, etc... MUST READ!" he wrote.

Evidently defending his father, Flynn Jr. posted a tweet the same day that Comet Ping Pong was attacked that linked to the Twitter account of Jack Posobiec, the self-described "special projects director" for Citizens4Trump: "Until #Pizzagate proven to be false, it'll remain a story. The left seems to forget #PodestaEmails and the many 'coincidences' tied to it."

Flynn Jr., adamant that the Pizzagate theories were substantive, subsequently posted close to a dozen Pizzagate-related tweets.

Some alt-right figures also indicated they intended to double down on the claims as well. Alex Jones posted a video apparently in response to the Comet Ping Pong attack without directly addressing it. With a Christmas tree as his backdrop, Jones launched into a lascivious recounting of the sex acts putatively described in Podesta's emails. He concluded with a wild-eyed attack on CNN and other mainstream-media outlets, suggesting that they were the real purveyors of fake news.

"Just, as for CNN and everybody else," he said, "look, I know the mainstream media is dead. You're dead. Your response now is to be state-run media, Obama has said it, and then try to shut us down. Good luck!"

Alefantis remained shaken after the Sunday incident, but refused to be cowed. "What happened today demonstrates that promoting false and reckless conspiracy theories comes with consequences," he said in a statement. "I hope that those involved in fanning these flames will take a moment to contemplate what happened here today, and stop promoting these falsehoods right away."

Richard Spencer always insisted that he had never intended to make Whitefish, the small western Montana town in the Flathead Valley where he spends half the year, a center of activity for the white-nationalist movement.

Spencer's Hitler-like salute in Washington had made him so notorious nationally that people in Whitefish became concerned that their town, a ski resort, would become associated with his cause. Local residents, including a real estate agent who is prominent in the area's Jewish community and a local rabbi, wondered whether there was a connection between the business presence of Spencer's mother, Shirley Spencer, and Spencer's white-nationalist organization.

Shirley Spencer exchanged emails with the real estate agent in which she said that her son's "actions have been a source of anguish within her family." The two discussed ways that the community could support her business without concerns that it might be funding racism, and possibly support a local anti-hate group called Love Lives Here, which had been organized several years before, partly in response to Spencer's presence in the town.

While this correspondence was taking place, a Missoula TV station ran a story detailing the exchanges, and in short order Shirley Spencer cut off the conversations and began adopting an adversarial stance. She accused Love Lives Here of "causing financial damage" and adding, "We unequivocally do not agree with the extreme positions espoused by Richard." She said she was now considering selling the building. She also published, through Richard, a number of the email exchanges she'd had with the local real estate agent, claiming they demonstrated an attempt to coerce her into denouncing her son.

Then Andrew Anglin became involved. In a December 16 post at the *Daily Stormer*, he published the names and addresses of the real estate agent, her children, and several prominent Jewish leaders in Whitefish, alongside their photos and superimposed Star of David patches, claiming they were responsible for the Spencers' problems. Simultaneously, an online army of trolls descended en masse on some of the people in Whitefish who had been identified as opposing Shirley Spencer's business. Their Twitter and email accounts were flooded with anti-Semitic and misogynistic threats.

"So Then—Let's Hit Em Up. Are y'all ready for an old fashioned Troll Storm?" Anglin wrote. Anglin stated that he was not advocating "violence or threats of violence or anything even close to that," but a week later he published a post in which he claimed he was preparing to bus in skinheads from the Bay Area of California. "We are continuing our barrage against the criminal Jews of Whitefish," he tweeted. "We are planning an armed protest in Whitefish ... We can easily march through the center of the town carrying high-powered rifles."

Anglin's threats initially spurred the Whitefish police chief to step up patrols, particularly for the people Anglin named in his posts. Other members of Love Lives Here reported that they had also been the recipients of harassing tweets.

The concerns in the community sharpened when Spencer announced that he was considering running as an independent for the congressional seat being vacated by Congressman Ryan Zinke, a Republican. "This would be an insurgent campaign," Spencer told the *Los Angeles Times*. "My candidacy would be something everyone would be talking about and would observe."

Montana Republicans made clear that they were not on board. The state party chairman, Jeff Essmann, told the *Missoulian* that he couldn't comment on "the merits of any candidate or share my personal views on any of them," but added that "in most corners of Montana, a Spencer candidacy would be viewed skeptically." Tellingly, the state organization had not denounced the candidacy of another white nationalist from the Flathead Valley, Taylor Rose, during his 2016 run for a seat in the state house of representatives.

Other Montana politicians also stepped up to denounce Spencer's presence and Anglin's threats and vows to hold a march. One of them was Ryan Zinke, Trump's choice for secretary of the interior. Zinke, the Democratic governor Steve Bullock, Republican senator Steve Daines, and many other Montana politicos released a statement on December 28 that said in part: "We say to those few who seek to publicize anti-Semitic views that they shall find no safe haven here."

Spencer attempted to tamp down the controversy—by heaping blame on his critics while rationalizing Anglin's behavior and suggesting the whole thing was a "joke" and a "troll" prank. Appearing on David Duke's radio program, Spencer claimed he wanted to try to keep his part-time Montana home out of the limelight created by his activism on behalf of white nationalism. "I don't host conferences, I don't hand out fliers here," he said. "It's just a place I go to get my work done. I like being out here. I don't want my daughter growing up in Washington, DC—I don't need to tell you why."

He claimed that the cause of the conflict was local Montana activists who had organized against him and his mother several years before, namely Love Lives Here and the Helena-based Montana Human Rights Network. He claimed they had attempted to strong-arm his mother into denouncing him but failed.

On YouTube Spencer called for the controversy to just go away: "I'm just saying this—let's just end this. Let's put it to bed. The controversy's over. Don't bring it up again. I won't bring it up again. I've said all I need to say."

Of Anglin, Spencer said: "He's wild. We have different styles. But this is one thing I will say, and I will say this with confidence. Andrew Anglin is a rational person. Andrew Anglin has specifically stated that this is nonviolent and that no laws are broken. This is—this *was* a troll. So that's what it is. People were pushing back."

Even though Spencer apparently still harbored an ambition to represent Montana as a congressman, he was adamant that he did not want Whitefish to become associated with his cause. "I do not want to change Whitefish. I do not want to make Whitefish the center of white nationalism."

That claim rather starkly contradicted what he had said on Duke's show four days before. In his glowing introduction of Spencer, Duke recalled the 1930s Louisiana politician Huey P. Long, a populist known as "the Kingfish." Henceforth Duke referred to Spencer, "the most famous man in Whitefish, Montana," as "the Whitefish … He is our Whitefish, he is a man standing up for us."

Spencer responded, "I like the name. I'm gonna run with it."

The larger Whitefish community responded decisively to the threats to Jewish community members. "It's important to know that the businesses that were hit by this were strongly supported in the community," said Will Randall of Love Lives Here. "Their businesses are booming now. They were hit at the beginning and were frightened, scared. And then the community came in and said, 'Well, I'm going to buy your product. I'm going to buy your soap, or your services. We've got your back.'"

Randall told me that it was his impression that any of the local Spencer sympathizers who had initially participated in the "troll storm" began to back away after Anglin announced plans for the march. "I don't know how kindly Montanans will take to California skinheads coming in and stirring things up. We'll see."

The threats created a national stir for a couple of news cycles, as various media organizations ranging from CNN and the *Washington Post* to local Montana news outfits picked up the story and magnified it. Eventually it emerged that Anglin had not obtained the proper permit for a march, and he announced it was being postponed. He promised to file for a permit later, but never did.

Marches and protests erupted nationwide in the weeks following the election. The day after the results were announced, protesters took to the streets in twenty-five cities to denounce Trump's election. New York, Los Angeles, San Francisco, Seattle, Miami all saw crowds in the tens and sometimes hundreds of thousands decrying the president-elect. Most of them remained peaceful demonstrations, although in two cities there were some outbreaks of violence. In Oakland, some forty fires were set, and in Portland, Oregon, some property damage and fistfights occurred. These were later attributed to the tactics of so-called "Black Bloc" anarchist protesters. Trump supporters and Fox News pundits began calling all these protests riots and claimed that the protesters were being paid by left-wing nonprofits.

The paranoia among Trump's far-right supporters began to mount as the day of Trump's inauguration, January 20, neared, particularly among the conspiracy-fueled Patriot bloc. Their deeply bred apocalyptic fear of a Communist takeover of the federal government is one of their longtime, original staples. Although Trump was the antithesis of such an outcome, that paranoia spiked.

The week before the inauguration, the anti-government group the Oath Keepers shouted out warnings on its website and Facebook page: "Communists Intend to Overthrow the United States Before Inauguration Day"; "10,000 Men with Guns to Prevent Coup on Inauguration Day"; "In Just 10 Days, the Radical Left Will Attempt to Overthrow the US Government."

At Alex Jones's *Infowars* conspiracy mill, the theories were multifarious as well as frantic: "Anarchists Are Hoping to Turn Donald Trump's Inauguration on January 20th into One of The Biggest Riots In US History"; "Will the CIA Assassinate Trump?"; "Alex Jones' Emergency Message to President Donald Trump to Deter Martial Law."

Other right-wing conspiracists and Trump supporters started getting into the act. The far-right Bikers For Trump organization, which had a permit to participate in the Inauguration-related protests, said it planned to protect Trump supporters and attendees at the events from protesters. Chris Cox, the founder of Bikers for Trump, told Fox News, "In the event we are needed, we certainly will form a wall of meat."

Fears that radical leftists might prevent Trump's ascension to the presidency were rampant among antigovernment activists. Many were the same militiamen who had vowed to undertake armed rebellion against the government in the event of a "rigged" Hillary Clinton victory.

When Trump won, the focus of their concern became instead a series of anti-Trump protests organized by a group of far-left activists calling themselves Refuse Fascism. As the Oath Keepers website explained, these activists were planning a series of continuing protests against Trump's election with the express purpose of preventing him from taking office.

One of the Oath Keepers' primary sources for their information about the planned disruptions of the inauguration came from "Health Ranger" Mike Adams, a longtime conspiracy theorist and onetime associate of Jones's *Infowars*. In 2013, just before the second inauguration of Barack Obama, Adams warned antigovernment

Patriots that the president would soon be issuing a "mass of kill orders" for them.

"What I am hearing is that there is an actual planned coup attempt," Adams told his audience in a video that was promoted by the Oath Keepers. He then conflated the Refuse Fascism protests with the long-announced "Women's March on Washington" scheduled for the day after the inauguration and expected to attract 200,000, saying that the "cover story" for the coup would be "the women's march, the labor union march, whatever it is."

"What's really happening is that they are hoping to foment enough anger and amass enough people on that day that it flips over into a popular uprising and they literally flood into the capital buildings—not just the Capitol building itself, but they try to take over, perhaps, the White House," he said.

Instead, Refuse Fascism turned out to be a tiny group that, on its best day, attracted about two dozen participants to its protest. It seemed that what really most disturbed Trump's would-be defenders was the massing of large numbers of women and women's rights supporters who planned to march in Washington.

On Friday, January 20, Trump was inaugurated in relative tranquillity. The crowd was small, especially compared to that at Barack Obama's 2008 inauguration, and a tiny handful of protesters created some small ripples of dissent. Chris Cox's bikers were nowhere to be found, but also nowhere needed.

But there was violence elsewhere that day.

An alt-right event was planned for Inauguration Day on the University of Washington campus in Seattle. Milo Yiannopoulos was scheduled to talk at Kane Hall that night. It had been on the schedule for months, but no one had really anticipated that he would be speaking in Seattle on the night Donald Trump was inaugurated until the date approached. The *Breitbart* tech editor and alt-right provocateur was close to wrapping up his nationwide "Dangerous Faggot" speaking tour with the Seattle appearance.

That evening, the crowds began assembling: those who wanted to hear the speech, and those who wanted to prevent them from doing so. As I looked around Red Square—the large red-brick plaza at the heart of the campus—I had an ominous feeling.

Even though it seemed peaceful enough at the outset, when the number of would-be audience members for Yiannopoulos's talk lining up outside Kane Hall was roughly equal to that of the anti-Milo protesters who began surrounding them and blocking their entry, it nonetheless seemed like a situation ripe for violence. Many of the protesters were coming into pretty close proximity with the alt-right Milo fans and there were plenty of verbal exchanges.

Yiannopoulos's presence, at the invitation of the school's College Republicans chapter, had created a controversy beforehand, and many critics had questioned the university's decision to permit hate speech on campus. UW officials were firm in their decision, defending their decision as a First Amendment matter.

The shouts, chants, and angry behavior clearly discomfited many of the now-surrounded Yiannopoulos and Trump fans, but early on, they responded by singing the National Anthem and chanting "Trump! Trump! Trump!" and "USA! USA! USA!"

When the doors to the event opened, the counter-protesters quickly moved to block the entrance to the event. The *Seattle Times* reported that about 200 attendees managed to make it in, but the remaining would-be attendees, who had bought tickets to the event, remained stuck outside, facing a hostile crowd of protesters.

Eventually, the verbal exchanges became physical shoves, and then punches. One young attendee made the mistake of directly approaching a phalanx of masked anarchist Black Bloc protesters and was punched in the mouth and hit in the face with a blue paint ball before being rescued by his father.

The event attendees were understandably frustrated that they couldn't get in to see Yiannopoulos. One of the alt-righters pulled out a Pepe banner—in that setting, the rough equivalent of waving a red flag in front of an angry bull. The Yiannopoulos fans chanted "Pepe! Pepe! Pepe!" knowing that Pepe the Frog symbolized the smirking face of alt-right white nationalism.

That was when things began to get ugly. More of the alt-righters and their friends began shoving the protesters, and several minor tussles began breaking out. A group of dedicated peacekeepers, wearing helmets and backpacks to protect themselves, intervened in several of these brewing fisticuffs, one of which broke out right next to me. Josh Dukes, thirty-four, an imposing man with an anti-fascist tattoo, was one of the peacekeepers. His interference was effective in dealing with some of the more violently inclined protesters and alt-righters. I'd been observing Dukes throughout the event as well, and he had only been intervening peacefully in every situation.

Just then, I was whacked from behind by a young woman in a masked black outfit, even as the melee began to spread and I heard more shouting. Then I heard a muffled bang. Suddenly, people were clearing away and Josh Dukes lay on the ground, critically wounded. (Dukes survived, but just barely; he suffered a .22 wound to his vital organs and has undergone multiple surgeries since. He remained in serious condition for months afterward.)

The man involved in the shooting of Dukes was someone else I'd been observing all evening, who was wearing a black leather jacket and a maroon hoodie. I took note of him early because most of the alt-right crowd was white, but this man was Asian. Just before the shooting, he had donned a yellow baseball cap and joined the people chanting, "Pepe!" He somehow ended up in the middle of the melee that erupted next to me.

Upon being told that a protester had been shot, Yiannopoulos briefly stopped his talk to confirm the news, and then continued, telling the crowd, "If we don't continue, they have won. If I stopped my event now, we are sending a clear message that they can stop our events by killing people. I am not prepared to do that."

Yiannopoulos's pronouncement at the speech clearly attempted to cast the alt-right as the victims of the shooting. *Breitbart News*, where Yiannopoulos was a celebrity editor, reported the shooting as having been perpetrated by the anti-fascist protesters. That was clearly not the case.

One of Milo's young fans, bedecked in furs and sunglasses, afterward gave an interview conveying that similarly confused mischaracterization of the events outside and enthusing that the show had gone on despite the shooting outside: "He decided to let the show go on despite somebody being shot, and compared it almost to a spoiled child, showing them what's OK. Pretty much saying it's OK to kill people, if you are willing, um—it's OK to kill people, because that would shut down our events, and he was—I mean, it was amazing, because it was almost like a movie, everyone stood up and clapped in accordance. It was really exciting to see that. It's one of the best things of Milo's I've ever heard, actually."

In the days afterward, both sides blamed the other for the violence, though it seemed the Red Caps were unhappy and freaked out merely by the presence of protesters peacefully asserting their own free-speech rights—which, in their worldview, constituted an assault on their free speech. Certainly the Black Bloc escalated the tension into violence, but in the end, there also was little question about who showed themselves willing to resort to lethal force: the alt-right contingent.

That was underscored a few days later when the College Republicans at the University of Washington—the sponsors of the event—issued a public statement that made no mention of the shooting victim or concern for his well-being or recovery, but instead warned the anti-fascists that "it's time your flame is put out. If you keep prodding the right you may be unpleasantly surprised what the outcome will be."

Police eventually charged the wife of the man I'd been observing throughout the evening; video footage apparently revealed her pulling out a gun and shooting Josh Dukes as he was tussling with her husband. Two months after the shooting, Elizabeth "Lily" Hokoana and her husband, Marc, both twenty-nine, were charged with an array of felonies in the case.

◆

Meanwhile, the Women's Marches on the day after the inauguration attracted millions of people peacefully carrying signs, most of them anti-Trump in nature, and wearing pink knitted "pussy hats" commemorating Trump's crude remarks about women that had been revealed during the campaign. The big march in Washington drew an estimated 500,000 people, and marches in cities around the nation drew similarly large numbers of participants: 750,000 in Los Angeles, 150,000 in San Francisco, 200,000 in Denver, 400,000 in New York, 175,000 in Seattle.

Worldwide, thousands of cities and an estimated 5 million people participated, 2.6 million of them in the United States. It marked the nation's largest political demonstrations since the Vietnam War.

The protests aggravated the new president. "Watched protests yesterday but was under the impression that we just had an election," he tweeted. "Why didn't these people vote?"

He was apparently even more annoyed by press reports and social media memes pointing out that the day-after protest significantly outsized the crowd at his inauguration, estimated at about 150,000.

The day after the inauguration, as thousands of women marched outside, Trump's press secretary, Sean Spicer, held his first White House briefing. Spicer took no questions from the assembled reporters but instead used the event to lecture the journalists about what he incorrectly termed "deliberately false reporting" on Trump's inauguration. He shouted, "We're going to hold the press accountable."

"This was the largest audience ever to witness an inauguration, period," said Spicer, in one of several statements contradicted by photographs and transit data. "These attempts to lessen the enthusiasm of the inauguration are shameful and wrong." When he was finished ranting, he walked off and left a stunned press room behind.

It was a classic authoritarian display: insisting that up is down, right is wrong, the White House's numbers were the *real* numbers, and reporters' numbers were wrong—like Trump's claims about the popular vote. Trump was laying claim to being the source of reality, displacing the "fake news" press, as he began calling it.

It worked quite well with people who considered themselves Trump supporters. The *Washington Post* conducted a study of the president's voters in which they were shown side-by-side crowd shots of Obama's inauguration with Trump's, which clearly demonstrated a substantially smaller crowd in 2017; and yet when asked a series of questions about the photos, most Trump voters stated that the Trump crowd was larger.

Trump's longtime adviser and campaign manager, Kellyanne Conway, went on NBC's *Meet the Press* to explain what Spicer was doing at that press conference. She said, "You're saying it's a falsehood. And they're giving—Sean Spicer, our press secretary—gave alternative facts."

The NBC host, Chuck Todd, responded, "Alternative facts aren't facts, they are falsehoods."

Later in the interview, Todd pressed Conway further, asking her, "What was the motive to have this ridiculous litigation of crowd size?"

"Your job is not to call things ridiculous that are said by our press secretary and our president. That's not your job," Conway said.

Todd persisted: "Can you please answer the question? Why did he do this? You have not answered it—it's only one question."

Conway said, "I'll answer it this way: think about what you just said to your viewers. That's why we feel compelled to go out and clear the air and put alternative facts out there."

Alt-Americans knew exactly what Conway meant.

The bomb threats to Jewish community centers had begun shortly after the new year. They were usually phoned in, using a voice anonymizer. One typical call went like this:

> It's a C-4 bomb with a lot of shrapnel, surrounded by a bag, a bag of marbles. In a short time, a large number of Jews are going to be slaughtered. Their heads are going to be blown off from the shrapnel. There's a lot of shrapnel. There's going to be a bloodbath that's going to take place in a short time. I think I told you enough. I must go.

The threats forced evacuations and created panic among Jewish communities around the nation—in Orlando, Florida; Albany, New York; Syracuse, New York; West Orange, New Jersey; Milwaukee; San Diego; and Salt Lake City. Over the next month of January, forty-eight Jewish community centers in twenty-six states and one Canadian province received nearly sixty bomb threats. Most were made in rapid succession on three days: January 9, 18, and 31. A number of centers received multiple threats.

On February 20, another wave of bomb threats hit eleven Jewish community centers across the country.

In the meantime, the Southern Poverty Law Center continued to record a steady drumbeat of hate incidents. By mid-February, its count had surpassed 1,300 hate incidents. "Mr. Trump claims he's surprised his election has unleashed a barrage of hate across the country," said SPLC president Richard Cohen in November. "But he shouldn't be. It's the predictable result of the campaign he waged."

During a joint press conference with the Israeli Prime Minister Benjamin Netanyahu on February 15, a reporter asked Trump, "Mr. President, since your election campaign and even after your victory, we've seen a sharp rise in the anti-Semitic incidents across the United States, and I wonder, what do you say to those among the Jewish community in the states and Israel, and maybe around the world, who believe and feel that your administration is playing with xenophobia and maybe racist tones?"

Trump replied with a rambling discourse on his Electoral College victory: "Well, I just want to say that we are very honored by the victory that we had, three hundred six electoral college votes," he said. "We were not supposed to crack two twenty, you know that, right? There was no way to two twenty-one, but then they said there's no way to two seventy. And there's tremendous enthusiasm out there.

"I will say that we are going to have peace in this country," he continued. "We are going to stop crime in this country. We are going to do everything within our power to stop long-simmering racism and every other thing that's going on. A lot of bad things have been taking place over a long period of time."

The next day, Trump held his first open press conference in Washington, and the president again was pressed on the subject. Jake Turx, a reporter for *Ami* magazine, said:

Despite what so many colleagues might be reporting, I haven't seen anybody in my community accuse either yourself or anyone on your staff of being anti-Semitic. However, what we are concerned about and what we haven't really heard you address is an uptick in anti-Semitism and how in this climate you're going to take care of it. There have been reports out that forty-eight bomb threats have been made against Jewish centers all across the country in the last couple of weeks. There are people who are committing anti-Semitic acts or threatening to—

Trump cut him off:

Sit down. I understand the rest of your question. So here's the story, folks.

Number one, I'm the least anti-Semitic person you've seen in your entire life. Number two, racism, the least racist person … Let me just tell you something, that I hate the charge. I find it repulsive.

A short while later, as the conference was wrapping up, Sirius XM reporter Jared Rizzi asked the president, "I'll follow up on my colleague's question about anti-Semitism. It's not about your personality or your beliefs. We're talking about a rise in anti-Semitism around the country. Some of it by supporters in your name. What can you do to deter that?"

Trump blamed the incidents on "the other side":

And some of it—and can I be honest with you? And this has to do with racism and horrible things that are put up, some of it written by our opponents. You do know that? Do you understand that? You don't think that anybody would do a thing like that.

Some of the signs you'll see are not put up by the people that love or like Donald Trump. They're put up by the other side. And you think it's, like, playing it straight? No. You have some of those signs and anger that is caused by the other side. They'll do signs and they'll do drawings that are inappropriate. It won't be my people. It will be the people on the other side to anger people like you.

Finally, as the press began discussing Trump's refusal to act and Jewish civil rights groups began applying more pressure, the president addressed the issue briefly at the end of a February 21 tour of the National Museum of African American Museum and Culture. "The anti-Semitic threats targeting our Jewish community and community centers are horrible and are painful and a very sad reminder of the work that still must be done to root out hate and prejudice and evil," Trump said.

The next day, on February 22, in the Kansas City suburb of Olathe, Adam Purinton, a white man, shot two Indian high-tech workers. Purinton had been shouting racial slurs at the victims and later told a bartender he had shot "two Iranians." His shots left Srinivas Kuchibhotla, thirty-two, a Garmin engineer from Overland Park, dead, and his co-worker, Alok Madasani, and Ian Grillot, twenty-four, who attempted to intervene, critically wounded.

Purinton shouted at his victims, "Get out of my country!" The FBI is investigating the case as a hate crime, though Kansas has no hate-crime statute.

The shootings set off shock waves in India, where many families have members working and living in the United States. It was reported in India that many students were reportedly rethinking their plans to come to work in the United States. "I used to think of America as a place where there is greater racial equality than exists in India," Dhriti Ahluwalia, twenty-six, told the *Washington Post*. "Now people are afraid ... There is racism."

Kuchibhotla's brother-in-law, Venumadhav Gajula, told the *Los Angeles Times* that he blamed the shooting on "a growing climate of racial intolerance in the United States."

The shock waves spread nationally, and the press began asking why Trump was failing to address the growing waves of hate crimes. On February 28, in his first official address to Congress, he attempted to lay the controversy to rest:

Tonight, as we mark the conclusion of our celebration of Black History Month, we are reminded of our nation's path toward civil rights and the work that still remains. Recent threats targeting Jewish Community Centers and vandalism of Jewish cemeteries, as well as last week's shooting in Kansas City, remind us that while we may be a nation divided on policies, we are a country that stands united in condemning hate and evil in all its forms.

Earlier in the day, however, Trump had made remarks suggesting he believed the threats to Jewish community centers were part of a domestic "false flag" campaign by his political enemies to make him look bad. At a gathering of state attorneys general that morning, when Pennsylvania attorney general Josh Shapiro asked him about the toppling of nearly a hundred headstones in a Philadelphia Jewish cemetery, he had reportedly said, "Sometimes it's the reverse."

The president reportedly promised the attorneys general that he would lay the matter to rest that evening, but in his speech he did not clarify what he had meant by "the reverse." In fact, his denunciation of "hate and evil in all its forms" was basically a generic statement.

Earlier, Jonathan Greenblatt, the president of the Anti-Defamation League, had said, "We are astonished by what the president reportedly said. It is incumbent upon the White House to immediately clarify these remarks. In light of the ongoing attacks on the Jewish community, it is also incumbent upon the President to lay out in his speech tonight his plans for what the federal government will do to address this rash of anti-Semitic incidents."

The Anne Frank Center for Mutual Respect, which had earlier criticized Trump's slowness to address the issue, was unimpressed with Trump's words to Congress. "We give him credit for doing the right thing tonight by beginning his speech to address anti-Semitism and other hate," said executive director Steven Goldstein. "But … the president didn't say exactly what he would do to fight anti-Semitism—how could he have stayed so vague?"

But the alt-right knew exactly how to interpret Trump's response. Most sites ignored his anodyne remarks about anti-Semitism and hate, and focused instead on his earlier remarks to the attorneys general. At the *Daily Stormer*, Andrew Anglin exulted, "Anyone who thinks Trump is not the real deal at this point is either nuts or a shill. He just called-out the Jews for hoaxing attacks against themselves."

Anglin, like Trump, believed the wave of hate crimes were inflicted by liberals to make Trump supporters look bad.

"It is obvious to us that these 'attacks' are almost certainly being done by the Jews themselves to gain sympathy," he wrote. "They want to use them to attack Trump, to claim that he has inspired violence against them. We have [to] stress the need for Trump to call them out on this, so they are not able to use them as a battering ram against him."

From the first day that Trump assumed the presidency, the White House was embroiled in one or another kind of chaos—some of it the result of internal wrangling, some of it a product of the press responding to his provocations. Longtime Beltway observers were shocked by all the turmoil.

But Trump—wielding his Twitter account, which he described as his way of "speaking directly to the people"—also demonstrated that he was masterful at creating distractions that kept his critics and the press hopping from one outrage to another, paying little attention while he quietly enacted his agenda on a broad array of policy fronts.

Trump's first real foray into enacting his agenda came when he followed through on his campaign promises to sign a Muslim immigration ban when he became president. One of his first executive orders, issued January 27, banned all entry to the United States for citizens of seven Muslim-majority nations: Iraq, Iran, Libya, Somalia, Sudan, Syria, and Yemen.

Several states sued to block the order. Trump's legal team argued that the order was not a "Muslim ban"—a religion-based ban would violate the Constitution's Establishment Clause—but soon ran aground on the shoals of Trump's own campaign rhetoric. The federal judges who reviewed the case all cited Trump's vows to institute a "Muslim ban" as evidence that the order was intended to apply a religious test and therefore was likely unconstitutional, and ordered it blocked.

The judges' rulings infuriated the president, who tweeted after the ruling February 4: "The opinion of this so-called judge, which essentially takes law-enforcement away from our country, is ridiculous and will be overturned!"

Yet Trump's legal arguments foundered again when the case went before the Ninth Circuit Court of Appeals. The appellate court upheld the order blocking Trump's order.

That weekend, the Trump team sent out one of his senior advisers, Stephen Miller, thirty-one, to act as the administration's spokesman on the news talk programs. Miller is a former Jeff Sessions staffer closely associated with Stephen Bannon, with a background of dalliances with white nationalists. Miller made an indelible impression.

"The president's powers here are beyond question," he told Chris Wallace on *Fox News Sunday with Chris Wallace*. "We don't have judicial supremacy in this country. We have three coequal branches of government."

He also criticized the appellate court. "The Ninth Circuit has a long history of being overturned and the Ninth Circuit has a long history of overreaching," he said. "This is a judicial usurpation of power."

A week later, on February 21, Miller told Martha MacCallum at Fox that any executive order that superseded the first one would follow the same template: "Fundamentally, you're still going to have the same basic policy outcome for the country, but you're going to be responsive to a lot of very technical issues that were brought up by the court and those will be addressed. But in terms of protecting the country, those basic policies are still going to be in effect."

On March 6, Trump filed a second executive order banning travel from Muslim nations, but Iraq was dropped from the list. In his order Trump claimed that Islamist terrorists posed the greatest domestic threat to Americans, and that those six nations had a history of producing immigrants who later committed terror crimes. That order, too, was struck down by a federal judge, who ruled that

Miller's February 21 comments were evidence that the order's intent had not changed.

Such floundering displays of incompetence became part of the daily White House circus. In mid-February, National Security Adviser Mike Flynn was accused of lying to Vice President Mike Pence about his contacts with Russian officials during a November meeting. After a weekend of turmoil, Flynn was fired. Trump eventually replaced him with a more respected national security figure, General H. R. McMaster (ret.). Trump's cabinet pick for labor secretary, Andrew Pudzer, was forced to withdraw after allegations of abuse of his ex-wife emerged. Thousands of open government jobs went unfilled because, Trump explained, the administration wasn't even trying to fill them.

Tension between the White House and the press intensified. Trump attempted to control his message to the public by regularly asserting the Alt-America version of reality, making himself the final authority of what was "factual" in that universe. The concept of "fake news" had entered the mainstream lexicon in 2015, growing out of real news accounts describing business enterprises built on fabricating news stories out of whole cloth, often pertaining to celebrities, and publishing them on websites that rely on heavy traffic counts for their ad revenues; some of these sites, in fact, were later credited with spreading a number of false smears about Clinton that were widely believed, and thus contributing to her election defeat. Trump turned the idea on its head by labeling the mainstream press "fake." While the press scrambled to make sense of his seemingly open dissembling, his real audience—his red-capped Alt-America followers—received the message clearly: Don't believe the lying press. The only person you can believe is Trump.

Thus, Trump's response to the increasing blizzard of stories detailing his incompetence was to blame the institutions recording it. At his contentious February 16 press conference, he went to open war with the media.

"The press has become so dishonest that if we don't talk about it, we are doing a tremendous disservice to the American people," he said. "We have to talk about it, to find out what's going on, because the press honestly is out of control. The level of dishonesty is out of control." The next morning, he tweeted: "The FAKE NEWS media (failing @nytimes, @NBCNews, @ABC, @CBS, @CNN) is not my enemy, it is the enemy of the American People!"

Trump's Twitter account ended up being an agent of chaos as his tweets whipped up storms of media and diplomatic controversies that became the focus of much of the daily news reportage on the new president. On March 4, he launched what became his most notorious tweet storm:

Terrible! Just found out that Obama had my "wires tapped" in Trump Tower just before the victory. Nothing found. This is McCarthyism!

Is it legal for a sitting President to be "wire tapping" a race for president prior to an election? Turned down by court earlier. A NEW LOW!

I'd bet a good lawyer could make a great case out of the fact that President Obama was tapping my phones in October, just prior to Election!

How low has President Obama gone to tap my phones during the very sacred election process. This is Nixon/Watergate. Bad (or sick) guy!

It later emerged that Trump was inspired to send out these tweets after reading a story on *Breitbart News*, based on anonymous sources, alleging that Obama had tapped Trump's phones during the campaign. Fact-checkers found the story to be groundless.

Obama adamantly denied the allegation, as did everyone in the intelligence community. James Clapper, the former director of national intelligence under Obama, told NBC's *Meet the Press* on March 5 that in the national intelligence activity he oversaw, "There was no such wiretap activity mounted against the president, the president-elect at the time, as a candidate or against his campaign." FBI director James Comey asked the Justice Department to issue a statement refuting Trump's claim.

In reality, Trump's tweets had put his incompetence on public display: anyone acquainted with contemporary surveillance technology knows that wiretapping is an extremely limited practice, legal only after evidence is presented to a federal surveillance court panel that then approves or rejects the wiretapping warrant. If Trump really had been surveilled by the Obama administration, as he claimed, that meant there was enough evidence for a court to approve it.

Nonetheless, the White House continued to insist that other evidence was going to emerge demonstrating that Trump had been right. Sean Spicer spun Trump's tweets for reporters, using "air quotes" to claim that he hadn't been referring to wiretapping specifically: "The President used the word 'wiretaps' in quotes to mean, broadly, surveillance and other activities."

Spicer then berated reporters for not picking up on news reports that vindicated Trump, notably a report the night before by the Fox News pundit Andrew Napolitano, who claimed that the surveillance had actually been conducted by Government Communications Headquarters (GCHQ), a British signals intelligence agency: "Judge Andrew Napolitano made the following statement, quote, 'Three intelligence sources have informed Fox News that President Obama went outside the chain of command (to spy on Trump). He didn't use the NSA, he didn't use the CIA ... He used GCHQ.'"

Intelligence officials in the UK were outraged, dismissing the allegation as "utterly ridiculous." Fox News backed away from Napolitano's claims, and shortly afterward suspended him from appearing on the network. But Trump adamantly refused to apologize, claiming that Spicer had only read the news story to reporters.

As the media tried to make sense of it all, Kellyanne Conway's phrase "alternative facts" was heard often. Pundits and late-night comics had enjoyed a field day with the term, using it to scornfully refer to the administration's growing record of spinning a spurious version of reality.

Conway herself had grown weary of being the butt of their jokes. "Excuse me, I've spoken 1.2 million words on TV, okay?" she told Olivia Nuzzi of *New York* magazine. "You wanna focus on two here and two there, it's on you, you're a f—ing miserable person."

What Conway's critics missed was that, despite their derision—and to some extent, because of it—the gambit was working, despite the fact that overall, Trump's travails seemed to hurt him badly in the polls. By mid-March, according to Gallup, only 37 percent of Americans approved of his performance, while 58 percent disapproved. Those were shockingly low numbers, especially compared to other first-term presidents at similar junctures in their tenures, who were generally in high-approval zones: 62 percent for Obama, 58 percent for George W. Bush, 60 percent for Ronald Reagan.

And yet in the places where it really mattered—in the congressional districts of Republican, Trump-backing lawmakers—Trump's ratings remained well over 50 percent. Conservative-oriented polls by Rasmussen put Trump's approval rating at 55 percent. Among Republicans, 81 percent found Trump "honest and trustworthy."

"I think he's doing good," Gary Pelletier, a Buffalo, New York, retiree told a local reporter. "People are complaining that he's not doing enough, but I'm all for whatever he's doing."

"He's doing everything he said he was going to do," said Phil Pantano, sixty, also of Buffalo.

Alt-America has always functioned as a refuge for people who reject factual reality, a place where they can convene and reassure one another of their fabricated version of how the world works. From its beginnings in the 1990s as an alternative universe with its own set of "facts" to its growth during the early part of the new century through the spread of antigovernment conspiracism, through its evolution into the mainstream of conservatism through the Tea Party, and finally its ultimate realization as a political force through the ascension of Donald Trump, Alt-America's primary usefulness has been as a ready tool for right-wing authoritarianism. The army of followers was already fully prepared by 2015, when Trump picked up their waiting scepter.

It was also the real-life manifestation of Robert Altemeyer's "lethal union" of right-wing authoritarian followers with a "social-dominance-oriented" authoritarian leader: that moment, Altemeyer says, when "the two can then become locked in a cyclonic death spiral that can take a whole nation down with them."

Other experts on authoritarianism fear the outcome of Trump's authoritarianism. "You submit to tyranny," writes the Yale historian Timothy Snyder, "when you renounce the difference between what you want to hear and what is actually the case." Snyder warns that "accepting untruth is a precondition of tyranny. Post-truth is pre-fascism [and] to abandon facts is to abandon freedom."

Snyder sees Trump's insistence on setting the terms of reality as a classic ploy: "This whole idea we're dealing with now about the alternative facts and post-factuality is pretty familiar to the 1920s," he told Sean Illing, the owner of the website *Vox*, in May. "It's a vision that's very similar to the central premise of the fascist vision. It's important because if you don't have the facts, you don't have the rule of law. If you don't have the rule of law, you can't have democracy.

"And people who want to get rid of democracy and the rule of law understand this because they actively propose an alternative vision. The everyday is boring, they say. Forget about the facts. Experts are boring. Let's instead attach ourselves to a much more attractive and basically fictional world."

The political reality on the ground, however, will depend on how Trump responds to challenges to his authority. A longtime Democratic presidential adviser, Ron Klain, told Ezra Klein of *Vox*: "If Trump became a full-fledged autocrat, it will not be because he succeeds in running the state. It'll be that he fails, and he has to find a narrative for that failure. And it will not be a narrative of self-criticism. It will not be that he let you down. He will figure out who the villains are, and he will focus the public's anger at them."

Afterword

Fascism and Our Future

People who have studied the extremist right as a historical and sociopolitical phenomenon in depth are acutely aware of a simple truth: America has been very, very lucky so far when it comes to fascistic political movements.

And now, with the arrival of the Donald Trump presidency, that luck appears to have finally run out.

This didn't happen overnight—Trump is the logical end result of a years-long series of assaults by the American right, not just on American liberalism but on democratic institutions themselves. With Trump the long-term creeping radicalization of the right has come home to roost.

Americans' attitudes about fascism have always been based on the assumption that fascism, as occurred in Germany when Hitler came to power, "can't happen here," that we love our freedom so much we would never give in to an authoritarian populist regime. We never stopped to consider what might happen if Americans' conception of freedom became so twisted that it came to embody the "freedom" to deprive other people of their freedoms, while preserving your own.

Fascism is not just a historical relic. It remains a living and breathing phenomenon that, for the generations since World War II, had only maintained a kind of half-life on the fringes of the American right. Its constant enterprise, during all those years, was to return white supremacism to the mainstream, restore its previous legitimacy, and restore its own power within the nation's political system. With Trump as its champion, it has finally succeeded.

It's important, first, to understand just what fascism is and what it is not. The word "fascist" has been so carelessly and readily applied as a shorthand way to demonize one's political opposition that the word has become almost useless: used to meaning anything, it has almost come to mean nothing.

One commonly, and wrongly, cited definition of fascism is attributed to Benito Mussolini: "Fascism should more appropriately be called Corporatism because it is a merger of state and corporate power." According to the investigative reporter John Foster "Chip" Berlet, Mussolini never said nor wrote such a thing. And neither did the fascist philosopher Giovanni Gentile, to whom it is also often attributed.

"When Mussolini wrote about corporatism," Berlet writes, "he was not writing about modern commercial corporations. He was writing about a form of vertical syndicalist corporatism based on early guilds." The terms "corporatism" and "corporate" meant an entirely different thing in 1920s Italy than they mean today: "corporations" were not individual businesses, but rather were sectors of the economy, divided into corporate groups, managed and coordinated by the government. "Corporatism," Berlet says, "meant formally 'incorporating' divergent interests under the state, which would resolve their differences through regulatory mechanisms."

In fact, says Berlet, this supposed definition of fascism directly contradicts many of the things that Mussolini actually did write about the nature of fascism.

Another thing that fascism decidedly is *not* is what the right-wing pundit Jonah Goldberg says it is: a kind of socialism and therefore "properly understood as a phenomenon of the left." This notion is such a travesty of the idea of fascism that it functionally negates its meaning. George Orwell wrote that "the idea underlying Fascism is irreconcilably different from that which underlies Socialism. Socialism aims, ultimately, at a world-state of free and equal human

356

beings. It takes the equality of human rights for granted. Nazism assumes just the opposite."

Not only did Goldberg's book, *Liberal Fascism: The Secret History of the American Left, From Mussolini to the Politics of Meaning*, published in 2009, become a *New York Times* bestseller, but its thesis became widely accepted on the American right among Patriots and Tea Partiers in the years leading up to Trump's ascension, who eagerly accused President Obama and liberal Democrats of being the *real* fascists.

Historians of fascism were scathing in their assessment. For example, Robert O. Paxton, an American political scientist who is professor emeritus at Columbia University and the author of seminal studies of fascism, wrote: "Goldberg simply omits those parts of fascist history that fit badly with his demonstration. His method is to examine fascist rhetoric, but to ignore how fascist movements functioned in practice."

In reality, fascism is a much more complex phenomenon than Goldberg's or the "corporate state" definition would have it. Historians have for years struggled to nail down its essential features, partly because, as Paxton notes, fascism in the 1920s "drew on both right and left, and tried to transcend that bitter division in a purified, invigorated, expansionist national community." In the postwar years of the 1950s and '60s, political scientists and historians tried to define it primarily by assembling a list of traits common to historical fascists.

The problem with this approach was that as historians examined the record more closely, they grasped that fascism was constantly acquiring and shedding one or another of these traits. It was a protean, shape-shifting phenomenon, and a simple list of traits failed to capture this dynamic quality.

In response, some scholars, notably Roger Griffin, a modern historian and political theorist at Oxford Brookes University in England, have attempted to distill fascism into a singular quality, an underlying principle that remained constant all throughout its various permutations. Griffin ultimately zeroed in on what he called "palingenetic ultranationalism": a revolutionary movement based on the belief that a nation can be restored to glory via a process of phoenix-like rebirth by activating, or creating, national myths of original greatness ("palingenesis" is the doctrine of continual rebirth).

Griffin explains fascism further as a "modern political ideology that seeks to regenerate the social, economic, and cultural life of a country by basing it on a heightened sense of national belonging or ethnic identity. Fascism rejects liberal ideas such as freedom and individual rights, and often presses for the destruction of elections, legislatures, and other elements of democracy. Despite the idealistic goals of fascism, attempts to build fascist societies have led to wars and persecutions that caused millions of deaths."

While Griffin's approach is extraordinarily useful and insightful, it still fails to fully explain the dynamic nature of fascism. Robert Paxton's 2005 book *The Anatomy of Fascism*, widely considered to be a definitive text on the subject, attempted to tackle that aspect of the phenomenon. His definition of fascism is placed in the context of the reality of its behavior: that is, fascism cannot be explained solely by its ideology; it is also identified and explained by *what it does*. By examining the historical record, Paxton has been able to describe its constantly mutating nature as occurring in five identifiable stages:

1. Intellectual exploration. Disillusionment with popular democracy manifests itself in discussions of lost national vigor.
2. Rooting. A fascist movement, aided by political deadlock and polarization, becomes a player on the national stage.
3. Arrival to power. Conservatives seeking to control rising leftist opposition invite the movement to share power.
4. Exercise of power. The movement and its charismatic leader control the state in balance with state institutions such as the police and traditional elites such as the clergy and business magnates.
5. Radicalization or entropy. The state either becomes increasingly radical, as did Nazi Germany, or slips into traditional authoritarian rule, as did fascist Italy.

Paxton explains that "each national variant of fascism draws its legitimacy ... not from some universal scripture but from what it considers the most authentic elements of its own community identity." He also examines the underlying principles that fueled the rise of fascism, and determines that there are nine "mobilizing passions" that have fed the fires of fascist movements wherever they have arisen:

1. A sense of overwhelming crisis beyond the reach of any traditional solutions

2. The primacy of the group, toward which one has duties superior to every right, whether universal or individual, and the subordination of the individual to it

3. The belief that one's group is a victim, a sentiment which justifies any action, without legal or moral limits, against the group's enemies, both internal and external

4. Dread of the group's decline under the corrosive effect of individualistic liberalism, class conflict, and alien influences

5. The need for closer integration of a purer community, by consent if possible, or by exclusionary violence if necessary

6. The need for authority by natural leaders (always male), culminating in a national chief who alone is capable of incarnating the group's destiny

7. The superiority of the leader's instincts over abstract and universal reason

8. The beauty of violence and the efficacy of will, when they are devoted to the group's success

9. The right of the chosen people to dominate others without restraint from any kind of human or divine law, right being decided by the sole criterion of the group's prowess in a Darwinian struggle

This last "passion" was explored as an essential aspect of Nazism by the Norwegian social scientist and philosopher Harald Ofstad, whose interviews with former Nazis led him to write *Our Contempt for Weakness: Nazi Norms and Values—And Our Own* (English translation, 1989). It described the logical extension of that Darwinian struggle against the "lesser" that pervades so much fascist literature: the deep-seated hatred and contempt in which all persons deemed "weaker"—ethnically, racially, medically, genetically, or otherwise—are held, and the desire to eliminate them entirely that it fuels.

Paxton ultimately summed this all up in a single paragraph: "Fascism may be defined as a form of political behavior marked by obsessive preoccupation with community decline, humiliation, or victimhood and by compensatory cults of unity, energy, and purity, in which a mass-based party of committed nationalist militants, working in uneasy but effective collaboration with traditional elites, abandons democratic liberties and pursues with redemptive violence and without ethical or legal constraints goals of internal cleansing and external expansion.

Fascism is both a complex and a simple phenomenon. In one sense, it resembles a dynamic human psychological pathology in that it's made up of a complex constellation of traits that are interconnected and whose presence and importance rise and fall according to the often fast-changing stages of development it goes through; and in another, it can in many ways be boiled down to the raw, almost feral imposition of the organized violent will of an angry and fear-ridden human id upon the rest of humankind.

Throughout history, it has only ever achieved real power when it was able to coalesce its many contentious and often warring factions under the banner of a unifying charismatic leader. The lack of such a figure at those periods when fascist tendencies were ascendant in the United States is one of the primary reasons historians believed that fascism never could obtain the "political space" required for obtaining power in the United States: "It can't happen here."

That's where Donald Trump comes in.

Fascist elements and tendencies have always been part of the nation's political DNA, even though many Americans cannot admit this. Indeed, it can be said that some of the worst traits of European fascism were borrowed from America, particularly the elimination-ist tendencies, manifested in the form of genocidal violence toward indigenous peoples and racial and ethnic segregation.

Hitler acknowledged at various times his admiration for the American genocide against Native Americans; for the segregation-ist Jim Crow regime in the South, on which the Nazis modeled the Nuremberg Race Laws; and for the deployment of mob violence by the Ku Klux Klan, which was the inspiration for the murderous street thuggery of the German Brownshirts and the Italian Black-shirts. According to Ernst Hanfstaengl, a German American who was a confidant of Hitler's for a time, Hitler was "passionately inter-ested in the Ku Klux Klan ... He seemed to think it was a political movement similar to his own." And it was.

Despite these tendencies, the United States had never yet given way to fascism at the national level. No doubt this, in the second half of the twentieth century at least, was due to horror at what ulti-mately transpired under the Hitler regime—namely, the Holocaust. We were appalled by racial and ethnic hatred, by segregation and eliminationism, because we saw the pile of corpses that they pro-duced in Europe. We didn't make the connection with our own piles of corpses, until the civil rights movement finally redressed our own national wrongs.

However, that was a different generation, one that grew up in the shadow of World War II and experienced not only McCarthyism but also the civil rights struggle. Today, it is not uncommon to see Nazi regalia treated as a kind of fashion statement and outrageous genocidal racial sentiments tossed about like popcorn, dismissed as a kind of naughtiness. White nationalism and supremacism, nativism, misogyny, conspiracism, sexual paranoia, and xenophobic hatred, once embodied in German National Socialism, have experienced a revival in twenty-first-century America in the form of the alt-right and Patriot-militia movements.

Relatively early in the campaign, a flood of observers began using the word "fascist" to describe Trump's campaign. Not all of these concerns were coming from the left: in November 2015, a number of conservatives began sounding the alarm as well, especially in response to Trump's vows to crack down on Muslim immigrants.

"Trump is a fascist. And that's not a term I use loosely or often. But he's earned it," the conservative pundit Max Boot, a Marco Rubio campaign adviser, tweeted in November 2015, after Trump had retweeted a graphic from #WhiteGenocide.

Steve Deace, a Ted Cruz supporter and conservative Iowa radio host, tweeted in November 2015, "If Obama proposed the same religion registry as Trump every conservative in the country would call it what it is—creeping fascism."

Even the staid, Republican-owned *Seattle Times* used the term to describe Trump in a November 2015 editorial: "There is a bottom line, and it's simple: Trump's campaign message reflects a kind of creeping fascism. It needs to be rejected."

Of course liberals, too, were alarmed: the historian Rick Perlstein, in a *Washington Spectator* piece titled "Donald Trump and the F Word," explored the question of Trump's fascist tendencies in depth, concluding that although Trump himself might not be a fascist, the phenomenon he was empowering was troublingly close to meeting Paxton's condition of fascism at the power-acquisition stage. Trump was tapping into a wellspring of discontent: "If he's just giving the people what they want, consider the people," he wrote. "Consider what they want."

There is little doubt that there is a significant resemblance between Trump's ascendance and that of previous fascist figures in history beyond Hitler, including Mussolini, Francisco Franco, and Miklos Horthy, partly because the politics he engenders indeed fill out so many of the key components that collectively create genuine fascism, as we've come to understand it through deep historical scholarship.

A careful examination of Trump's campaign and post-election messages in light of Paxton's definition reveals a raft of fascist traits:

1. Eliminationist rhetoric is the backbone of Trump's appeal. His opening salvo in the campaign—the one that first catapulted him

to the forefront in the race, in the polls, and proved wildly popular with Republican voters—was his vow, and subsequent proposed program, to deport all 12 million of the United States' undocumented immigrants (he used the deprecatory term "illegal alien") and to erect a gigantic wall on the nation's southern border. The language he used to justify such plans—labeling those immigrants "criminals," "killers," and "rapists"—is classic rhetoric designed to dehumanize an entire group of people by reducing them to objects fit only for elimination.

Trump's appeal ultimately is about forming a "purer" community, and it has been relentless and expansive: When an audience member asked him at a town-hall-style appearance when and how he was going to "get rid of all the Muslims," he responded that "we're going to be looking at a lot of different things." He also claimed that if elected, he would send back all the refugees from Syria who had arrived in the United States: "If I win, they're going back," he told one of his approval-roaring campaign crowds. He told an interviewer that the Black Lives Matter movement was "looking for trouble" and later suggested that maybe a Black Lives Matter protester should have been "roughed up."

2. Palingenetic ultranationalism, after race-baiting and ethnic fearmongering, is the most obviously fascistic component of Trump's presidential election effort, embodied in those trucker hats proclaiming, "Make America Great Again." Trump amplifies the slogan this way: "The silent majority is back, and we're going to take the country back. We're going to make America great again."

That's almost the letter-perfect embodiment of palingenesis: the promise of the phoenix-like rebirth of a nation from the ashes of its "golden age."

3. Trump's deep contempt for both liberalism and establishment conservatism allows him to go over the heads of established political alignments. The conservative talk-show host Rush Limbaugh has noted, "In parlaying this outsider status of his, he's better at playing the insiders' game than they are ... He's running rings around all of these seasoned, lifelong, highly acclaimed professionals in both the

consultant class, the adviser class, the strategist class, and the candidate class. And he's doing it simply by being himself."

4. Trump exploits a feeling of victimization, constantly proclaiming that America is in a state of crisis that has made it "the laughingstock" of the rest of the world, and contends that this has occurred because of the failures of (primarily liberal) politicians.

5. He himself embodies the concept of a lone male leader who considers himself a man of destiny. His refusal to acknowledge the lack of factual basis of many of his comments embodies the fascistic notion that the leader's instincts trump logic and reason in any event.

6. Trump's contempt for weakness was manifested practically every day on the campaign trail, ranging from his dissing of John McCain as "not a hero" because "I like people who weren't captured," to his onstage mockery of Serge Kovaleski, a *New York Times* reporter who has a disability.

This list is thought-provoking—and it is meant to be thought-provoking—but as part of our exercise in examining the attributes of real fascism, we also can begin to discern the difference between that phenomenon and the Trump candidacy.

For example, fascists have, in the past, always relied upon an independent, movement-driven paramilitary force capable of intimidating their opponents with various types of thuggery. In Italy these were the Blackshirts; Hitler imitated the Italian units with the formation of the Brownshirts, the Storm Division. Trump has no such paramilitary force at his disposal.

Members of various white-supremacist organizations and bona fide paramilitary organizations such as the Oath Keepers and the Three Percent movement are avid Trump backers. Trump has never made known any desire to form an alliance with or to make use of such groups.

However, via wink-wink nudge-nudge cues Trump has on occasion encouraged or failed to condemn spontaneous violence by some of his supporters against both protesters at rallies and groups they consider undesirable, such as when "enthusiastic supporters" committed anti-Latino hate crimes.

Encouraging extralegal vigilante violence can be classified as a fascistic response. Yet a serious fascist would have called upon not just the crowd to respond with violence, but also his paramilitary allies to respond with retaliatory strikes. Trump didn't do that.

Another perhaps more basic reason that Trump cannot be categorized as a true fascist is that he is not an ideologue who acts out of a rigid adherence to a consistent worldview, as do all real fascists. Trump's only real ideology is worship of himself, "the Donald." He will do and say just about anything that appeals to any receptive segment of the American body politic to attract their support. One segment of the body could be called the nation's id—groups that live on paranoia and hatred regarding those different from themselves and also the political establishment.

There's no question that these supporters brought a visceral energy to the limited universe of the GOP primary, though I don't know anyone who, in 2015, expected that such a campaign could survive the oxygen and exposure of a general election. Those observers, including me, were all proved wrong. Few observers had any clue how successfully the Alt-America worldview could become in muscling its way into the national spotlight.

However, the reason why Trump has never yet called upon the shock troops of a paramilitary wing for support, and why he has attempted to keep an arm's-length distance from the overtly racist white nationalists and neo-Nazis who have become some of his most enthusiastic backers, is simple: he isn't really one of them.

What he is, says Chip Berlet, is a classic right-wing nativist populist demagogue: "His ideology and rhetoric are much more comparable to the European populist radical right, akin to Jean-Marie Le Pen's National Front, the Danish People's Party, or Vladimir Zhirinovsky's Liberal Democratic Party of Russia. All of them use the common radical right rhetoric of nativism, authoritarianism, and populism."

Trump himself is not a fascist primarily because he lacks any kind of coherent, or even semi-coherent, ideology, nor has he agitated for a totalitarian one-party state. What he represents instead is a sort of gut-level reactionism that lacks the rigor and absolutism, the demand for ideological purity, that are characteristic of full-bore fascism.

But that does not mean that the movement he has unleashed is not potentially dangerously proto-fascist, nor that he is not dangerous to American democracy. Indeed, he has now proved to be more dangerous than an outright fascist, because such a figure would be far less appealing and far less likely to succeed in the current milieu. What Trump has succeeded in doing, by exploiting the strands of right-wing populism in the country, has been to make the large and growing number of proto-fascist groups in America larger and more vicious. In other words he is simultaneously responding to and creating the conditions that could easily lead to the genuine growth of fascism.

The journalist Milton Mayer, in *They Thought They Were Free: The Germans 1933–1945* (1955), describes how these changes happen not overnight, but incrementally:

> "You see," my colleague went on, "one doesn't see exactly where or how to move. Believe me, this is true. Each act, each occasion, is worse than the last, but only a little worse. You wait for the next and the next. You wait for one great shocking occasion, thinking that others, when such a shock comes, will join with you in resisting somehow. You don't want to act, or even talk, alone; you don't want to 'go out of your way to make trouble.' Why not?—Well, you are not in the habit of doing it. And it is not just fear, fear of standing alone, that restrains you; it is also genuine uncertainty ...
>
> "Now you live in a world of hate and fear, and the people who hate and fear do not even know it themselves; when everyone is transformed, no one is transformed. Now you live in a system which rules without responsibility even to God. The system itself could not have intended this in the beginning, but in order to sustain itself it was compelled to go all the way."

We lose our humanity incrementally, in small acts of meanness. The Nazis' regime ultimately embodied the ascension of demonic inhumanity, but they didn't get that way overnight. They got that way through, day after day, attacking and demonizing and urging the elimination of those they deemed their enemies.

And this has been happening to America—in particular, to the conservative movement and the Republican Party—for a very long time. Donald Trump represents the culmination of a trend that really began in the 1990s.

That was when we first saw the popular rise of eliminationist hate talk. It was first heard in Patrick Buchanan's 1992 declaration of a "culture war"; it was then wielded with thoughtless glee and great regularity by an increasingly rabid set of right-wing pundits led by Rush Limbaugh; then it was deeply codified by a new generation of talking heads who have subsequently marched across the sound stages at Fox News. It surfaced particularly with the birth of the Tea Party, which became perhaps the single most significant manifestation of right-wing populism in the nation's history, certainly since the Ku Klux Klan of the 1920s.

Trump aligned himself very early with the Tea Party elements, remarking in 2011, "I represent a lot of the ingredients of the Tea Party." And indeed he does—in particular, its obeisance to the captains of industry and their untrammeled right to make profits at the expense of everyone else.

Right-wing populism is essentially predicated on what today we might call the psychology of celebrity worship: convincing working-class schlubs that they, too, can someday become rich and famous—because when they do, would they want to be taxed heavily? It's all about dangling that lottery carrot out there for the poor stiffs who delude themselves about their chances of hitting the jackpot.

The thing about right-wing populism is that it's manifestly self-defeating: those who stand to primarily benefit from this ideology are the wealthy, which is why they so willingly underwrite it.

One might be inclined to dismiss it as a kind of "sucker populism." But that would be to overlook the reasons for its appeal, which run much deeper, and are really in many ways more a product of people's attraction to an authoritarian system. Those psychological needs often are a product of the levels of general public fear, much more so than of economic well-being or other factors. That fear is generated by a large number of factors, including the spread of unfiltered social media, as well as the rapid decline in basic journalistic standards of factuality in the larger mainstream media, as well as the mainstream media's increasing propensity to promote information that, producers say, reflects what people want to see rather than what responsible journalistic ethics would consider more important: what they need to know. That's how Alt-America became so powerful a political force.

This right-wing populism, largely lurking on the periphery and gradually building an audience, was whipped into life by Ron Paul's and Sarah Palin's 2008 candidacies, and then became fully manifest as a national movement in short order with the rise of the Tea Party in 2009. Not only was the Tea Party an overtly right-wing populist movement, it soon became a major conduit for a revival of the populist Patriot-militia movement. Many of these "Tea Party Patriots" are now Oath Keepers and Three Percenters whose members widely supported Trump's candidacy, and are now vowing to defend his presidency with their own arms.

Most of these extremists are only one step removed, ideologically speaking, from the neo-Nazis and other white supremacists of the racist right, and both of those segments of the right lean heavily on nativist and authoritarian rhetoric. It's only somewhat natural that Trump's right-wing populism would be mistaken for fascism—they are closely related. Not every right-wing populist is a fascist, but every fascist is a right-wing populist.

Thus, Donald Trump may not be a fascist, but with his vicious brand of right-wing populism he is not just empowering the latent fascist elements in America, he is leading his followers merrily down a path that leads directly to fascism. If the final result is fascism, the distinction between right-wing populism and fascism is not really significant except in understanding how it happened in the first place.

The United States, thanks to Trump, has now reached a fork in the road where it must choose down which path its future lies—with democracy and its often fumbling ministrations, or with the appealing rule of plutocratic authoritarianism, ushered in on a tide of fascistic populism (if history serves as a example, the fascistic populists will eventually overwhelm their plutocrat sponsors).

Trump may not be a fascist, but he is an authoritarian who, intentionally or not, is empowering the existing proto-fascist elements in American society; even more dangerously, his alt-right–Tea Party brand of right-wing populism is helping these groups grow their ranks and their potential to recruit new members by leaps and bounds. Not only that, he is making thuggery seem normal and inevitable. And that *is* a serious problem.

How can you talk with a diehard Alt-American if you are a dedicated mainstream liberal? Many Americans confronted that question over their family Thanksgiving tables a couple of weeks after the election. The conversations often did not turn out well.

But it is no longer a question we can pretend away, perhaps by choosing to stay away from those tables altogether. The American radical right is a real force with real power—both political and cultural—and it is no longer alarmist to point that out. Nor is it a problem that we can hope to attack head-on through blunt political force, though without question the barrage of attacks on Americans' civil rights that very likely now await us in the coming years will require our most vocal opposition.

It will be incumbent upon this political opposition to be totally dedicated to the principles of nonviolent resistance. During the anti-Trump protests that immediately followed his election, the liberal mainstream media characterized a handful of violent incidents as riots. That undermines the aims of the anti-Trump protest. Fascist movements have a long-documented history of converting any violence they encounter after having provoked it into a justification for further violence that far outpaces anything that the opposing left might be capable of mustering.

The rise of the radical right is a symptom of problems more deep-seated than the purely political level. Fascism, at its base, is fueled by hate and the pure objectification of an utter lack of empathy for other human beings. Thus, the negation of this negative emotion is not love, but empathy. Confronting fascism—as J. K. Rowling suggests with a theme running through her popular "Harry Potter" series of children's books—means first embracing humanity, both ours and theirs; from that embrace we can make the personal choices that define what kind of people we are. We need to be able to put ourselves in other people's shoes, even if we do not agree with them, for our own sake as well as theirs. Harry's experiences observing young Tom Riddle, the nascent Lord Voldemort, through the magical "Pensieve" gave these stories a surprisingly profound depth of meaning.

Empathy as an essential political principle actually comes naturally to progressives as a policy imperative. Certainly the liberal social policies that have created wealthy liberal urban enclaves that were the base of the Democratic Party's support in the 2016 election reflect that empathetic impulse, in the form of broad social safety nets, supportive urban-oriented programs, high-powered educational systems, and bustling economies. The impulse behind most modern liberal programs has been to raise the standard of living for ordinary people and to defend the civil rights of everyone, especially those who have not enjoyed them for much of the nation's history. That's a fairly empathetic agenda.

Liberals' dealings regarding rural and Rust Belt America, however, have over the past forty years largely been characterized by at best benign neglect, in terms of both economic policy and culture: wealthy urbanites do often look down their noses at rural and working-class citizens and consider their concerns and attitudes at best antiquated and at worst backward and stupid. This political disconnect emerges in all kinds of cultural expressions, from movie stereotypes to thoughtless remarks from liberal politicians.

Which is perhaps why the conversations around our Thanksgiving tables were so deeply awkward, if not deeply disturbing, in the wake of Donald Trump's surprise election. And yet that is the kind of place where the deeper change that needs to occur in our relationships with each other as Americans can happen. One healing conversation at a time.

If Americans of goodwill—including mainstream conservatives who recognize how their movement has been hijacked by radicals—can learn to start talking to each other again, and maybe even pull a few Alt-Americans out of their abyss along the way, then perhaps we can start to genuinely heal our divisions instead of relegating each other into social oblivion and, maybe eventually, civil war. Some kind of cultural or political civil war is clearly already on many minds.

The bottom-line issue is really an epistemological one: how is a rational exchange possible when we can't even agree on what constitutes a fact and factuality? Most liberals (certainly not all) tend to prefer traditional standards of factuality and evidence in which concrete information from reliable sources is accepted as fact, and scientific evidence obtained through peer-reviewed methods is considered the gold standard for presentable evidence in a discussion.

Pretty much the opposite is true in Alt-America. Science and scientists are viewed with suspicion as participants in the "conspiracy," and so their contributions are instantly discarded as worthless, as is the work of any kind of academic in any field, including history and the law. The only sources of information they accept as "factual" are tendentious right-wing propaganda riddled with false facts, wild distortions, and risible conspiracist hyperbole. Fox News—whose mass failures regarding factual accuracy are now the stuff of legend—is considered by Alt-Americans to be the only "balanced and accurate" news source, though even it is viewed with deep suspicion by alt-righters, Patriots, and Alex Jones acolytes.

Breaking through that wall is at best difficult, and in the case of dedicated and fanatical Alt-Americans, probably not worth the personal costs in terms of the emotional abuse they like to heap on those with whom they disagree. But finding people who remain within reach—those for whom common decency and respectful discourse and Christian kindness are still important values, even though they may have voted for Trump—may provide an avenue for deeper social change.

At some point, there will have to be a discussion about just what is a fact and what isn't, because that eventually will determine whether or not you can ever come to a rational common ground. But getting there first will take a lot of empathy.

The communications expert Sharon Ellison specializes in what she calls "powerful nondefensive communication"; she has developed an effective empathy-driven model that she has shown can be effective in at least breaking down the interpersonal barriers that modern politics have erected, and upon which the radical right thrives. The starting place, she says, is curiosity:

> Instead of blasting Trump or insulting the morality or intelligence of his supporters, first, just get curious. You don't have to agree; you're simply gathering information and trying to understand where they're coming from, even if you believe they're deeply misguided.
>
> Make it a dialogue, not a debate or an inquisition. No matter how true and rational your analysis is, force-feeding it will not go down well. Nor will a premeditated series of sugar-coated questions designed to subtly lead the person to "get it." The right question, skillfully and non-aggressively posed, could prompt someone to gain unexpected insights, and when they realize something for themselves, they can more easily accept it.
>
> Your questions should be very specific but posed in a non-judgmental way. (Note that I'm calling the questions "specific" rather than "pointed," which implies that a question is a weapon.)

Ellison cautions against using general, open-ended questions such as whether people can ever learn to get along. Some of us gravitate toward these because they feel softer, but they can wind up serving as an invitation to rant.

The key to understanding people who have become drawn into the Alt-America universe is the role that the hero myth plays in framing their worldview. Dedicated Patriots and white nationalists, just like the hate criminals they inspire, genuinely envision themselves as heroes. They are saving the country, or perhaps the white race, or perhaps just their local community. And so anything, *anything* they might do in that act of defense is excusable, even laudable.

This embrace of the heroic is what ultimately poisons us all. The sociologist James Aho has explored this concept of the hero:

> The warrior needs an enemy. Without one there is nothing against which to fight, nothing from which to save the world, nothing to give his life meaning. What this means, of course, is that if an enemy is not ontologically present in the nature of things, one must be manufactured. The Nazi needs an international Jewish banker and conspiratorial Mason to serve his purposes of self-aggrandizement, and thus sets about creating one, at least unconsciously. By the same token, the radical Zionist locks himself in perverse symbiosis with his Palestinian "persecutors," the Communist with his "imperialistic capitalist running dogs," the capitalist with his Communist "subversives."

Aho goes on to describe how the enemy is constructed as embodying "putrefaction and death," is experienced "as issuing from the 'dregs' of society," whose "visitation on our borders is tantamount to impending pestilence ... The enemy's presence in our midst is a pathology of the social organism serious enough to require the most far-reaching remedies: quarantine, political excision, or, to use a particularly revealing expression, liquidation and expulsion."

What Aho describes is a dynamic latent in all sectors of American society but finding a virulent expression in right-wing extremism. It is one in which both sides—the heroic exemplars of the far right and their named "enemies," that is, Jews, civil-rights advocates, and the government—essentially exchange roles in their respective perceptions; the self is always heroic, the other always the enemy. Each sees the other as the demonic enemy, feeding the other's fears and paranoias in an increasingly threatening spiral that eventually breaks out in the form of real violence.

There is, as Aho suggests, a way to escape this dynamic, to break the cycle. And it requires, on the part of those seeking to oppose this kind of extremism, a recognition of their own propensity toward naming the enemy and adopting the self-aggrandizing pose of the hero:

As [the cultural anthropologist] Ernest Becker has convincingly shown, the call to heroism still resonates in modern hearts. However, we are in the habit of either equating heroism with celebrity ("TV Actress Tops List of Students' Heroes") or caricaturing the hero as a bluff-and-swagger patriot/soldier making the world safe for, say, Christian democracy. In these ways heroism is portrayed as a rather happy if not entirely risk-free venture that earns one public plaudits. Today we are asked to learn that, in the deepest and truest sense, heroism is really none of these things, but a largely private vocation requiring stamina, discipline, responsibility, and above all courage. Not just the ascetic courage to cleanse our personal lives of what we have been taught is filth, or even less to cleanse society of the alleged carriers of this filth, but, as Jung displayed, the fortitude to release our claim on moral purity and perfection. At a personal and cultural level, I believe this is the only way to transcend the logic of enemies.

For all of its logic and love of science, modern liberalism as a social force is weighed down by its most consistent flaw: an overweening belief in its own moral superiority, its heroism, as it were. (Not, of course, that conservatives are any better in this regard; if one factors in the religious right and the "moral values" vote, they are objectively worse.) This tendency becomes especially noticeable in urban liberal societies, which for all their enlightenment and love of tolerance are maddeningly smug, intolerant of the "ignorance" of their rural and "fly-over country" counterparts. It's not an omnipresent attitude, but it is pervasive enough that others' perceptions of it are certainly not without basis. There's a similar stigma attached to religious beliefs as well, especially among more secular liberals, and that in turn has given birth to a predictable counterreaction that is only partially a result of misunderstanding.

If we look at the 2016 electoral map, and see all those red rural counties and come to terms with the reasons why none of them ever turn blue, it's important to come to terms with our own prejudices and our easy willingness to treat our fellow Americans—the ones who are not like us—with contempt and disrespect. Simply beginning the change will require both humility and empathy.

That's not to suggest that we respond to racist or violent

provocations with touchy-feely attempts at "reaching out" to the other side; these are always rejected with contempt, or viewed as a sign of weakness. Certainly it does not mean we need to "reach out" to the rural haters and the conspiracy-spewing Patriots. I grew up in rural America, and I'm all too familiar with the bullies and swaggering ignoramuses who hold too much sway in that culture, and whose politics and worldview are now ascendant beyond their wildest imaginings (and they are wild, trust me). There's really no point in trying to reach out to people who will only return your hand as a bloody stump. The only thing they understand, in the end, is brute political force: being thrashed at the ballot box, and in the public discourse.

So it is vital for liberals, progressives, moderates, and genuine conservatives to link arms in the coming years to fight back against the fascist tide. It will require organizing, and it will require real outreach. And if this coalition wants to succeed, its members will need to break the vicious circular social dynamic that right-wing extremists always create, particularly in rural communities where their bullying style of discourse can stifle honest discourse. To do that, some self-reflection will go a long way.

Respecting those from rural areas, those who hold deep religious beliefs, doesn't force progressives to compromise their own beliefs or standards. It simply means being part of a democracy, which is enriched by its diversity. It means once again empowering the many rural progressives who have lived there all along, fighting the good fight against all odds, because they are the people who are best equipped to have those many dinner-table conversations.

Certainly traditional rural values such as communitarianism, common decency, mutual respect, and respect for tradition should have a place among all that diversity that liberals are fond of celebrating. Because until urban progressives learn to accord them that respect, they are doomed to remain trapped in the vicious cycle being fueled on both sides. For liberals and moderates, breaking out may be a matter of survival—especially as the rabid right's fantasies begin coming to fruition.

Alt-America, thanks to Donald Trump, is no longer merely the stuff of these fantasies. It will take the best of us, the most decent part of us—the better angels of our nature, as Abraham Lincoln invoked in his first inaugural address—to prevent right-wing dreams from becoming realities.

Notes

Chapter 1: Into the Abyss

p. 1   **Hopefully, he's going to sit there and say:** Alan Blinder, "Donald Trump Fails to Fill Alabama Stadium, but Fans' Zeal Is Unabated," *New York Times*, Aug. 21, 2015.

p. 2   **This robocall goes out:** Gideon Resnick, "White Nationalists Launch Trump Hotline," *Daily Beast*, March 22, 2016.

p. 2   **The march to victory:** Jonathan Mahler, "Donald Trump's Message Resonates with White Supremacists," *New York Times*, Feb. 29, 2016.

p. 2   **Get all of these monkeys:** Ashley Feinberg, "Top Neo-Nazi Website Applauds 'Glorious Leader' Trump's Call to Ban All Muslims," Gawker. com, Dec. 8, 2015.

p. 2   **Donald Trump was right:** Sara DiNatale and Maria Sacchetti, "South Boston Brothers Allegedly Beat Homeless Man," *Boston Globe*, Aug. 19, 2015.

p. 2   **People who follow me:** Justin William Moyer, "Trump Says Fans Are 'Very Passionate' after Hearing One of Them Allegedly Assaulted Hispanic Man," *Washington Post*, Aug. 21, 2015.

p. 4   **Right-wing populism:** See Chip Berlet and Matthew N. Lyons, *Right-Wing Populism in America: Too Close for Comfort* (New York: Guilford Press, 2000), pp. 6–9, 19–51, 175–303.

p. 4   **Thus, the Tea Party:** See Devin Burghart, "Tea Party Nationalism: A Critical Examination of the Tea Party Movement and the Size, Scope, and Focus of Its National Factions," report, Institute for Research and Education on Human Rights, Fall 2010, www.irehr.org/2010/10/12/tea-party-nationalism-report-pdf/.

p. 4   **The Patriots have always specialized in:** See David Neiwert, *In God's*

Country: The Patriot Movement and the Pacific Northwest (Pullman: Washington State University Press, 1999), pp. 22–40.

p. 5   **"I think the people":** David Neiwert, "Donald Trump Claims to Be the Ideal Tea Party Candidate: 'I Represent a Lot of the Ingredients of the Tea Party,'" Crooksandliars.com, April 7, 2011.

p. 6   **"He is defying":** Chris Stegall, "Donald Trump Defying the Laws of Political Gravity," CBSPhilly, Jan. 25, 2016.

p. 6   **"The U.S. has become":** Washington Post staff, "Full text: Donald Trump Announces a Presidential Bid," *Washington Post*, June 16, 2015.

p. 7   **Longtime nativists:** See, for example, Ann Coulter, "America Nears El Tipping Pointo," Anncoulter.com, Dec. 5, 2012.

p. 8   **In fact, Coulter had made:** "Ann Coulter Cites White Nationalists, Anti-Muslim Activists and Other Racists in New Book," *Hatewatch*, Southern Poverty Law Center, Splcenter.org, June 29, 2015.

p. 8   **Coulter also credited:** Jared Taylor, "¡Adios, America!: Coulter's Call for Immigration Sanity," *American Renaissance*, June 16, 2015.

p. 8   **"get used to your little girls being raped":** See Brian Tashman, "Ann Coulter: 'Get Used to Your Little Girls Being Raped' Due to Immigration," *Right Wing Watch*, June 8, 2015.

p. 8   **"Americans should fear immigrants":** Catherine Taibi, "Ann Coulter Believes Americans Should Fear 'Illegal Immigrants' More Than ISIS," *Huffington Post*, Feb. 26, 2015.

p. 8   **She denied that:** Scott Eric Kaufman, "Ann Coulter: Mexican Culture 'Is Obviously Deficient,' and Hispanics Are 'Not Black, So Drop the Racism Crap'," Salon.com, May 27, 2015.

p. 9   **Coulter, who had been an ardent:** Mikayla Bean, "Ann Coulter: A 'Trump-Romney' Ticket Would Stop 'Foreigners' From Outvoting 'White Americans'," *Right Wing Watch* (People For the American Way), Aug. 6, 2015, rightwingwatch.org.

p. 9   **It was apparently:** Carlos Lozada, "Did Ann Coulter's New Book Help Inspire Trump's Mexican 'Rapists' Comments?," *Washington Post*, Aug. 3, 2015.

p. 9   **One of the solutions:** See Coulter, "Immigration Hawks Frightened by 99-Pound Blonde," syndicated column, June 3, 2015, anncoulter.com.

p. 9   **Another ardent Trump admirer:** See Southern Poverty Law Center, "Kyle Rogers," Extremist Profile, splcenter.org.

p. 10   **Rogers seemed to make:** See Dartagnan, "Leader of Group That Inspired Dylann Roof Hawked Trump T-Shirts Day Before Charleston Massacre," *Daily Kos*, Sept. 5, 2015, dailykos.com.

p. 10   **Dylann Roof was:** See Mark Berman, "Prosecutors Say Dylann Roof 'Self-Radicalized' Online, Wrote Another Manifesto in Jail," *Washington Post*, Aug. 22, 2016, washingtonpost.com.

p. 10   **In the days before:** See "Dylann Roof's Manifesto," *New York Times*, Dec. 13, 2016, nytimes.com.

p. 12 **Adkisson was driven:** See CNN staff, "Affidavit: Man Admits Church Shooting, Says Liberals Should Die," CNN, July 28, 2008, cnn. com. See also Adkisson's manifesto, online at http://web.knoxnews.com/pdf/021009church-manifesto.pdf.

p. 13 **In the seven and a half years:** See David Neiwert, "Home Is Where the Hate Is: Trump's Fixation on Demonizing Islam Hides True Homegrown US Terror Threat," Reveal Radio/Center for Investigative Reporting, June 21, 2017.

p. 14 **After the elections of 2010:** See David Neiwert, "No, Rep. King, We Indeed Cannot Be In Denial," Crooksandliars.com, March 10, 2011.

p. 15 **King ignored this plea:** See David Neiwert, "Domestic Terrorism: Senate Hears Testimony About the Rise of the Right-Wing Threat," Crooksandliars.com, Sept. 21, 2012.

p. 15 **The Southern Poverty Law Center:** "Hate Map," Southern Poverty Law Center, https://www.splcenter.org/hate-map.

p. 16 **In March 2015, Mark Potok:** See Mark Potok, "The Year in Hate and Extremism," *Intelligence Report*, March 9, 2015, www.splcenter.org/fighting-hate/intelligence-report/2017/year-hate-and-extremism.

p. 16 **Dylann Roof had hardly seemed:** See Frances Robles and Nikita Stewart, "Dylann Roof's Past Reveals Trouble at Home and School," *New York Times*, July 16, 2015. See also Kevin Wadlow, "Charleston Shooter Roof Left Little Fingerprint on the Keys," *Florida Keys News*, June 27, 2015; Associated Press, "Charleston Shooting Suspect Led Troubled Life Long Before Radicalization," June 27, 2015.

p. 17 **Another old friend:** See Bruce Wright, "Who Is Dalton Tyler? Dylann Storm Roof's Roommate Says Alleged Charleston Church Shooter Planned Shooting for 6 Months," *International Business Times*, June 18, 2015, ibtimes.com.

p. 18 **When he set out:** See Charlotte Krol, "Dylann Roof's Friend: Charleston Church 'Wasn't Primary Target,'" *Telegraph*, June 20, 2015.

p. 18 **When he walked into the church:** See Enjoli Francis and Mary Bruce, "New Police Documents Reveal Deadly Minutes Inside South Carolina Church," ABC News, October 29, 2015.

p. 20 **On the day after:** See Justin Wm. Moyer, "Why South Carolina's Confederate Flag Isn't at Half-Staff after Church Shooting," *Washington Post*, June 19, 2015.

p. 20 **The Trayvon Martin shooting:** See Pew Research Center, "Big Racial Divide over Zimmerman Verdict," July 22, 2013.

p. 21 **The heated conversation turned into a bonfire:** See Chris Branch, "Looking Ahead after the Ferguson Protests: What Next?," *Huffington Post*, Dec. 2, 2014, huffingtonpost.com. See also Frank Newport, "Gulf Grows in Black-White Views of U.S. Justice System Bias," Gallup, July 22, 2013, gallup.com.

p. 21 **There were other similar incidents:** See J. David Goodman,

"Difficult Decisions Ahead in Responding to Police Chokehold Homicide," *New York Times*, Aug. 4, 2014; Elahe Izadi and Peter Holley, "Video Shows Cleveland Officer Shooting 12-Year-Old Tamir Rice within Seconds," *Washington Post*, Nov. 26, 2014; Richard Perez-Pena, "Lawyers Square Off in Tulsa as Reserve Deputy Surrenders in Unarmed Man's Death," *New York Times*, April 14, 2015; David A. Graham, "The Mysterious Death of Freddie Gray," *Atlantic*, April 22, 2015.

p. 21 **The incidents kept mounting:** See Jessica Guynn, "Meet the Woman Who Coined #BlackLivesMatter," *USA Today*, March 4, 2015.

p. 21 **South Carolina had had its own moment:** See Frances Robles and Alan Blinder, "Pastor Denounces Racism at Walter Scott's Funeral One Week after Police Shooting," *New York Times*, April 11, 2015.

p. 21 **As it happened:** See M. Delatorre, "Dylann Roof and Michael Slager Are Jail Neighbors, Police Confirm," KFOR-TV, June 21, 2015, kfor.com.

p. 22 **At the funerals:** See Nikita Stewart and Richard Perez-Pena, "In Charleston, Raw Emotion at Hearing for Suspect in Church Shooting," *New York Times*, June 19, 2015.

p. 22 **President Obama came:** See Ashley Alman, "Obama on Charleston Shooting: 'This Type of Mass Violence Does Not Happen in Other Advanced Countries,'" *Huffington Post*, June 18, 2015.

p. 22 **The Confederate flag:** See Jessica Taylor, "The Complicated Political History of the Confederate Flag," National Public Radio, June 22, 2015.

p. 23 **The historian Gordon Rhea writes:** See Gordon Rhea, "Why Non-Slaveholding Southerners Fought," *Civil War Trust*, Jan. 25, 2011, civilwar.org.

p. 23 **"Today we are here":** See "Transcript: Gov. Nikki Haley of South Carolina on Removing the Confederate Flag," *New York Times*, June 22, 2015.

p. 23 **Even some of the flag's staunchest:** See Frances Robles, Richard Faussett, and Michael Barbaro, "Nikki Haley, South Carolina Governor, Calls for Removal of Confederate Battle Flag," *New York Times*, June 22, 2015.

p. 24 **On June 23:** See Michael E. Miller, "Jenny Horne: How a Descendant of the President of the Confederacy Helped Vanquish His Flag," *Washington Post*, July 9, 2015. See also Meg Wagner and Corey Siemaszko, "South Carolina Removes Confederate Flag from Statehouse as Crowd Cheers, Sings: 'Hey, Hey, Hey, Goodbye'," *New York Daily News*, July 10, 2015.

p. 24 **Governor Robert Bentley of Alabama:** See Krishnadev Calamur, "Alabama Governor Orders Removal of Confederate Flags From Capitol," National Public Radio, June 24, 2015.

p. 24 **Retailers around the country:** See Sarah Kaplan, "Wal-Mart, American Bellwether, and the Confederate Flag," *Washington Post*, June 23, 2015.

p. 24   **Monuments to the Confederacy:** See Kirsten West Savali, "New Orleans Mayor Mitch Landrieu's Speech on Terrorist, Genocidal Confederate Symbolism Is One for the History Books," *The Root*, March 17, 2017; *Daily Beast*, "Removal of Confederate Monuments Compared to ISIS," Dec. 19, 2015.

p. 24   **In Memphis:** See "Memphis City Council OKs Removal of Confederate Monument," *The Courier*, Aug. 12, 2015. See also Jay Miller, "Nathan Bedford Forrest Statue Won't be Relocated," *Knoxville News Sentinel*, Oct. 21, 2016.

p. 24   **In pop culture:** See Joe Otterson, "Confederate Flag Gets 'Dukes of Hazzard' Yanked," *USA Today*, July 1, 2015. See also Fox Motor Sports, "Pro Golfer Bubba Watson Removing Confederate Flag From 'General Lee,'" July 6, 2015, foxsports.com.

p. 24   **As for real cars:** See "NASCAR Chair Brian France Wants 'Insensitive Symbol' Eliminated at Races," ESPN.com, June 27, 2015.

p. 25   **As the weeks went by:** See Lindsey Bever and Justin William Moyer, "NASCAR Faces 'Southern Thunder' as Confederate Flags Fly at Daytona," *Washington Post*, July 6, 2015.

p. 25   **The backlash to the backlash:** See Jeremy Borden, "KKK Met with Skirmishes at Rally to Protest Confederate Flag Removal," *Washington Post*, July 18, 2015.

p. 26   **Some of the most eager:** See Heidi Beirich, "Furling the Flag," *Intelligence Report*, Oct. 27, 2015, splcenter.org.

p. 26   **In Alabama:** See Andrew J. Yawn, "Rally for State Secession Falls Flat," *Montgomery Advertiser*, Aug. 29, 2015.

p. 27   **On July 14, when President Obama:** See Katie Zezima, "Obama Greeted by Protesters Waving Confederate Flags in Oklahoma," *Washington Post*, July 16, 2015.

p. 27   **Things turned frightening:** See Tom McKay, "Confederate Flag-Wavers Crashed a Black Child's Birthday Yelling 'Kill Y'all N*ggers'," *Mic*, July 29, 2015, mic.com.

p. 28   **It was all caught on video:** See Tyler Estep, "Stories Differ in Douglas County Confederate Flag Flap," *Atlanta Journal Constitution*, July 27, 2015.

p. 28   **The movie:** See Armond White, "The Politics Behind *Trainwreck* and *Irrational Man*," *National Review*, July 27, 2015.

p. 28   **A young writer:** See Katie Yoder, "Media Love Affair with Amy Schumer Is a 'Trainwreck' for Women," Fox News Opinion, July 16, 2015, foxnews.com/opinion.

p. 28   **In his room:** See Richard Burgess, "Cryptic Phrases, 'Trainwreck' Mentions, More Revealed in Lafayette Theater Shooter's Journal, Motel Photos," *Acadiana Advocate*, Jan. 21, 2016. See also Elliott Hannon, "Hate-Filled Journal of Louisiana Theater Shooter Praises Dylann Roof for 'Wake Up Call'," *Slate*, Jan. 13, 2016.

p. 30 **On July 23:** See Ashley Cusick, "'Slow and Methodical': Officials Describe Deadly La. Theater Shooting," *Washington Post*, July 24, 2015.

Chapter 2: Alt-America

p. 37 **And privileged they are:** See D'Vera Cohn and Andrea Caumont, "10 Demographic Trends That Are Shaping the US and the World," Pew Research Center, March 31, 2016.

p. 37 **They are similarly impervious:** See, for example, Linda Qui, "How Much Do Undocumented Immigrants Pay in Taxes?," *PunditFact*, Oct. 2, 2016; Lisa Christensen Gee, Matthew Gardner, and Meg Wiehe, "Undocumented Immigrants' State & Local Tax Contributions," Institute on Taxation and Economic Policy, February 2016, https://itep.org/wp-content/uploads/immigration2016.pdf.

p. 37 **You can explain to them:** For information about green cards and unskilled workers, see Ilona Bray, "EB-3 Visa for Professional, Skilled, and Unskilled Workers," *NOLO*, www.nolo.com/legal-encyclopedia/eb-3-visa-professional-skilled-unskilled-workers.html. For information about the unskilled-labor market, see Michael Clemens, "More Unskilled Workers, Please: The New Immigration Bill Doesn't Do Nearly Enough to Address America's Real Labor Shortage," *Foreign Policy*, July 8, 2013.

p. 37 **You can show them:** See, for example, Alex Nowsrateh, "Immigration and Crime—What the Research Says," Cato Institute, July 14, 2015.

p. 38 **Alex Jones and his *Infowars* outfit:** See Alexander Zaitchik, "Meet Alex Jones: The Most Paranoid Man in America Is Trying to Overthrow the 'Global Stasi Borg State,' One Conspiracy Theory at a Time," *Rolling Stone*, March 2, 2011.

p. 39 **The political scientist:** See J. Eric Oliver and Thomas J. Wood, "Conspiracy Theories and the Paranoid Style(s) of Mass Opinion," *American Journal of Political Science*, March 5, 2014. See also John Sides, "Fifty Percent of Americans Believe in Some Conspiracy Theory. Here's Why," *Washington Post*, Feb. 19, 2015.

p. 40 **The legal scholars:** See Cass R. Sunstein and Adam Vermeule, "Conspiracy Theories," *Chicago Unbound*, University of Chicago Public Law and Legal Theory Working Paper, No. 199, 2008.

p. 41 **The personality trait:** See Robert Altemeyer, *The Authoritarians*, University of Manitoba, Spring 2006, theauthoritarians.org.

p. 42 **The psychologist Robert Altemeyer:** See Robert Altemeyer, "Donald Trump and His Authoritarian Followers," The Authoritarians. org, July 18, 2016, theauthoritarians.org.

p. 44 **One study found:** See Maggie Koerth-Baker, "Why Rational People Buy Into Conspiracy Theories," *New York Times Magazine*, May 21, 2013; Karen Douglas and Robbie Sutton, "Does It Take One to Know One? Endorsement of Conspiracy Theories Is Influenced by Personal

Willingness to Conspire," *Journal of Social Psychology* 50, no. 3 (September 2011): 544–52.

p. 44 **Another study found:** See Joseph Parent and Joseph Uscinski, "People Who Believe in Conspiracy Theories Are More Likely to Endorse Violence," *Washington Post*, Feb. 5, 2016.

p. 45 **I call this desire eliminationism:** See David Neiwert, *The Eliminationists: How Hate Talk Radicalized the American Right* (New York: PoliPoint Press, 2009).

p. 46 **Polling data helps:** See "Conspiracy Theory Poll Results," Public Policy Polling, April 2, 2013, and "Democrats and Republicans Differ on Conspiracy Theory Beliefs," Public Policy Polling, April 2, 2013, publicpolicypolling.com.

p. 47 **In 2014:** See J. Eric Oliver and Thomas Woods, "Conspiracy Theories and the Paranoid Style(s) of Mass Opinion," *American Journal of Political Science* 58, no. 4 (October 2014); Sides, "Fifty Percent of Americans Believe in Some Conspiracy Theory."

p. 47 **By August 2016:** See Josh Clinton and Carrie Roush, "Poll: Persistent Partisan Divide Over 'Birther' Question," NBC News, Aug. 10, 2016.

p. 48 **A May 2016 Public Policy Polling survey:** See Alex Gangitano, "Poll: Two-Thirds of Trump Backers Think Obama Is Muslim," *Roll Call*, May 10, 2016.

p. 48 **An October 2016 Fairleigh Dickinson poll found:** See "Fairleigh Dickinson Poll Shows 90 Percent of Trump and Clinton Supporters Believe in Conspiracies That Smear the Candidate They Oppose," Public Mind Poll, Oct. 11, 2016, http://publicmind.fdu.edu/2016/161011/final.pdf.

p. 48 **An August 2016 Public Policy Polling survey:** See "Clinton Leads in NC for First Time since March," Public Policy Polling, Aug. 9, 2016, www.publicpolicypolling.com/pdf/2015/PPP_Release_NC_80916.pdf.

Chapter 3: Black Helicopters and Truck Bombs

p. 51 **Trochmann had been living under the shadow of the law:** See the court documents filed in Sanders County under Trochmann's name: a felony warrant from Wright County detailing Trochmann's alleged role in hiding his daughter from the girl's mother, filed Jan. 24, 1992; and Trochmann's own "Affidavit of Facts" in the case, filed Feb. 24, 1992, plus another affidavit from Trochmann regarding his complaints over his arrest, filed Feb. 7, 1992.

p. 51 **The Trochmann brothers:** See Jess Walter, *Every Knee Shall Bow: The Truth and Tragedy of Ruby Ridge and the Randy Weaver Family* (New York: ReganBooks, 1995), pp. 108–9.

p. 51 **Rumors that Dave Trochmann:** John and Randy Trochmann vehemently deny that they or David Trochmann were involved in any gun-running activity (author's interview, Feb. 1996). The Trochmanns were never charged in the investigation.

p. 51   **It soon emerged:** This was a key point in Randy Weaver's eventual trial. Weaver claims the informant, William Fadeley, approached him about providing the guns. Fadeley claims the contrary. The jury believed Weaver, but there is evidence in their later taped conversations—the first meeting in which the subject arose was not taped—that Fadeley's version is correct. See court testimony, *United States v. Randy Weaver and Kevin Harris*, U.S. District Court, Boise, Idaho, 1993.

p. 52   **One day in August 1992:** The most thorough account of the Weaver standoff is Jess Walters's *Every Knee Shall Bow: The Truth and Tragedy of Ruby Ridge and the Randy Weaver Family* (New York: ReganBooks, 1995). See also Walters's analysis, "Warning Shot: The Lessons of Ruby Ridge," *Spokesman-Review*, Nov. 19, 1992. For other factually accurate accounts see James Aho, *This Thing of Darkness: A Sociology of the Enemy* (Seattle: University of Washington Press, 1994), pp. 50–67, which also offers a strong sociological analysis of the affair; Kenneth S. Stern, *A Force upon the Plain: The American Militia Movement and the Politics of Hate* (New York: Simon & Schuster, 1996), pp. 19–34.

p. 52   **Gritz was a bluff, colorful camera hound:** See David Neiwert, *In God's Country: The Patriot Movement and the Pacific Northwest* (Pullman: Washington State University Press, 1999), pp. 66–8, 137–47.

p. 54   **"The second violent American revolution":** See Howard Kurtz and Dan Balz, "Clinton Assails Spread of Hate through Media; Americans Urged to Stand against 'Reckless Speech'; Conservatives Take Offense," *Washington Post*, April 25, 1995.

p. 54   **Limbaugh generally eschewed:** See "Koppel Covers for Limbaugh's Rumor-Mongering," *Fairness and Accuracy in Reporting*, Fair.org, July 1, 1994; "Clinton Body Bags," Snopes.com; Gabe Wildau and Nicole Castau, "Anatomy of a Smear: Sandy Berger 'Socks' Shocker; Lies, Blind Quotes, and Innuendo Rampant in Berger Coverage," *Media Matters*, July 23, 2004.

p. 54   **Alex Jones later told the reporter:** See Zaitchik, "Meet Alex Jones."

p. 55   **Similar speakers:** See Neiwert, *In God's Country*, pp. 30–32.

p. 57   **Bo Gritz was one of the most prominent:** See Neiwert, *In God's Country*, pp. 137–55.

p. 57   **He eventually confessed:** See Lou Michel and Dan Herbeck, *American Terrorist: Timothy McVeigh and the Oklahoma City Bombing* (New York: HarperCollins, 2001), pp. 223–7.

p. 60   **In a widely covered speech:** See William J. Clinton, "Remarks to the American Association of Community Colleges in Minneapolis, Minnesota, April 24, 1995," American Presidency Project, http://www.presidency. ucsb.edu/ws/?pid=51270.

p. 60   **Years later:** See Ann Coulter, *Slander: Liberal Lies about the American Right* (New York: Three Rivers Press, 2002), pp. 92–93.

p. 61 **In Roundup, Montana:** Neiwert, *In God's Country*, pp. 101–14.

p. 61 **It lasted eighty-one days:** Neiwert, *In God's Country*, pp. 240–60. For an assessment of law-enforcement techniques in handling the Patriots contemporary with the events in western Montana, see Erik Churchman, "Showdown versus Slowdown: Montana Law Enforcement Struggles to Decide How to Take On the Armed Right Wing," *Missoula Independent*, March 23, 1995.

p. 62 **Shortly after the Freemen standoff ended:** See "Olympic Officials Express Sorrow at Bombing," CNN, July 27, 1996; Marc Brenner, "The Ballad of Richard Jewell," *Vanity Fair*, February 1997.

p. 62 **Then, on January 16, 1997:** See "The Hunt for Eric Rudolph," CNN, June 15, 2002; Bill Torpy and Don Plummer, "Finally Caught: 5 Year Hunt for Eric Rudolph Ends," *Atlanta Journal-Constitution*, June 1, 2003.

p. 64 **He explained in a statement:** "Full Text of Eric Rudolph's Confession," National Public Radio, April 14, 2005.

p. 64 **Militia activity had dropped:** "The World of the Patriots," *Intelligence Report*, June 15, 1999.

p. 64 **But this didn't seem to discourage:** See David Neiwert, "'What Kind of Life Do I Have without My Bride?,'" *Salon*, Sept. 28, 1998.

p. 66 **Gritz's stumble had little effect:** See "Y2K Paranoia: Extremists Confront the Millennium," Anti-Defamation League, 1999.

p. 67 **A number of right-wing websites:** See, for example, Joseph Farah, "Y2K and Martial Law," *World Net Daily*, Dec. 8, 1998.

p. 67 **No one could quite match:** See Matt Novak, "Remember That Time Alex Jones Tried to Start a Y2K Riot?," *Paleofuture*, July 16, 2015, paleofuture.gizmodo.com/remember-that-time-alex-jones-tried-to-start-a-y2k-riot-1693454677.

Chapter 4: 9/11 and the Dark Invaders

p. 69 **The smoke and the dust:** See Alexander Zaitchik, "Meet Alex Jones: The Most Paranoid Man in America Is Trying to Overthrow the 'Global Stasi Borg State,' One Conspiracy Theory at a Time," *Rolling Stone*, March 2, 2011; also, Tim Murphy, "How Donald Trump Became Conspiracy Theorist in Chief," *Mother Jones*, November/December 2016.

p. 70 **This element:** See Meyssan, *9/11: The Big Lie* (London: Carnot Publishing, 2002); David Ray Griffin, *The New Pearl Harbor: Disturbing Questions About the Bush Administration and 9/11* (Northampton, MA: Interlink Publishing, 2004); and David Ray Griffin, *The 9/11 Commission Report: Omissions and Distortions* (Northampton, MA: Olive Branch Press, 2004).

p. 71 **In addition to his radio show:** See "Alex Jones," Southern Poverty Law Center, Extremist Profile, splcenter.org.

p. 71 **Limbaugh in particular:** "Rush Limbaugh Says 9/11 Truthers Need Rehab," YouTube video, March 16, 2007.

p. 72 **At Fox News:** Stephen C. Webster, "Geraldo 'Much More Open Minded' about 9/11 Thanks to NYC Television Ads," *Raw Story*, Nov. 14, 2010; "Fox Host Napolitano Is a 9-11 Truther: 'It Couldn't Possibly Have Been Done the Way the Government Told Us,'" *Media Matters*, Nov. 24, 2010.

p. 72 **The radio pundit Michael Reagan:** See Michael Reagan, *The Michael Reagan Show*, June 10, 2008. Transcript and audio file available at www.fair.org/index.php?page=3552.

p. 73 **Even back then, Rush Limbaugh:** This quotation formerly appeared on Limbaugh's website but has since been removed. A similar version was reported in the *Denver Post*, December 29, 1995.

p. 73 **In one of his nightly Fox broadcasts:** See Sam Gill, "O'Reilly on NY Times 'Kristof: "How Nuts Is this Guy?,"'" *MediaMatters*, December 20, 2005.

p. 74 **At one point, O'Reilly:** See "Ward Churchill Blames O'Reilly for Being Fired from University of Colorado," Fox News, March 13, 2009.

p. 74 **For example, the popular:** See "Hannity on Abu Ghraib photos: 'Was that a DNC plot too?,'" *Media Matters*, Sept. 15, 2004.

p. 74 **The eliminationist rhetoric:** See, for example, Sean Hannity, *Deliver Us from Evil: Defeating Terrorism, Despotism, and Liberalism* (New York: HarperCollins, 2004); Dinesh D'Souza, *The Enemy at Home: The Cultural Left and Its Responsibility for 9/11* (New York: Doubleday, 2007); Michael Savage, *The Enemy Within: Saving America from the Liberal Assault on Our Churches, Schools, and Military* (Nashville, TN: Nelson Current, 2003); Ann Coulter, *Treason: Liberal Treachery from the Cold War to the War on Terrorism* (New York: Crown Forum, 2003).

p. 74 **Between 1990 and 2000:** See "U.S. Immigration Trends," Migration Policy Center Data Hub, migrationpolicy.org/programs/data-hub/us-immigration-trends.

p. 75 **NAFTA, approved under:** See Armando Navarro, *The Immigration Crisis: Nativism, Armed Vigilantism, and the Rise of a Countervailing Movement* (Walnut Creek, CA: Rowman Altamira, 2009), pp. 125–30, 167; Terry Greene Sterling, *Illegal: Life and Death in Arizona's Immigration War Zone* (Guilford: Lyons Press, 2010), pp. x–xiii; United States Government Accountability Office, "GAO-06-770 Illegal Immigration: Border-Crossing Deaths Have Doubled Since 1995," August 2006, gao.gov/new.items/d06770.pdf; Karl Eschbach, Jacqueline Hagan, and Nestor Rodriguez, "Causes and Trends in Migrant Deaths along the U.S.-Mexico Border, 1985–1998," Center for Immigration Research, University of Houston, 2001.

p. 77 **These changes at the border were creating:** See Linda Lobao and Curtis W. Stofferahn, "The Community Effects of Industrialized Farming: Social Science Research and Challenges to Corporate Farming Laws,"

Agriculture and Human Values 25, no. 2 (June 2008): 219–40; Daniel T. Lichter, "Immigration and the New Racial Diversity in Rural America," *Rural Sociology* 77, no. 1 (March 2012): 3–35.

p. 77 **By 2000, anti-immigration organizations:** See "Anti-Immigration Groups," *Intelligence Report*, March 21, 2001.

p. 78 **David Duke, a former Ku Klux Klansman:** See "David Duke: In His Own Words," Anti-Defamation League Report, May 2000.

p. 78 **These myths nonetheless came:** "Ten Myths About Immigration," *Teaching Tolerance* (Southern Poverty Law Center), Spring 2011; "Myths and Facts about Immigrants and Immigration," Anti-Defamation League; Alex Nowsrateh, "Immigration Myths—Crime and the Number of Illegal Immigrants," Cato Institute, March 20, 2017.

p. 80 **On one of his:** "O'Reilly Claimed NY Times, Other 'Lefty Zealots' Believe 'the White Christians Who Hold Power Must Be Swept Out by a New Multicultural Tide,'" *Media Matters*, May 17, 2006.

p. 80 **"We believe very strongly":** Tyler Bridges, *The Rise of David Duke* (Oxford: University Press of Mississippi, 1994), p. 67.

p. 80 **Duke and a couple of carfuls:** Leonard Zeskind, *Blood and Politics: The History of the White Nationalist Movement from the Margins to the Mainstream* (New York: Farrar Straus Giroux, 2009), pp. 34–5.

p. 80 **The concept, however:** David Neiwert, *And Hell Followed with Her: Crossing the Dark Side of the American Border* (New York: Nation Books, 2013), pp. 24–6.

p. 81 **Chris Simcox was a:** See Susy Buchanan and David Holthouse, "Minuteman Civil Defense Corps Leader Chris Simcox Has Troubled Past," *Intelligence Report*, no. 120, (Winter 2005), splcenter.org, and Max Blumenthal, "Vigilante Injustice," *Salon*, May 22, 2003. See also Dennis Wagner, "Minuteman Leader Found New Calling after 9/11 Attacks," *Arizona Republic*, June 1, 2006.

p. 82 **One of the people listening in:** See Jim Gilchrist and Jerome R. Corsi, *Minutemen: The Battle to Secure America's Borders* (Los Angeles: World Ahead Publishing, 2006), pp. 5–6.

p. 82 **The media reportage:** See "Bush Decries Border Project," *Washington Times*, March 24, 2005.

p. 83 **The whole thing came together:** "Minutemen, Other Anti-Immigrant Militia Groups Stake Out Arizona Border," *Intelligence Report*, no. 118 (Summer 2005).

p. 83 **The most exciting thing:** Holthouse, who was on the scene, described this incident in the author's interview with him, but it is also described by several Minuteman sympathizers in their online accounts. See, for instance, Spiff, "Report of Some Activities of Day 10 of the Minuteman Project," *Free Republic*, April 11, 2005, freerepublic.com.

p. 83 **By the second week of April:** See Marc Cooper, "The 15-Second Men," *Los Angeles Times*, May 1, 2005.

p. 83 **Acually, the two men:** See Hernan Rozemberg, "Minutemen Bordering on Chaos," *San Antonio Express-News*, May 6, 2005.

p. 84 **One of the people:** See David Neiwert, *And Hell Followed With Her: Crossing the Dark Side of the American Border* (New York: Nation Books, 2013), pp. 123–9; 241–50; Scott North, "No Boundaries: Shawna Forde and the Minutemen Movement," *The Herald*, October 25, 2009.

p. 86 **The Minuteman name:** Gaiutra Bahadur, "Nativist Militias Get a Tea-Party Makeover," *Nation*, Oct. 28, 2010.

p. 86 **The final nail:** David Neiwert, "Chris Simcox's Fall From Minuteman Heights Ends in 19 1/2-Year Sentence for Molesting Girls," *Hatewatch*, Southern Poverty Law Center, July 13, 2016.

p. 86 **A reporter for Mother Jones:** Shane Bauer, "I Went Undercover with a Border Militia. Here's What I Saw," *Mother Jones*, November/December 2016.

Chapter 5: A Black President and a Birth Certificate

p. 87 **Jim David Adkisson:** See J. J. Stambaugh, "Takedown of Alleged Shooter Recounted," *Knoxville News Sentinel*, July 29, 2008; Hayes Hickman and Don Jacobs, "Suspect's Note Cites 'Liberal Movement' for Church Attack," *Knoxville News-Sentinel*, July 29, 2008; Neiwert, *The Eliminationists*, pp. 1–5.

p. 89 **Right from the start:** FoxNews Chicago, "KKK Warns of Death Threat against Obama," May 21, 2007.

p. 90 **In fact, they began claiming:** Heidi Beirich and Mark Potok, "Silver Lining: Not All White Supremacists Oppose Black President," *Intelligence Report*, Southern Poverty Law Center, Fall 2008.

p. 90 **Rush Limbaugh ran ditties:** See "Barack the Magic Negro Explained," *Rush Limbaugh Show*, March 23, 2007.

p. 90 **In the *Washington Times*:** Steve Sailer, "The Rise of Obama," *Washington Times*, Dec. 25, 2007.

p. 91 **At mainstream news sites:** See Brian Montopoli, "CBSNews.com Turns Off Comments on Obama Stories," CBS News, May 4, 2007.

p. 91 **Upon hitting the hustings:** Jimmy Orr, "Palin: Obama 'Palling Around with Terrorists,'" *Christian Science Monitor*, Oct. 5, 2008; Mark Leibovich, "Palin Visits a 'Pro-America' Kind of Town," *The Caucus* (blog), Oct. 17, 2008.

p. 92 **And the crowds responded:** David Neiwert, "McCain/Palin Supporters Let Their Racist Roots Show," CrooksandLiars.com, Oct. 16, 2008.

p. 92 **Such sentiments weren't unique:** David Neiwert, "Racism, Hate Bubble Up Yet Again at Palin's Rally in Vegas," CrooksandLiars.com, Oct. 25, 2008.

p. 93 **In Texas:** Jade Ortego, "Noose Ignites Tempers on Campus," *The Lariat* (Baylor University), November 6, 2008.

p. 94 **On the North Caroline State University campus:** Robert Shibley, "N.C. State in Uproar over Racist Messages in 'Free Expression Tunnel,'" Foundation for Individual Rights in Education, November 24, 2008.

p. 94 **But such student antics:** Christine Hauser, "After a Hate Crime Spree, an Intense Effort to Make Arrests," *New York Times*, January 11, 2009.

p. 94 **All four men:** Frank Donnelly, "Teen in Election Night Rampage Sentenced on State Hate-Crime Charges," *Staten Island Advance*, December 23, 2009.

p. 94 **There were cross burnings:** "Hate Crime Incidents: From Election Day to Inauguration Day," *Trends in Hate* (blog), February 7, 2009.

p. 94 **On election night:** Nicole Gonzales and Tom Callan, "Police Investigating So. Ogden Flag Burning," KSL.com, November 6, 2008.

p. 94 **Two days before:** Julie Arrington, "Racial Graffiti Found at Fire: Homeowner in DC for Inauguration," *Gainesville Times*, January 19, 2009.

p. 95 **On Inauguration Day:** Denise Gibson, "Clippings of Obama Torched on Apt. Door," *Jersey Journal*, January 21, 2009.

p. 95 **The next day:** John Ellement, "Killing 'Nonwhite People' Was Motive in Brockton Shooting Spree, Police Say," *Boston Globe*, January 22, 2009.

p. 95 **The Southern Poverty Law Center:** See Larry Keller, "Racist Backlash Greets President Barack Obama," *Intelligence Report*, February 26, 2009; David Neiwert, "The Racist Backlash to Obama's Presidency," Crooks andLiars.com, Nov. 17, 2008.

p. 95 **The spike in racially motivated violence:** Associated Press, "Obama Has More Threats Than Any Other President-Elect," NewsOne.com, November 15, 2008.

p. 96 **In Georgia:** Jesse Washington, "Obama Election Spurs Race Crimes around Country," Associated Press, November 21, 2008.

p. 97 **The viral anonymous e-mail:** Christopher Hayes, "The New Right-Wing Smear Machine," *Nation*, October 25, 2007.

p. 97 **The Obama campaign responded:** See Agence France-Presse, "Obama Hits Back at Internet Slanders," June 13, 2008.

p. 97 **Some of them noticed:** Amy Hollyfield, "For True Disbelievers, the Facts Are Just Not Enough," *Tampa Bay Times*, June 28, 2008.

p. 97 **Naturally, a fresh:** David Weigel, "Change They Can Litigate: The Fringe Movement to Keep Barack Obama from Becoming President," *Slate*, Dec. 4, 2008; Jess Henig with Joe Miller, "Born in the U.S.A.: The Truth about Obama's Birth Certificate," FactCheck.org, Aug. 21, 2008.

p. 98 **Jerome Corsi:** "Corsi's Claim that Obama Posted 'False, Fake Birth Certificate' Flatly Rejected by Hawaii Health Department," Media Matters.org, August 15, 2008.

p. 98 **The Obama campaign:** Henig and Miller, "Born in the U.S.A."

p. 98 **Hawaii state officials:** "Obama's Birth Certificate Verified by State," KITV.com (Honolulu), October 31, 2008.

p. 98   **Of course, there are always:** "No Doubt about Obama's Birth," *Honolulu Star-Bulletin*, editorial, July 29, 2009.

p. 98   **Jones and his fellow "Truthers":** Zaitchik, "Meet Alex Jones."

p. 99   **In addition to the Zeitgeist films:** See Peter Joseph, *Zeitgeist: The Movie* (2007), *Zeitgeist: Addendum* (2008), and *Zeitgeist: Moving Forward* (2011). See also Jeremy Stahl, "You're Not Paranoid If It's True: What Happens When Believers in 9/11 Conspiracy Theories Change Their Minds," *Slate*, Sept. 8, 2011; Matt Taibbi, *The Great Derangement: A Terrifying True Story of War, Politics, and Religion* (New York: Random House, 2008), pp. 177–83; Will Storr, "The 9/11 Conspiracy Theorist Who Changed His Mind," *Daily Telegraph*, May 29, 2013.

p. 99   **Infowars began drawing:** Zaitchik, "Meet Alex Jones."

p. 100   **In August 2009:** Paul Joseph Watson, "Obama Calls for National Civilian Stasi," Prison Planet, July 17, 2008.

p. 100   **The convergence:** Weigel, "Change They Can Litigate"; Sara Olkon and James Janega, "Tax Activist's Ad Challenges Obama's Eligibility for Office," *Chicago Tribune*, Dec. 3, 2008.

p. 100   **Orly Taitz:** See Daniel Schulman and Rachel Morris, "Meet the Birthers: Who Are These People, Really?," *Mother Jones*, Aug. 10, 2009.

p. 101   **When the Army:** David Neiwert, "Hannity Gleefully Promotes Birther Soldier's Get-out-of-Service Scam as Legitimate," Crooksand Liars.com, July 16, 2009.

p. 101   **Rush Limbaugh too:** "Limbaugh: 'God Does Not Have a Birth Certificate. Neither Does Obama,'" MediaMatters.org, June 10, 2009.

p. 101   **Dobbs kicked off:** Eric Hananoki, "Dobbs Repeatedly Makes Obama Birth Certificate Claims His CNN Colleagues Call 'Total Bull,'" MediaMatters.org, July 17, 2009.

p. 101   **However, filling in for Dobbs:** Heather, "Lou Dobbs Tonight with a Double Dose of Birther Crazies—Orly Taitz and Alan Keyes," Crooksand Liars.com, July 18, 2009.

p. 101   **Despite the debunking:** Heather, "After (R) Mike Castle Shoots Down Birther, Lou Dobbs Raises Questions about Obama's Birth Certificate," CrooksandLiars.com, July 21, 2009.

p. 101   **Rather than back down:** "Dobbs Says Obama Could 'Make the Whole ... Controversy Disappear ... by Simply Releasing His Original Birth Certificate,'" MediaMatters.org, July 22, 2009.

p. 101   **On his radio show:** "Dobbs Persists," MediaMatters.org, July 24, 2009.

p. 101   **When the resulting:** Chris Ariens, "Jon Klein on Birthers: 'It Seems This Story Is Dead,'" *TVNewser*, July 24, 2009.

p. 101   **That night:** Heather Digby Parton, "Lou Dobbs: The 'Left Wing Media' Has Attacked Me—While He Continues His Birther Attack on Obama," CrooksandLiars.com, July 24, 2009.

p. 102   **As the controversy raged:** David Neiwert, "Now Lou Dobbs Wants to Pretend He Was Just 'Reporting' Birther Claims," CrooksandLiars. com, July 29, 2009.

p. 102 **Dobbs eventually:** Howard Kurtz, "Lou Dobbs Resigns from CNN Broadcast," *Washington Post*, Nov. 12, 2009.

p. 102 **Beck already had:** See Rob Dietz, "CNN's Beck to First-Ever Muslim Congressman: '[W]hat I Feel Like Saying Is, 'Sir, Prove to Me That You Are Not Working with Our Enemies'," MediaMatters.org, Nov. 15, 2006.

p. 102 **He also was open:** Glenn Beck, "What Is the Government Hiding in Imprisoned Border Patrol Case? Survivor of Home Invasion Discusses Connecticut Tragedy; TSA Warns of Terrorist Dry Runs," CNN, July 25, 2007, transcript, http://transcripts.cnn.com/TRANSCRIPTS/0707/25/gb.01.html.

p. 103 **Still, he gave the public:** See David Neiwert, "BillO and Beck's Excellent Adventure on Planet Bizarro," CrooksandLiars.com, November 16, 2008.

p. 103 **The show also featured:** David Neiwert, "The Eyes of Glenn Beck Are upon You," CrooksandLiars.com, February 4, 2009.

p. 103 **When Stephen Colbert parodied:** David Neiwert, "Stephen Colbert Does Glenn Beck One Better: Peer Deeeep into His Gut," Crooksand Liars.com, February 12, 2009.

p. 103 **A few weeks after this:** David Neiwert, "They Call Him Mr. Maudlin: Glenn Beck, You Are a Nut a Loon," CrooksandLiars.com, March 14, 2009.

p. 103 **Beck devoted most of his energy:** David Neiwert, "Beck: Obama Has Us on the Road Not Just to Socialism but Communism," CrooksandLiars.com, February 5, 2009.

p. 104 **He frequently fretted:** David Neiwert, "Malkin-Beck Freakout: Imminent Mexico Collapse Could Doom America!," CrooksandLiars. com, January 29, 2009.

p. 104 **At other times:** David Neiwert, "Glenn Beck's Latest Looming Apocalypse: Iran," CrooksandLiars.com, February 10, 2009.

p. 104 **Soon Beck's paranoia:** David Neiwert, "FEMA Concentration Camps? The Militia Good Times Are Rollin' Again," CrooksandLiars. com, March 17, 2009.

p. 104 **This, eventually:** David Neiwert, "Credit Where It's Due: Glenn Beck's Thorough Debunking of FEMA Camps Confirms C&L's Report-age," CrooksandLiars.com, April 7, 2009.

p. 104 **On March 24:** David Neiwert, "Birchersville: John Bolton Helps Glenn Beck Whip Up 'One World Government' Paranoia," Crooksand Liars.com, March 25, 2009.

p. 105 **Taking away guns:** David Neiwert, "Beck and NRA's LaPierre Warn of Insidious Obama Plot to Grab Our Guns," CrooksandLiars.com, March 19, 2009.

p. 105 **In April 2009:** See "Wayne LaPierre Rejects 'Extremist' Label; Defends Second Amendment," Fox News, April 17, 2009, transcript, www. foxnews.com/story/2009/04/17/wayne-lapierre-rejects-extremist-label-defends-second-amendment.html.

p. 105 **The paranoia whipped up:** Peter Baker, "Economy May Delay Work on Obama's Campaign Pledges," *New York Times*, January 10, 2009.

p. 106 **The initial spike:** Judson Berger, "Obama Driving Surge in Gun Sales, Firearms Groups Say," Fox News, January 16, 2009.

p. 106 **The only time:** David Theroux, "Halbrook to Testify in Hearings on Eric Holder for Attorney General," *The Beacon* (blog, The Independent Institute), January 14, 2009.

p. 106 **What upset the gun crowd:** Eric Holder, "Keeping Guns Away from Terrorists," *Washington Post*, October 25, 2001.

p. 106 **"Barack Obama would be":** Chris J. Cox, "Obama and Guns: Words Matter and the Record Doesn't Match," *Washington Times*, October 30, 2008.

p. 106 **Warnings like that:** See Josh Wingrove, "Obama Win Spurs U.S. Gun Sales Boom," *Globe and Mail* (Toronto), Nov. 12, 2008.

p. 106 **The National Rifle Association's big annual:** Kevin Bohn, "NRA Thrives amid Fears of Heightened Gun-Control Efforts," CNN, May 15, 2009.

p. 107 **"Right now is":** Tim Gaynor, "US Gun Owners Wary of Obama at NRA Convention," Reuters, May 15, 2009.

p. 107 **Video footage from the NRA:** David Neiwert, "The NRA Thrives on Paranoia, and the Rest of Us Will Pay," CrooksandLiars.com, May 18, 2009.

Chapter 6: Mad Hatters and March Hares

p. 109 **Even before the inauguration:** See David Neiwert, "The Obama 'Resistance': Wingnuttery Never Sleeps," CrooksandLiars.com, December 26, 2008.

p. 109 **Leading the charge:** *Rush Limbaugh Show*, January 16, 2009.

p. 110 **Limbaugh's wish:** See David Neiwert, "Limbaugh's Excuse for Hoping Obama Fails—'Dems Did It Too'—Is Baloney," Crooksand Liars.com, March 3, 2009.

p. 110 **Paul announced his candidacy:** Stephen Dinan, "Paul Breaks Single-Day Online Fundraising Record," *Washington Times*, November 6, 2007.

p. 111 **Paul also drew:** See David Neiwert, "The Dark Side of the 'Paul Phenomenon,'" *Orcinus*, November 14, 2007, dneiwert.blogspot.com.

p. 111 **Paul's appeal:** See David Neiwert, "Ron Paul vs. the New World Order," *Orcinus*, June 8, 2007, dneiwert.blogspot.com; David Neiwert, "Ron Paul's Record in Congress," *Orcinus*, November 11, 2007, dneiwert. blogspot.com.

p. 112   **Paul's history:** See Jamie Kirchick, "Angry White Man," *New Republic*, January 7, 2008.

p. 112   **Political observers** Michael Levenson, "Ron Paul's Tea Party for Dollars," *Boston Globe*, December 16, 2007.

p. 113   **In the wake:** Mark Landler and Steven Lee Myers, "Buyout Plan for Wall Street Is a Hard Sell on Capitol Hill," *New York Times*, September 23, 2008.

p. 113   **Finally, on February 11:** See David M. Herszenhorn and Carl Hulse, "Deal Reached in Congress on $789 Billion Stimulus Plan," *New York Times*, February 11, 2009.

p. 113   **At around the same time:** See Jane Hamsher, "A Brief History of Tea Bagging," Firedoglake.com, April 15, 2009.

p. 114   **A protest on:** See "President Signs Massive Stimulus in Denver: Republicans Protest Stimulus at State Capitol," ABC7 News, February 17, 2009. At her blog Malkin described the Denver Tea Party as being organized by these groups. See Michelle Malkin, "'Yes, We Care!' Porkulus Protesters Holler Back," February 17, 2009, michellemalkin.com.

p. 114   **The spark that finally lit:** See Steven Perlberg, "Rick Santelli Started the Tea Party with a Rant Exactly 5 Years Ago Today—Here's How He Feels about It Now," Business Insider.com, Feb. 19. 2014.

p. 115   **Santelli's rant went viral:** Brian Beutler, "FreedomWorks' Long History of Teabagging," TalkingPointsMemo.com, April 14, 2009.

p. 115   **So what Fox offered:** See "'Fair and Balanced' Fox News Aggressively Promotes 'Tea Party' Protests," MediaMatters.org, April 8, 2009.

p. 116   **On March 13:** See David Neiwert, "They Call Him Mr. Maudlin: Glenn Beck, You Are A Nut A Loon," CrooksandLiars.com, March 14, 2009.

p. 116   **On March 18:** See "'Fair and Balanced' Fox News Aggressively Promotes 'Tea Party' Protests," MediaMatters.org, April 8, 2009.

p. 116   **On March 20:** See David Neiwert, "Yes, Glenn Beck, Militias Can Be Very Ordinary-Seeming. That's Their Purpose," CrooksandLiars. com, March 20, 2009.

p. 117   **Beck turned out to be:** "Beck Says You Can 'Celebrate with Fox News' at Any of Four 'FNC Tax Day Tea Parties,'" MediaMatters.org, April 6, 2009.

p. 117   **Beck's fellow Fox hosts:** "Hosting the Party: Fox Aired at Least 20 Segments, 73 Promos on 'Tea Party' Protests—in Just 8 days," Media Matters.org, April 15, 2009.

p. 117   **Fairly typical was:** See "'Fair and Balanced' Fox News Aggressively Promotes 'Tea Party' Protests," MediaMatters.org, April 8, 2009.

p. 118   **April 4, 2009:** Jon Schmitz and Moriah Balingit, "Affidavit Outlines Shootings That Left Three Pittsburgh Police Officers Dead," *Pittsburgh Post-Gazette*, April 6, 2009; Dennis B. Roddy, "Poplawski Was 'Braced for Fate' in Days Leading to Attack," *Pittsburgh Post-Gazette*, April 6, 2009.

p. 119   **Outside the home:** "Gunman Kills Three Pittsburgh Police Officers," Associated Press, April 4, 2009.

p. 119   **Poplawski, it soon emerged:** David Neiwert, "The Emerging Portrait of Richard Poplawski: A White-Supremacist Radical," CrooksandLiars.com, April 5, 2009.

p. 120   **Mark Pitcavage:** Mark Pitcavage, "Richard Poplawski: The Making of a Lone Wolf," Anti-Defamation League, April 8, 2009.

p. 120   **However, an astonishing thing:** David Neiwert, "Poplawski's Neo-Nazi Activism Included Posting Glenn Beck Video, but Media Talk about Dog Pee," CrooksandLiars.com, April 7, 2009.

p. 121   **Moved to action in part:** "Rightwing Extremism: Current Economic and Political Climate Fueling Resurgence in Radicalization and Recruitment," Department of Homeland Security, Office of Intelligence and Analysis Assessment, April 7, 2009.

p. 121   **This assessment had first:** See Daryl Johnson, *Right Wing Resurgence: How a Domestic Terrorist Threat Is Being Ignored* (Lanham, MD: Rowan & Littlefield, 2012), pp. 195–220.

p. 122   **But the report's unambiguous language:** Audrey Hudson and Eli Lake, "Federal Agency Warns of Radicals on Right," *Washington Times*, April 14, 2009.

p. 122   **The howls:** See Michelle Malkin, "Confirmed: The Obama DHS Hit Job on Conservatives Is Real," MichelleMalkin.com, April 14, 2009.

p. 123   **In a July 2008 report:** Federal Bureau of Investigation, "White Supremacist Recruitment of Military Personnel since 9/11," Intelligence Assessment, July 7, 2009.

p. 124   **Mainstream conservatives:** *The O'Reilly Factor*, Fox News, April 16, 2009. Transcript of video at David Neiwert, "Is the DHS Watching Returning Veterans? Only When They Join Far-Right Hate Groups," CrooksandLiars.com, April 17, 2009.

p. 124   **On his nightly:** *Lou Dobbs Tonight*, CNN, April 14, 2009.

p. 125   **Even the televangelist:** See David Neiwert, "Pat Robertson Urges His Callers to Crash Homeland Security Hotline," CrooksandLiars.com, April 17, 2009.

p. 125   **Initially Napolitano defended:** David Neiwert, "Napolitano Rebuts the Fearmongering over DHS Domestic-Terror Bulletin," CrooksandLiars.com, April 19, 2009.

p. 125   **However, the clamor:** Spencer S. Hsu, "Napolitano Apologizes to Veterans," *Washington Post*, April 16, 2009.

p. 125   **She later told:** Michael O'Brien, "Napolitano: DHS Memo Based on Past Experience," *The Hill*, April 16, 2009.

p. 125   **Fox hosts, though:** See David Neiwert, "That DHS Domestic-Terror Report Isn't about the Tea Parties—It's About the Poplawskis," CrooksandLiars.com, April 15, 2009.

p. 126   **Amid all this wild speculation:** Robin Abcarian and Nicholas

Riccardi, "Abortion Doctor George Tiller Is Killed; Suspect in Custody," *Los Angeles Times*, June 1, 2009.

p. 126 **The April 15 Tax Day:** See Janie Lorber and Liz Robbins, "Tax Day Is Met with Tea Parties," *New York Times*, April 15, 2009.

p. 126 **The analyst Nate Silver:** See Nate Silver, "Tea Party Nonpartisan Attendance Estimates: Now 300,000+," FiveThirtyEight.com, April 16, 2009.

p. 127 **Fox's coverage:** "Live from Alamo Tea Party, Beck Hosts Joe Horn, Who 'Shot 2 Illegals Burglarizing Home,' " MediaMatters.org, April 15, 2009.

p. 127 **Hannity also hooked up:** See David Neiwert, "Tea Tantrum Indeed: The Right-Wing Populists Have Officially Taken Over Movement Conservatism," CrooksandLiars.com, April 16, 2009.

p. 127 **The slogans:** See Kombiz, "How I Missed the 2 Million Man Teabagging Flash Mob Today," CrooksandLiars.com, September 12, 2009.

p. 128 **The Tea Party events:** See Kevin Poulsen, "Oklahoma Man Arrested for Twittering Tea Party Death Threats," *Wired*, April 24, 2009. For screen shots of Hayden's tweets see David Neiwert, "Fox News' 'Tea Party' Hysteria Really Did Whip Up the Far-Right Nutcases," Crooksand Liars.com, April 27, 2009.

p. 128 **Greta Van Susteren:** See *On The Record with Greta Van Susteren*, Fox News Channel, February 27, 2009, transcript at " 'Fair and Balanced' Fox News Aggressively Promotes 'Tea Party' Protests," MediaMatters.org, April 8, 2009. See also David Neiwert, "Will the 'Tea Party' Tantrums Become a Vehicle for Right-Wing Thuggery?," CrooksandLiars.com, July 29, 2009.

p. 129 **Within days:** David Neiwert, "Will the 'Tea Party' Tantrums Become a Vehicle for Right-Wing Thuggery?," CrooksandLiars.com, July 29, 2009.

p. 129 **It soon emerged:** Lee Fang, "Right-Wing Harassment Strategy against Dems Detailed in Memo: 'Yell,' 'Stand Up and Shout Out,' 'Rattle Him,'" ThinkProgress.org, July 31, 2009.

p. 130 **On August 1:** Richard Dunham, "Dogging Doggett: Conservative Protesters Disrupt Health Event," *Houston Chronicle*, August 3, 2009.

p. 130 **The congressman later:** W. Gardner Selby, "Doggett Says He's More Resolved Than Ever to Pass a Health-Care Plan," *Austin American-Statesman*, August 3, 2009.

p. 130 **On August 6:** Adam Smith, "Mayhem, Amid Protesters at Kathy Castor, Betty Reed Town Hall Meet," *The Buzz* (blog, *Tampa Bay Times*), August 6, 2009, tampabay.com.

p. 131 **It left an impression:** Beau Zimmer, "Healthcare Reform Sparks Meeting Mayhem," 10Connects.com (WTSP-TV), August 15, 2009.

p. 131 **In late August:** See David Neiwert, " 'Tea Party Express' Ads Showing Up on Fox Broadcasts," CrooksandLiars.com, August 27, 2009.

p. 131   **This tour was sponsored:** Diane Farsetta, "Our Country Deserves Better: The Russo Marsh Crowd Bashes Obama from Coast to Coast," CommonDreams.org, October 29, 2008.

p. 132   **In July 2009:** Kyle, "Obama Worse Than Hitler and Ahmadinejad," *Right Wing Watch*, July 2, 2009, rightwingwatch.org.

p. 132   **District of Columbia:** Joe Markman, "Crowd Estimates Vary Wildly for Capitol March," *Los Angeles Times*, September 15, 2009.

p. 132   **Afterward, Beck and his supporters:** See "Beck Claims 9–12 Protests 'Largest March on Washington Ever' Based on 'Overseas' Reporting," MediaMatters.org, September 14, 2009.

p. 132   **On *Fox and Friends*:** See "Beck, Limbaugh Run wild with Estimates on Size of 9/12 protests," MediaMatters.org, September 14, 2009.

p. 132   **Some of the signs:** See Kombiz, "How I Missed the 2 Million Man Teabagging Flash Mob Today," CrooksandLiars.com, September 12, 2009.

p. 132   **Journalist Max Blumenthal:** See Max Blumenthal, "'Get the Government Out of My Social Security!' Inside the 9.12 Teabagger Rally," *Huffington Post*, September 14, 2009.

p. 133   **During one of Giffords's:** See "Political Notebook: Giffords' following of Conservative Activists Grows," *Arizona Daily Star*, August 8, 2009.

p. 133   **Giffords's health-care vote:** See David Neiwert, "Eliminationist Rhetoric and the Shooting of Gabrielle Giffords: There Were Plenty of Precursors," CrooksandLiars.com, January 8, 2011.

p. 133   **In hopes of healing:** See "Arizona Congresswoman Giffords Shot; Doctors 'Optimistic' about Recovery Chances," *Arizona Republic*, January 8, 2011; "Routine Event Turned Deadly Fast," *Star-Tribune*, January 10, 2011.

p. 134   **The dead included:** See "Arizona Congresswoman Gabrielle Giffords: The Victims," *Arizona Republic*, January 8, 2011; Katie Couric, "Strangers Linked by Tragedy in Tucson Rampage," CBS News, January 10, 2011.

p. 135   **It shortly emerged:** See Eric Lipton, Charlie Savage, and Scott Shane, "Arizona Suspect's Recent Acts Offer Hints of Alienation," *New York Times*, January 10, 2011.

p. 135   **"The killer, Jared Loughner":** See Bill O'Reilly, "Murder in Arizona and the Gross Exploitation of It," Fox News, January 10, 2011.

p. 135   **It also soon emerged:** See Dan Barry, "Looking behind the Mug-Shot Grin," *New York Times*, January 21, 2011; Torie Bosch, "Jared Lee Loughner's Worldview a Conspiracy Theory Laundry List," AOL News, January 12, 2011.

p. 135   **"The whole thing stinks":** Zaitchik, "Meet Alex Jones."

Chapter 7: The Return of the Militias

p. 137   **This did not seem to be your ordinary:** David Neiwert, "'We Are at War': How Militias, Racists and Anti-Semites Found a Home in the Tea Party," AlterNet.org, November 21, 2010.

p. 138   **Lawrence D. Pratt:** See "Larry Pratt" (extremist profile), Southern Poverty Law Center (splcenter.org).

p. 139   **Most observers of the movement had counted:** See "Active Anti-government Groups in the United States," Southern Poverty Law Center.

p. 140   **According to Mark Potok:** Mark Potok, "Rage on the Right," *Intelligence Report*, March 2, 2010.

p. 140   **Mark Pitcavage:** Neiwert, "'We Are at War'."

p. 140   **David Barstow:** See David Barstow, "Tea Party Lights Fuse for Rebellion on Right," *New York Times*, February 15, 2010.

p. 141   **Travis McAdam:** See David Neiwert, "'We Are at War': How Militias, Racists and Anti-Semites Found a Home in the Tea Party," *AlterNet*, November 21, 2010.

p. 142   **A common organizational theme:** See David Neiwert, "'Molon Labe': Folks on the Fringe Right Are Fearfully Fingering Their Triggers," CrooksandLiars.com, January 17, 2009.

p. 142   **One of these veterans:** Mark Potok, "Marine's Arrest Again Raises Issue of Extremists in the Military," *Intelligence Report*, February 12, 2009.

p. 143   **The bright yellow banner:** Rob Walker, "The Shifting Symbolism of the Gadsden Flag," *New Yorker*, October 2, 2016; Neiwert, *And Hell Followed with Her*, p. 160.

p. 144   **On July 4, 2009:** See David Weigel, "Tea Party Movement Loses Steam," *Washington Independent*, July 4, 2009.

p. 144   **Glenn Beck, on his June 19 show:** "Beck Hosts 'Disenfranchised Democrat' to Promote Tea Parties," MediaMatters.org, June 15, 2009.

p. 144   **Even before the July events:** Anti-Defamation League, "White Supremacists May Attempt to Co-Opt July 4 'Tea Parties' to Promote a Hateful Agenda," press release, July 2, 2009.

p. 145   **These warnings:** David Neiwert, "As 'Tea Parties' Lose Steam, Fringe Conspiracists Step Up to the Fore," CrooksandLiars.com, July 6, 2009.

p. 146   **The credo that Dyer:** David Neiwert, "Delusions of Grandeur: Militia Video Warns President Obama to Leave the Country by Oct. 15," *Crooks andLiars.com*, October 10, 2009; Neiwert, "Will Ex-military 'Patriots' Form a More Dangerous Kind of Militia?," CrooksandLiars.com, March 5, 2009.

p. 148   **On January 21, 2010:** David Neiwert, "'Oath Keepers' Leader Arrested for Child Rape; Cops Find Stolen Grenade Launcher in His House," CrooksandLiars.com, January 21, 2010.

p. 148　**Immediately, the Oath Keepers:** David Neiwert, "After Dyer's Rape Arrest, 'Oath Keepers' Disavow Any Association with Onetime Key Figure," CrooksandLiars.com, January 21, 2010.

p. 148　**Dyer skipped out:** Ryan Lenz, "Mistrial in Child Rape of Antigovernment Activist," *Hatewatch*, Southern Poverty Law Center, January 24, 2012; Ryan Lenz, "Oklahoma Oath Keeper Convicted of 6-Year-Old Daughter's Rape," *Hatewatch*, Southern Poverty Law Center, April 20, 2012.

p. 149　**Like John Trochmann:** See "Elmer Stewart Rhodes," Southern Poverty Law Center, Extremist Profile.

p. 150　**"You need to be alert":** Justine Sharrock, "Oath Keepers and the Age of Treason," *Mother Jones*, March/April 2010.

p. 151　**Rhodes has an affable:** David Neiwert, "After Dyer's Rape Arrest, 'Oath Keepers' Disavow Any Association with Onetime Key Figure," CrooksandLiars.com, January 21, 2010; David Neiwert, "'Oath Keepers' Chief Points to Katrina Response to Justify Paranoia: 'They Disarmed Americans over Some Bad Weather,'" CrooksandLiars.com, February 20, 2010.

p. 152　**In March 2010, Justine Sharrock:** See Justine Sharrock, "Oath Keepers and the Age of Treason," *Mother Jones*, March/April 2010.

p. 153　**One of the participants:** See "Gun Rights Advocates, 'Patriots' Mix in April Protests," *Intelligence Report*, May 30, 2010.

p. 153　**He called the concept:** Spencer Sunshine, "Profiles on the Right: Three Percenters," Political Research Associates, January 5, 2016; see also "Michael Brian Vanderboegh," Southern Poverty Law Center, Extremist Profile.

p. 153　**What made it stand out:** Tim Murphy, "Gun Rally Too Extreme for Oath Keepers," *Mother Jones*, April 14, 2010; see also Nick Wing, Arthur Delaney, and Sam Stein, "Gun Rally: Second Amendment Activists Swarm DC, VA Rallies," *Huffington Post*, June 19, 2010.

p. 154　**Vanderboegh had been:** See "Michael Brian Vanderboegh," Southern Poverty Law Center, Extremist Profile.

p. 155　**However, Kerodin and Vanderboegh:** See Bill Morlin, "Convicted Extortionist a Key Figure in Idaho Citadel 'Patriot' Project," *Hatewatch*, Southern Poverty Law Center, January 18, 2013.

p. 156　**Richard Mack:** See Mark Potok and Ryan Lenz, "Line in the Sand," *Intelligence Report* , June 13, 2016.

p. 157　**Mack is a devotee:** See "Meet the Patriots," *Intelligence Report*, May 20, 2010; Ryan Lenz, "Former Arizona Sheriff Richard Mack Seeks 'Army' of Sheriffs to Resist Federal Authority," *Intelligence Report*, December 22, 2014.

p. 157　**In his magisterial:** Daniel Levitas, *The Terrorist Next Door: The Militia Movement and the Radical Right* (New York: St. Martin's Griffin, 2004), p. x.

p. 160 **The key to Mack's recruitment:** Rural Organizing Project, "Up in Arms: A Guide to Oregon's Patriot Movement—Key Organizing Themes in the Movement," Political Research Associates, September 2016; Heather Digby Parton, "2nd Amendment Fanatics Are Just This Desperate: How Wing-nuts with Guns Are Trying to Hijack the Constitution," *Salon*, November 5, 2015.

p. 160 **The recuitment scheme:** See Mark Potok and Ryan Lenz, "Line in the Sand," *Intelligence Report*, June 13, 2016.

Chapter 8: The Bundy Pandora's Box

p. 161 **Cliven Bundy was:** Adam Nagourney, "A Defiant Rancher Savors the Audience That Rallied to His Side," *New York Times*, April 23, 2014.

p. 161 **He was also an ardent:** Jack Jenkins, "The Bundy Family's Odd Mormon Connection, Explained," *Think Progress*, January 24, 2016.

p. 161 **The BLM canceled:** Lenz, "War in the West."

p. 162 **In April 2012:** "Trespassing Cattle Set Stage for Federal Land Showdown," Associated Press, April 16, 2012.

p. 162 **The letter unnerved:** Jamie Fuller, "The Long Fight between the Bundys and the Federal Government, from 1989 to Today," *Washington Post*, January 4, 2016.

p. 162 **In late March 2014:** See Ryan Lenz, "War in the West," *Intelligence Report*, Southern Poverty Law Center, August 19, 2014, splcenter.org.

p. 162 **On April 5:** Zach Whitney, "Delta Man Arrested, Released after Protesting BLM's Cattle Roundup," Fox13 Salt Lake City, April 7, 2014.

p. 163 **Alex Jones's *Infowars*:** Lenz, "War in the West." *Intelligence Report*, August 19, 2014; Alex Jones, "Cliven Bundy: Domestic Patriot," Infowars. com, April 19, 2014.

p. 163 **Even the *Drudge Report*:** Timothy Johnson, "Drudge Report Recklessly Hypes Confrontation between Rancher and Federal Government," MediaMatters.org, April 11, 2014; Max Strasser, "For Militiamen, the Fight for Cliven Bundy's Ranch Is Far From Over," *Newsweek*, April 24, 2014.

p. 163 **BLM officials, meanwhile:** See John Glionna, "'Range War' with BLM: Hundreds Rally for Nevada Cattle Rancher," *Los Angeles Times*, April 7, 2014.

p. 163 **On April 9:** Lenz, "War in the West"; Paul Joseph Watson, "'Red Dawn: Supporters Rally to Defend Family Facing Showdown with Feds," *Infowars*, April 8, 2014.

p. 166 **A week of endeavoring:** See Liz Fields, "Nevada Cattle Rancher Wins 'Range War' with Feds," ABC News, April 12, 2014.

p. 166 **Richard Mack later told:** See David Neiwert, "Richard Mack Explains Nevada 'Range War' Strategy: 'Put All the Women Up Front,'" *Hatewatch*, Southern Poverty Law Center, April 15, 2014.

p. 167 **The Patriot movement:** See David Neiwert, "Federal Retreat in Nevada 'Range War' Gives Green Light to Extremists," *Hatewatch*, Southern Poverty Law Center, April 17, 2014.

p. 167 **The blog *Bearing Arms*:** See Bob Owens, "Cowboys and Communists," *Bearing Arms*, April 13, 2014; see also Mike McDaniel, "Of Cows, Tortoises and the Rule of Law," *Stately McDaniel Manor*, April 12, 2014, statelymcdanielmanor.wordpress.com.

p. 167 **Leading the parade:** See Mike Vanderboegh, "Courage Is Contagious, Defiance Is Contagious, Victory Is Contagious. The Huge Win in the Desert at the Bundy Ranch," *Sipsey Street Irregulars*, April 12, 2014, sipseystreetirregulars.blogspot.com.

p. 168 **That was the sentiment:** See "Historic! Feds Forced to Surrender to American Citizens," *Infowars*, April 14, 2014.

p. 168 **In the meantime:** See World Net Daily, "Sheriff: Feds Strategize for 'Raid' on Ranch," *Infowars*, April 15, 2014.

p. 168 **At the slightly more mainstream:** See John Ransom, "War on Federal Bureaucrats Opens at the Bundy Ranch," *Town Hall*, April 16, 2014, townhall.com.

p. 168 **Meanwhile, Oath Keepers:** See David Neiwert, "Federal Retreat in Nevada 'Range War' Gives Green Light to Extremists," *Hatewatch*, Southern Policy Law Center, April 17, 2014.

p. 169 **In Nevada:** See Steve Sebelius, "Let's Be Honest About What Bundy Is, and Is Not," *Las Vegas Review-Journal*, April 15, 2014.

p. 169 **Cliven Bundy continued:** See Nathan Baca, "Political Cause Growing in Bundy's Dispute with BLM," KLAS-TV (Las Vegas), April 12, 2014.

p. 169 **Fox News's Sean Hannity:** See "Cliven Bundy Fires Back After Ranch Standoff Comes to an End," Fox News, April 14, 2014.

p. 169 **Back at the Bundy Ranch:** See David Neiwert, "Back at the Bundy Ranch: More Militiamen Gather, Things Get Crazier," *Hatewatch*, Southern Poverty Law Center, April 23, 2014.

p. 170 **The media reports:** See David Neiwert, "Right-Wing Media Eagerly Promote Cliven Bundy and His Anti-Federal Faceoff," *Hatewatch*, Southern Poverty Law Center, April 11, 2014.

p. 170 **The speakers came:** See David Neiwert, "Indiana Sheriff With Antigovernment Views Creates Stir by Traveling to Bundy Ranch," *Hatewatch*, Southern Poverty Law Center, May 7, 2014.

p. 170 **Then Cliven Bundy gave them one:** See David Neiwert, "Bundy Doubles Down on 'Negro' Talk, and Supporters Flee in Droves," *Hatewatch*, Southern Poverty Law Center, April 25, 2014.

p. 173 **On April 24:** See Andy Borowitz, "Republicans Blast Nevada Rancher for Failing to Use Commonly Accepted Racial Code Words," *New Yorker*, April 24, 2014.

p. 173 **Ryan Payne:** See Ted McDermott, "Freedom Fighter: When Rancher Cliven Bundy Engaged in a Standoff with the BLM, a Montana

Man Initiated a Call to Action to Militia across the Country. He Considers It Just the First Battle in a War to Reclaim America," *Missoula Independent*, June 12, 2014.

p. 173 **A couple of weeks afterward:** See George Knapp, "I-Team: Police Faced Possible 'Bloodbath' at Bundy Protest," KLAS-TV (Las Vegas), April 30, 2014.

p. 174 **By late April:** See David Neiwert, "Back at the Bundy Ranch: More Militiamen Gather, Things Get Crazier," Southern Poverty Law Center, *Hatewatch*, April 23, 2014; also, see David Neiwert, "Militiamen and Oath Keepers Drew Weapons, Threatened to Kill Each Other," *Hatewatch*, Southern Poverty Law Center, May 2, 2014.

p. 177 **One of the people:** See "Trial and Terror," *Reveal Radio*, June 24, 2017 (30:00–44:30), revealnews.org; see also David Neiwert, "Las Vegas Shooting Suspect Jerad Miller Threatened Violence in Interview at the Bundy Ranch," *Hatewatch*, Southern Poverty Law Center, June 12, 2004.

p. 175 **Chan recalled later:** Author's interview with Melissa Chan, October 21, 2016.

p. 178 **Howard Scheff:** See Travis Gettys, "Jerad Miller Cried 'Hysterically' When He Was Asked to Leave Bundy Ranch, Candidate Says," *Raw Story*, June 10, 2014.

p. 179 **Melissa Chan later reflected:** Author's interview with Melissa Chan, October 21, 2016.

p. 180 **The next morning:** See "Trial and Terror," *Reveal Radio*, June 24, 2017 (30:00-44:30), revealnews.org.

Chapter 9: Bad Days on the Malheur

p. 183 **Donald Trump had appeared:** "Donald Trump: Bundy Should Make a Deal, Putin 'Toying' with Obama," *Fox News Insider*, April 16, 2014.

p. 183 **"This was a watershed moment":** Shane Dixon Kavanaugh, "American Militias Emboldened by Victory at Bundy Ranch," Vocativ.com, April 14, 2014.

p. 183 **Larry Pratt:** See Matt Gertz, "Prominent Gun Activist Calls Bundy Standoff A 'Turning Point In Modern America,'" MediaMatters.org, April 27, 2014.

p. 184 **He announced he was leaving:** Philip Bump, "Cliven Bundy Has Officially Left the Republican Party Herd," *Washington Post*, May 27, 2014.

p. 184 **Later that fall:** David Neiwert, "Cliven Bundy in Bizarre Video for Black Candidate: 'It's Almost Like Black Folks Think White Folks Owe Them Something,'" *Hatewatch*, Southern Poverty Law Center, October 20, 2014.

p. 184 **Speaking at a gathering:** See Ryan Lenz, "Six Months after Standoff in Nevada, the Federal Government Has Not Yet Responded," *Hatewatch*, Southern Poverty Law Center, October 17, 2014.

p. 184 **Just one month after:** John M. Glionna, "Protesters in Utah Drive ATVs onto Federal Land—but Find No Showdown," *Los Angeles Times*, May 10, 2014. See also Dennis Romboy, "Judge Orders Recapture Canyon ATV Protest Riders to Pay $96K in Damages," *Deseret News*, October 28, 2015; Michael McFall, "Phil Lyman Begins 10-Day Jail Sentence for ATV Protest Conviction," *Salt Lake Tribune*, April 19, 2016; Ben Winslow, "Lyman Wants Conviction Overturned, Insists Recapture Canyon Was Not Closed to OHVs," KSTU-TV, September 15, 2016.

p. 185 **While driving along Interstate 15:** David Neiwert, "In Wake of Bundy Standoff, Utah BLM Wrangler Threatened by Armed Men in Pickup," *Hatewatch*, Southern Poverty Law Center, May 8, 2014.

p. 185 **A few weeks later:** Mark Binelli, "Lone Star Crazy: How Right-Wing Extremists Took Over Texas," *Rolling Stone*, July 1, 2014.

p. 185 **At about the same time:** Lauren Villagran, "NM Ranchers Confront Feds over Water," *Albuquerque Journal*, May 8, 2014.

p. 185 **In mid-June:** David Neiwert, "Brother of 'Sovereign Citizen' Who Reportedly Shot a BLM Ranger Traces a Loved One's Transformation," *Hatewatch*, Southern Poverty Law Center, June 19, 2014.

p. 185 **That July:** Bill Morlin, "DHS Says Nevada Stand-Off Inspired Antigovernment Extremists," *Hatewatch*, Southern Poverty Law Center, August 19, 2014.

p. 186 **In early April 2015:** David Neiwert, "Oath Keepers Descend upon Oregon with Dreams of Armed Confrontation over Mining Dispute," *Hatewatch*, Southern Poverty Law Center, April 22, 2015.

p. 186 **A protest rally:** David Neiwert, "'Patriots' Rally for Oregon Mine Owners Turns Out a Tepid Affair," *Hatewatch*, Southern Poverty Law Center, April 23, 2015.

p. 187 **People in Grants Pass:** David Neiwert, "Oath Keepers Come Out to Heckle Oregon Resident Who Want Armed Gathering to Disband," *Hatewatch*, Southern Poverty Law Center, April 26, 2015.

p. 187 **Finally, on May 25:** David Neiwert, "'Patriots' Declare Victory for Oregon Mine after Judge Issues Stay for BLM Enforcement," *Hatewatch*, Southern Poverty Law Center, May 25, 2015.

p. 187 **The Patriots' next attempt:** David Neiwert, "'Patriots' Heed 'Call to Action' to 'Protect' Montana Mine from a Baffled U.S. Forest Service," *Hatewatch*, Southern Poverty Law Center, August 11, 2015.

p. 187 **On August 5:** David Neiwert, "Dispatch from Lincoln: 'Patriots' Lost in the Haze at Contested Montana Mine Site," *Hatewatch*, Southern Poverty Law Center, August 27, 2015.

p. 189 **After the fizzled standoff attempts:** David Neiwert, "Antigovernment 'Patriots' Show Up at Military Recruiting Centers Nationwide to 'Protect the Protectors,'" *Hatewatch*, Southern Poverty Law Center, August 3, 2015.

p. 189 **The object of the militiamen's ire:** David Neiwert, "Idaho Town Divided by Fears over Refugees, 'Sharia Law,'" *Hatewatch*, Southern Poverty Law Center, September 24, 2015.

p. 189 **The Three Percenters:** David Neiwert, "'III Percenters' Ride Wave of Islamophobia in Idaho to Lead Anti-Refugee Protests," *Hatewatch*, Southern Poverty Law Center, November 4, 2015.

p. 190 **Three weeks later:** David Neiwert, "Idahoans Rally to Support Refugees, While Extremists' Counter-Protest Gets Ugly," *Hatewatch*, Southern Poverty Law Center, November 27, 2015.

p. 191 **Two Burns-area ranchers:** Brian Denson, "Controversial Oregon Ranchers in Court Wednesday, Likely Headed Back to Prison in Arson Case," *Oregonian*, October 7, 2015.

p. 191 **The Hammond family:** See Kathie Durbin, "Ranchers Arrested at Wildlife Refuge," *High Country News*, October 3, 1994.

p. 192 **In 2001:** Brian Denson, "Controversial Oregon Ranchers in Court Wednesday"; Les Zaitz, "Militiamen, Ranchers in Showdown for Soul of Burns," *Oregonian*, December 30, 2015.

p. 192 **The case caught the attention:** See Carli Brousseau, "Oregon Occupation Planned for Months by Ammon Bundy and Montana Militia Leader," *Oregonian*, January 11, 2016.

p. 194 **An Arizona militiaman:** See "Jon Ritzheimer Bids a Tearful and Angry Goodbye at Scene of Oregon Militia Takeover," YouTube, January 7, 2016.

p. 194 **Ritzheimer had already:** David Neiwert, "Militiamen Plan to Bring Guns to Mosques Around Nation in 'Global' Protest of Islam," *Hatewatch*, Southern Poverty Law Center, October 9, 2015; Peter Holley, "The 'Unhinged' Oregon Protester That the FBI Has Been Tracking for Month," *Washington Post*, January 5, 2016.

p. 195 **Saturday was a frigid:** See Brousseau, "Oregon Occupation Planned for Months"; Bill Morlin, "Bundy Sons Lead Antigovernment Extremists, Militia in Takeover of Federal Wildlife Headquarters in Oregon," *Hatewatch*, Southern Poverty Law Center, January 4, 2016.

p. 196 **As they were departing:** This scene was captured on two videos. See Valley Forge Network, *Burns Oregon Video Documentary—3—Jan 2nd Post Rally, Evening at Refuge*, YouTube, posted February 20, 2016. The other, *Burns Oregon Rally for Hammonds*, published January 3, 2016, by the *Pete Santilli Show*, has been removed. It is described in Brousseau, "Oregon Occupation Planned for Months."

p. 197 **Walter Eaton was:** Conrad Wilson and Bryan M. Vance, "Threat against Harney County Sheriff Described in Testimony," Oregon Public Broadcasting, September 14, 2016.

p. 197 **Ammon Bundy told:** Les Zaitz, "Militia Takes Over Malheur

National Wildlife Refuge Headquarters," *Oregonian*, January 2, 2016.

p. 198   **One of the more colorful:** Kate Ng, "Oregon Militia Gunman Holes Himself Up under a Tarp on Live TV during Anti-Government Protest," *Independent*, January 6, 2016.

p. 195   **Sheriff Ward ordered:** Kelly House, "Sheriff to Oregon Militants: 'Go Home,'" *Oregonian*, January 4, 2016.

p. 198   **But the Bundy brothers:** Ryan Lenz, "After Three Weeks, the FBI Promises 'Deliberate and Measured' Response to Oregon Standoff," *Hatewatch*, Southern Poverty Law Center, January 22, 2016.

p. 198   **The plea went viral:** Daniel Wallis, "Oregon Occupiers Ask Public for Supplies: Get Glitter, Sex Toys," Reuters, January 14, 2016.

p. 199   **Indeed, the occupation:** David Neiwert, "Infighting over Oregon Militia Takeover Reveals Deep Divisions Among Patriots," *Hatewatch*, Southern Poverty Law Center, January 7, 2016.

p. 199   **Brandon Curtiss and his:** Fedor Zarkhin, "'Buffer Zone' in Oregon Standoff: Ex-Cop Brandon Curtiss Says He's a Peacemaker," *Oregonian*, January 15, 2016.

p. 201   **Over the next couple of weeks:** Joe Heim, "'These Buildings Will Never, Ever Return to the Federal Government,'" *Washington Post*, January 16, 2016.

p. 202   **Several of them:** David Neiwert, "Oregon Militants Try to Recruit a 'Constitutional' Sheriff From Neighboring County, but Fail," *Hatewatch*, Southern Poverty Law Center, January 15, 2016.

p. 202   **In the meantime:** Jacqueline Keeler, "'It's So Disgusting' Malheur Militia Dug Latrine Trenches among Sacred Artifacts," *Indian Country Today*, February 17, 2016; Sam Levin, "Fresh Outrage after Militia Seen Rifling through Tribal Artifacts at Oregon Refuge," *Guardian*, January 21, 2016.

p. 203   **Two weeks into the standoff:** Bill Morlin, "Possible Federal Crimes Numerous at Oregon Refuge Takeover," *Hatewatch*, Southern Poverty Law Center, January 15, 2016.

p. 203   **The Bundys had remained:** Luke Hammill, "Update: Oregon Standoff Meeting Interrupted with Announcement That Altercation Stopped Speakers," *Oregonian*, January 26, 2016.

p. 204   **Oregon State Police sprung:** See Evan Perez and Holly Yan, "Ammon Bundy, Other Protesters Arrested in Oregon; LaVoy Finicum Killed," CNN, January 27, 2016.

p. 204   **LaVoy Finicum began yelling:** Deschutes County Sheriff's Office, *Synced Investigation Video*, YouTube, March 8, 2016.

p. 205   **The next day:** Kyung Lah and Brad Parks, "Woman Says She Was Feet Away When Shots Killed Oregon Occupier FINICUM," CNN, February 3, 2016.

p. 206   **Michele Fiore:** David Neiwert, "Antigovernment Movement's Rank and File Want Retaliation for Arrests, Death in Oregon, but Their Leaders Are Reluctant," *Hatewatch*, Southern Poverty Law Center, January 28, 2016.

p. 206 **Within a few days:** Bill Morlin, "Oregon Shooting Video May Galvanize, Incite Antigovernment Fringe," *Hatewatch*, Southern Poverty Law Center, January 29, 2016.

p. 206 **A few weeks later:** Bill Morlin, "Fatal Shooting of Refuge Occupier Justified, but State Report Questions FBI's Role," *Hatewatch*, Southern Poverty Law Center, March 9, 2016.

p. 207 **In no time at all:** Bill Morlin, "'Cascade of Threats' Directed at Public Officials Involved with Oregon Occupation," Southern Poverty Law Center, *Hatewatch*, March 28, 2016.

p. 207 **The FBI moved swiftly:** David Neiwert, "Anger, Threats over Malheur Arrests, Death Spur Feds to Issue Warning to Law Enforcement, Federal Workers," *Hatewatch*, Southern Poverty Law Center, February 17, 2016.

p. 208 **Four holdouts would not budge:** Bill Morlin, "Bundy Patriarch Urges Refuge Occupiers to Stay Put," *Hatewatch*, Southern Poverty Law Center, February 2, 2016.

p. 208 **Another video:** Southern Poverty Law Center, *Hatewatch*, "Malheur Militiaman Warns of 'Bloodbath,' Calls for Fellow Patriots to Join 'History in the Making,'" YouTube, uploaded January 30, 2016.

p. 209 **Fiore spent much:** John Sepulvado, "GOP Politicians Planned and Participated in Key Aspects of Refuge Occupation," Oregon Public Broadcasting, March 16, 2016.

p. 209 **The day before:** Bill Morlin, "Cliven Bundy Arrested as Remaining Wildlife Refuge Occupiers Set to Surrender," *Hatewatch*, Southern Poverty Law Center, February 11, 2016; Bill Morlin, "Four Arrests at Oregon Refuge End 41-Day Standoff," *Hatewatch*, Southern Poverty Law Center, February 11, 2016.

p. 210 **The flow of hate mail:** Neiwert, "Anger, Threats over Malheur Arrests, Death."

p. 211 **On February 1:** See David Neiwert, "The Right-Wing Oregon Occupiers Have a Martyr Now, and That Should Worry Everyone," *Washington Post*, February 10, 2016.

p. 212 **The following Saturday:** "In the Aftermath of LaVoy Finicum's Death, Growing Number of Rallies Push Martyrdom Narrative," *Hatewatch*, Southern Poverty Law Center, May 3, 2016.

Chapter 10: The Alt-Right Reinvention

p. 213 **The anti-Semite has chosen:** Jean-Paul Sartre, *Anti-Semite and Jew: An Exploration of the Etiology of Hate* (New York: Schocken Books, 1948), pp. 13–14.

p. 213   **On October 10, 2014:** Andrew Hart, "Game Developer Brianna Wu Flees Home after Death Threats," *Huffington Post*, Oct. 12, 2014.

p. 214   **The threats directed at:** Dean Takashi, "Brianna Wu Speaks Up about Death Threats and Personal Cost of Opposing #GamerGate," *VentureBeat*, February 9, 2015.

p. 214   **One of the feminists' chief:** Milo Yiannopoulos, "Feminist Bullies Tearing the Video Game Industry Apart," *Breitbart News*, September 1, 2014.

p. 216   **The Internet made possible:** Chip Berlet and Matthew Lyons, "Hard Right Conspiracism and Apocalyptic Millennialism," *Public Eye*, December 19, 2001.

p. 217   **The media-sciences expert:** Judith Donath, "Identity and Deception in the Virtual Community," *MIT Media Lab*, November 12, 1996.

p. 219   **The personality profile of trolls:** Erin E. Buckels, Paul D. Trapnell, and Delroy L. Paulhus, "Trolls Just Want to Have Fun," *Personality and Individual Differences*, September 2014, pp. 97–102.

p. 220   **The original 1994 study:** See Jim Sidanius and Felicia Pratto, "Social Dominance Orientation: A Personality Variable Predicting Social and Political Attitudes," *Journal of Personality and Social Psychology* 94, no. 4 (1994): 741–63.

p. 220   **The psychologist Robert Altemeyer:** See Bob Altemeyer, "Highly Dominating, Highly Authoritarian Personalities," *Journal of Social Psychology* 144, no. 4 (2004): 425.

p. 220   **White nationalism had been lurking:** See Leonard Zeskind, *Blood and Politics: The History of the White Nationalist Movement from the Margins to the Mainstream* (New York: Farrar, Straus and Giroux, 2009), pp. 367–9, 393–8. See also "White Nationalists," Southern Poverty Law Center.

p. 222   **Jared Taylor epitomized:** "Jared Taylor," Southern Poverty Law Center, Extremist Profile; "American Renaissance," Southern Poverty Law Center, Extremist Profile; Anti-Defamation League, "Extremism in America: Jared Taylor/American Renaissance," report, January 11, 2011. See also Nina Burleigh, "Steve Bannon, Jared Taylor, and the Radical Right's Ivy League Pedigree," *Newsweek*, March 23, 2017.

p. 222   **Peter Brimelow also fit:** "Peter Brimelow," Southern Poverty Law Center, Extremist Profile; "The Nativists Are Restless," *New York Times*, editorial, January 31, 2009. See also Peter Brimelow, "America's Immigration Policy—Hitler's Revenge?," *VDare*, August 22, 2006.

p. 223   **MacDonald is a white nationalist:** "Kevin MacDonald," Southern Poverty Law Center, Extremist Profile; Heidi Beirich, "California State University, Long Beach Psychology Professor Kevin MacDonald Publishes Anti-Semitic Books," *Intelligence Report*, April 22, 2007.

p. 224   **The phrase "cultural Marxism":** Bill Berkowitz, "Cultural Marxism Catching On," *Intelligence Report*, August 15, 2003.

p. 224   **One of the subscribers:** Jason Wilson, "'Cultural Marxism': A

Uniting Theory for Rightwingers Who Love to Play the Victim," *Guardian*, January 18, 2015.

p. 225   **David Duke:** "David Duke," Southern Poverty Law Center, Extremist Profile.

p. 226   **Stormfront is:** Heidi Beirich, "White Homicide Worldwide: Stormfront, the Leading White Supremacist Web Forum, Has Another Distinction—Murder Capital of the Internet," Southern Poverty Law Center, March 31, 2014. Also see "Stormfront," Southern Poverty Law Center, Extremist Profile.

p. 226   **The Knights Party:** "Thomas Robb," Southern Poverty Law Center, Extremist Profile; "Knights of the Ku Klux Klan," Southern Poverty Law Center, Extremist Profile; Eve Conant, "Hate Groups Are Benefiting from Obama's Election," *Newsweek*, April 24, 2009.

p. 227   **The Council of Conservative Citizens:** "Council of Conservative Citizens," Southern Poverty Law Center, Extremist Profile; Anti-Defamation League, "Extremism in America"; Anti-Defamation League, "The Council of Conservative Citizens: Declining Bastion of Hate," June 25, 2015.

p. 228   **Vanguard News Network:** See Don Terry, "Vanguard News Network: A History of Violence," *Hatewatch*, Southern Poverty Law Center, April 14, 2014; "Alex Linder," Southern Poverty Law Center, Extremist Profile; Anti-Defamation League, "Neo-Nazi Aryan Alternative Newspaper Reappears," June 15, 2009.

p. 230   **The audience for conspiracy theories:** See Bob Altemeyer, *The Authoritarians* (University of Manitoba, 2006), pp. 75–92, 176; Bob Altemeyer, "Donald Trump and Authoritarian Followers," *Daily Kos*, March 2, 2016.

p. 232   **It all began, really:** Aric Suber-Jenkins, "How 4Chan, a Small Anime Forum, Became Donald Trump's Most Rabid Fan Base," Mic.com, October 31, 2016.

p. 233   **The "manosphere":** "Misogyny: The Sites," *Intelligence Report*, March 1, 2012.

p. 233   **So it was unsurprising:** Simon Parkin, "Zoe Quinn's Depression Quest," *New Yorker*, September 9, 2014; Adam Smith, "Mostly Indescribable: Depression Quest," *Rock, Paper, Shotgun*, February 14, 2013.

p. 234   **Quinn's media fame:** Nick Wingfield, "Feminist Critics of Video Games Facing Threats in 'GamerGate' Campaign," *New York Times*, October 15, 2014.

p. 235   **Quinn's previous flood:** Radhika Sanghani, "Misogyny, Death Threats and a Mob of Trolls: Inside the Dark World of Video Games with Zoe Quinn—Target of #GamerGate," *Daily Telegraph*, September 10, 2014.

p. 235   **The harassment didn't end:** Wingfield, "Feminist Critics of Video Games."

p. 236   **Richard Spencer, an editor:** Kevin DeAnna, "The Alternative Right," *Taki's Magazine*, July 26, 2009.

p. 237   **Spencer grew up:** "Richard Bertrand Spencer," Southern Poverty Law Center, Extremist Profile; "Alternative Right," Southern Poverty Law Center, Extremist Profile.

p. 238   **Spencer moved his end:** David Neiwert, "Small-Town Montana Residents Organize to Oppose Presence of White Nationalists," *Hatewatch*, Southern Poverty Law Center, November 19, 2014.

p. 239   **Brad Griffin:** Hunter Wallace, "My Alt-Right Biography," *Occidental Dissent*, December 15, 2016 .

p. 239   **In 2008, Griffin:** See "Bradley Dean Griffin," Southern Poverty Law Center, Extremist Profile.

p. 240   **Griffin later explained:** Richard B. Spencer, "AltRight and Its Enemies," *Radix Journal*, March 5, 2010.

p. 240   **Notwithstanding the congenial:** Hunter Wallace, "Should White Americans Prepare For 'Race War'?," *Occidental Dissent*, May 8, 2015.

p. 241   **Griffin is also married:** Keegan Hankes, "Future of the Council of Conservative Citizens Unknown after Founder's Passing," *Hatewatch*, Southern Poverty Law Center, March 9, 2015.

p. 241   **Born in 1991:** See "Matthew Heimbach," Southern Poverty Law Center, Extremist Profile.

p. 242   **After graduating college:** See "Traditionalist Worker Party," Southern Poverty Law Center, Extremist Profile.

p. 243   **Andrew Breitbart built:** Rebecca Mead, "Rage Machine: Andrew Breitbart's Empire of Bluster," *New Yorker*, May 24, 2010; Noah Shachtman, "How Andrew Breitbart Hacked the Media," *Wired*, March 11, 2010; David Carr, "The Provocateur," *New York Times*, April 13, 2012; "How Andrew Breitbart Helped Launch Huffington Post," *BuzzFeed*, March 1, 2012.

p. 244   **Despite its mainstream position:** Dean Obeidallah, "Steve Bannon Contributed to Anti-Muslim Hate. American Media Must Call Him Out," *Huffington Post*, November 17, 2016.

p. 244   **It eventually emerged:** See Chris Rovyar, "Damaging Brooklyn ACORN Sting Video Ruled 'Heavily Edited,' No Charges to Be Filed," *New York*, March 2, 2010; Andy Newman, "Advice to Fake Pimp Was No Crime, Prosecutor Says," *New York Times*, March 1, 2010.

p. 244   **The uproar:** See "House Votes to Strip Funding for ACORN," Fox News, September 17, 2009.

p. 244   **Breitbart also was able:** Maggie Haberman, "Breitbart Takes Over Weiner Presser," *Politico*, June 6, 2011; Dana Bash, "Weiner Resigns after Sexting Scandal," CNN, June 16, 2011.

p. 244   **Later, unedited videos:** See Christine Schwen et al., "Timeline of Breitbart's Sherrod Smear," MediaMatters.org, July 22, 2010.

p. 245   **But on March 1, 2012:** Christina Ng, "Publisher and Author Andrew Breitbart Dead," *ABC News*, March 1, 2012.

p. 245   **After a couple of weeks:** Keach Hagey, "Breitbart to Announce New Management," *Politico*, March 19, 2012.

p. 245   **Bannon was a former:** See Joshua Green, "This Man Is the Most Dangerous Political Operative in America," *Bloomberg Businessweek*, October 8, 2015.

p. 245   **Bannon reportedly became:** See Jason M. Breslow, Miles Alvord, and Carla Borras, "Who Is Steve Bannon? The View from Four Breitbart Staffers," *Frontline*, May 23, 2017.

p. 245   **After a white journalist:** "Breitbart News Posts Factual Headline About 'Race War' Double Murder, Internet Melts Down," *Breitbart News*, August 27, 2015.

p. 246   **Breitbart also portrayed:** Ben Shapiro, "Media Pay Homage to Trayvon Martin on 21st Birthday. Here's the Real Story," *Breitbart News*, February 5, 2016.

p. 246   **Per Breitbart, Michael Brown:** John Nolte, "'Ferguson Effect': America's New Crime Wave Is All Part of the Plan," *Breitbart News*, May 30, 2015.

p. 246   **Breitbart's headline:** Tom Tancredo, "Political Correctness Protects Muslim Rape Culture," *Breitbart News*, January 2, 2016.

p. 246   **Over a Milo:** Milo Yiannopoulos, "Silicon Valley's Startup Culture Explains Why Mass Muslim Immigration Must Stop," *Breitbart News*, August 3, 2016.

p. 246   **A Yiannopoulos anti-feminist rant:** Milo Yiannopoulos, "The Solution to Online 'Harassment' Is Simple: Women Should Log Off," *Breitbart News*, July 5, 2016.

p. 246   **When the uproar:** Gerald Warner, "Hoist It High and Proud: The Confederate Flag Proclaims a Glorious Heritage," *Breitbart News*, July 1, 2015.

p. 246   **Breitbart.com rarely:** Stephen Piggott, "Is Breitbart.com Becoming the Media Arm of the 'Alt-Right'?," Southern Poverty Law Center, *Hatewatch*, April 28, 2016.

p. 246   **A fairly typical example:** See "Even More Racism from Breitbart News, Now with 20% More Neo-Nazis!," AngryWhiteMen.com, August 30, 2015; Daniel Nussbaum, "Tarantino: 'Finally, the Issue of White Supremacy Is Being Talked about and Dealt With,'" *Breitbart News*, August 24, 2015.

p. 247   **The website's staff:** See TBogg, "'Slaves Built the US the Way Cows Built McDonald's'—and Other Historical 'Facts' from Katie McHugh," *Raw Story*, June 5, 2017.

p. 247   **However, Breitbart's primary connection:** Milo Yiannopoulos, "Welcome to Breitbart Tech, A New Vertical Covering Tech, Gaming and Internet Culture," *Breitbart News*, October 127, 2015.

p. 247   **He more or less cemented:** Allum Bokhari and Milo Yiannopoulos, "An Establishment Conservative's Guide to the Alt-Right," *Breitbart News*, March 29, 2016.

p. 248 **Andrew Anglin:** See "Andrew Anglin," Southern Poverty Law Center, Extremist Profile.

p. 248 **Around 2010:** See Andrew Anglin, "Andrew Anglin Exposed!," *Daily Stormer*, March 14, 2015.

p. 249 **The new site was named:** See Heidi Beirich, "Blog Wars: The Daily Stormer and Its Racist Frenemies," *Hatewatch*, Southern Poverty Law Center, March 10, 2015.

p. 249 **Anglin wrote in February 2014:** Andrew Anglin, "Blacks Loved Slavery and Regretted Its End," *Daily Stormer*, February 20, 2014.

p. 250 **One of the website's regular visitors:** Keegan Hankes, "Dylann Roof May Have Been a Regular Commenter at Neo-Nazi Website the Daily Stormer," *Hatewatch*, Southern Poverty Law Center, June 21, 2015.

p. 250 **But Anglin's agenda was more:** See Andrew Anglin, "A Normie's Guide to the Alt-Right," *Daily Stormer*, August 31, 2016.

p. 251 **The Right Stuff:** Amanda Head, "For the Alt-Right, the Message Is in the Punctuation," *New York Times*, June 10, 2016.

p. 251 **Danger and Play:** Andrew Marantz, "Trolls for Trump," *New Yorker*, October 31, 2016.

p. 251 **RamZPaul:** "Paul Ray Ramsey," Southern Poverty Law Center, Extremist Profile; Don Terry, "The Smiling Nationalist," *Intelligence Report*, August 21, 2013.

p. 252 **The Political Cesspool:** "James Edwards," Southern Poverty Law Center, Extremist Profile.

p. 252 **@RickyVaughn:** Keegan Hankes and Alex Amend, "Alt-Right Celebrity @Ricky_Vaughn99 Suspended from Twitter," *Hatewatch*, Southern Poverty Law Center, October 65, 2016; Hannibal Bateman, "The Man behind the Meme," *Radix Journal*, January 20, 2016.

p. 253 **RooshV:** See "Misogyny: The Sites," *Intelligence Report*, March 1, 2012; Joanna Adams, "Roosh V's Toronto Lecture Held in Mississauga, Despite Protests: Report," *Huffington Post*, August 17, 2015.

p. 253 **weev:** See Sam Biddle, "iPad Hacker and 'Troll' Weev Is Now a Straight-Up White Supremacist," *Gawker*, October 7, 2014.

p. 254 **Anglin was especially vicious:** Anglin, "A Normie's Guide"; "Alternative Right," Southern Poverty Law Center, Extremist Profile.

p. 254 **A *Washington Post* profile:** Philip Beam, "Hillary Clinton Plans to Tie Donald Trump to the 'Alt-Right' and the Worst of the Web," *Washington Post*, August 23, 2016; Andrew Anglin, "Ahead of Clinton Speech, WaPo Does Another Alt-Right Article," *Daily Stormer*, August 24, 2016.

p. 255 **More feuds broke out:** Keegan Hankes, "Eating Their Own: Several Feuds Erupt Among White Nationalists," Southern Poverty Law Center, *Hatewatch*, October 21, 2014.

p. 255 **After recounting:** Hunter Wallace, "Beefs in the WN Movement," *Occidental Dissent*, October 9, 2014.

p. 255 **Pepe the Frog:** Olivia Nuzzi, "How Pepe the Frog Became a Nazi Trump Supporter and Alt-Right Symbol," *Daily Beast*, May 25, 2016.

p. 256 **In September 2016:** Matt Miller, "Exclusive: The Creator of Pepe the Frog Is Voting for Hillary," *Esquire*, September 28, 2016.

p. 258 **Domestic terrorism attacks:** Kathy Gilsinan, "ISIS and the 'Internet Radicalization' Trope," *Atlantic*, December 8, 2015; Ed Pilkington and Dan Roberts, "FBI and Obama Confirm Omar Mateen Was Radicalized on the Internet," *Guardian*, June 14, 2016.

p. 258 **But the massive:** David Neiwert, "Home Is Where the Hate Is," Reveal Radio/Center for Investigative Reporting, June 22, 2017; Naomi Braine, "Terror Network or Lone Wolf? Disparate Legal Treatment of Muslims and the Radical Right," Political Research Associates, June 19, 2015.

p. 258 **Both media accounts:** Rick Gladstone, "Many Ask, Why Not Call Church Shooting Terrorism?," *New York Times*, June 28, 2015; Kevin Cirilli, "FBI Head Won't Call Charleston Shooting a Terrorist Act," *The Hill*, June 20, 2015.

p. 258 **Similarly, when an anti-abortion:** Eric Tucker and Sadie Gurman, "Why the Planned Parenthood Shooting Isn't Legally Referred to as 'Domestic Terrorism,'" Associated Press, December 1, 2015.

p. 259 **One of these theories:** Katelyn Y. A. McKenna and John A. Bargh, "Coming Out in the Age of the Internet: Identity 'Demarginalization' through Virtual Group Participation," *Journal of Personality and Social Psychology* 75 (1998): 681–94; Daveed Gartenstein-Ross and Nathaniel Barr, "The Social Science of Online Radicalization," *War on the Rocks*, October 29, 2015.

p. 259 **A 2012 study:** Neal Caren, Kay Jowers, and Sarah Gaby, "A Social Movement Online Community: Stormfront and the White Nationalist Movement," *Research in Social Movements, Conflicts and Change* 33 (2012): 163–93.

p. 260 **According to J. M. Berger:** J. M. Berger, "Tailored Online Interventions: The Islamic State's Recruitment Strategy," Combating Terrorism Center, October 23, 2015.

p. 260 **The process of radicalization:** Abi Wilkinson, "We Need to Talk about the Online Radicalisation of Young, White Men," *Guardian*, November 15, 2016.

p. 260 **Keegan Hankes:** Keegan Hankes, interviewed by author, October 22, 2016.

p. 261 **Berger, whose focus:** J. M. Berger, "The Social Apocalypse: A Forecast," *IntelWire*, August 31, 2016.

Notes

Chapter 11: "Hail Emperor Trump!"

p. 263   **A Trump candidacy:** See Bradford Richardson, "Trump as George H. W. Bush's Running Mate? 'I Was Asked That Question'," *The Hill*, November 8, 2015.

p. 263   **Then in 1999:** See Matt Bai, "Jesse Finds His Big Guy," *Newsweek*, July 18, 1999; see also "Trump Offers Details on Possible Presidential Bid," CNN, November 28, 1999; also see "Donald Trump Says He Will Not Run for President in 2000," NBC News (*Today* Show), February 14, 2000.

p. 263   **He started taking the idea:** See Maggie Haberman, "Trump Tops Romney, Pawlenty," *Politico*, March 7, 2011; also see Aliyah Shahid, "Donald Trump Takes Lead in GOP Primary Poll, Beats Romney, Huckabee, Palin, Gingrich, Bachmann, Paul," *New York Daily News*, April 15, 2011; also see Jason Linkins, "Donald Trump Brings His 'Pretend to Run for President' Act to CPAC," *Huffington Post*, February 11, 2011.

p. 263   **Trump began making headlines:** See "Trump Claims Obama Birth Certificate 'Missing'," CNN, April 25, 2011; also see Ashley Parker and Steve Eder, "Inside the Six Weeks Donald Trump Was a Nonstop 'Birther'," *New York Times*, July 2, 2016; also see Alana Abramson, "How Donald Trump Perpetuated the 'Birther' Movement for Years," ABC News, September 15, 2016.

p. 263   **"Here is what the Republican party":** See video of US senator Lindsey Graham speaking before the *Atlantic's* First Draft of History conference, October 1, 2009, link.brightcove.com/services/player/bcpid30183074001?bctid=42981023001.

p. 264   **None of this deterred:** See David Jackson, "Trump Keeps Beating 'Birther' Drum against Obama," *USA Today*, April 7, 2011.

p. 264   **There was an immediate backlash:** See Erik Ortiz, "Trump Kept 'Birther' Beliefs Going Long After Obama's Birth Certificate Was Released," NBC News, September 16, 2016.

p. 264   **Trump soon announced:** See Mollie Reilly, "There's Still No Evidence That Trump Sent Investigators to Hawaii to Dig Up Dirt on Obama," *Huffington Post*, September 16, 2016.

p. 264   **Later he said:** See "Trump: My Investigators in Hawaii Can't Believe What They Are Finding," *The Right Scoop*, April 6, 2011.

p. 264   **Joseph Farah:** See Ben Smith, "Trump and the Blacks," *Politico*, April 14, 2011.

p. 264   **The controversy kept swirling:** See "Trump Claims Obama Birth Certificate 'Missing'," CNN, April 25, 2011.

p. 265   **Three days later:** See Chris Megerian, "What Donald Trump Has Said through the Years about Where President Obama Was Born," *Los Angeles Times*, September 16, 2016.

p. 265   **Obama opened the night:** See Maggie Haberman and Alexander

412

Burns, "Donald Trump's Presidential Run Began in an Effort to Gain Stature," *New York Times*, March 12, 2016; see also Adam Gopnik, "Trump and Obama: A Night to Remember," *New Yorker*, September 12, 2015; also see Amy B. Wang, " 'It Was Fantastic': Trump Denies 2011 White House Correspondents' Dinner Spurred Presidential Bid," *Washington Post*, February 28, 2017.

p. 266 **Few among the pundit class:** See Peter Grier, "Donald Trump Says He Might Run for president. Three Reasons He Won't," *Christian Science Monitor*, February 10, 2011.

p. 266 **In mid-May 2011:** See "Trump Not Running for President," CNN, May 16, 2011.

p. 266 **But Trump did not relent:** See Michael Scherer, "Birtherism Is Dead, but the Birther Industry Continues," *Time*, April 27, 2011.

p. 266 **In August 2011:** See Stephen Lemons, "Joe Arpaio Birther Posse Probes President Obama's Birth Certificate," *Phoenix New Times*, September 19, 2011; also see Sarah Anne Hughes, "Sheriff Joe Arpaio Tasks 'Cold Case Posse' to Investigate Obama's Birth Certificate," *Washington Post*, September 20, 2011.

p. 266 **He sent a couple:** See Alex Pareene, "Arpaio Goons Sent to Hawaii for Important Birther Investigation," *Salon*, May 22, 2012.

p. 266 **On March 31, 2012:** See Linda Bentley, "Arpaio's Cold Case Posse Vows 'Team Will Not Quit Until This Is Finished'," *Sonoran News*, April 4, 2012; also see "Sheriff Joe Arpaio Press Conference March 31," YouTube, March 31, 2012.

p. 266 **Trump wrote a personal letter:** See "Donald Trump: Say It Is So, Sheriff Joe," *WorldNetDaily*, March 14, 2012.

p. 266 **Trump also continued:** See Michael Barbaro, "Donald Trump Clung to 'Birther' Lie for Years, and Still Isn't Apologetic," *New York Times*, September 16, 2016.

p. 267 **Alex Jones:** See "Alex Jones: CIA, El Chapo, and Donald Trump in Conspiracy against Rand Paul," MoFo Politics, July 14, 2015.

p. 267 **Andrew Anglin:** See Sarah Posner and David Neiwert, "How Trump Took Hate Groups Mainstream," *Mother Jones*, October 14, 2016.

p. 267 **However, Trump began gaining:** See "Michael Savage Interviews Donald Trump on The Savage Nation—2/20/14," YouTube.com, February 20, 2014.

p. 267 **Throughout 2014:** See Brian Tashman, "Michael Savage: Obama Is Wiping Out Americans Through Diseases Carried By Migrant Kids," *Right Wing Watch*, September 10, 2014; also see Brian Tashman, "Michael Savage: Obama Wants to Bring Ebola Epidemic to America, Should Resign," *Right Wing Watch*, October 2, 2014; also see Eric Hananoki, "Michael Savage's Disgusting Rant: PTSD and Depression Sufferers Are 'Weak,' 'Narcissistic,' 'Losers'," *Media Matters*, October 21, 2014.

p. 267   **Savage and Trump formed:** See "Michael Savage Interviews Donald Trump on The Savage Nation—2/20/14," YouTube.com, February 20, 2014.

p. 267   **Soon enough, support:** See Matthew Richer, "For Better or Worse, Donald Trump May Be the Only Immigration Patriot Running for President," *VDare*, April 12, 2015.

p. 268   **When Trump made his candidacy official:** See Sarah Posner and David Neiwert, "How Trump Took Hate Groups Mainstream," *Mother Jones*, October 14, 2016.

p. 268   **It wasn't until later in the week:** See Adam Gabbatt, "Donald Trump's Tirade on Mexico's 'Drugs and Rapists' Outrages US Latinos," *Guardian*, June 16, 2015.

p. 268   **Officials in Mexico:** See Ishaan Tharoor, "Top Mexican official Blasts Donald Trump's 'Absurd' Comments on Migrants," *Washington Post*, June 17, 2015.

p. 268   **Trump shortly responded:** See Tai Koppan, "What Donald Trump Has Said about Mexico and Vice Versa," CNN, August 31, 2016.

p. 269   **The *Washington Post* awarded:** See Michelle Yee Hee Lee, "Donald Trump's False Comments Connecting Mexican Immigrants and Crime," *Washington Post*, July 8, 2015.

p. 270   **"I can never apologize for the truth":** See "Trump on Immigration Comments: 'I Can Never Apologize for the Truth'," *Fox News Insider*, July 5, 2015.

p. 270   **The next day:** See Michelle Yee Hee Lee, "Donald Trump's False Comments Connecting Mexican Immigrants and Crime," *Washington Post*, July 8, 2015.

p. 270   **"I urge all readers":** See Andrew Anglin, "The *Daily Stormer* Endorses Donald Trump for President," *Daily Stormer*, June 28, 2015.

p. 270   **The godfather:** See Patrick Buchanan, "Out With the Old Parties and Politicians," *American Conservative*, June 19, 2015.

p. 270   **Peter Brimelow's:** See James Kirkpatrick, "We Are All Donald Trump Now—Left Moves to Ban Truth About Immigration," *VDare*, July 9, 2015.

p. 271   **Other white nationalists:** See Gregory Hood, "Why We Need a Troll as President," *Radix Journal*, July 22, 2015.

p. 271   **Writers at the alt-right website:** See Hunter Wallace, "The Donald Announces," *Occidental Dissent*, June 16, 2015.

p. 271   **Trump chased away:** See Jeremy Diamond and Sara Murray, "Trump Outlines Immigration Specifics," CNN, August 17, 2015.

p. 271   **Trump's position paper:** See Jared Taylor, "Is Trump Our Last Chance?," *American Renaissance*, August 21, 2015.

p. 272   **David Duke enthused:** See Sara Jerde, "White Supremacist David Duke: Trump Has Said 'Some Incredibly Great Things'," August 25, 2015.

p. 272 **Brad Griffin promptly:** See Hunter Wallace, "Trump's White Walkers," *Occidental Dissent,* August 16, 2015.

p. 272 **Peter Brimelow's *VDare*:** See Peter Brimelow, "The Trump Wrecking Ball, the Washington Cartel, and the Jews," *VDare,* August 19, 2015.

p. 272 **Trump fever quickly spread:** See Rachel Monroe, "How Does a White Supremacist See America Today?," *New York Magazine,* October 12, 2015; also see "ANP Report for September 20, 2015," *American Nazi Party,* September 20, 2015; also see Peter Holley and Sara Larimer, "How America's Dying White Supremacist Movement is Seizing on Donald Trump's Appeal," *Washington Post,* February 29, 2016.

p. 272 **Richard Spencer's:** See Richard B. Spencer, "Our Big, Fat, Beautiful Dog Whistle," *Radix Journal,* September 5, 2015.

p. 273 **Another leading white nationalist:** See Kevin MacDonald, "Donald Trump's Breakthrough Statement on Immigration," *Occidental Observer,* August 16, 2015.

p. 273 **Matthew Heimbach:** See Matthew Heimbach, "The Trump Train and the Southern Strategy: The Only Hope for the GOP," *Traditionalist Youth Network,* October 2015.

p. 274 **Donald Trump loves to portray:** See Theodore Schleifer, "Trump Doesn't Challenge Anti-Muslim Questioner at Event," CNN, September 18, 2015.

p. 274 **polls then showed:** See "Trump Supporters Think Obama Is a Muslim Born in Another Country," Public Policy Polling, September 1, 2015.

p. 274 **Trump answered:** See Eugene Scott, "Trump Says He's Not 'Morally Obligated' to Defend Obama Against Claims," CNN, September 19, 2015.

p. 274 **Muslims-rights groups:** See "CAIR Calls on Donald Trump to Clarify 'Looking At' Getting Rid of Muslims," Council on American-Islamic Relations (press release), September 18, 2015.

p. 274 **Then another:** See "Meet the Press Transcript—September 20, 2015," NBC News, September 20, 2015.

p. 275 **That, too, provoked:** See Jeremy Diamond, "Muslim-American group Calls on Ben Carson to Drop Out," CNN, September 21, 2015.

p. 275 **Islamophobia had gradually:** See Richard Fausset, "Refugee Crisis in Syria Raises Fears in South Carolina," *New York Times,* September 25, 2015; see also David Neiwert, "Idaho Town Divided by Fears Over Refugees, 'Sharia Law'," *Hatewatch,* September 24, 2015.

p. 275 **One incident that caught:** See Ken Kalthoff, "Irving Teen Says He's Falsely Accused of Making a 'Hoax Bomb'," NBC Dallas-Fort Worth, September 16, 2015.

p. 275 **It soon emerged:** See Travis Gettys, "The Mayor of Ahmed Mohamed's Town Is a Well-Known Conservative Folk Hero for Fighting Fake Muslim 'Threats'," *Raw Story,* September 16, 2015.

p. 275 **She continued to defend:** See Matt Ferner, "Irving Mayor Defends School and Cops, Doesn't Apologize for Arrest of Muslim Teen over Clock," *Huffington Post*, December 19, 2015.

p. 275 **Eventually, the conspiracists:** See Avi Selk, "Craze over Teen Clockmaker from Irving Shifts from Celebrity to Conspiracy," *Dallas Morning News*, September 22, 2015.

p. 275 **Local media fueled:** See David Neiwert, "How the Candidates, the Haters, and the Media Have Cooked Up a Perfect Storm of Islamophobia," *Hatewatch*, October 2, 2015.

p. 275 **The day after Trump's town hall:** See Brian Tashman, "Larry Klayman: Retired Military Leads Weighing Anti-Obama Coup," *Right Wing Watch*, September 18, 2015.

p. 276 **The spread of Islamophobia:** See David Neiwert, "How the Candidates, the Haters, and the Media Have Cooked Up a Perfect Storm of Islamophobia," *Hatewatch*, October 2, 2015.

p. 277 **Mike Huckabee:** See Nick Wing, "Mike Huckabee: Muslims Depart Mosques Like 'Uncorked Animals,' Throwing Rocks, Burning Cars," *Huffington Post*, August 9, 2013.

p. 277 **Governor Bobby Jindal:** See Adam B. Lerner, "Jindal Won't Back Down on 'No-Go Zone' Comments, " *Politico*, January 21, 2015.

p. 277 **Former governor Jeb Bush:** See Olivia Nuzzi, "Jeb's Anti-Muslim, Anti-Gay New Hire," *Daily Beast*, March 15, 2015.

p. 277 **Senator Ted Cruz:** See Adam B. Lerner, "Ted Cruz Under Fire for Tennessee Campaign Chairman," *Politico*, June 11, 2015.

p. 277 **Rick Santorum, too:** See Scott Kaufman, "Rick Santorum Slams Muslims: 'You Don't See Baptist Ministers Going on Jihad'," *Raw Story*, September 28, 2014; also see Stephanie Condon, "Rick Santorum Endorses Muslim Profiling," CBS News, November 23, 2011.

p. 277 **In September he had told:** See Nick Gass, "Trump Calls for Taking In Syrian Refugees," *Politico*, September 9, 2015.

p. 277 **On October 1, at a rally:** See "Donald Trump: I Would Send Syrian Refugees Home," BBC News, October 1, 2015.

p. 278 **On November 22, 2015:** See Sarah Posner and David Neiwert, "How Trump Took Hate Groups Mainstream," *Mother Jones*, October 14, 2016.

p. 278 **The tweet originated:** See Jon Greenberg, "Trump's Pants on Fire Tweet that Blacks Killed 81% of White Homicide Victims," *PolitiFact*, November 23, 2015.

p. 278 **The alt-right video blogging star:** See RamZPaul, Twitter, January 22, 2016, twitter.com/ramzpaul/status/690572476045099008.

p. 278 **James Edwards:** See Sarah Posner and David Neiwert, "How Trump Took Hate Groups Mainstream," *Mother Jones*, October 14, 2016.

p. 279 **This is what he did:** See "O'Reilly Confronts Trump on Retweeting

Inaccurate Stats About Black Murder Rate," *Fox News Insider,* November 23, 2015.

p. 279   **Two months later:** See Nolan D. McCaskill, "Trump Retweets Another White Supremacist," *Politico,* February 27, 2016.

p. 279   **Among the white nationalists:** See Andrew Anglin, "Happening: Trump Retweets Two More White Genocide Accounts Back-to-Back," *Daily Stormer,* January 25, 2016.

p. 279   **The account @NordicNation:** See Sarah Posner and David Neiwert, "How Trump Took Hate Groups Mainstream," *Mother Jones,* October 14, 2016.

p. 279   **Earlier in January:** See Richard B. Spencer, "That Robocall," *Radix Journal,* January 13, 2016.

p. 279   **But Jared Taylor and William Johnson:** See Eric Hananoki, "White Nationalists Behind Pro-Trump Robocall: Trump's Response Was 'Wonderful' and Validating," *Media Matters,* January 19, 2016.

p. 280   **This tango:** See Eliza Collins, "David Duke: Voting against Trump Is 'Treason to Your Heritage'," *Politico,* February 25, 2016.

p. 280   **When asked about:** See "Transcripts: State of the Union, February 28, 2016," CNN, February 28, 2016.

p. 280   **The Monday after:** See Jesse Byrnes, "Trump: 'David Duke Is a Bad Person'," *The Hill,* March 3, 2016.

p. 280   **At Occidental Dissent:** See Hunter Wallace, "The Trumpening Is at Hand," *Occidental Dissent,* February 29, 2016.

p. 280   **Duke himself:** See Anna Merod, "David Duke 'Laughs Off' Trump's Disavowal, Continues Praise," MSNBC, March 1, 2016.

p. 280   **In July, when he announced:** See Stephen Piggott, "Former Klan Leader David Duke Announces U.S. Senate Bid," *Hatewatch,* July 22, 2016.

p. 280   **When Trump disparaged:** See Theodore Schleifer, "Trump Defends Criticism of Judge with Mexican Heritage," CNN, June 5, 2016.

p. 287   **when he refused to condemn:** See Katherine Krueger, "Trump Won't Condemn Anti-Semitic Threats on Journo Who Profiled His Wife," *Talking Points Memo,* May 5, 2016.

p. 281   **when he claimed that 'some people':** See Meghan Keneally, "Donald Trump Claims 'Some People' Called for a Moment of Silence for the Dallas Gunman," ABC News, July 13, 2016.

p. 281   **when his son and campaign chief:** See Ari Feldman, "Donald Trump Jr. Retweets the 'Neo-Nazi Movement's Favorite Academic'," *Forward,* September 1, 2016.

p. 281   **On July 9:** See "Donald Trump Event Phoenix Sheriff Joe Arpaio July 11, 2015," YouTube.com, July 11, 2015.

p. 282   **The next day:** See M. J. Lee, "Trump Says He Still Doesn't Know Where Obama Was Born," CNN, July 9, 2015.

p. 282 **Now leading the parade:** See Tim Murphy, "How Donald Trump Became Conspiracy Theorist in Chief," *Mother Jones,* November/December 2016; see also "Trump Insider Exposes Bushes and Clintons," YouTube.com (Alex Jones Channel), November 9, 2015 (youtube.com); also "Alex Jones and Donald Trump Bombshell Full Interview," YouTube.com, December 2, 2015.

p. 283 **Jones later claimed:** See Sam Levine, "Conspiracy Theorist Alex Jones Boasts About Advising Donald Trump," *Huffington Post,* September 3, 2016; also see "Alex Jones Says He 'Personally Talked to' Trump and Encouraged Him to Push Rigged Election Conspiracy Theory," *Media Matters,* August 31, 2016.

p. 283 **"The kind of conspiracism":** See David Neiwert, "At Trump Events, Conspiracist-Devised 'Hillary for Prison' Chant Becomes an Obsessive Theme," *Orcinus,* September 6, 2016.

p. 284 **When Cruz finally folded:** See David Neiwert, "Right-Wing Extremists Hail the Ascension of 'Emperor Trump' as GOP Nominee," *Hatewatch,* May 6, 2016.

p. 285 **Anglin, posting at:** See Andrew Anglin, "For Jews, Trump Win Is Like Another Holocaust," *Daily Stormer,* May 4, 2016.

p. 285 **Other white supremacists:** See Brian Tashman, "David Duke Hails Donald Trump for Thwarting the 'Jewish Supremacists Who Control Our Country'," *Right Wing Watch,* May 4, 2016.

p. 286 **Trump rebuked:** See Maggie Haberman, "Donald Trump 'Disavows' David Duke's Remarks on 'Jewish Extremists'," *New York Times,* May 5, 2016.

p. 286 **James Kirkpatrick:** See James Kirkpatrick, "Trump Victorious as GOP Transformed into a National Conservative Party," *VDare,* May 4, 2016.

p. 286 **Matthew Heimbach:** See David Neiwert, "Right-Wing Extremists Hail the Ascension of 'Emperor Trump' as GOP Nominee," *Hatewatch,* May 6, 2016.

p. 287 **Matthew Heimbach told reporters:** See Brendan O'Connor, "White Nationalists at the RNC Don't Think Trump Goes Far Enough," *Gawker,* July 18, 2016.

p. 287 **A contingent of armed militiamen:** See Peter Larson, "This Militia Group Walked Around the RNC with AR-15s, AK-47s, and G3s," *Vice,* July 18, 2016.

p. 287 **Inside the convention hall:** See Josh Israel, "Everything You Need To Know About the Extremists Who Will Highlight Trump's Republican Convention," *Think Progress,* July 14, 2016; also see Elizabeth Dias, "Trump's Prosperity Preachers," *Time,* April 14, 2016.

p. 287 **The most noteworthy:** See David Neiwert, "Sheriff David Clarke Plays a Straight-Talking Cop on Cable TV, But His Agenda Springs From Far-Right Extremism," *Hatewatch,* October 30, 2015.

p. 288   **Spurred in part:** See "FULL SPEECH: Sheriff David A. Clarke Jr. Republican National Convention," YouTube.com, July 18, 2016.

p. 288   **Sarah Posner of Mother Jones:** See Sarah Posner, "How Donald Trump's New Campaign Chief Created an Online Haven for White Nationalists," *Mother Jones*, August 22, 2016; also see "Exploring the Nationalistic and Christian Right Influences on Trump," *Fresh Air*, National Public Radio, February 2, 2017; also see Sarah Posner and David Neiwert, "How Trump Took Hate Groups Mainstream," *Mother Jones*, October 14, 2016.

p. 288   **Richard Spencer was there:** See Sarah Posner, "Meet the Alt-Right 'Spokesman' Who's Thrilled with Trump's Rise," *Rolling Stone*, October 18, 2016.

p. 289   **At a screening:** See Sarah Posner, "How Donald Trump's New Campaign Chief Created an Online Haven for White Nationalists," *Mother Jones*, August 22, 2016.

p. 289   **Three weeks later:** See Jonathan Martin, Jim Rutenberg, and Maggie Haberman, "Donald Trump Appoints Media Firebrand to Run Campaign," *New York Times*, August 17, 2016.

Chapter 12: The Id Unleashed

p. 291   **In the summer of 2016:** See Eder Kampuzano, "Oregon Man Who Drove Swastika-Emblazoned Truck Repaints to Support Donald Trump," *Oregonian*, September 7, 2016; also see Brad Reed, "'Do the White Thing': Infamous Oregon neo-Nazi Covers His Truck in Racist Pro-Trump Slogans," *Raw Story*, September 8, 2016.

p. 291   **He described:** See Shane Dixon Kavanaugh, "Pro-Trump Swastika Truck Is Driving Up and Down the West Coast," *Vocativ*, September 7, 2016.

p. 292   **"We interpret that as an endorsement":** See Jessica Schulberg, "Trump's Neo-Nazi and Jewish Backers Are Both Convinced He's Secretly on Their Side," *Huffington Post*, May 26, 2016.

p. 292   **Pendergraft endorsed:** Author's email exchange with Pendergraft, August 25, 2016, and October 7, 2016.

p. 293   **In late August:** See Hunter Wallace, "The Case for Trump: Visibility, Eroding Taboos, Coming Out," *Occidental Dissent*, August 21, 2016.

p. 294   **The violent trend began:** See Ben Mathis-Lilley, "A Continually Growing List of Violent Incidents at Trump Events," *Slate*, April 25, 2016.

p. 294   **After a March 9, 2016, rally:** See Justin Wm. Moyer, Jenny Starrs, and Sarah Larimer, "Trump Supporter Charged after Sucker-Punching Protester at North Carolina Rally," *Washington Post*, March 11, 2016.

p. 294   **In Cedar Rapids, Iowa:** See Nolan D. McCaskill, "Trump Urges Crowd to 'Knock the Crap out of' Anyone with Tomatoes," *Politico*, February 1, 2016; also see Michael E. Miller, "Donald Trump on a Protester:

'I'd like to Punch Him in the Face'," *Washington Post,* February 23, 2016; also see Ashley Parker, "In 'Good Old Days,' Donald Trump Says, Campaign Protesters Got More Than Just an Escort Out," *New York Times,* February 27, 2016.

p. 294 **But when Jake Tapper confronted him:** See Hannah Levintovah, "After Violence, Trump Says Protesters at His Rallies Are 'Bad Dudes'," *Mother Jones,* March 11, 2016. Also see "Transcript of Republican Debate in Miami, Full Text," CNN, March 10, 2016.

p. 294 **A video of flag-waving:** See David Ferguson, "'Burn Every Single Ni**er!': This Is How Trump Supporters Talk When They Think Nobody's Listening," *Raw Story,* August 17, 2016.

p. 295 **Such vicious ideas were soon expressed:** See "US Hate Crimes Up 20 Percent in 2016, Fueled by Election Campaign: Report," Reuters, March 14, 2017.

p. 295 **Those fears were realized:** See Reuters and *Vice News,* "The Boston Bros Who Said 'Trump Was Right' after Beating and Pissing on a Mexican Man Are Headed to Prison," *Vice,* May 17, 2016.

p. 295 **Trump responded:** See Donald Trump, Twitter.com, August 21, 2015, twitter.com/realDonaldTrump/status/634765744673267712.

p. 295 **But the next day:** See Justin Wm. Moyer, "Trump Says Fans Are 'Very Passionate' after Hearing One of Them Allegedly Assaulted Hispanic Man," *Washington Post,* August 21, 2015.

p. 295 **Muslims were a special target:** See Christopher Mathias, "Police Are Looking for an Alleged Trump Supporter Who Attacked a Muslim Woman," *Huffington Post,* May 3, 2016; also see Josh Marshall, "Crazed Trumper Assaults Muslim Women in Brooklyn," *Talking Points Memo,* September 10, 2016.

p. 296 **The evidence was not merely anecdotal:** See Engy Abdelkader, "When Islamophobia Turns Violent: The 2016 U.S. Presidential Elections," *Bridge Initiative* (Georgetown University Center for Muslim-Christian Understanding), May 2016.

p. 296 **The Monday after the tragedy:** See Jeremy Diamond, "Donald Trump: Ban All Muslim Travel to US," CNN, December 8, 2015.

p. 297 **It's impossible to establish:** See David Neiwert, "A Firestorm of Vicious Behavior Toward Muslims Rages in the Wake of San Bernardino Rampage," *Hatewatch,* December 10, 2015.

p. 298 **Trump's wink-wink suggestions:** See Nick Corasaniti and Maggie Haberman, "Donald Trump Suggests 'Second Amendment People' Could Act against Hillary Clinton," *New York Times,* August 9, 2016.

p. 298 **"This is a political movement":** See "Trump on Uproar Over 2nd Amendment Remark: 'Give Me a Break'," *Fox News Insider,* August 9, 2016.

p. 298 **Unchastened, Trump:** See Sean Sullivan and Jenna Johnson, "Trump: Clinton's Bodyguards Should 'Disarm Immediately' and 'See What Happens to her'," *Washington Post,* September 16, 2016.

p. 298   **He understood the importance:** See Jesse Byrnes, "Trump Supporter Fears 'Civil War' if Clinton Wins," *The Hill*, August 16, 2016.

p. 299   **Hillary Clinton was not:** See Alan Rappeport, "Hillary Clinton Denounces the 'Alt-Right,' and the Alt-Right Is Thrilled," *New York Times*, August 26, 2016.

p. 299   **"The alt-right as a moniker of resistance":** See David Weigel, "The Alt-Right's Take on Clinton's Speech: Botched, but Legitimizing," *Washington Post*, August 28, 2016.

p. 300   **However, the speech also led:** Author's interview with Potok, September 20, 2016.

p. 300   **On September 9:** See Angie Drobnic Holan, "In Context: Hillary Clinton and the 'Basket of Deplorables'," *PolitiFact*, September 11, 2016.

p. 301   **On CNN with Wolf Blitzer:** See Philip Bump, "Mike Pence Declines to Say whether David Duke Is 'Deplorable' Because He 'Is Not in the Name-Calling Business'," *Washington Post*, September 12, 2016.

p. 301   **Clinton soon apologized:** See Angie Drobnic Holan, "In Context: Hillary Clinton and the 'Basket of Deplorables'," *PolitiFact*, September 11, 2016.

p. 301   **The political analyst Nate Silver:** See "How Many of Trump's Supporters Really Are 'Deplorable'?," *FiveThirtyEight*, September 14, 2016.

p. 301   **Donald Trump Jr.:** See Paulina Firozi, "Trump Jr. and Top Supporter Share White Nationalist Image on Social Media," *The Hill*, September 10, 2016.

p. 301   **Trump's dance with Birtherism:** See Nick Gass, "Trump Concedes Obama Was Born in the US," *Politico*, September 15, 2016.

p. 302   **With that, he urged:** See Cooper Allen, "Trump Birther Event Blasted as Hotel 'Infomercial'," *USA Today*, September 16, 2016.

p. 302   **Trump fared reasonably well:** See Stephen Collinson, "Clinton Puts Trump on Defense at First Debate," CNN, September 27, 2016.

p. 302   **Alt-righters groused:** See Dr. Patrick Slattery, "Debate Over, Media Commences Psy-Op Shilling for Abominable Shillary," *Daily Stormer*, September 27, 2016; also see Hunter Wallace, "Review: First 2016 Presidential Debate," *Occidental Dissent*, September 27, 2016; see also Andrew Anglin, "All Polls: Trump Won Debate," *Daily Stormer*, September 27, 2016.

p. 302   **Clinton eventually brought:** See Meghan Keneally, Veronica Stracqualursi, Shushannah Walshe, Meredith McGraw, and Julia Jacobo, "2nd Presidential Debate: 11 Moments That Mattered," ABC News, October 9, 2016; also see Aaron Blake, "The Final Trump-Clinton Debate Transcript, Annotated," *Washington Post*, October 19, 2016.

p. 304   **When it was all over:** See "Viewers Say Clinton Wins Second Debate," Gallup Polls, October 13, 2016; also see Anna Palmer and Jake Sherman, "Poll: Hillary Clinton Won the Second Debate," *Politico*, October 11, 2016.

p. 304   **That moment deeply disturbed:** See Charlie Savage, "Threat to Jail Clinton Smacks of 'Tin-Pot Dictators,' Experts Say," *New York Times*, October 10, 2016.

p. 304   **But his supporters:** See Andrew Anglin, "88%," *Daily Stormer*, October 10, 2016.

p. 304   **"November 8, we better":** See Linda Qiu, "Donald Trump's Baseless Claims about the Election Being 'Rigged'," *PolitiFact*, August 15, 2016.

p. 305   **After the second debate:** See Stephen Collinson, "Why Trump's Talk of a Rigged Vote Is So Dangerous," CNN, October 19, 2016.

p. 305   **He told the *New York Times*:** See Patrick Healy and Maggie Haberman, "Donald Trump Opens New Line of Attack on Hillary Clinton: Her Marriage," *New York Times*, September 30, 2016.

p. 305   **At a campaign rally in Green Bay:** See Jenna Johnson, "Donald Trump Says the Election Is 'Rigged.' Here's What His Supporters Think That Means," *Washington Post*, October 18, 2016.

p. 306   **Trump took a wildly conspiracist turn:** See Alex Kaplan, "Trump's Anti-Semitic Speech Came from Breitbart, the Alt-Right, and Alex Jones," *Media Matters*, October 14, 2016; also see "FULL: Donald Trump Speech in Columbus, OH.Oct. 13. 2016. Donald Trump Rally in Columbus today," YouTube.com, October 13, 2016.

p. 306   **So the subject:** See "Full Transcript: Third 2016 Presidential Debate," *Politico*, October 20, 2016.

p. 307   **Once again, polls found:** See Jennifer Agiesta, "Hillary Clinton Wins Third Presidential Debate, According to CNN / ORC Poll," CNN, October 20, 2016; see also "Clinton Wins Third Debate, Gains Ground as 'Presidential'," Gallup Polls, October 24, 2016.

p. 308   **SPLC'S Ryan Lenz:** See Ryan Lenz, "With Three Weeks to Go, Talk of 'Rigged Election' Leads to Promises of Violence," *Hatewatch*, October 20, 2016.

p. 308   **"You have 1.8 million people":** See " 'Hannity' Exclusive: Trump Talks WikiLeaks, Sexual Assault Allegations, Media Bias and the 'Rigged System'," *Fox Nation*, October 22, 2016.

p. 308   **He also now claimed:** See Darren Samuelson, "A Guide to Donald Trump's 'Rigged' Election," *Politico*, October 25, 2016.

p. 309   **Trump's followers came fervently to believe:** See Ben Schreckinger, "White Nationalists Plot Election Day Show of Force," *Politico*, November 2, 2016.

p. 309   **However, a number of:** See David Neiwert and Sarah Posner, "Meet the Horde of Neo-Nazis, Klansmen, and Other Extremist Leaders Endorsing Donald Trump," *Mother Jones*, September 21, 2016.

p. 310   **Stewart Rhodes has a sensitive:** See "Oath Keepers Promise to Patrol the Polls on Election Day," *Hatewatch*, October 26, 2016.

p. 310   **Another group of militiamen:** See Stephen Piggott, "3 Men

Arrested in Plot to Bomb Kansas Apartment Complex, Mosque Following Presidential Election," *Hatewatch*, October 14, 2016.

p. 311 **The plan was to position:** See Cleve R. Wootson Jr., "'It Will Be a Bloodbath': Inside the Kansas Militia Plot to Ignite a Religious War," *Washington Post*, October 15, 2016.

p. 311 **In the meantime:** See David Zucchino, "A Militia Gets Battle Ready for a 'Gun-Grabbing' Clinton Presidency," *New York Times*, November 4, 2016.

p. 312 **These sentiments:** See Zack Beauchamp, "Make America Violent Again: Trump's Rhetoric Could Cause Election Day Mayhem—and Worse," *Vox*, October 26, 2016.

p. 312 **"I will be there":** See Justin Mitchell and Andy Sullivan, "US Militia Girds for Trouble as Presidential Election Nears," Reuters, November 2, 2016.

p. 312 **That ended suddenly:** See Hal Bernton, "Jury Acquits Leaders of Malheur Wildlife-Refuge Standoff," *Seattle Times*, October 27, 2016; also see Allegra Kirkland, "Anti-Gov't Activists See Vindication in Acquittal of Oregon Occupiers," *Talking Points Memo*, October 28, 2016.

p. 312 **Still, outside the courtroom:** See Frad Barbash, " 'Off the Charts Unbelievable': Will Acquittal of Oregon Refuge Occupiers Embolden Extremists, Militias?," *Washington Post*, October 28, 2016.

p. 312 **Mainstream observers:** See Judy L. Thomas, "Monitors of Militant Groups Fear Bundy Verdict in Oregon Could Embolden Extremists," *Kansas City Star*, October 28, 2016.

p. 313 **Jessica Campbell:** See Zoe Carpenter, "The Bundy Acquittal Is Dangerous," *Nation*, November 1, 2016.

p. 313 **"This is it, folks":** See David Jackson, "Trump Conducts Election Eve Campaign Marathon," *USA Today*, November 7, 2016.

p. 313 **He also kept refusing:** See Jacob Pramuk, "On Election Day, Trump Still Says It's 'Largely a Rigged System'," CNBC, November 8, 2016.

p. 313 **A Sky News reporter:** See Ajay Nair, "'She's Going to Prison!' Trump Supporter Warns of 'Rebellion' if Clinton Becomes President," *Express*, November 5, 2016.

p. 314 **Clinton had already called Trump:** See "Here's the Full Text of Donald Trump's Victory Speech," CNN, November 9, 2016.

Chapter 13: The Aftermath

p. 317 **To the Children of Satan:** See an example of this letter at Hailey Branson-Potts, "Letters Threatening Genocide against Muslims and Praising Trump Sent to Multiple California Mosques," *Los Angeles Times*, November 26, 2016.

p. 317 **Heidi Beirich:** Author's email exchange with Beirich, January 11, 2017.

p. 318   **Every day they poured in:** All examples are taken directly from the Southern Poverty Law Center's post-election hate incident database. See "Update: 1,094 Bias-Related Incidents in the Month following the Election," *Hatewatch*, December 16, 2016; also see "Post-Election Bias Incidents up to 1,372; New Collaboration with ProPublica," *Hatewatch*, February 10, 2017.

p. 319   **The most striking pattern:** The author obtained this statistic by combing through the Southern Poverty Law Center's post-election hate incident database.

p. 319   **When asked:** See Amy B. Wang, " 'Stop It,' Trump Tells Supporters Who Are Spreading Hate. Is It Enough?," *Washington Post*, November 14, 2016.

p. 320   **Most Trump supporters:** See Sara Rathod, "Militia Groups Are Basking in Trump's Victory," *Mother Jones*, November 10, 2016.

p. 321   **Several of Trump's alt-right:** See Ben Collins, "Alt-Right Declares Total Victory: 'We're the Establishment Now'," *Daily Beast*, November 9, 2016.

p. 321   **Andrew Anglin:** See Andrew Anglin, "We Won," *Daily Stormer*, November 9, 2016.

p. 321   **However, very few political analysts:** See Michael J. Coren, "I Read Hundreds of Articles about Why Donald Trump Won and What's Coming Next. Here Are the Best," *Medium*, December 16, 2016.

p. 321   **FBI Director James Comey's:** See Rebecca Savransky, "Nate Silver: Clinton 'Almost Certainly' Would've Won before FBI Letter," *The Hill*, December 11, 2016.

p. 321   **The news that Russian:** See Arsad Mohammed and Jonathan Landay, "U.S. Obtained Evidence after Election That Russia Leaked Emails: Officials," Reuters, January 4, 2017.

p. 321   **A flood of fake news:** See "How Online Hoaxes and Fake News Played a Role in the Election," *PBS Newshour*, November 17, 2016; also see Craig Silverman, "This Analysis Shows How Viral Fake Election News Stories Outperformed Real News on Facebook," *BuzzFeed*, November 16, 2016; also see Craig Timberg, "Russian Propaganda Effort Helped Spread 'Fake News' during Election, Experts Say," *Washington Post*, November 24, 2016.

p. 322   **Analysts gleaned some meaning:** See Philip Bump, "Donald Trump Will Be President Thanks to 80,000 People in Three States," *Washington Post*, December 1, 2016.

p. 322   **However, that analysis papered over:** See Janet Adamy and Paul Overberg, "Places Most Unsettled by Rapid Demographic Change Are Drawn to Donald Trump," *Wall Street Journal*, November 1, 2016.

p. 324   **Overall, Trump won among:** See Jon Henley, "White and Wealthy Voters Gave Victory to Donald Trump, Exit Polls Show," *Guardian*, November 9, 2016.

p. 324 **One of the persistent myths:** See "Roots of Hate: Recent Studies Sharply Challenge the Notion That Hate Crimes—or Hate Groups—Are Linked to Economic Hardship," *Intelligence Report*, Southern Poverty Law Center, March 2, 2002, splcenter.org.

p. 324 **This was particularly illustrated:** See Michele Stacey, Kristin Carbone-López, Richard Rosenfeld, "Demographic Change and Ethnically Motivated Crime: The Impact of Immigration on Anti-Hispanic Hate Crime in the United States," *Journal of Contemporary Criminal Justice*, 27, no. 3, July 19, 2011.

p. 324 **"There are a couple of things":** See Chauncey DeVega, "Trump's Election Has Created 'Safe Spaces' for Racists: Southern Poverty Law Center's Heidi Beirich on the Wave of Hate Crimes," *Salon*, March 8, 2017.

p. 324 **The contemporary Klan:** Author's email exchange with Rachel Pendergraft, October 7, 2016.

p. 325 **"Critics See":** See Michael D. Shear, Maggie Haberman, and Michael S. Schmidt, "Critics See Stephen Bannon, Trump's Pick for Strategist, as Voice of Racism," *New York Times*, November 14, 2016.

p. 325 **The Anti-Defamation League:** See Jose A. DelReal, "Trump Draws Sharp Rebuke, Concerns over Newly Appointed Chief White House Strategist Stephen Bannon," *Washington Post*, November 13, 2016.

p. 325 **David Duke told CNN:** See Andrew Kaczynski and Chris Massie, "White Nationalists See Advocate in Steve Bannon Who Will Hold Trump to His Campaign Promises," CNN, November 15, 2016.

p. 325 **Bannon helped defuse:** See Kimberly A. Strassel, "Steve Bannon on Politics as War," *Wall Street Journal*, November 18, 2016.

p. 326 **Michael Flynn:** See Stephen Piggott, "Trump's National Security Advisor's Twitter Account Shows Extent of Anti-Muslim Beliefs," *Hatewatch*, December 20, 2016; also see Julian Hattem, "Trump's Pick for Security Adviser Praised Controversial 'Alt-Right' Figure," *The Hill*, November 29, 2016.

p. 326 **Senator Jeff Sessions:** See Stephen Piggott, "Jeff Sessions: Champion of Anti-Muslim and Anti-Immigrant Extremists," *Hatewatch*, November 18, 2016; also see "New HRC Report Details Jeff Sessions' Alarming Anti-LGBTQ Record," Human Rights Campaign, January 9, 2017; also see Mark Potok, "Sessions' Embrace of Racist Law One More Reason to Reject His Confirmation as Attorney General," *Hatewatch*, January 31, 2017; also see Emily Bazelon, "The Voter Fraud Case Jeff Sessions Lost and Can't Escape," *New York Times Magazine*, January 9, 2017.

p. 326 **Rex Tillerson:** See Josh Rogin, "Inside Rex Tillerson's Long Romance with Russia," *Washington Post*, December 13, 2016; also see Matt Egan, Julia Horowitz, and Chris Isidore, "Behind the Deep Ties between Exxon's Rex Tillerson and Russia," CNN, December 11, 2016; also see Andrew E. Kramer and Clifford Krauss, "Rex Tillerson's Company,

Exxon, Has Billions at Stake Over Sanctions on Russia," *New York Times,* December 12, 2016.

p. 326 **Betsy DeVos:** See Catherine Brown and Ulrich Boser, "The DeVos Dynasty: A Family of Extremists," Center for American Progress, January 23, 2017; also see Kristina Rizga, "Betsy DeVos Wants to Use America's Schools to Build 'God's Kingdom'," *Mother Jones,* March/April 2017.

p. 327 **Scott Pruitt:** See Marianne Lavell, "Scientists Call Out Pruitt's False View of Climate Change," *Inside Climate News,* March 13, 2017.

p. 327 **Sonny Perdue:** See Natasha Geiling, "Trump Fills His Final Cabinet Post with Another Climate Denier," *Think Progress,* January 19, 2017.

p. 327 **All these developments:** See Pema Levy, "White Nationalists Celebrate Trump's Victory and Early Appointments," *Mother Jones,* November 19, 2016.

p. 327 **Spencer and his cohorts decided:** See Joseph Goldstein, "Alt-Right Gathering Exults in Trump Election with Nazi-Era Salute," *New York Times,* November 20, 2016; also see Katie Glueck, "Alt-right Celebrates Trump's Election at DC Meeting," *Politico,* November 19, 2016.

p. 328 **Spencer shrugged off:** See Lindsey Ellefson, "For White People, 'It's Conquer or Die': Richard Spencer Defends 'Hail Trump' Salute," *Mediaite,* March 8, 2017.

p. 328 **On November 23:** See "Donald Trump's *New York Times* Interview: Full Transcript," *New York Times,* November 23, 2016.

p. 328 **Jones also defended:** See Paul Joseph Watson, "Report: Three Million Votes in Presidential Election Cast by Illegal Aliens," *Infowars,* November 14, 2016; also see "Proof Donald Trump Won the Popular Vote," YouTube.com, November 23, 2016; also see Alison Graves, "Fact-Check: Did 3 Million Undocumented Immigrants Vote in This Year's Election?," *PunditFact,* November 8, 2016.

p. 329 **The president-elect himself:** See Cleve R. Wootson Jr., "Donald Trump: 'I Won the Popular Vote If You Deduct the Millions of People Who Voted Illegally'," *Washington Post,* November 27, 2016.

p. 329 **Trump cited Philips:** See "Knock the Vote: Zero Evidence Has Been Put Forth to Support the Widely Parroted Claim that 3 Million 'Illegal Aliens' Voted in the 2016 Presidential Election," Snopes.com, November 16, 2016.

p. 329 **The national media:** See Philip Bump, "The Twitter-Born Conspiracy Theory Driving Donald Trump's Explanation for Losing the Popular Vote," *Washington Post,* January 27, 2017.

p. 329 **Trump spokesperson:** See Erik Wemple, "CNN Commentator Scottie Nell Hughes: Facts No Longer Exist," *Washington Post,* December 1, 2016.

p. 330 **In November, just before the election:** See Celia Kang, "Fake News Onslaught Targets Pizzeria as Nest of Child-Trafficking," *New York Times,* November 21, 2016.

p. 330 **A month later:** See Eric Lipton, "Man Motivated by 'Pizzagate' Conspiracy Theory Arrested in Washington Gunfire," *New York Times*, December 5, 2016.

p. 330 **One of the theories' chief promoters:** A search for "Pizzagate" at Infowars.com produced about 100 entries in July 2017; typical headlines include "Pizzagate Is Global," December 1, 2016, and "Pizzagate: The Mysterious Death of a Human Trafficking Investigator," December 3, 2016. Also see Jon Browne, "Pizzagate: The Bigger Picture," *Infowars*, December 1, 2016.

p. 330 **Alefantis told:** See Celia Kang, "Fake News Onslaught Targets Pizzeria as Nest of Child-Trafficking," *New York Times*, November 21, 2016.

p. 331 **The claims kept ratcheting:** See Glenn Kessler, " 'Pizzagate' Rumors Falsely Link Death of Sex-Worker Advocate to Nonexistent Clinton Probe," *Washington Post*, December 6, 2016.

p. 331 **Soon, even nearby businesses:** See "'Pizzagate' Shows How Fake News Hurts Real People," *Washington Post* (editorial), November 25, 2016.

p. 331 **On his Facebook page:** See Tim Mak, "'Pizzagate' Gunman Liked Alex Jones," *Daily Beast*, December 4, 2016.

p. 331 **Soon it came out:** See "13-Year-Old Struck by Vehicle in Salisbury, Airlifted to Hospital," WBTV-TV (Charlotte, NC), October 24, 2016.

p. 331 **The theories also were promoted:** See Allegra Kirkland, "How 'Pizzagate' Evolved from a Fringe Online Conspiracy to a Real-Life Threat," *Talking Points Memo*, December 5, 2016.

p. 332 **Some alt-right figures:** See Brian Tashman, "Alex Jones Defends 'Pizzagate' Truthers after Conspiracy Theory Leads to Armed Attack," *Right Wing Watch*, December 5, 2016.

p. 332 **Alefantis remained:** See Faiz Siddiqui and Susan Svrluga, "NC Man Told Police He Went to DC Pizzeria with Gun to Investigate Conspiracy Theory," *Washington Post*, December 5, 2016.

p. 332 **Spencer's Hitler-like salute:** See "A Truce in the Battle for the Soul of American White Nationalism?," *Hatewatch*, December 20, 2016.

p. 333 **The two discussed ways:** See David Neiwert, "Small-Town Montana Residents Organize to Oppose Presence of White Nationalists," *Hatewatch*, November 19, 2014.

p. 333 **While this correspondence was taking place:** See David Winter, "We Investigate: Whitefish, Family Torn Apart by White Nationalist's Notoriety," ABC/Fox Montana (Missoula, MT), December 12, 2016.

p. 333 **Then Andrew Anglin became:** See Chuck Tanner, "White Nationalist Group Targets Whitefish, Montana," Institute for Research and Education on Human Rights, December 25, 2016; also see "Website Author Fills Out Permit Paperwork for March against Whitefish Jews," ABC/Fox Montana (Missoula, MT), January 2, 2016; updated January 26, 2016.

p. 333 **Anglin stated:** See Chuck Tanner, "White Nationalist Announces Plans to Bus White Power Skinheads to Whitefish," Institute for Research and Education on Human Rights, December 29, 2016.

p. 334 **Anglin's threats:** See Christine Hauser, "After Neo-Nazi Posting, Police in Whitefish, Mont., Step Up Patrols," *New York Times*, December 20, 2016.

p. 334 **The concerns in the community:** See Vince Devlin and Andrew Schneider, "White Nationalist Spencer Says He May Seek Zinke's Seat," *Missoulian* (MT), December 16, 2016; also see Kurtis Lee, "White Nationalist Richard Spencer Considers a Run for Congressional Seat," *Los Angeles Times*, December 20, 2016.

p. 334 **Tellingly, the state organization:** See David Neiwert, "Montana Republicans Warmly Embrace a White Nationalist's Legislative Candidacy," *Hatewatch*, October 10, 2016.

p. 334 **Other Montana politicians:** See Eric M. Johnson and Keith Coffmann, "Montana Lawmakers Denounce Plans for Neo-Nazi Rally," Reuters, December 27, 2016.

p. 334 **Spencer attempted to tamp down:** See "White Nationalists Roil Small Montana Town With Threats, Vow to March," YouTube.com, January 3, 2017.

p. 336 **The threats created:** See "Whitefish, Montana's Most Infamous Resident," *Anderson Cooper 360* (CNN), December 15, 2016; see also David Weigel, "Montana Governor, Legislators Condemn Plans for White-Nationalist March," *Washington Post*, December 27, 2016; also see Eli Sanders, "Neo-Nazis Postpone Threatened Rally in Whitefish, Montana," *The Stranger*, January 12, 2017; see also Anne Helen Petersen, "Neo-Nazis Came for This Small Town: Can You Keep Them from Coming for Yours?," *BuzzFeed*, February 12, 2017.

p. 336 **Marches and protests:** See Euan McKirdy, "Thousands Take to the Streets to Protest Trump Win," CNN, November 10, 2016; see also Madison Park, Ralph Ellis, Khushbu Shah, and Azadeh Ansari, "Anti-Trump Protests Move Through Fifth Day," CNN, November 14, 2016; see also Abigail Hauslohner and Mark Berman, "Anti-Trump Demonstrators Say Nationwide Protests Are 'Just a Taste of Things to Come'," *Washington Post*, November 16, 2016.

p. 336 **In Oakland:** See Max Blau, Euan McKirdy, and Holly Yan, "Protesters Target Trump Buildings in Massive Street Rallies," CNN, November 11, 2016; also see Jim Ryan, "Portland's Anti-Trump Protest Turns Violent, as Rioters Rampage in Pearl," *Oregonian*, November 10, 2016 (updated November 11, 2016).

p. 336 **Trump supporters and Fox News:** See " 'Professional Protesters' Riot Over Trump's Election, Attacking Bystanders and Vandalizing Cars, Property," *Fox News*, November 11, 2016.

p. 336 **The paranoia among:** See David Neiwert, "'Communist Takeover'

Paranoia Gets a Final Resuscitation for Trump's Inauguration," *Hate-watch*, January 17, 2017.

p. 337 **Other right-wing conspiracists:** See David Neiwert, "'Communist Takeover' Paranoia Gets a Final Resuscitation for Trump's Inauguration," *Hatewatch*, January 17, 2017.

p. 337 **Many were the same militiamen:** See Justin Mitchell and Andy Sullivan, "U.S. Militia Girds for Trouble as Presidential Election Nears," Reuters, November 2, 2016.

p. 338 **In 2013:** See Mark Potok, "White Hot: For the Radical Right, Obama Victory Brings Fury and Fear," *Intelligence Report*, February 14, 2013.

p. 338 **"What I am hearing":** See " 'Health Ranger' Adams Warns of Communist Plan to Mount Inauguration-Day Coup," YouTube, January 16, 2017

p. 338 **Instead, Refuse Fascism:** See David Neiwert, "'Communist Takeover' Paranoia Gets a Final Resuscitation for Trump's Inauguration," *Hatewatch*, January 17, 2017.

p. 338 **An alt-right event:** See David Neiwert, "Alt-Right Event in Seattle Devolves into Chaos and Violence Outside, Truth-Twisting Inside," *Hatewatch*, January 23, 2017.

The *Seattle Times* reported: See Katherine Long, Lynn Thompson, and Jessica Lee, "Man Shot during Protests of Breitbart Editor Milo Yiannopoulos' Speech at UW; Suspect Arrested," *Seattle Times*, January 20, 2017.

p. 340 **Upon being told:** See Katherine Long, Lynn Thompson, and Jessica Lee, "Man Shot during Protests of Breitbart Editor Milo Yiannopoulos' Speech at UW; Suspect Arrested," *Seattle Times*, January 20, 2017.

p. 340 **Yiannopoulos' pronouncement:** See "At UW, Milo Misleadingly Portrays Alt-Right as the Victims of Shooting Outside," YouTube.com, January 21, 2017.

p. 340 **Breitbart News:** See Lucas Nolan, "Suspect in Shooting Outside MILO Event Claims Self Defence, Released Without Charges," *Breitbart News*, January 21, 2017.

p. 341 **One of Milo's young fans:** See "At UW, Milo Misleadingly Portrays Alt-Right as the Victims of Shooting Outside," YouTube.com, January 21, 2017.

p. 341 **That was underscored:** See Sean Nelson, "UW Republicans to Protestors After Shooting: 'It's Time Your Flame Is Put Out'," *The Stranger*, January 25, 2017.

p. 341 **Police eventually charged:** See David Neiwert, "Husband and Wife Accused of Planning Violence in Shooting at UW Milo Protest," *Hatewatch*, April 26, 2017. Footage captured by the author at the protest played a critical role in the decision to file charges.

p. 342 **Meanwhile, the Women's Marches:** See Sophie Tatum, "Women's

March on Washington: What You Need to Know," CNN, January 17, 2017; see also Anemona Hartocollis and Yamiche Alcindor, "Women's March Highlights as Huge Crowds Protest Trump: 'We're Not Going Away'," *New York Times,* January 21, 2017; see also Perry Stein, Steve Hendrix, and Abigail Hauslohner, "Women's Marches: More Than One Million Protesters Vow to Resist President Trump," *Washington Post,* January 22, 2017; see also Kaveh Waddell, "The Exhausting Work of Tallying America's Largest Protest," *Atlantic,* January 23, 2017.

p. 342 **The protests aggravated:** See Donald J. Trump (@realDonald Trump), Twitter, January 22, 2017, 4:47 a.m., twitter.com/realDonald Trump/status/823150055418920960.

p. 342 **The day after the inauguration:** See Chris Cilizza, "Sean Spicer Held a Press Conference. He Didn't Take Questions. Or Tell the Whole Truth," *Washington Post,* January 21, 2017.

p. 343 **The *Washington Post* conducted:** See Brian Schaffner and Samantha Luks, "This Is What Trump Voters Said When Asked to Compare His Inauguration Crowd with Obama's," *Washington Post,* January 25, 2017.

p. 343 **Trump's longtime adviser:** See "Conway: Press Secretary Gave 'Alternative Facts'," *Meet the Press* (NBC News), January 22, 2017.

p. 343 **The bomb threats:** See JTA, "This Is What a JCC Bomb Threat Sounds Like," *Jewish Journal,* February 1, 2017.

p. 344 **The threats forced evacuations:** See "At Least 17 Bomb Threats Called In to JCCs Nationwide in Third Wave of Harassment," *Jewish Telegraphic Agency,* January 31, 2017; see also "Scores of Jewish Community Centers Received Bomb Threats in the Last Month," *Hatewatch,* February 22, 2017.

p. 344 **On February 20:** See "Another Wave of Bomb Threats Hit Jewish Institutions, Worrying and Uniting Communities," *Hatewatch,* February 28, 2017.

p. 344 **In the meantime:** See "Post-Election Bias Incidents up to 1,372; New Collaboration with ProPublica," *Hatewatch,* February 10, 2017.

p. 344 **During a joint press conference:** See "Remarks by President Trump and Prime Minister Netanyahu of Israel in Joint Press Conference," The White House, Office of the Press Secretary, February 15, 2017.

p. 345 **The next day:** See "Full Transcript: President Donald Trump's News Conference," CNN, February 17, 2017. See also David Neiwert, "Trump Still Refusing to Address Post-Election Wave of Anti-Semitism, Hate Incidents," *Hatewatch,* February 17, 2017.

p. 346 **Finally, as the press:** See Julie Hirschfield Davis, "In First, Trump Condemns Rise in Anti-Semitism, Calling It 'Horrible'," *New York Times,* February 21, 2017.

p. 346 **The FBI is investigating:** See Mark Berman, "FBI Investigating Shooting of Two Indian Men in Kansas as a Hate Crime," *Washington Post,* February 28, 2017.

p. 346   **The shootings set off:** See Annie Gowen, " 'Everyone's Nervous': Some Students in India Rethink US Study Plans after Kansas Shooting," *Washington Post*, February 25, 2017; also see Shashank Bengali, "Kansas Shooting Shocks an Indian City Where 'Every Other House' Has Someone in America," *Los Angeles Times*, February 24, 2017.

p. 346   **On February 28:** See "Remarks by President Trump in Joint Address to Congress," The White House, Office of the Press Secretary, February 28, 2017.

p. 347   **Earlier in the day:** See David Neiwert, "Trump Condemns Attacks On Jews—After Earlier Suggesting They Are Meant to Make Him Look Bad," *Hatewatch*, March 1, 2017.

p. 347   **But the alt-right knew:** See Andrew Anglin, "Glorious Leader Donald Trump Calls Out "Anti-Semitic Attacks" as False Flag Hoaxes!," *Daily Stormer*, February 28, 2017.

p. 348   **Trump's first real foray:** See Amy B. Wang, "Trump Asked for a 'Muslim Ban,' Giuliani Says—and Ordered a Commission to Do It 'Legally'," *Washington Post*, January 29, 2017; also see Kyle Blaine and Julia Horowitz, "How the Trump Administration Chose the 7 Countries in the Immigration Executive Order," CNN, January 30, 2017.

p. 348   **Several states sued to block:** See Alexander Burns, "Legal Challenges Mount Against Trump's Travel Ban," *New York Times*, January 30, 2017.

p. 348   **The federal judges:** See Fred Barbash and Derek Hawkins, "Trump's Loose Talk about Muslims Gets Weaponized in Court against Travel Ban," *Washington Post*, February 7, 2017.

p. 349   **The judges' rulings:** See Amy B. Wang, "Trump Lashes Out at 'So-Called Judge' Who Temporarily Blocked Travel Ban," *Washington Post*, February 4, 2017.

p. 349   **Yet Trump's legal arguments:** See Adam Liptak, "Court Refuses to Reinstate Travel Ban, Dealing Trump Another Legal Loss," *New York Times*, February 9, 2017.

p. 349   **That weekend:** See Josh Harkinson, "Trump's Newest Senior Adviser Seen as a White Nationalist Ally," *Mother Jones*, December 14, 2016.

p. 349   **"The president's powers":** See Tom Howell Jr., "In Power Struggle with Judicial Branch, Trump Pursues 'All Options' to Extreme Vetting," *Washington Times*, February 12, 2017.

p. 349   **A week later:** See "Stephen Miller Says Trump's New Travel Ban Will Be 'Fundamentally' the Same as His First Travel Ban," *The Week*, February 22, 2017; also see Betsy Woodruff, "Stephen Miller May Have Made It Easier to Sue Trump's Travel Ban," *Daily Beast*, March 15, 2017.

p. 349   **On March 6, Trump filed:** See David Neiwert, "Trump's Second Travel Ban Once Again Misidentifies Source of Domestic Terrorist Threat," *Hatewatch*, March 13, 2017.

p. 350 **Thousands of open government jobs:** See Jonathan Karl and Jordyn Phelps, "Trump's Empty Administration: What's Behind the High Number of Vacant Government Jobs," ABC News, June 16, 2017.

p. 350 **At a contentious February 16:** See "Full Transcript: President Donald Trump's News Conference," CNN, February 17, 2017.

p. 351 **The next morning:** See Michael M. Grynbaum, "Trump Calls the News Media the 'Enemy of the American People'," *New York Times*, February 17, 2017.

p. 351 **On March 4, he launched:** See Jana Heigl, "A Timeline of Donald Trump's False Wiretapping Charge," *PolitiFact*, March 21, 2017.

p. 351 **It later emerged:** The story in question is by Joel B. Pollak, "Mark Levin to Congress: Investigate Obama's 'Silent Coup' vs. Trump," *Breitbart News*, March 3, 2017.

p. 351 **Fact-checkers:** See Glenn Kessler, "Trump's 'Evidence' for Obama Wiretap Claims Relies on Sketchy, Anonymously Sourced Reports," *Washington Post*, March 5, 2017.

p. 351 **James Clapper:** See "Former DNI James Clapper: 'I Can Deny' Wiretap of Trump Tower," NBC News, March 5, 2017.

p. 352 **Sean Spicer spun:** See Jeremy Diamond, "Spicer: Trump Didn't Mean Wiretapping When He Tweeted about Wiretapping," CNN, March 14, 2017.

p. 352 **Intelligence officials in the UK:** See Peter Baker and Steven Erlanger, "Trump Offers No Apology for Claim on British Spying," *New York Times*, March 17, 2017.

p. 352 **Conway herself had grown:** See Mary Kay Linge, "Conway: 'Alternative Fact' Critics Are 'F—Ing Miserable' People," *New York Post*, March 18, 2017.

p. 353 **By mid-March, according to Gallup:** See Jessica Estepa, "Poll: President Trump's Approval Rating Hits a New Low," *USA Today*, March 20, 2017.

p. 353 **And yet in the places:** See Russell Berman, "Where Trump's Popularity Matters—and Where It Doesn't," *Atlantic*, March 15, 2017; see also Nikita Vladimirov, "Two New Polls Find Wildly Different Trump Approval Ratings," *The Hill*, February 16, 2017; also see Cynthia Tucker, "Trump's Supporters Still Back Him, Regardless of His Lies," *UExpress*, March 16, 2017.

p. 353 **"I think he's doing good":** See Jerry Zremski, "Die-Hard Local Trump Voters Stand By Their Man," *Buffalo News*, February 27, 2017.

p. 354 **Other experts on authoritarianism:** See Timothy Snyder, *On Tyranny: Twenty Lessons from the Twentieth Century* (New York: Tim Duggan Books, 2016), p. xx.

p. 354 **Snyder sees Trump's insistence:** See Sean Illing, "'Post-Truth Is Pre-Fascism': A Holocaust Historian on the Trump Era," *Vox*, March 9, 2017.

p. 354 **The political reality on the ground:** See Ezra Klein, "Donald Trump Is Dangerous When He's Losing," *Vox*, February 22, 2017.

Afterword: Fascism and Our Future

p. 356 **One commonly, and wrongly:** See Chip Berlet, "Mussolini: The Fake Quote," *Research for Progress*, November 4, 2015; also see Chip Berlet, "Mussolini on the Corporate State," *Political Research Associates*, January 12, 2005.

p. 356 **Another thing that fascism decidedly is not:** See "HNN Special: A Symposium on Jonah Goldberg's Liberal Fascism," *History News Network*, February 2010, hnn.com. See especially David Neiwert, "Introduction," *History News Network*, February 2, 2010; Robert Paxton, "The Scholarly Flaws of 'Liberal Fascism'," *History News Network*, February 2, 2010; and Roger Griffin, "An Academic Book—Not!," *History News Network*, February 2, 2010. Jonah Goldberg responded with "Definitions and Double Standards," *History News Network*, February 2, 2010.

p. 357 **In response, some scholars:** See Roger Griffin, *The Nature of Fascism* (London: Routledge, 1993); see also Roger Griffin, *Modernism and Fascism: The Sense of a Beginning under Mussolini and Hitler* (New York: Palgrave Macmillan, 2007).

p. 358 **While Griffin's approach:** See Robert O. Paxton, *Anatomy of Fascism* (New York: Alfred Knopf, 2004), p. 23.

p. 358 **By examining the historical record:** See Robert O. Paxton, "The Five Stages of Fascism," *Journal of Modern History*, 70, no. 1 (March, 1998): 1–23.

p. 359 **He also examines:** See Robert O. Paxton, *The Anatomy of Fascism* (New York: Alfred Knopf, 2004), pp. 41–2.

p. 359 **This last passion:** See Harald Ofstad, *Our Contempt for Weakness: Nazi Norms and Values—and Our Own* (London: Almqvist and Wiksell, 1989).

p. 361 **Hitler acknowledged:** See Asher Keren, "Anti-Semitism and the Native American Genocide," *Israel Rising*, March 16, 2016; also see James Whitman, "Why the Nazis Loves America," *Time*, March 21, 2017; also see Sean Braswell, "When the Nazis Courted the KKK," *Ozy*, May 13, 2015; also see "Adolf Hitler Quotes: Quotes By and About Hitler," CelebrityTypes, citing Ernst Hanfstaengl: "Hitler wanted to hear all about the [American] skyscrapers ... but failed utterly to draw logical conclusions from the information ...[He was] passionately interested in the Ku Klux Klan ... He seemed to think it was a political movement similar to his own."

p. 361 **Relatively early in the campaign:** See M. J. Lee, "Why Some Conservatives Say Trump Talk Is Fascist," CNN, November 25, 2015.

p. 362 **Even the staid:** See "Donald Trump's Creeping Fascism Needs to Be Rejected," *Seattle Times* (editorial), November 24, 2015.

p. 362   **Of course liberals too:** See Rick Perlstein, "Donald Trump and the 'F-Word'," *Washington Spectator,* September 30, 2015.

p. 363   **The conservative talk-show host:** See Joe Kovacs, "Limbaugh: Why Trump Is Clobbering Establishment GOP," *WorldNetDaily,* October 20, 2015.

p. 364   **For example:** See David Neiwert, "Today's History Lesson: How the Brownshirts Used Street Violence as Martyrdom Propaganda," *Orcinus,* August 9, 2009.

p. 365   **What he is:** See Chip Berlet, "Trump, Fascism, and Right-Wing Populism," *Research for Progress,* August 10, 2016.

p. 366   **The journalist Milton Mayer:** See *They Thought They Were Free: The Germans 1933–1945* (Chicago: University of Chicago Press, 1955), pp. 170–1.

p. 372   **The communications expert:** See Erica Etelson, "How to Flip a Trump Voter Without Pushing Too Hard," *AlterNet,* September 17, 2016.

p. 373   **The embrace of the heroic:** See James Aho, *This Thing of Darkness: A Sociology of the Enemy* (Seattle: University of Washington Press, 1994), p. 26.

Index

Index